A SERIOUSLY GROOVY MOVIE CHRISTMAS

Thomas A. Christie

Other Books by Thomas A. Christie

Liv Tyler: Star in Ascendance

The Cinema of Richard Linklater

John Hughes and Eighties Cinema

Ferris Bueller's Day Off: The Pocket Movie Guide

The Christmas Movie Book

Notional Identities

The Shadow in the Gallery

The James Bond Movies of the 1980s

Mel Brooks: Genius and Loving It!

The Spectrum of Adventure

A Righteously Awesome Eighties Christmas

Contested Mindscapes

John Hughes FAQ

The Golden Age of Christmas Movies

The Heart 200 Book
[with Julie Christie]

A Very Spectrum Christmas

Mysteries and Secrets of the Heart 200 Route
[with Julie Christie]

A Totally Bodacious Nineties Christmas

Scotland's Christmas
[with Murray Cook]

A SERIOUSLY GROOVY MOVIE CHRISTMAS

Festive Cinema of the 1960s and 70s

Thomas A. Christie

A Seriously Groovy Movie Christmas: Festive Cinema of the 1960s and 70s by Thomas A. Christie.

First published in Great Britain in 2024 by Extremis Publishing Ltd.,
Suite 218, Castle House, 1 Baker Street, Stirling, FK8 1AL, United Kingdom.
www.extremispublishing.com

Extremis Publishing is a Private Limited Company registered in Scotland (SC509983) whose Registered Office is Suite 218, Castle House, 1 Baker Street, Stirling, FK8 1AL, United Kingdom.

Copyright © Thomas A. Christie, 2024.

Thomas A. Christie has asserted the moral right under the Copyright, Designs and Patents Act 1988 to be identified as the author of this work.

The views expressed in this work are solely those of the author, and do not necessarily reflect those of the publisher. The publisher hereby disclaims any responsibility for them.

This book is a work of non-fiction. Unless otherwise noted, the author and the publisher make no explicit guarantees as to the accuracy of the information included in this book. All hyperlinks indicated in the text were considered to be live and accurately detailed at time of publication.

This book may include references to organisations, feature films, television programmes, popular songs, musical bands, novels, reference books, and other creative works, the titles of which are trademarks and/or registered trademarks, and which are the intellectual properties of their respective copyright holders.

All rights reserved. No part of this publication may be reproduced, stored in a retrieval system, or transmitted, in any form or by any means, electronic, mechanical, photocopying, recording or otherwise, without the prior permission in writing of the publisher.

This book is sold subject to the condition that it shall not, by way of trade or otherwise, be lent, re-sold or hired out, or otherwise circulated without the publisher's prior consent in any form of binding or cover other than that in which it is published and without a similar condition including this condition being imposed on the subsequent purchaser.

A CIP catalogue record for this book is available from the British Library.

ISBN: 978-1-7394845-7-6

Typeset in Goudy Bookletter 1911, designed by The League of Moveable Type.

Printed and bound in Great Britain by IngramSpark, Chapter House, Pitfield, Kiln Farm, Milton Keynes, MK11 3LW, United Kingdom.

Front cover artwork is Copyright © Suat Gursozlu at Shutterstock.
Back cover artwork from Pixabay.
Cover design and book design is Copyright © Thomas A. Christie.
Author image is Copyright © Julie Christie.
Incidental illustrations from Pixabay and Copyright © Fabio Pagani at Shutterstock.

The copyrights of third parties are reserved. All third party imagery and textual quotations are used under the provision of Fair Use for the purposes of commentary and criticism. While every reasonable effort has been made to contact copyright holders and secure permission for all images reproduced in this work, we offer apologies for any instances in which this was not possible and for any inadvertent omissions.

This book is dedicated to
my dear friend

Mr Eddie Small
(1951–2020)

Eternally a scholar and a gentleman,
and one of the kindest people
ever to grace the academic world.

Contents

Introduction .... Page 1

1. *The Apartment* (1960) .... Page 7
2. *Pocketful of Miracles* (1961) .... Page 45
3. *Santa Claus Conquers the Martians* (1964) ...... Page 77
4. *The Magic Christmas Tree* (1964) .... Page 103
5. *The Christmas That Almost Wasn't* (1966) .... Page 123
6. *The Lion in Winter* (1968) .... Page 145
7. *Scrooge* (1970) .... Page 181
8. *Whoever Slew Auntie Roo?* (1971) .... Page 213
9. *Santa and the Ice Cream Bunny* (1972) .... Page 245
11. *Silent Night, Bloody Night* (1972) .... Page 279
10. *Black Christmas* (1974) .... Page 307
12. *The Silent Partner* (1978) .... Page 345
13. Other Christmas Films of the 1960s and 70s .... Page 387

Filmography .... Page 391
Bibliography .... Page 401
Index .... Page 423
Acknowledgements .... Page 447

Also in This Series:

'When we recall Christmas past, we usually find that the simplest things – not the great occasions – give off the greatest glow of happiness.'

Bob Hope

A SERIOUSLY GROOVY MOVIE CHRISTMAS

Festive Cinema of the 1960s and 70s

Introduction

THINK of the 1960s and 70s, and you can't help but be immediately confronted by some of the most transformative events in recent history. The Space Race, the Vietnam War, the Watergate scandal, the Summer of Love, the Civil Rights movement, multiple tragic and world-shaking assassinations of major public figures, and heightened Cold War tensions all contributed to a period in history which profoundly reshaped society, culture and politics. For the Christmas movie, however, these two decades formed a kind of wilderness period for the genre, sandwiched between its glory days in the immediate post-War era and its popular resurgence throughout the eighties. Yet while this period has come to be regarded as a kind of Bermuda Triangle of festive cinema – often forgotten or unfairly overlooked – it was also witness to some bold and experimental film-making which repeatedly and intensely challenged audience expectations of this category of cinema.

There are numerous reasons why Christmas movies became reasonably scarce in cinemas throughout the sixties and seventies. For one, major shifts were taking place in the popular cultural landscape of the time which were causing attitudes towards the themes of traditional festive cinema to change and evolve. Suddenly the key, time-honoured premises of the genre – celebrating nuclear family dynamics, scepticism towards unfettered consumerism, and the coming together of friends and local communities – had begun to seem out of step with a rapidly-fluctuating cultural zeitgeist. While Hollywood became more intently focused on reflecting the social and political disruptions of the time, the carefree whimsy which had characterised so much early Christmas cinema now seemed less relevant than in the genre's heyday. The major economic uncertainty caused by geopolitical factors such as the Oil Crisis also led to a downturn in studios prepared to invest in big budget Christmas films, with commercial factors leading to an unwillingness to allocate resources to the kind of sumptuous set designs, elaborate costumes and intricate special effects that had come to be associated with the cinema of the festive season.

Perhaps the principal reason for the paucity of Christmas movies in cinemas was the growing dominance of television sets in homes, which had become the prevailing medium for broadcasting festively-themed entertainment during this period. Much commercial effort was expended on selling colour television sets to a mass public audience, and cinema no longer held quite the same degree of dominance over live action festive narratives. With perennially popular Christmas-themed programming emerging throughout the 1960s and 70s, families rapidly discovered new favourites which became annual traditions in their homes every December. While film theatres were often largely devoid of festive fare throughout the decade, sixties television provided fertile ground for the emergence of many well-regarded Christmas animated features, including *Rudolph the Red-Nosed Reindeer* (Kizo Nagashima and Larry Roemer, 1964); *A Charlie Brown Christmas* (Bill Melendez, 1965); *How the Grinch Stole*

Christmas (Chuck Jones and Ben Washam, 1966); and *Frosty the Snowman* (Jules Bass and Arthur Rankin Jnr, 1969). During the seventies, on the other hand, the Christmas film continued to thrive in the form of numerous made-for-television productions, with many high-quality features finding an enthusiastic audience. These included TV movies featuring some prominent star names, such as *It Happened One Christmas* (Donald Wrye, 1977), with Orson Welles and Cloris Leachman; *The House Without a Christmas Tree* (Paul Bogart, 1972) and *A Christmas to Remember* (George Englund, 1978), both of which starred Jason Robards; *The Gathering* (Randal Kleiser, 1977), with Edward Asner; *An American Christmas Carol* (Eric Till, 1979), which featured an excellent central performance from Henry Winkler; and *The Homecoming: A Christmas Story* (Fielder Cook, 1971), which was to be the precursor to the long-running and immensely popular television series *The Waltons* (1972-81).

The late 1950s had seen the beginnings of a transitional phase in the early life of the Christmas movie, where themes such as the festive season's perennial capacity for character transformation were retained while others, including specific explorations of spirituality and the religious origins of Christmas, started to be downplayed by film-makers. The key features of that decade had been the development and repackaging of traditional Christmas themes in order to keep pace with the increasing social change of the post-War era. By the arrival of the sixties, however, Christmas cinema had found itself in a state of commercial impasse which led to a significant re-evaluation of how the festive season was depicted on the big screen. This creative reassessment continued into the seventies, with the traditional themes of the holiday season being countered – and sometimes subverted – by the changing cultural and social values of the time.

Although many of the timeless premises which have come to be associated with the holiday season were preserved, often as overarching themes, several of the Christmas movies of the era would rely on the festivities as a background setting for the action rather than celebrating the holidays quite as directly as had been the case in the genre's golden age. The comparative rarity of Christmas films during this era has also meant that a number of low-budget independent features managed to earn themselves a degree of notoriety that may otherwise not have been the case in other periods, where they would almost certainly have been overlooked due to the proximity of more aggressively-marketed competitors.

Christmas features throughout the sixties and seventies would often riff on characteristic themes of the genre while playfully – or sometimes meaningfully – challenging them in surprisingly consequential ways. Character transformation may predictably be key to Ebenezer Scrooge's personal journey in Ronald Neame's musical *Scrooge* (1970), for instance, but it would prove to be every bit as relevant (albeit in wildly different ways) to the complex emotional development of Bud Baxter in Billy Wilder's *The Apartment* (1960). Overall, however, movies produced in these decades have become renowned more for their subversive qualities than their fidelity to the thematic traditions of Christmas cinema. Films such as Anthony Harvey's *The Lion in Winter* (1968), for example, tease the importance of family bonding and spending time together during the holiday season, only to turn this festive convention on its head by depicting a royal family at war during a medieval Christmas Court – thus confronting the time-honoured depiction of families coming together to celebrate and support one another, despite any challenges they may face, over Christmas. Similarly, festive conventions of community and unity were correspondingly challenged by movies such as Theodore Gershuny's *Silent Night, Bloody Night* (1972) and Bob Clark's *Black Christmas* (1974). While numerous Christmas features over the years have emphasised the idea of coming together as a community and supporting one another during the festive season, Gershuny's feature instead considers dark secrets which threaten to destabilise an isolated town when they unexpectedly re-emerge during one fateful December, while Clark's film depicts characters finding strength and solace through community, during the most challenging of holiday periods, in an entirely unexpected way.

Many other traditional Christmas themes are examined and often subverted by the holiday movies of his era. In films such as Richard C. Parish's *The Magic Christmas Tree* (1964), we see the spirit of generosity and giving reflected through acts of kindness towards others or learning the joy of giving rather than receiving, with characters learning valuable lessons about the importance of generosity during the festive season. Others, including Frank Capra's *Pocketful of Miracles* (1961), presents an unconventional meditation on themes of redemption and second chances, where characters are given the opportunity to make amends for self-interested choices and thus to change for the better. As in the 1940s golden age of Christmas cinema, protagonists continued to show an ability to undergo character transformation after experiencing a change of heart thanks to the festive season... but now, in a new and uncertain age, this process often took place in surprisingly unanticipated ways. Christmas movies of the sixties and seventies frequently highlighted the magic and wonder of the holiday season, emphasising the importance of maintaining a sense of wonder and awe – even in a world that was proving to be increasingly full of complex domestic and geopolitical challenges. Whereas films such as Nicholas Webster's *Santa Claus Conquers the Martians* (1964) and Rossano Brazzi's *The Christmas That Almost Wasn't* (1966) celebrate the power of belief and imagination, especially in children, later features including Curtis Harrington's *Whoever Slew Auntie Roo?* (1971) and Daryl Duke's *The Silent Partner* (1978) were to consciously disrupt it, putting a decidedly adult spin on shadowy events playing out against the otherwise ebullient backdrop of the festive season.

As this book focuses on full-length cinematic features, it does not discuss documentaries or short films, and nor does it address the numerous animated movies and made-for-TV films produced throughout the decade. It is, however, intended to showcase the sheer diversity of creative output being produced within the genre of festive cinema during this tumultuous and transformative period in world history.

Overall, the Christmas movies of the 1960s and 70s reflected a variety of traditional themes that still resonate with audiences of all ages, capturing the spirit of the holiday season while also conveying important messages about love, kindness, and the human experience. It was a time of surprising creative highs and stultifying critical lows. However, these films remain at their most memorable when showcasing creative inventiveness, confronting long-held audience assumptions about the customs of festive cinema and then deftly undermining them – often to striking effect. This bold artistic approach would prove to be highly influential, and would help to shape the genre as it continued to develop and diversify into the titan of the box-office it would eventually become.

1

The Apartment (1960)

The Mirisch Corporation

Director: Billy Wilder
Producer: Billy Wilder
Screenwriters: Billy Wilder and I.A.L. Diamond

IT seems only fitting to begin this study of the Christmas cinema of the 1960s and 70s with one of the most critically celebrated cinematic features of the early sixties – and one of the all-time great New York-based holiday movies, at that. There are some films which concern themselves specifically with the meaning and the effects of the festive season, whereas others tend to be situated within the holiday period but offer a rather more muted appraisal of themes related to the inspiration of the festive season and the influence of the Christmas spirit. *The Apartment*, it is fair to say, falls squarely into the latter category of festive movie. Yet it has nonetheless come to be regarded as one of the central Christmas films of the 1960s, its prominence assured by its touching, warm-hearted exploration of the holiday season's ability to turn around even the bleakest of personal circumstances. A lasting story of hope in the face of impersonal corporate detachment, it is often easy to forget that the bulk of the film's narrative takes place between Christmas and the New Year. But by its conclusion, *The Apartment* leaves the audience in no doubt that it is among the most life-affirming of festive tales; one that firmly elevates the optimism of the human spirit over mundane drudgery, allowing a ray of optimism to shine into the struggle of everyday life.

The Apartment was the brainchild of celebrated writer, producer and director Billy Wilder. A hugely talented and prolific film-maker, by the early 1960s the multiple award-winning Wilder had become particularly well-known for producing features which dealt uncompromisingly with complex moral subject matter and complicated, often uncomfortable social issues. He regularly explored these topics within a comedic framework, but always proved to be resolutely unafraid of courting controversy with the investigation of his chosen themes. Especially well-known at the time for his hugely popular romantic comedy-dramas *Sabrina* (1954), *The Seven Year Itch* (1955) and *Some Like It Hot* (1959), *The Apartment* was a hotly anticipated film on its release, with much media speculation centring on the new production.

Wilder's inspiration for *The Apartment* has been famously discussed over the years by his fans; as the film-maker himself explained to the American Film Institute, 'The genesis of *The Apartment* I remember very, very vividly. I saw David Lean's *Brief Encounter*, which was based on a one-act play by Noel Coward, and in the play Trevor Howard was the leading man. A married man has an affair with a married woman, and he uses the apartment of a chum of his for sexual purposes. I always had it in the back of my mind that the friend of Trevor Howard's, who only appears in one or two tiny scenes, who comes back home and climbs into the warm bed the lovers have just left, would make a very interesting character'.[1] From this kernel of an idea, Wilder would lean in to his exceptional cinematic gifts of deftly-crafted characterisation and supremely witty dialogue to produce what, for many critics, was to become one of his crowning achievements.

Wilder chose as his charismatic lead performer Jack Lemmon, an actor who was eminently well-qualified for an appearance in a Christmas film following his critically successful and good-natured supporting performance in Richard Quine's whimsical, festively-situated *Bell, Book and Candle* (1958) alongside James Stewart a few years earlier. However, *The Apartment* was to be anything but a typical Christmas film; as Andrew Pulver has explained, while the movie's employment of the festive season was far from orthodox, it was to riff on the established tropes of the holidays expertly as it achieved its creative aims:

> Billy Wilder's Oscar-winning romance-farce isn't a Christmas movie exactly – elves, Santa and reindeer are in very short supply – but the holiday season, as it specifically manifested itself in the drunken, libidinous era of the *Mad Men* early 1960s, is central to its maudlin, sentimental tone. Which is, of course, what makes it absolutely brilliant, as if the entire cast and crew were operating through a fug of whisky fumes and a cacophony of party tooters. [...] Sticking this bedroom-shuffling scenario – with its potential for misunderstandings, embarrassments and humiliations – into the Christmas/New Year week, with its heady atmosphere, booze-fuelled fumblings and lowered inhibitions, was a stroke of genius, and makes the whole film hum brilliantly.[2]

It's the first of November 1959 in New York City, and junior office worker Calvin Clifford 'Bud' Baxter (Jack Lemmon) is at his desk on the nineteenth floor of the headquarters of Consolidated Life, a big-city insurance firm. Bud often works late at his office, not because of any gratuitous diligence on his part, but because he has come to an unorthodox arrangement with his superiors at the same workplace to make use of his apartment as a venue to conduct extra-marital affairs – safely concealed from the knowledge of their wives. He does this in the hope of currying favour with his ethically-dubious bosses, including managers such as Al Kirkeby (David Lewis), who is conducting an affair with company telephonist Sylvia (Joan Shawlee). However, Bud's efforts to please his supervisors do not even engender in Kirkeby the basic courtesy of remembering his name. The arrangement works out well for his superiors, but less so for Bud who is often left waiting around in the cold before he can regain access to his own home if (or, rather, when) his bosses' liaisons should over-run. The pact is also raising the suspicions of Bud's neighbours, especially Mildred Dreyfuss (Naomi Stevens), who are apprehensive about the suspicious noises emanating from his apartment while he is apparently away at work.

When Kirkeby discovers that Sylvia has left her galoshes at Bud's apartment, he returns later that evening to retrieve them. Bud meekly asks him if he would consider being more punctual in future, given that he has had to hang around outside in the freezing winter weather to accommodate his manager's out-of-office activities. In a facile attempt to salve his tattered conscience, Kirkeby assures Bud that he has put in a good word for him with Jeff Sheldrake (Fred MacMurray), director of the company's personnel department, and that Bud is sure to be in line for a promotion in the near future. However, he follows this up with new requests for Bud to stock the apartment with more alcohol and snacks, even though it becomes obvious that the unlucky Bud has been having to fund these lavish demands out of his own pocket. Later, as he deposits a bin full of empty bottles outside his apartment, he meets his well-meaning neighbour Dr Dreyfuss (Jack Kruschen), who – on sight of the copious contents of Bud's trash – believes him to be an alcoholic. Without much subtlety, the doctor advises Bud to take more care of himself: having heard the endless succession of liaisons going on from the next apartment, he obviously suspects that Bud is also massively promiscuous.

Bud has retired to bed when he is startled by a late phone call. Joe Dobisch (Ray Walston), one of the office's administration managers, has met a beautiful and rather inebriated blonde woman (Joyce Jameson) at a bar nearby, and requires urgent use of Bud's apartment. This does not sit well with Bud, who is already exhausted and does not exactly relish waiting around outside in the middle of the night. However, Dobisch makes it clear that he is unwilling to take no for an answer, giving Bud his assurance that he will make sure that his name will be on the efficiency rating top ten if he should help him out. Bud soon realises that he has no choice, and reluctantly departs his home to make way for Dobisch and his new acquaintance. Pausing only to leave a warning note on his record player (the loud late night music has been causing his neighbours to protest), he departs from the building just as Dobisch's cab arrives.

While the shady Dobisch makes himself at home, explaining to his guest that the apartment actually belongs to his mother, the fatigued Bud is left with no option but to wander the streets of New York in sub-zero temperatures. The next morning he arrives at work with a heavy cold, looking rather the worse for wear. While waiting for the elevator, he attempts to engage Kirkeby in conversation, but is indifferently brushed off. However, his spirits brighten when he sees the beautiful Fran Kubelik (Shirley MacLaine), who operates one of the building's elevators. His attraction to her is obvious, not least from his lively flirting. Once he reaches the floor where he works, the bitter Kirkeby voices his disdain at the fact that no man in the firm appears able to win over the independently-minded Fran with their charms.

Later that day, Bud's cold appears to be getting worse. He calls up Dobisch on an internal line and tells him that because he had left the wrong key under the welcome mat, Bud was unable to regain access to his apartment and thus had to wake his landlady in the middle of the night. Dobisch assures him that the correct key will soon be on its way in the internal mail, and that he is already in the process of sending a report to Sheldrake which will recommend Bud's efficiency. As Bud's fever continues to become inflamed, he calls Mr Vanderhoff (Willard Waterman) of the public relations department; Vanderhoff was due to use the apartment that night, but Bud is forced to cancel due to the state of his health. Vanderhoff is reluctant to agree, but eventually is left with no alternative and rearranges his 'appointment' instead. This encroaches onto another booking by Mr Eichelberger (David White), who is forced to rearrange in turn, clashing with yet another arrangement – this time with Kirkeby. Fortunately Kirkeby is amenable to the change, meaning that Bud's heavily-packed diary of apartment reservations is finally rebalanced thanks to some frantic organisation.

Bud is called to Sheldrake's office in the personnel department. Taking Fran's elevator, he tries to gently talk her into a date, but she offers no reply. However, his tangible enthusiasm at the prospect of promotion means that even this subtle rebuff to his advances can't make a dent in his excitement. Sheldrake's secretary, Miss Olsen (Edie Adams), frostily orders Bud into the office. Once there, the slick but entirely insincere Sheldrake congratulates Bud on his efficiency and popularity within the company. Several executives have personally requested that Bud be transferred to their own departments. However, Sheldrake is suspicious of Bud's merits, having already deduced the real source of the young man's supposed high esteem. He offers Bud the chance to explain himself. Bud tells Sheldrake that about a year ago, while attending a night-school class in advanced accounting, he had well-meaningly offered an employee the use of his apartment in order to change his clothing prior to an appointment. However, little realising the true motives at hand, he was soon receiving requests from other high-up members of staff to similarly make use of his home, and the situation escalated into its current state. Bud fully expects to receive at least a reprimand from Sheldrake, but instead the senior manager offers him two theatre tickets to see *The Music Man* on Broadway; he too wants the use of Bud's apartment. Left with no real option but to comply, Bud accedes to Sheldrake's request. In return, the unscrupulous director promises Bud that he considers him to be a worthy candidate for promotion when the company's next personnel shake-up takes place the following month.

More out of hope than expectation, Bud hangs around the building after work in the hope of catching Fran when she leaves. On meeting her, he asks if she will join him at the theatre. At first she declines, telling him that she is due to meet someone else that evening, but sensing his eagerness she relents and tells him that while she has business to attend to first, she will meet him at the theatre just before the show starts. Bud is overjoyed, though Fran seems much more reserved in her affections. Once they have parted company, Fran heads for a restaurant nearby. There, she meets a supremely furtive Sheldrake – her unnamed date for the evening. It soon becomes apparent that she and Sheldrake had been involved in a rather intense affair during the summer, but that Fran had broken it off when she realised that it was not sustainable: she knows that Sheldrake would never have voluntarily left his wife and children. However, Sheldrake emphasises that his feelings for her continue to run deep. Fran is resistant to the force of his personality, assuring him that a break between them was for the best, but Sheldrake seems unable to contemplate that there is no hope of rekindling their romance. He tells her that he has been in contact with his lawyer about a divorce, and that he will set the legal proceedings in motion if Fran will admit that she is still in love with him. Fran tells him that she reciprocates his affections, having never believed that he would actually go ahead with ending his marriage. They leave the restaurant when it starts to become crowded; one of the newcomers is Miss Olsen, who coldly observes the fact that Sheldrake and Fran have been at the same table together. Fran tells Sheldrake that she must head off for her other arrangement (although he is unaware that she plans to meet Bud for a date). Sheldrake instead persuades her to join him at the apartment, calling a cab for this purpose. Unknown to either of them, Bud has been left out in the cold again – he is waiting patiently outside the theatre, even although the show has started, in the vain hope that Fran will still show up late to meet him.

Bud's exasperated persistence eventually pays off when, some time later, he is given a promotion to Second Administrative Assistant. He has barely enough time to relish having a tiny office of his own, however, before he is visited by Dobisch, Kirkeby, Vanderhoff and Eichelberger. They have come, ostensibly, to offer their congratulations on his promotion... but it soon becomes apparent that they are displeased that Bud has been gradually making his apartment less available to them. Unable to tell them about Sheldrake's use of his home for fear of exposing the senior boss's extra-marital activities, he instead tries to fob them off by telling them that he appreciates his own personal space from time to time. They are unhappy with his seemingly carefree attitude, however, and warn him that just as they have made possible the elevation of his position within the company, so too can they diminish his stature as they see fit.

Their thinly-veiled threats are interrupted by the arrival of Sheldrake; Bud quickly encourages the other men to leave when the personnel director comes into the office, keen to keep their new arrangement private. Sheldrake asks Bud to have a second key to the apartment cut for the executive's own personal use, and books the use of Bud's home for Thursday night. Bud agrees to both of Sheldrake's demands, little realising that the affair his boss is conducting is actually with Fran. Bud also returns a compact to Sheldrake that he had found in his apartment, assuming that it belongs to the woman that he had been entertaining. He points out that it has a cracked mirror, but that he found it that way on returning home. Sheldrake admits that it was broken when his companion for the evening threw it at him in a fit of anger.

Christmas Eve arrives at Consolidated Life, and a rowdy party is taking place on the nineteenth floor. As the water cooler is being merrily augmented with copious amounts of liquor, Bud decides to take a drink to Fran, who is still operating one of the elevators in spite of the ongoing festive hijinks. Fran is surprised to see him, given that he has been avoiding her for weeks, but he tells her that in spite of initially being hurt at the way that she stood him up at the theatre in November, he forgives her, understanding that she must have had good reason not to have made the date. He whisks her out of the elevator and into the partying crowd. Promising to get more drinks, he momentarily leaves Fran on the periphery of the multitude, where she is accosted by the tipsy Miss Olsen. Resentfully, Olsen needles Fran, telling her that she is fully aware of her surreptitious affair with Sheldrake and admitting that a few years ago he had conducted a similar liaison with her. Indeed, she goes on to reveal that Sheldrake has been something of a serial womaniser within the company, and that Fran should eventually expect to be treated no differently than any of his many other previous conquests — casually and callously discarded when Sheldrake inevitably moves on to a new target.

Unaware of the intense conversation between Fran and Miss Olsen, the still-merry Bud returns with new refreshments. The now-very-uncomfortable Fran tells him that she feels a little claustrophobic in the crowd, so he ushers her into his cramped office and promptly shows off his new bowler hat — a status symbol that he has purchased to celebrate his new position as a (very) junior executive. He tries again to ask Fran out on a date, but — not unkindly — she turns him down once more. He tells her that he has growing influence with Sheldrake and will put in a good word on her behalf, in the hope of assuring her promotion within the company. She seems reluctant about him doing so, however, but doesn't divulge her own relationship with Sheldrake. However, when Bud jokily rearranges his hat to a more jaunty angle, she produces her compact to give him an idea of how he looks; on seeing the cracked mirror, he immediately puts two and two together – to his immense dismay. Bud is shocked by the discovery of Fran's affair with Sheldrake, but doesn't confront her with this knowledge. Instead, their meeting is interrupted by a call from Sheldrake himself, who asks Bud if he has made all the necessary arrangements for his next meeting at the apartment – including putting up a Christmas tree. Still stunned by the revelation of Fran being involved with the personnel director, Bud leaves the office in a daze while the raucous party continues to rage around him.

Bud is drowning his sorrows in a busy bar. He is so miserable, and indeed so inebriated, that even a visit from a jovial Santa Claus (Hal Smith) is unable to raise a smile. A woman in a fur coat, Margie MacDougall (Hope Holiday), tries to attract Bud's attention with all the subtlety of a breeze-block through a plate glass window. After much cajoling, she eventually leaves him with no option but to buy her a drink, while she plays a song on the bar's jukebox and strikes up a wearying conversation about the Cuban Revolution. As they chat, Bud explains that he is unmarried and has no family, but unfortunately for him even that doesn't mean that his home is vacant – he can't even be miserable with the benefit of solitude.

Meanwhile, back at that very apartment, Sheldrake is growing frustrated by Fran's behaviour; she is deeply upset and can't stop crying. Believing that her distress is borne out of his constant delay over instigating her divorce, Sheldrake assures her that the timing just isn't right – he'll start the ball rolling with his lawyers only once the conditions are favourable for him (whenever that may be). Fran then tells him about her conversation with Miss Olsen, and rings off the names of some of the women in the company that Sheldrake has previously conducted affairs with. He brushes off her concerns with glib platitudes, but his furtive glances at his watch give the lie to his obvious awkwardness; clearly he is expected at home. She gives him a carefully-selected vinyl record album as a Christmas gift, though he elects to leave it in the apartment to avoid having to explain its presence to his wife. In return, he gives her a hundred dollar bill and tells her to buy something nice with it, though she is too thoroughly disillusioned to bother making her distaste at his shoddy gesture apparent.

Sheldrake sets off, knowing that he has already missed his train, but he grows impatient with Fran's genuine upset. Before he departs, he tells her that their relationship will not always be composed of clandestine meetings; one day the love he feels for her will win out, and they can celebrate openly. But Fran clearly no longer believes a word he tells her. With a parting wish for a Merry Christmas, Sheldrake leaves, but Fran decides to stay a while longer in the apartment. She puts on the album that she had given Sheldrake, and – now that she is alone – finally vents her pent-up feelings of anger and hurt. Weeping inconsolably, she heads for the bathroom to freshen up. There, she discovers Bud's well-stocked supply of sleeping tablets and appears to consider them very closely.

Back at the bar, Bud and Mrs MacDougall are ejected by Charlie the bartender (Benny Burt) due to the lateness of the hour. Margie asks Bud if he'd like to come back to her home, but Bud remarks that they may as well return to his – after all, it seems to be a popular enough venue with everyone else. Once they arrive at the apartment, Bud asks Margie to get the drinks while he puts on some music. He is surprised to discover Fran's album on the turntable, but soon exchanges it for something a little more up-tempo. He then finds Fran's gloves lying on his coffee table, which perplexes him even more. But his confusion reaches a crescendo when he puts the gloves into his bedroom for safe-keeping and discovers Fran lying unconscious on his bed. At first, believing her to be asleep, he angrily tells her to get out of his apartment; after all, even he can have company to entertain sometimes. But on discovering the empty bottle of sleeping tablets next to her prone form, he soon realises that she has attempted to commit suicide. Quickly sobering up, he races next door to Dr Dreyfuss and begs him to revive Fran, then unceremoniously ejects a deeply confused Mrs MacDougall.

Dr Dreyfuss checks out Fran's condition and takes her into the bathroom in the hope of clearing the tablets from her system. Sure enough, Bud soon hears vomiting and realises that the doctor has got to her just in time. Taking the woozy Fran back through to the living room, Dreyfuss administers some medication to stabilise her condition. Unaware of the (admittedly rather complicated) truth behind the situation, the doctor voices disdain at what he perceives to be Bud's lax morals; his assumption is that following an argument with Fran, which had prompted her to overdose on the tablets, Bud had obviously gone to a bar with the goal of picking up another woman as quickly as possible. Telling Bud to fetch some coffee, he adds that another half hour would have made all the difference between them saving Fran's life and her suicide attempt being successful. Eventually they manage to revive her to the point where she regains semi-consciousness, but Dreyfuss warns that they must keep her awake for a few hours until the sleeping tablets lose their effectiveness. After this has passed, and Fran is safely back in Bud's bed, the doctor again warns Bud that it's time for him to stop behaving so irresponsibly. The next time such an incident happens, he cautions, it may be too late to turn things around.

On Christmas morning, Bud finds his livid landlady Mrs Lieberman (Frances Weintraub Lax) demanding to know the source of the previous evening's commotion. Bud manages to sidestep the issue and assure her that it won't happen again, though her temper is clearly at breaking point. However, his own anger – with regard to Fran's narrow escape from death, and its underlying cause – is barely held in check. He rings up Sheldrake, who is at home playing with his children and their Christmas presents. Bud explains the desperation of the previous night's events to Sheldrake, but he makes it perfectly clear that he wants nothing to do with Fran's recovery – only that it is essential that his name be kept out of any subsequent investigations. Bud is clearly disgusted by Sheldrake's complete lack of regard for Fran's predicament or wellbeing, but has little recourse but to accede to his office superior's craven desire to avoid any engagement with the situation.

Fran tries to get up, but Bud discovers her stumbling around just in time to save her from collapsing. She wants to brush her teeth, so Bud finds her a new toothbrush while surreptitiously sweeping the bathroom for any razor blades and other potentially dangerous items that might incline her to harm herself. While Fran freshens up, Bud tries to persuade a hostile Mrs Dreyfuss to let him borrow some coffee. Concerned at Fran's condition, Mrs Dreyfuss instead brings her over a meal, although Fran is in no mood to eat it. Bud tries to entertain Fran with conversation and, eventually, card games. But she is so deeply depressed with her current situation that she responds poorly to both. Fran explains that although she knows Sheldrake to be a cold and unfeeling liar, she still loves him in spite of his dishonesty, moral cowardice, and multitude of other failings. Over a game of gin rummy, she tells Bud that she feels doomed to never find a suitable partner; every romance she has had has ended in disappointment. Bud attempts to assure Fran that Sheldrake was anxious about the state of her health when they spoke on the phone, but she knows only too well that he is lying to spare her feelings.

Bud is aware that he must keep Fran safe at his home for a few days until she has fully recuperated. However, he has completely forgotten that his apartment has been booked for an afternoon appointment by Kirkeby, who arrives unannounced with Sylvia. Kirkeby is initially angered by Bud's presence, particularly when he is ordered to leave, but his attitude softens slightly when he realises that Bud has female company himself. Glancing through to the bedroom and seeing Fran asleep in Bud's bed, Kirkeby is righteously impressed that his underling has managed to romance the one woman in the company whose affections have always been considered singularly unwinnable. He promises to keep this knowledge a secret, though Bud seems to be long past caring about the tiresome office politics of Consolidated Life.

Once Christmas has passed, Sheldrake returns to his office and wastes no time in unceremoniously firing Miss Olsen. He tells her that he will not tolerate any interference in his private life; for her part, she is too contemptuous of his behaviour to argue with him. Sheldrake calls Bud at home and asks about Fran's condition, again reiterating his desire for his name to be kept out of things. However, Bud encourages Sheldrake to speak with Fran on the phone and encourage her recovery. Fran is extremely reluctant to join the conversation, but eventually finds the courage. Sheldrake is distant and condescending towards her, insisting that they put the incident behind them and effectively profess that their Christmas Eve meeting had never happened in the first place. Fran's utter disgust is evident. Neither of them are aware that Miss Olsen is silently listening in on the conversation using her internal phone. Once Sheldrake has rung off, the vengeful Olsen – now with nothing to lose – calls up the executive's wife and arranges to meet her in the near future.

Bud has gone out for some groceries when he returns to find an anxious Mrs Lieberman at the apartment door. Having smelt gas, she was all set to use the pass key. Alarmed that Fran may be trying to gas herself with his oven, Bud races into the apartment to discover that she was using the hob and had simply forgotten to light it. Fran is eager to return to her family, who are presumably worried sick about her unexplained absence, but Bud encourages her to remain there for one more day – Dr Dreyfuss had recommended a full 48 hours of rest before her health was likely to return to normal. He promises her that he will make dinner for her that evening, as a parting gift before she leaves the following morning.

Back at Consolidated Life, a concerned man named Karl Matuschka (Johnny Seven) arrives in search of Fran. Eventually directed to Dobisch's office, he explains that he is Fran's brother-in-law, and that his wife has been concerned about her sister's unexplained whereabouts over the past couple of days. Kirkeby is also present in the office, and is still smarting about having been ejected by Bud the previous day. He and Dobisch are also clearly envious of Bud's success in romancing Fran, so they decide to hand over the details of his home address to Karl as an act of pure spite.

With the aid of a tennis racquet, Bud is preparing a rather unconventional spaghetti dinner for Fran. However, the candles on the table have barely been lit before a furious Karl turns up and demands to know what is going on. Fran manages to keep his anger under control until she can get dressed, but the situation becomes complicated when Dr Dreyfuss arrives and asks how the patient is doing. When the situation with the sleeping tablets is brought up, Karl insists on knowing what has happened to his sister-in-law. Bud lies to spare Fran's feelings and claims that he was responsible for her malady, which earns him a beating from Karl but saves Fran from explaining what had happened previously with Sheldrake. Karl marches Fran out of the apartment while a melancholic but blissfully oblivious Dreyfuss tells Bud that due to his lifestyle, he probably had it coming all along.

The next morning, sporting an impressive black eye, Bud returns to work. He arranges to meet with Sheldrake in the hope of persuading him that he will take the 'problem' of Fran out of his hands – that is to say, that by entering into a relationship with her, Bud will save any embarrassment from bleeding into Sheldrake's private life. But he is caught flat-footed when he arrives in Sheldrake's office and discovers that it is full of luggage; Miss Olsen had carried out her intended plan to inform Mrs Sheldrake of her husband's many affairs, meaning that he really is now heading for a divorce whether he wants one or not. Thus Sheldrake still plans to pursue Fran anew, though he makes it clear to Bud that he also intends to enjoy the single life for a while before he thinks of settling down with anyone.

Sheldrake has a further surprise for Bud: his current aide has been transferred to Consolidated Life's Denver office, meaning that he has a vacancy for an assistant director in the personnel department. Sheldrake shows Bud through to his plush new office and reels off the many new perks of the executive experience that he can enjoy, but is puzzled by the younger man's apparent lack of enthusiasm. Later that night,

Bud meets Fran in the building's foyer. She seems to find the encounter uncomfortable, but tells Bud that she is happy to know that Sheldrake's divorce is finally underway; the two of them are planning to keep their relationship quiet until the legal proceedings have all been tied up. Bud is clearly crushed by her credulous gullibility, but puts on a brave face.

On New Year's Eve, Sheldrake calls Bud into his office and asks him for the use of his apartment yet again – he's planning a romantic *tête-à-tête* with Fran, but his temporary accommodation is too public a venue. However, Bud stands up to his amoral boss for once, refusing to give up his home when he knows how hollow Sheldrake's intentions towards Fran really are. Sheldrake makes the choice clear to Bud: either he hands over the key to his apartment right away, or he will be fired with immediate effect. Disgusted, Bud hands over a key… but Sheldrake quickly realises that it is the key to the executive washroom. Bud explains to him that he has decided to take Dr Dreyfuss's advice and start behaving like a human being rather than the unthinking corporate drone that he is in danger of becoming. In short, Bud has realised that it's time to put the petty machinations of Consolidated Life behind him.

Bud decides to pack up his things at the apartment. Dr Dreyfuss arrives to borrow some ice-cubes for his New Year's party, and is surprised to see that all of Bud's possessions have been loaded into boxes. Bud tells him that although he is unsure of his destination, he needs to make a clean break from the apartment and everything it represents. The doctor kindheartedly invites him to join his family and friends at the party, but Bud politely declines, feeling in no mood to celebrate. He doesn't realise that at the same time, Fran is at another party – Sheldrake has taken her to their usual restaurant to ring in the new year of 1960. He tells her that he has had to arrange a hotel room in Atlantic City, due to everywhere in town being booked up. Disdainfully, he explains that there was no way that he could use the apartment due to Bud's defiance of him, and seems bewildered at how his newly-assertive minion could be so ungrateful (completely unmindful of the many personal sacrifices that Bud had previously made for him). It is clear that Sheldrake regards adultery as being simply one of the perks of his job; like access to the executive canteen, he feels that it is his right to use and abuse people as he sees fit, and cannot remotely fathom Bud's objection to his behaviour. Fran brightens when she hears of the way that Bud had finally decided to stand up to Sheldrake's amoral misbehaviour, particularly when she deduces the true depth of the younger man's feelings toward her. The restaurant's patrons perform a boisterous rendition of 'Auld Lang Syne' as the midnight bells approach. Sheldrake joins in but, upon turning to join Fran in a toast to the year ahead, discovers that his companion has disappeared.

Fran races along the street towards Bud's apartment. On entering the building she hears what sounds like a gunshot and, believing that her erstwhile colleague has decided to end it all, desperately hammers at his door. Puzzled, Bud appears in the doorway with a newly-opened bottle of champagne – much to Fran's relief. Entering the apartment, she asks where he's headed now that he has packed up and ready to go. When Bud replies that he isn't entirely sure, she responds that she feels exactly the same way; indirectly, she confirms that her relationship with Sheldrake is over. Deciding to complete their unfinished game of gin rummy, she cuts the cards just as Bud tells her with absolute determination how he feels about her. Smiling, and knowing that she feels exactly the same way,

Fran tells him that it's time to stop talking and deal a new hand of cards.

The *Apartment* is, to say the least, far removed from typical Christmas cinema. A mature film with distinctly adult themes, withering in its social commentary and articulate disdain for the spiteful, shallow nature of office politics, on the surface it appears to engage only sporadically with the festive season. Yet the classic Christmas theme of the holiday season's power to improve the lives of individuals and communities is still very much at the core of *The Apartment*. Wilder uses the Christmas revelries and New Year festivities of the film as more than simply a backdrop; Bud and Fran's low-key engagement with the festive season, celebrating at work but privately discontented, contrasts very effectively with Sheldrake's perfunctory acknowledgement of the holidays, whether playing half-heartedly with his boisterous young children, casually ordering Bud to decorate his apartment with a tree at a specific time, or giving Fran – almost as an afterthought – a perfunctory monetary gift that requires no deliberation or emotional consideration whatsoever. So too is Bud's domestic misery surrounding his superiors' misuse of his home brilliantly accentuated by the bumptious Kirkeby thinking nothing of using the apartment on, of all times, Christmas Day. The intoxication of the office party gives Sheldrake's vengeful secretary Miss Olsen the perfect opportunity that she has been seeking to attempt to sabotage his fling with Fran, while the film's New Year's Eve conclusion seems like just the right point for Bud and Fran to celebrate the end of their old professional lives and the start of a blossoming new romance.

The Apartment is an outstanding exploration of the human condition, given the way that it so expertly alternates between themes of love, loneliness and corporate culture. While Christmas serves as a backdrop to the film, it also plays a significant role in shaping the narrative and influencing the main characters' emotions. Wilder shrewdly uses the holiday season as a contrasting element to highlight the stark and often uncomfortable realities of the various characters' lives. In the midst of festive cheer and yuletide celebrations, Bud finds himself a solitary and isolated figure, and his aching awareness of this fact lends poignancy to the film's exploration of loneliness and alienation in the modern society of the time. (Never do two people seem more alone in a crowd than Bud and Fran during the raucous, jam-packed office Christmas party.) The juxtaposition of the festive season with Bud's joyless and empty apartment underscores the emptiness and emotional void he finds himself experiencing, despite being surrounded by the otherwise exuberant hustle and bustle of Christmas.

Furthermore, Christmas in *The Apartment* serves as a clever metaphor for false appearances and superficiality; the festive season has depth and significance which is entirely dispensed with in favour of shallow ostentation by the self-serving corporate world. Bud's increasingly-hesitant willingness to lend out his apartment to his superiors for their extramarital affairs reflects the moral ambiguity and personal corruption that is inherent in some corners of the hard-hearted business environment. The holiday period's awkward balance of joy and materialism lends an air of both seasonal exultation and acquisitive triviality to proceedings, ensuring that the Christmas backdrop to the characters' moral dilemmas and interpersonal compromises feels highly distinctive throughout.

Amidst the bleakness of personal isolation and the abuse of the corporate pecking order, Christmas also ultimately comes to symbolise hope and redemption for individuals in

The Apartment. Bud's growing affection for Fran, despite the inauspicious circumstances of their initial encounters, hints at the possibility of genuine connection and the eventual prospect of true emotional fulfilment. Their final scene together, set on New Year's Eve, suggests a promising and emancipatory new beginning for Bud and Fran which surpasses the sense of cynicism and unwilling seclusion that pervades so much of the film. Wilder deftly employs Christmas imagery and subverts the festive atmosphere – sometimes apparently skin-deep, but often surprisingly profound – to underscore *The Apartment*'s themes of loneliness, ethical dubiety and ultimately redemption. His masterful direction, and the nuanced performances of the talented cast, elevate the film far beyond its holiday setting, crafting a timeless exploration of human relationships and the search for meaning in a world that often seems depressingly phony and ruthlessly cold-blooded.

The film proved controversial at the time due to its depiction of Consolidated Life's executives as flawed, essentially corrupt individuals, a ragtag collection of immoral cowards who are only too willing to abuse their subordinates professionally and domestically in order to get what they want. As Glenn Erickson has explained, 'Perhaps the critics were shocked by the idea that the eager young Baxter doesn't believe that goodness will triumph without a little cheating. They might also then be repulsed by a heroine with low self-esteem, one always getting the fuzzy end of the lollypop like Marilyn Monroe in *Some Like it Hot*. Add this to an overall story that sees infidelity and sordidness unchallenged by a higher morality, and you can understand why they were dismayed. Baxter and Kubelik are decent enough, but not above petty dishonesties to try and get through the lonely nights –

what's so bad about that? America's never grown up out of the fairy tale mentality, where one good deed always results in an avalanche of reformed hearts and merry good will'.³ Instead, the audience is presented with the contentious notion that the dynamics of office life can behave like a naturally occurring soup – that is to say that it is scum, not cream, which has a tendency to rise to the top – which was a concept that created no small amount of dispute when the film was released to the public in the early sixties.

Wilder's depiction of dog-eat-dog office politics has remained fresh and germane more than sixty years later, casting a discomfiting light on interpersonal dynamics and the ways in which a toxic workplace can change people – and never for the better. Although the screenplay, a collaboration between Wilder and his long-time writing partner I.A.L. Diamond, is fecund in its elaboration of moral concerns, they never allow the film to become overtly preachy or didactic, instead allowing the audience to make up their own minds. As Richard Armstrong has put it, '*The Apartment* is about people who, by pursuing the post-modern deities of Money and Status, have departed from their humanity, that which they have in kind with others. Fran's "Why do people have to love people, anyway?" contains more than mere disappointment over a failed romance. It calls into question the very thrust of postwar American life. If the logic of commercial exchange attends Sheldrake's swapping tickets for *Music Man* for Bud's apartment key; his promise to divorce his wife in return for Fran's love; and Margie's wanting to "buy" Bud some music on the jukebox, Bud and Fran will become no less than an ethical Adam and Eve'.⁴ In fact, the narrative does at times seem to be at pains to emphasise that although Bud eventually takes up a more principled position than his supposed superiors, he too is an imperfect individual and certainly no saint. He may not have asked for the predicament he finds himself in, but he still exhibits enough flexibility in his principles to capitalise upon the opportunities it presents. Much time and creative effort is invested in his moral hand-wringing over the ethical considerations of allowing his bosses to make use of his home for their illicit affairs, and indeed this contrasts perfectly with Fran's conscience-wrestling as she balances her feelings for Sheldrake against the knowledge that their romance will, if successful, eventually destroy the cohesion of his family.

Moral tales are relatively common in the genre of the Christmas film, but rarely had audiences been exposed to quite such a cutting interpretation of executive machinations as Wilder had presented in *The Apartment*. Far from a Manichean construal of the managerial mind, the film focused not on corporate corruption but rather the dishonest nature of mendacious individuals who were entirely willing to abuse their positions of power to achieve profligate ends. Indeed, Wilder's use of the holiday season becomes particularly relevant in this regard; the traditional virtues of family and friendship that Christmas films so regularly promote are either neglected or rejected by Consolidated Life's managers (Sheldrake is barely interested in keeping his sons entertained with their new toys on Christmas morning, and Kirkeby uses Christmas Day as nothing more than a vehicle for yet another extra-marital tryst), while Bud and Fran both crave the comfort and solace that are offered by the ideals of togetherness endorsed by the festive season. As James Powers has discussed, the yuletide backdrop serves to make Wilder's interpretation of the human condition all the more pointed: 'Where else has social comment ever been so effective? Wilder hones his points to a piercing edge in such scenes as that in a grim saloon, on Christmas Eve, as the faithful ignore the jukebox blaring "Adestes Fideles" to jolt themselves into tranquility at the bar. The vulgar and graceless aspects of modern life, noted in the periphery before, get head-on examination here'.[5]

Because the action of *The Apartment* is set mainly around the bustling snake pit of the office environment and Bud's rather more modest (if somewhat impersonal) apartment, the interpersonal dynamics of the characters seem all the sharper when delineated through Wilder and Diamond's screenplay. The kindly concern of Dr Dreyfuss, the loneliness of Margie MacDougall and the punch-first-ask-questions-later familial concern of Karl Matuschka all stand in stark contrast to the self-serving egotism of the corporate managers and their petty-minded peccadilloes. Indeed, as Gerd Gemünden clarifies, even the central location of Bud's apartment is a carefully-considered creative choice on Wilder's part, as its contents and decoration say much about its occupant and his character:

> The generic nature of this title [...] signals that the true protagonist may not be Baxter but the place he lives in, and that the basic tension explored by the film is that between being a certain *type* of human being and what actually makes that being *human*. A Buddy-Boy without real friends, Baxter leads a solitary life of TV dinners, surrounded by run-of-the-mill furniture, minimal kitchen appliances, and posters of modern paintings, which we later understand to have been purchased while passing time in museums because his apartment is occupied. Clearly, places like these produce and shape types like Baxter, while types like Baxter

will seek out places like these to make their 'home'. The notion of home needs to be rendered in quotation marks, not only because Baxter's professional ambition literally makes him homeless, but also because even when occupied by himself, the apartment provides Baxter with only the most spurious sense of belonging.[6]

The main difference between the two protagonists and their superiors at Consolidated Life is that whereas Sheldrake and his ilk have already sold their souls to the corporate machine, and seem to have no moral issue in having done so, Bud and Fran are both seeking something better but indefinable that cannot be provided by the prestige of a promotion or the prospect of a better office. By the end of the film, both Fran and Bud have realised that it is they who define their jobs, not the other way around. But for the likes of Kirkeby and Dobisch, this distinction will probably always seem meaningless. This factor, as Roger Ebert explains, is the reason why Wilder marries together social commentary and the milieu of the festive season so expertly:

> There is a melancholy gulf over the holidays between those who have someplace to go, and those who do not. *The Apartment* is so affecting partly because of that buried reason: It takes place on the shortest days of the year, when dusk falls swiftly and the streets are cold, when after the office party some people go home to their families and others go home to apartments where they haven't even bothered to put up a tree. On Christmas Eve, more than any other night of the year, the lonely

person feels robbed of something that was there in childhood and isn't there anymore. [...] The valuable element in Wilder is his adult sensibility; his characters can't take flight with formula plots, because they are weighted down with the trials and responsibilities of working for a living. In many movies, the characters hardly even seem to have jobs, but in *The Apartment* they have to be reminded that they have anything else.[7]

The Apartment has a very great deal to recommend it, from Wilder's celebrated ability for skilful frame composition to Adolph Deutsch's powerful score, and especially Edward G. Boyle's fantastic set design, contrasting the stark and clinical corporate interiors of Consolidated Life with the oddly impersonal homeliness (and endearing clutter) of Bud's apartment. (The interior was deliberately designed to seem cramped and unpretentious, full of knick-knacks purchased from second-hand stores and allegedly even featuring old furniture items that had belonged to the director's personal collection, which he felt were a good match for Baxter's modest abode.) Given Wilder's famous perfectionism, it is no surprise to see so many memorably-composed sequences, from the unassuming Bud being visually sidelined into the corner of the shot as his apartment's brash guests arrive at the entryway steps through to the unusual perspective achieved by art director Alexander Trauner, who brought about the prodigious scale of the insurance office by fooling the camera; rather than an impossibly long working space crammed with individual workers at identical desks, the room was actually populated with increasingly shorter people leading up to the back of the room, where children dressed in business suits were placed at miniature desks to maintain the illusion of a very large occupied space. Even the setting was no mistake, with Wilder deciding to shoot the film during the Christmas of 1959 in order to capture the energy and atmosphere of the real festive season. This approach did not come without its challenges, as Gene D. Phillips has noted: 'Since *The Apartment* takes place during the Christmas season, the bitterly cold New York weather during location shooting was appropriate for the movie, but it was tough on cast and crew. Wilder had planned to shoot several exterior shots in front of Bud's apartment building, "but it was so cold that we were always running to the nearest bar to warm ourselves" with a shot of whiskey, says [production designer Alexander] Trauner in his autobiography; "we weren't making progress"'.[8]

However, the greatest success of *The Apartment* is arguably dependent upon the two remarkable central performances which drive it. Jack Lemmon has rarely been so memorable as he was in the role of the hapless, basically decent Bud Baxter, a man whose ambition is always tempered with humility, and who desires (as he eventually realises) the achievement of success through merit rather than by dishonest means. Lemmon's acting career started in television in the late 1940s. His performances on American TV were prolific throughout the early fifties, and he made his first appearance on film in George Cukor's *It Should Happen to You* (1954) soon after. His film career throughout the 1950s included roles in movies such as *Phffft* (Mark Robson, 1954), *Mister Roberts* (John Ford and Mervyn LeRoy, 1955), *Fire Down Below* (Robert Parrish, 1957), *Cowboy* (Delmer Daves, 1958), *Bell, Book and Candle* (Richard Quine, 1958), and – perhaps most memorably – as double bass player Jerry in Billy Wilder's earlier hit *Some Like It Hot* (1959). No stranger to industry recognition of his talents, Lemmon had won an Academy Award for Best Actor in a Supporting Role in 1956 for his performance in *Mister Roberts*, and had been nominated for Best Actor in a Leading Role for *Some Like It Hot*. He won the Best Actor in a Leading Role Academy Award again some years later for his appearance in John G. Avildsen's *Save the Tiger* (1973), and was nominated for the award on a staggering five further occasions; as well as his Oscar nomination for *The Apartment*, he was also nominated for performances in Blake Edwards's *Days of Wine and Roses* (1962), James Bridges's *The China Syndrome* (1979), Bob Clark's *Tribute* (1980) and Costa-Gavras's *Missing* (1982).

Lemmon even managed to persuade the painstakingly meticulous Wilder, who famously insisted on exacting fidelity to the screenplay when filming, to allow a couple of instances of inspired improvisation during *The Apartment*: firstly, when Bud smartly discharges a nasal spray into the air with adroit comic timing, and secondly, when the character serenades himself while cooking a spaghetti dinner. Sometimes this improvisational quality took his performance to unexpected places: in one sequence Bud was supposed to recoil from a punch, but Lemmon misjudged the reaction and, rather than miming the impact, was actually knocked off his feet as a result of the blow. Because of the sincerity of Lemmon's shocked reaction, Wilder decided to retain the scene as it was shot rather than remounting the sequence. Lemmon was to collaborate with Wilder many times in the future, in films which included *Meet Whiplash Willie* (1966), *Avanti!* (1972), *The Front Page* (1974) and *Buddy Buddy* (1981). He and Shirley MacLaine would both, of course, famously work again with Wilder just a few years later in *Irma la Douce*

(1963), an adaptation of the Alexandre Breffort play, which also claimed its own measure of success at the Academy Awards.

Shirley MacLaine was the perfect foil for Lemmon's likeable, slightly neurotic protagonist. Fran Kubelik is a smart and sassy character, but also sensitive and vulnerable. Her deep hurt at Sheldrake's malign machinations is tangible, as is her growing sense of disaffection with her treatment, which mirrors Bud's own dawning realisation and disillusionment at the way that he has been treated by his superiors. MacLaine made her cinematic debut in Alfred Hitchcock's *The Trouble with Harry* (1955), and later went on to perform in a wide variety of films which included *Around the World in Eighty Days* (Michael Anderson, 1956), *The Matchmaker* (Joseph Anthony, 1958), *Stranger with a Gun* (George Marshall, 1958) and *Can-Can* (Walter Lang, 1960) before appearing in *The Apartment*. MacLaine later won the Best Actress in a Leading Role Academy Award for her performance in James L. Brooks's *Terms of Endearment* (1983). She received numerous nominations for Best Actress in a Leading Role over the years, for performances in films including Vincente Minnelli's *Some Came Running* (1958) and Herbert Ross's *The Turning Point* (1977), as well as for her appearances in *The Apartment* and Wilder's aforementioned *Irma la Douce*. Additionally, she received an Academy Award nomination for her documentary film *The Other Half of the Sky: A China Memoir* (1975), co-directed with Claudia Weill.

The Apartment also benefits from an absolutely faultless supporting cast. The film is packed with excellent performances, including Edie Adams's turn as the bitterly aloof Miss Olsen; Jack Kruschen as the concerned, neighbourly Dr Dreyfuss; and Naomi Stevens as Mildred, his compassionate but formidable wife. However, it is Bud's selection of sleazy, philandering bosses who tend to linger longest in the memory. David Lewis is superb as the sordid Al Kirkeby, while Ray Walston – who was perhaps best known at the time for his performance as Luther Billis in Joshua Logan's *South Pacific* (1958) – is similarly impressive as the seedy, malicious admin manager Joe Dobisch. Central among this catalogue of grotesque corporate characters is, of course, the notorious Jeff D. Sheldrake. Screen veteran Fred MacMurray would have been a well-known face to audiences by the time of *The Apartment* due to his high-profile appearances in films such as *Alice Adams* (George Stevens, 1935), *The Trail of the Lonesome Pine* (Henry Hathaway, 1936) and *True Confession* (Wesley Ruggles, 1937). Here, he turns his wholesome, square-jawed persona well and truly on its head; MacMurray excels in creating a multifaceted scoundrel, projecting Sheldrake as a craven adulterer whose professional veneer and abuse of power do little to make the character seem any less pitiful or achingly insincere in the eyes of the audience.

The Apartment performed very impressively with both critics and the public, quickly becoming a solid box-office success. Ed Sikov observes that '[United Artists] was very pleased with *The Apartment*'s initial performance, and it would only get better as the year progressed: "10 regional premieres rack up over a quarter of a million dollars in the first week," a full-page ad in *Variety* proclaimed. Billy [Wilder] brought *The Apartment* in on (or near) budget at $2,825,965. By the end of 1963, the film had taken in a domestic gross of $6.5 million, with an additional $2.7 million coming in from abroad'.[9] Reviewers at the time praised the film almost universally, with particular acclaim for its strong lead performances – particularly in regard to Jack Lemmon's strong evocation of a troubled central character which managed to convey empathy and pathos without allowing the weight of the role to detract from the adroit implementation of his robust comic skills. Some, such as Bosley Crowther of *The New York Times*, commended the disciplined creativity of the film's central premise, opining that 'Mr Wilder and his co-author on the script, I.A.L. Diamond, have managed to keep the action and the dialogue tumbling with wit. [...] His direction is ingenious and sure, sparkled by brilliant little touches and kept to a tight, sardonic line'.[10] Others, such as *Life* magazine, applauded the way that Wilder had managed to wring such an inspired seam of comedy from a seemingly serious setting: 'The result shows in his films as "the Wilder touch", a mingling of gentle comedy, hilarious slapstick, and daring efforts to test the limits of good taste. His plot for *The Apartment*, for instance, is outrageous: a young man zooms up in a big insurance company because he happens to have a midtown apartment which he can lend to his bosses for their casual flirtations. This is a subject that calls for the utmost in deftness and taste and how well Wilder has managed can be questioned. But there is no questioning that, at its best, his film is very funny'.[11] *Variety* also joined the chorus of admiration for the many different complementary elements of the production, noting that 'to Wilder's striking credit, the picture has atmosphere, it creates a feeling about people, and, along the way, it makes a few pertinent comments about big businessmen and their infidelities. Joseph LaShelle's Panavision camera states its case skillfully with low-key work for loneliness, brightness for the efficient office sequences. Art director Alexander Trauner and set decorator Edward G. Boyle have effectively recreated a Gotham apartment house and a business office that is spectacular in its scope. Film editor Daniel

Mandell maintains smooth pace, and sound by Fred Lau is tops'.[12]

This appreciation for *The Apartment*'s impeccable quality has continued to be expressed in the writing of modern commentators, many of whom have emphasised the strong on-screen chemistry between Lemmon and MacLaine, the skills of the highly effective supporting ensemble cast, and the universality of the film's themes. Ruthe Stein, for instance, considered in *The San Francisco Chronicle* that the striking balance between comedic touches and serious drama that is achieved by the script and cast is what has kept audiences returning to the film decades after its initial release: 'Wilder keeps the tone light while addressing some serious issues, including an attempted suicide. Lemmon and MacLaine are magical together, and MacMurray more than holds his own as the third part of the triangle. He commands the office – and, not incidentally, the big screen – with a sexual energy he would scarcely have a chance to show again'.[13] *The Guardian*'s Colin Jacobson instead drew attention to Wilder's expert directorial sleight of hand which proves to be consistently compelling: 'In the hands of a lesser director, *The Apartment* could – and probably should – have been a mess. However, Wilder managed to dance between the humor and the pathos and make both sides of the coin believable and effective. Though the film's second half did become more serious, the picture lacked any form of abrupt change of pace. Instead, Wilder gently moved it into a different direction, and the shift worked nicely'.[14] Many critics, such as Scott Tobias, have instead pointed towards the depth and quality of the screenplay as being crucial to the film's success: 'The tonal wizardry of *The Apartment* is often miraculous, like the Christmas party where Fran's heartbreak over hearing of Sheldrake's past dalliances contrasts directly with Bud goofing around in a new bowler hat like Charlie Chaplin. Most films define themselves as one genre or another, but this one can be several of them at once. But that sort of high-level plate-spinning is true of the screenplay in general, which is immensely satisfying in the way it keeps planting and paying off turns of the plot'.[15]

Wilder's film went on to do extremely well at awards ceremonies, not least at the Academy Awards where it won five Oscars and was nominated for five more. In all, *The Apartment* won the Academy Award for Best Picture; Best Director; Best Film Editing; Best Writing (Story and Screenplay: Written Directly for the Screen), and Best Art Direction/Set Decoration (Black and White). It was thus one of the last monochrome films to receive the honour of a Best Picture Oscar, and its success was to see Billy Wilder becoming the first person to win Academy Awards for Best Picture, Best Director and Best Screenplay. Jack Lemmon was nominated for Best Actor in a Leading Role, Shirley MacLaine for Best Actress in a Leading Role, and Jack Kruschen for Best Actor in a Supporting Role. The film was also nominated for Best Cinematography (Black and White), and Best Sound. *The Apartment* achieved recognition at many other awards ceremonies, including wins at the Golden Globes and the BAFTA Awards. It has since come to be regarded as one of the most critically significant films of the sixties, and in 1994 it was selected for inclusion in the United States Library of Congress National Film Registry as being considered 'culturally, historically, or aesthetically significant'.

Not only has *The Apartment* remained one of Billy Wilder's most successful and commonly screened films, but its already-assured longevity has been enhanced by the release of *Promises, Promises*, a musical comedy production which premiered on Broadway at the Shubert Theater on Sunday 1st December 1968. Featuring Jerry Orbach as 'Chuck' Baxter, Jill O'Hara as Fran and Edward Winter as Sheldrake, the production ran until 1972, but was also performed successfully on London's West End in 1969. With music written by Burt Bacharach, lyrics by Hal David and the book by Neil Simon, the play adhered to the plot of the original film fairly closely. It has more recently been revived as a Broadway production in 2010, featuring Sean Hayes, Kristin Chenoweth and Tony Goldwyn in the three leading parts.

The Apartment has come to be regarded as one of the high points of Billy Wilder's stellar directorial career, and the film provided both Jack Lemmon and Shirley MacLaine with celebrated and memorable roles. With its highly impressive array of awards, its commercial success and critical acclaim, Wilder's movie had established that the Christmas film (or, at the very least, films with a prominent festive setting) remained relevant in the fast-moving new world of the 1960s. The film reflected the rapidly changing culture of an increasingly liberated society, highlighting new developments in professional living, sexual behaviour and moral attitudes while simultaneously emphasising that the traditional virtues of Christmas had not been forgotten or rendered obsolete by the relentless march of progress. The new decade may have promised transformational social and cultural progress, but it seemed that the Christmas movie would still have a part to play in it – even if its traditions were to be challenged to evolve in order to remain relevant to a rapidly-changing world.

REFERENCES

1. The American Film Institute, 'Dialogue on Film: Billy Wilder and I.A.L. Diamond', in *Billy Wilder: Interviews*, ed. by Robert Horton (Jackson: University Press of Mississippi), 110-31, p.111.

2. Andrew Pulver, 'My Favourite Christmas Film: *The Apartment*', in *The Guardian*, 23 December 2015.
   <https://www.theguardian.com/film/filmblog/2015/dec/23/my-favourite-christmas-film-the-apartment>

3. Glenn Erickson, '*The Apartment: Collector's Edition*', in *DVD Savant*, 4 February 2008.
   <https://www.dvdtalk.com/dvdsavant/s2503apar.html>

4. Richard Armstrong, *Billy Wilder, American Film Realist* (Jefferson: McFarland, 2000), p.102.

5. James Powers, '*The Apartment*: THR's 1960 Review', in *The Hollywood Reporter*, 15 June 2017.
   <https://www.hollywoodreporter.com/movies/movie-news/apartment-review-1960-movie-1011488/>

6. Gerd Gemünden, *A Foreign Affair: Billy Wilder's American Films* (Oxford: Berghahn Books, 2008), pp.127-28.

7. Roger Ebert, 'Great Movies: *The Apartment*', in *The Chicago Sun-Times*, 22 July 2001.
   <https://www.rogerebert.com/reviews/great-movie-the-apartment-1960>

8. Gene D. Phillips, *Wilder: The Life and Controversial Films of Billy Wilder* (Lexington: The University Press of Kentucky), p.241.

9. Ed Sikov, *On Sunset Boulevard: The Life and Times of Billy Wilder* (Jackson: University Press of Mississippi, 2017), p.449.

10. Bosley Crowther, 'Screen: Busy *Apartment*: Jack Lemmon Scores in Billy Wilder Film', in *The New York Times*, 16 June 1960.
    <https://www.nytimes.com/1960/06/16/archives/screen-busy-apartmentjack-lemmon-scores-in-billy-wilder-film.html>

11. Anon., 'The Wilder Touch: The Director Explains His Zany Method for Relaxing Actors', in *Life*, 30 May 1960, pp.40-41.

12. Anon., '*The Apartment*', in *Variety*, 18 May 1960.
    <https://variety.com/1960/film/reviews/the-apartment-1200419766/>

13. Ruthe Stein, 'DVD Review: *The Apartment: Collector's Edition*', in *The San Francisco Chronicle*, 6 April 2008.
    <https://www.sfgate.com/movies/article/DVD-review-The-Apartment-Collector-s-edition-3288284.php>

14. Colin Jacobson, '*The Apartment: Collector's Edition*', in *DVD Movie Guide*, 6 February 2008.
    <http://www.dvdmg.com/apartmentce.shtml>

15. Scott Tobias, '*The Apartment* at 60: Is This Billy Wilder's Finest Film?', in *The Guardian*, 15 June 2020.
    <https://www.theguardian.com/film/2020/jun/15/the-apartment-billy-wilder-jack-lemmon>

2

Pocketful of Miracles (1961)

Franton Productions

Director: Frank Capra
Producer: Frank Capra
Screenwriters: Hal Kanter and Harry Tugend, based on a screenplay by Robert Riskin from a story by Damon Runyon

CONSIDER Christmas cinema, and most people will immediately bring to mind Frank Capra's inimitable *It's a Wonderful Life* (1946) – the festive post-War masterpiece which has arguably done more than any other single film to define the key themes of the genre. However, what is less well-known is the fact that this legendary director was to return to the festive season near the end of his film-making career with *Pocketful of Miracles*: a movie which may not have reached the dizzying heights of his glory days in the 1930s, but which nonetheless was to celebrate the holiday period in ways that seemed a world apart from his earlier cinematic triumph.

While Capra's name will always be synonymous with *It's a Wonderful Life* (a film which, for many, has come to signify the very best that the Christmas movie genre can offer), by the early sixties that legendary James Stewart movie had all but disappeared into obscurity, still awaiting its storied revival with the public through copious screenings on television throughout the 1970s and 1980s which would eventually lead to its immortality in popular culture. Its inability to draw a vast audience on the scale of his earlier work at the time of its initial release was to mark the beginning of a significant creative shift in the career of Capra, who had established himself as one of Hollywood's leading directors of the time due to successive critical and commercial successes including *It Happened One Night* (1934), *Mr Deeds Goes to Town* (1936), *You Can't Take It with You* (1938), *Mr Smith Goes to Washington* (1939), *Meet John Doe* (1941) and *Arsenic and Old Lace* (1944). Also a highly accomplished writer and producer, he served as President of the Academy of Motion Picture Arts and Sciences between 1935 and 1939, and he was additionally recognised for his highly influential documentary work with the US Army Signal Corps during the Second World War. Capra served as President of the Directors Guild of America on three occasions between 1938 and 1941, and worked closely with the California Institute of Technology, where he produced innovative educational films with a scientific theme during the 1950s. Though his cinematic output slowed in the post-War period, he remained in the public eye thanks to films such as *Riding High* (1950) and *Here Comes the Groom* (1951), both starring Bing Crosby, and comedy *A Hole in the Head* (1959), which had been headlined by Frank Sinatra and Edward G. Robinson. The latter had been his first foray into colour film-making, and this approach would continue into his final full-length motion picture, *Pocketful of Miracles*.

Though it is rarely to be found named amongst his most popular or well-known features, *Pocketful of Miracles* was nonetheless an unusual feature for Capra – not least in the sense that it was one of only two films where he had directed the story years beforehand and then later decided to work on a remake (the other being 1934's Warner Baxter-starring *Broadway Bill*, which he was later to recreate in 1950 as *Riding High* with Bing Crosby in the lead role). *Pocketful of Miracles*, on the other hand, was to be a remake of Capra's earlier movie *Lady for a Day* (1933), which had been adapted by Robert Riskin from Damon Runyon's 1929 short story *Madame La Gimp*, which had first appeared in *Hearst's International-Cosmopolitan*.

The work of Runyon, an accomplished journalist and writer of short stories, had continued to be popular with the American public even following his death in 1946, with his colourful and larger-than-life depictions of New York life remaining embedded in the public consciousness. His tales of gangsters, hustlers and Broadway actors, usually set in and around the Prohibition era, were full of idiosyncratic dialogue and attention-grabbing situations, and his stories were eagerly translated to the big screen in many films which included *The Big Street* (Irving Reis, 1942), *Bloodhounds of Broadway* (Harmon Jones, 1952) and – perhaps most famous of all – *Guys and Dolls* (Joseph L. Mankiewicz, 1955), a stage musical adaptation which starred Frank Sinatra, Marlon Brando and Jean Simmons. More unexpected was the fact that an adaptation of Runyon's work had already proven to be a hit with Christmas movie audiences thanks to Sidney Lanfield's *The Lemon Drop Kid* (1951) a decade beforehand, which had featured Bob Hope in the title role as a fast-talking hustler with a surprising heart of gold.

Capra was said to have been eager to remake *Lady for a Day* for some years, but had been unable to persuade the film's rights owners, Columbia Pictures, of the creative need to revisit the story. He was approached by Paramount Pictures in the 1950s with a view to filming a remake, but was unable to agree with the studio on the details of a radically more modernised version of the story (which at this stage had been renamed *Ride the Pink Cloud*). Eventually, Capra decided to put up his own money to buy the rights from Columbia Pictures and struck an agreement with United Artists in 1960 to remake the story in colour. However, attempts to bring the plot up to date were abandoned, and it was decided that the new film would instead retain the Runyonesque 1930s setting of the original.

No less an acting luminary than Frank Sinatra had been intended for the lead role of Dave the Dude, but he and Capra failed to agree on matters relating to the character's interpretation. Numerous other famous stars were considered, including Jackie Gleason, Dean Martin and even Kirk Douglas, before Glenn Ford was eventually cast as the protagonist. This decision brought with it the advantage that movie veteran Ford owned his own production company, and was able to assist in the financing of the film. It also presented some creative conflicts, such as Ford's insistence that Shirley Jones – who had been cast in the role of Queenie Martin – be replaced by Hope Lange. There was also reportedly great personal friction between Ford and Bette Davis, the film legend who had been cast in the pivotal role of Apple Annie. Due to the ensuing on-set conflict between actors, Capra found the atmosphere of the production extremely difficult and was said to suffer severe and near-constant migraine headaches as a result of the stress involved in helming the increasingly difficult project.

Capra both produced and directed *Pocketful of Miracles*, which was filmed in Panavision, on a budget of $2.9

million – a considerable step up (even taking inflation into account) from the $300,000 that had been spent on *Lady for a Day*. The screenplay by Hal Kanter and Harry Tugend was based on Robert Riskin's earlier screenplay, and retained some plot points while developing and embellishing others (including, of course, leaning heavily into the Christmas backdrop). The film marked the final cinematic role of actor Thomas Mitchell, who had worked with Capra to great acclaim on *It's a Wonderful Life*, and also the debut of Ann-Margret. While Capra found the circumstances of the production to be less than ideal, he would later publicly state that he actually came to prefer *Pocketful of Miracles* to the original *Lady for a Day* – an opinion that was not shared by the vast majority of critics. Some, such as Joseph McBride, even went so far as to voice the view that 'the leaden and preachy *Pocketful of Miracles* [was] so shockingly inferior to *Lady for a Day* that it effectively ended [Capra's] Hollywood career'.[1]

Christmas is fast approaching in a cold and drizzly New York City, and down-at-heel fruit vendor Apple Annie (Bette Davis) is wrapped up against the elements as she sells apples to the passing public. Annie has become a sort of mother figure to many of the homeless drifters who occupy the streets of New York, and even in her uncertain financial state she still gives to charity over the holidays. She hears that local organised crime kingpin Dave the Dude (Glenn Ford) is looking for her, and makes her way through the festively-decorated streets in search of him.

Arriving at a well-appointed backroom speakeasy, Annie meets with Dave's crumpled, permanently cantankerous sidekick Joy Boy (Peter Falk), but barely has time to ask for the boss before the room is rocked by a controlled explosion. The snappily-dressed Dave emerges from his office with a safety deposit box which has just been blown open by an expert safecracker. The once-locked box belonged to fellow gangster Rudy Martin, whose corpse has recently been recovered from the Hudson River, and contains evidence of substantial gambling debts. Dave is puzzled by an additional note asking whoever finds the papers to take care of 'Queenie', and decides to look into it.

Deeply superstitious, Dave believes that the apples he buys from Annie bring him good luck – and given that he is clearly on the up-and-up, he might be on to something. She presents him with an especially large and shiny apple, and he pays her handsomely for it. Annie notes that the generous Dave, who grew up in grinding poverty, seems determined to believe in something bigger than himself, which is why he is such a popular figure amongst the citizens of New York (if not necessarily the authorities).

Just as Annie is leaving, a striking young woman arrives to thank Dave for having paid for Rudy Martin's recent burial. Joy Boy believes she must be chasing up an unpaid debt, but she explains that she is Martin's daughter, Queenie (Hope Lange). Travelling all the way from Maryland, having only just learned of her father's demise, Queenie tells Dave that she had been instructed that if anything should befall Rudy, she should present Dave with the deeds to her late father's club. However, Joy Boy explains that this will do little to recompense Dave for the $20,000 owed to him by the ill-fated Rudy. Queenie explains that she works as a cashier in a cafeteria and is willing to pay Dave back for her father's debts, though she can only afford $5 per week. The speakeasy owner is surprised by her honesty and agrees to her terms, even though it will take her decades at that rate to repay him for her father's arrears. But then he hatches another plan: by persuading the attractive Queenie into becoming a performer in the nightclub she has been bequeathed from her father, he can make her a star and ensure that her efforts become much more profitable than her current employment.

Much to the apprehensive Joy Boy's surprise, Queenie's talents as a singer and dancer transform the ailing club into a success, and it is soon turning a brisk profit which means that she is able to pay Dave back much faster than anticipated. Within two years, the club has become such a phenomenon in New York that it starts coming under attack from Dave's underworld rivals. However, everything changes when Prohibition ends and the sale of alcohol becomes legal once again. To safeguard his long-term business interests, Dave sets up a meeting with a mysterious 'Big Man', but is unwilling to attend until he has procured an apple from Annie to ensure his good luck.

Annie, meanwhile, is illicitly procuring letterheaded notepaper from a contact who works as a porter in an upmarket hotel in the city. He is baffled that she continually asks him to act as a conduit for letters from Spain, but she refuses to enter into details. Before he can pry any further, however, Joy Boy arrives and drags Annie away so that she can supply Dave with one of her apples. The good-humoured gangster, meanwhile, is celebrating the nightclub's success with Queenie – though he laments that since alcohol has become legal, champagne doesn't hold quite the same level of illicit excitement. Queenie has now sold the nightclub at the height of its success, which has enabled her to repay Dave in full. Her father's debts are finally recompensed after two years of hard graft.

Queenie tells Dave that she wants to get married, and has made arrangements not just for a wedding ceremony but also for them to leave the underworld behind and relocate to the rather more peaceful State of Maryland, where they can start a family away from the gangland violence of the city. Dave initially seems reluctant to leave his lucrative life of organised crime, but his love for Queenie eventually wins out and he agrees to her vision of a life of domestic bliss.

An agitated Joy Boy arrives and beseeches Dave to pick up the pace; Steve Darcey (Sheldon Leonard), the notorious Chicago gangland leader, has arrived to meet with him. Queenie is aghast: Darcey has a nationwide reputation for murder and violence. Dave tries to reassure her that he will be safe; he has had to expend every effort to smuggle the infamous mobster into New York right under the collective noses of the police department, which will buy him goodwill. A self-made man who has worked his way up through the perilous hierarchy of organised crime, Dave is determined to reach the top at any cost.

Pausing only to purchase the requested apple from Annie on the way to his car, Dave speeds off for his illicit rendezvous with Darcey. The Chicagoan mob boss is holed up in a custom-designed transport truck, and is none too happy about having been kept waiting. The pair enter into a game of verbal brinkmanship, and Darcey reveals that he is looking to grant the rights to his New York business interests to one single successful candidate. With the bootlegging business now obsolete, the mobster intends to syndicate his crime operations across the country, and Dave stands to benefit by becoming his representative in New York. Darcey demands $50,000 from Dave as a sign of good faith, but he refuses and instead tells his guest that he will require $100,000 himself as a guarantee of their access to his territory. Dumbstruck by Dave's audacity, Darcey watches the New Yorker leave and resolves to recruit him to his side... or else ensure that he can't do business at all. Privately, Dave reflects that he dislikes Darcey's dictatorial attitude, and would be just as happy to bring down the Chicago kingpin as work with him.

After attending Mass at her local chapel, the hard-drinking Annie returns to her run-down home – an alleyway flophouse – and pens a letter to her daughter Louise on the high class hotel notepaper she procured earlier. It becomes clear that Annie is masquerading as a wealthy socialite, and she is using the money she has accumulated from her street operations as a monthly allowance for her daughter. She becomes tearful at not having seen her daughter in person for many years, but insists in the letter that she is under medical advice not to make the transatlantic journey to Spain, where Louise is living. She also responds approvingly to the news that Louise has fallen deeply in love with a new partner.

Annie heads for the hotel to send the letter to Europe, but discovers that her porter contact has been fired; due to acting as her go-between, he was suspected by his employers of interfering with the mail for personal gain. Unperturbed, she barges into the main reception, her tattered appearance causing the well-dressed guests and employees to react in shock. She asks the aghast receptionist to check for incoming mail from Barcelona, giving her name as 'Mrs E. Worthington-Manville', but after a long altercation with increasingly senior members of staff she is horrified to discover that as the recipient was not recognised at the hotel, the letter has been sent back to Spain. Thankfully she is able to retrieve it – with no small amount of commotion – just before it reaches the mail, but she is sternly warned never to visit the hotel again. This embargo presents its own problems, she knows, as her subterfuge is now at an end; her daughter will inevitably discover that she is not resident there. Back on the streets, Annie initially reads the letter with gladness, but soon hits on a revelation so shocking that it causes her to faint onto the sidewalk.

At Dave's upscale apartment, things are even more chaotic. Joy Boy is desperately trying to arrange a contingent of bodyguards for his boss, but discovers that it is impossible to find anyone willing to risk their lives after Dave's perceived slight on the famously-unpredictable Darcey. Worse still, Queenie has heard of her fiancé's ambitions to become the King of New York and has decided to elope with a cafeteria owner named Howard Porter instead. Dave is outraged by her change of heart, and urges her to reconsider. Before the matter is resolved, Darcey sends word that he wants to resume negotiations. Dave, naturally, won't even consider another meeting unless he can buy a fresh apple from Annie beforehand to ensure his luck.

Joy Boy's slow-witted associate, Junior (Mickey Shaughnessy), is already in search of the elusive fruit trader, but finds Broadway curiously free of street dwellers. However, this is because the aforementioned homeless individuals are all converging on Dave's apartment. They explain that for years, Annie has been communicating with her daughter in Spain; Louise was given over to a convent as an infant, and has no idea of the reality of her mother's straitened, destitute existence. However, Louise has recently become engaged to a member of the Spanish aristocracy, and as Annie's contact in the hotel has been fired, she has no way of responding to her. All of her street-based associates consider themselves godparents to Annie's daughter, but Dave has done more than anyone to pay Louise's monthly allowance on account of the huge tips he pays for his apples.

Sending Joy Boy to stall Darcey, Dave heads to Annie's home and finds her heavily inebriated. Tearfully, she tells him that Louise is planning to visit New York in order to introduce Annie to the Spanish heir she is betrothed to. This has caused her to panic, knowing that her grandiose claims of being a big city socialite will be in tatters once the reality is revealed. Annie's homeless associates implore Dave to pay the upmarket hotel for a week's use of a suite so that Annie can continue her deception and fool her daughter into thinking that she is a wealthy figure. But Dave is too focused on the more immediate problem of parleying with Darcey to fully consider the fruit-seller's plight.

Dave asks Queenie to send for a doctor to take care of Annie, whose body has been badly ravaged by the long-term effects of alcoholism. However, Queenie – who has thus been contemptuous of Dave's superstitions – angrily throws his apple out of the car window and demands that he take action to help the despondent fruit vendor. Losing his nerve, Dave decides to collect Annie and drive her to the palatial hotel penthouse of one of his associates: a famous and wildly successful writer named Rodney Kent, who is currently staying in Havana. As the crime boss tries to sober her up, Joy Boy arrives, having had a rough ride from the increasingly querulous Darcey. He warns Dave that the Chicago mobster's patience is wearing decidedly thin. Meanwhile, Queenie arrives with a team of costumers and cosmetic artists and asks them to work their magic on the dishevelled Annie.

Some hours later, the makeover crew wearily depart the penthouse, and the miraculously transformed Annie emerges – now looking every inch the sophisticated grandee. Dave is speechless as the classily-dressed Annie sells him a fresh apple to grant him some much-needed luck as he finally heads for his meeting with Darcey. However, before he can leave, Queenie interjects that in order to make the fraud complete, they will also need to recruit a stand-in husband for Annie; in her letters, she has referred to Louise's stepfather (conveniently unnamed, as no such person actually exists).

Exasperated, but knowing that his future luck is dependent on Annie continuing to be able to sell apples, Dave seeks out Judge Henry G. Blake (Thomas Mitchell) – a well-spoken pool hustler with a dignified demeanour and an expert eye for a swindle. Blake is somewhat unkempt and scruffy, but is also highly cultured and has a mind like a steel trap. He is soon enlisted to the cause, and Dave promises payment for his efforts. The judge is initially sceptical of attempting to play the part of Annie's husband for a week, but is persuaded once he sees the extent of her makeover.

Louise's ship docks at a harbour in New York – her arrival is made considerably easier thanks to Dave's plan to use his underworld associates to disperse press reporters keen to chronicle the presence of a Spanish aristocrat. Annie is elated when Louise (Ann-Margret) recognises her, waving excitedly from the deck. She is accompanied by her fiancé, Carlos Romero (Peter Mann) and his father, Count Alfonso Romero (Arthur O'Connell). Dave's attempts to keep the officious Spanish Consul (Jay Novello) at bay attract police attention, so he instructs Junior to distract the crowd with a staged fight while their oblivious visitors are spirited away from the harbour.

At Dave's apartment, Junior reports that everything is going faultlessly with the masquerade – the Count and his son have been treated to a VIP tour of New York and don't suspect a thing about the subterfuge that is underpinning their entire visit. An infuriated Joy Boy points out that while this urban fairy tale has been taking place, contact has been lost with Darcey for days. What can the mob boss be planning? At that moment, two of the Chicagoan henchmen arrive to pick up Dave for a meeting with Darcey – at gunpoint. Dave, who has just managed to thwart the Count's attempts to contact the Spanish Consul by phone (being desperate to avoid Annie's cover being blown), explains that he has to buy an apple before negotiations can resume... but the gun-toting gangsters have other ideas. With a bit of quick-thinking dexterity, Dave is able to turn the tables and has the pair locked up in his apartment, promising to return only once he has procured a new apple.

The determined Spanish Consul tracks down the Count to the hotel penthouse. The bureaucrat warns that 'Mrs Worthington-Manville' is a highly suspicious figure – he has been able to find no reference to her during his enquiries, and tells the Spanish aristocrat to take care, lest she be a fraud seeking to defraud or socially embarrass him. However, the Count takes great displeasure at the implication and points out that not only was the Consul not present to meet him at the pier (Dave having deflected him at the time), but his phone call to his official residence had also been fruitless. Indignant, the Count ejects the flustered bureaucrat from the penthouse, but not before the Consul reveals that he had questioned the hotel bellboy and discovered that the residence is actually that of the novelist Rodney Kent. The quick-thinking butler, Hudgins (Edward Everett Horton), who is completely aware of Dave's scheme to help Annie, confidentially claims that the award-winning 'Rodney Kent' is actually the writing pseudonym of Judge Blake, thus keeping up the façade.

Dave arrives to buy a fresh apple from Annie, teasing the others that it is a long-running family joke. Hudgins warns that a reporter has been waiting outside the penthouse, keen to interview 'Mrs Worthington-Manville'. Dave intercepts the journalist and, with the promise of a big scoop, manages to imprison him in a storage cupboard. As he is doing so, the Count suggests that the engagement of his son and Annie's daughter be formally recognised at a private reception. This alarms all present, as he insists on a 'modest' event for around a hundred friends and close acquaintances.

An increasingly unnerved Dave panics, knowing that all of their collective associates consist of either underworld racketeers or homeless drifters. How can they possibly gather together a hundred city socialites when none of them will have the faintest idea who Annie is? Back at his apartment, he orders Darcey's accomplices released, hoping that he can salvage enough remaining goodwill to strike a deal. He is interrupted when Louise and Carlos arrive to ask him if he will consider being godfather to their first child when the time comes, which he finds touching, but with Queenie's help he manages to get rid of them before Darcey's henchmen emerge from his backroom. Then Judge Blake hits on an idea: the only way to successfully carry off a reception without raising the Count's suspicions will be to draw in all of the members of Dave's gang – each of them dressed smartly and pretending to a level of societal sophistication they don't actually possess. Dave is hugely sceptical of this plan, given how rough and ready his lieutenants are, but Queenie seems convinced that with a bit of effort it can be carried out successfully.

Deciding to set Darcey's enforcers free, warning that he is willing to negotiate but will not be strong-armed into a deal, Dave gets to work tracking down a hundred guests for the reception. Queenie, the Judge and Joy Boy are all roped into this one last-ditch effort to allay the Count's suspicions. Little do they know that the police are growing increasingly frustrated by the mystery of missing reporters in the city – no less than three journalists have now disappeared without a trace after investigating Annie at the penthouse. The Mayor (Jerome Cowan) is under growing pressure from the city's newspaper editors, who are pressing for action and threatening to approach the State Governor, who is soon due to arrive in the city. The Police Commissioner (Barton MacLane) is warned that he will be fired if results aren't achieved as quickly as possible, but investigations have thus far turned up nothing. When the Police Chief (John Litel) hears witness accounts of Dave the Dude being present at the docks for the Count's arrival, he orders the gangster put under surveillance in the hope that his involvement can be ascertained.

At Queenie's recently-closed nightclub, she and Dave are feverishly trying to persuade a hall full of hardened mobsters to speak and behave like gentry. In reality, it's all he can do to temporarily separate them from their handguns as they don tuxedos to rehearse for the white-tie event. Joy Boy despairs as Dave's line-up reprobates and scoundrels tortuously practice bowing and exchanging pleasantries, each of them with a fake identity to keep up the pretence.

The next evening, the penthouse has been transformed into a social hub, complete with live chamber music. Annie starts to take cold feet, but Judge Blake promises her that with his improvisational ability, he will swiftly step in to obfuscate any *faux-pas* made by the fake socialite guests. However, it is he who soon finds himself tongue-tied when the Count points out that the parents of the bride will be expected to contribute a dowry for the forthcoming matrimonial arrangements...

and he estimates that $50,000 should be an adequate amount. His mood brightens when the Count reveals that he is a champion billiards player back in Barcelona and suggests that they have a friendly game before the reception begins. With some tactical thinking and a bit of sly persuasion, the Judge's legendary pool skills soon have the wealthy Count agreeing to pay for the entire dowry by himself.

Back at Queenie's nightclub, the bogus socialites are taking part in their final rehearsals – unaware that police detectives are watching their every movement very carefully. Darcey phones the club and finally relents in the long-running game of brinkmanship with Dave; he agrees to pay him in exchange for his collaboration in his criminal enterprises. Dave tells the mob boss that he will make the transaction at midnight. Queenie is disheartened to hear that the deal is going through, but agrees to keep a lid on any objections until the event is over.

Dave and Queenie depart the club for the penthouse, with the other 'society guests' instructed to head there at regular intervals thereafter. All of them have been given an assumed identity, ranging from the Postmaster General to the Secretary of the Interior. As soon as they head for their car, however, they are given a tip-off that the police have the whole block surrounded. Dave returns to the club and calls the Judge, warning him to stall the event as long as he can. He then hatches a plan to visit the Commissioner and throw the police off the scent, meaning that the reception guests will be able to leave for the penthouse without being tailed.

True to his word, Dave is allowed to meet with the Commissioner and admits that he is holding the three missing reporters. He offers to release them, safe and unharmed, the following day if the Commissioner will call off the surveillance team that is surrounding Queenie's nightclub. Unwilling to negotiate, the senior police official has Dave thrown into a cell and triumphantly calls the Mayor to tell him that the case has been solved. This also comes as a relief to the visiting Governor of New York (David Brian), who is attending a formal reception in his honour. However, when the Mayor learns that Dave has threatened to ensure that the three journalists disappear permanently unless he is released, he demands that the gangland kingpin be brought to him at the reception immediately.

Dave uses his one regulation phone call while in custody to contact Queenie and explain the situation. Crestfallen, and knowing that this development will blow Annie's deception apart, she tells all of the assembled mobsters that they can go home – there will be no reception to attend tonight. She then heads for the penthouse, where the start of the event has been delayed for so long that the Count and Carlos are becoming bewildered that nobody has arrived. Louise becomes upset, making Annie resolve to tell the visiting Spaniards the truth behind the situation. However, before she can confess there is a commotion as guests finally arrive. Far from gangster charlatans, though, these are real society figures – led by the Mayor of New York himself.

Annie is dumbstruck as the Mayor formally greets her and claims to recognise her from previous meetings. Even the Count is dumbfounded when the Governor arrives, exuding charm from every pore. Queenie looks on in shock at all the top-level officials who have attended, but the enigmatic Dave – who has turned up without fanfare – stays silent about his involvement. Clearly he has persuaded the officials to get in on the act, much to the stupefaction of everyone present.

A police motorcade accompanies the family as Louise, Carlos and the Count are driven back to the harbour to depart for Spain after the reception. Annie and the Judge bid their guests a tearful farewell, while Dave considers a very different challenge – Darcey has turned up in his mobile headquarters with the requested hundred thousand dollars, ready to seal the deal. However, at the last minute Dave changes his mind; after all their fevered promotion of family life over the past few days, the thought of a happy domestic existence with Queenie in Maryland now seems much more appealing than a wealthy but ultimately precarious career at the top of the criminal underworld. As the couple embrace, Annie puts to rest any concerns about her own future as she effortlessly reverts back to her street hustler persona, instructing her associates to get out there and start capitalising on the Christmas goodwill of the crowds at the pier.

Pocketful of Miracles may have inspired audiences with its portrayal of the holiday spirit and themes of emancipation and goodwill, but it has never seriously challenged the stature of Capra's earlier masterpiece *It's a Wonderful Life* amongst audiences. That may, in part, be due to its substitution of an everyman in small town America for a cast of larger-than-life characters in a frostily atmospheric New York City, creating a tonal shift that – to many viewers – might seem less directly relatable. The film employs Christmas as a backdrop to highlight the transformative power of love, kindness and generosity – especially in terms of its exploration of a mutually-supportive community existing at the heart of this bustling and densely-populated metropolis. Despite the humble circumstances of many of the characters, and the criminal underworld aspects which permeate much of the action, the holiday season brings out the best in these unconventional individuals as they each come together to help Apple Annie maintain her elaborate social deception and ensure a happy outcome for her daughter and her new fiancé.

Throughout the film, the festive season serves as a catalyst for acts of compassion and selflessness. Characters from all walks of life – including gangsters, street dwellers, swindlers, law enforcement officers and civic officials – unite and work together to support Annie and ensure that her pretence in masquerading as an upmarket socialite is a success. The sense of togetherness and camaraderie fostered by the holiday season underscores the film's central message of the importance of human connection and empathy. *Pocketful of Miracles* also lays emphasis on the theme of redemption and second chances; the characters are able – sometimes quite unexpectedly – to find hope and renewal amidst the festive atmosphere of Christmas. Through acts of kindness and generosity, characters experience personal growth and transformation, ultimately finding joy and fulfilment in often unanticipated ways. The film thus uses its Christmas backdrop effectively in order to convey themes of love, deliverance and the power of human connection. It celebrates the spirit of the holiday season and reminds viewers of the importance of compassion, altruism, and – indeed – to believe in the possibility of miracles.

The movie's uneven melange of comedy-drama and the communication of a moral message has proven to be almost certainly its most persistent criticism, with the heavy-handedness of the underlying ethical discourse baffling many critics who had recognised Capra's mastery of such subtexts of principle in years gone by. Dave Kehr, for instance, remarks that 'Capra's powers as a cunning audience manipulator largely deserted him after World War II, when – with the glorious exception of *It's a Wonderful Life* – he seemed to lose faith in the sentimental fables he told. This lumpy and depressing farewell film measures the extent of his fall from conviction; not a moment in it rings true'.[2] The reason for this scepticism, of course, may be that the actual moral lesson of the film seems muddied and confused on account of the grand subterfuge that underpins the plot, leading to very confused messaging. For a movie which puts so much emphasis on communicating the noble and unselfish actions of its characters, this muddled expression is especially problematic, particularly in the oddly rushed and poorly-explained *denouement* when Dave the Dude's scheme to present mobsters as ersatz socialites is scuppered only to be replaced by the sudden presence of the genuine cream of New York's cultural order – a conceit which is mishandled by Kanter and Tugend's screenplay. As James-Masaki Ryan has perceptively observed:

> At the end of the film, everyone including high ranking politicians come to the ceremony for Apple Annie. Her daughter Louise and the Romeros are utterly convinced that Annie is a very respectable woman. Eventually Louise and the Romeros sail back to Spain that evening, and are happy to see Louise's side of the family. But what is the moral of the story? That lower class individuals cannot earn the respect of the upper class unless they pretend to be in the upper class? A makeover and elaborate disguises can be the answer to everything? What will eventually happen when the wedding is to take place? Will Dave have to shell out money again to ship Annie along with her fake

husband Judge among a few others to Spain for the ceremony? How long would the charade have to last? From *Mrs Doubtfire* to *A Bug's Life*, they had stories of characters pretending to be someone else, and while things seemed fine for a while, the charade couldn't last forever. The truth was uncovered, but the characters had to prove that their intentions were good, even if the lying was not. Dozens of stories have a similar premise, but *Pocketful of Miracles* has none of that. Instead it tells audiences that they are basically nothing at the bottom and unless you can dress the part, become the part, and be accepted by the upper class, you're out of luck. While the story worked as a short story in a slightly fantastical Cinderella-esque setting in 1929, for a full length story, it doesn't have a satisfactory ending or message.[3]

When all is said and done, however, the fact that *Pocketful of Miracles* was not considered favourably by many critics, or indeed by audiences generally, has meant that it has been relegated to the status of a curio in the wider context of Capra's stellar filmography. A number of reasons for this have been mulled over the years, from the uneven momentum of the rather flabby and unrealised narrative (the film runs for a somewhat flaccid 137 minutes in comparison to *Lady for a Day*'s much leaner 96 minute duration) to the questionable wisdom of tacking so closely to the 1930s milieu of the original – a decision which not only invited unfavourable comparisons, but also suggested a surprising lack of inventiveness. Some, such as Raymond Carney, criticised the fact that Capra's creative efforts had unconsciously started to echo his earlier successes, essentially becoming an unintentional pastiche of themselves: 'Consider the bedroom fight between Dave the Dude and Queenie Martin in *Pocketful of Miracles*. [[...]] It is almost a parody of certain scenes in earlier Capra films. It goes through all the motions of being an improvised, exploratory, emotional, spontaneous interaction between two adults in love, but it lacks any important emotional content, which is why it only comes off as dramatic farce and silliness in the tradition of Danny Kaye, Jerry Lewis, or Doris Day'.[4]

While it can't be said for sure whether Capra's decision to revisit the 1930s (his own cinematic glory days) as the setting for *Pocketful of Miracles* was motivated by either nostalgia or over-familiarity, the decision baffled many critics who found that the creative stratagem sat awkwardly with the largely forward-looking cinema of the time. McBride, for instance, ventures the opinion that 'one reason his 1961 remake of *Lady for a Day*, *Pocketful of Miracles*, failed was that it was a period piece, set in 1933, and thus emotionally distant from its audience'.[5] With the film's lukewarm critical reception and disappointing box-office takings, it proved to mark a disappointing end to a legendary directorial career which had produced some of the best-regarded films of the mid-to-late thirties. It has been speculated by some commentators, such as Matthew C. Gunter, that Capra himself had failed to evolve as a director from the immediate post-War period onwards, leading his directorial efforts to appear increasingly hackneyed and out of touch with filmgoers of the time: 'Absurdly, while Capra blamed the poor reception of *Pocketful of Miracles* and the fall of his career on his lack of risk taking, he also condemned the Hollywood system for committing the same sin. Frank Capra, for all his intellect and understanding, simply failed to see the key reasons why he no longer sparked the imagination of the American people. In actuality, Capra's films had changed, not the American public'.[6]

Ultimately, while *Pocketful of Miracles* may have been a pleasant enough slice of 1960s Christmas cinema, and was certainly not forgotten at the awards ceremonies of the time, it was to be a strangely muted conclusion to such a storied directorial career. Its tortured production and strangely uneven tone have meant that it has never come close to having similar longevity to Capra's earlier festive triumph. As Andrew Gaudion has observed, 'A remake of his own film, 1933's *Lady for a Day*, [*Pocketful of Miracles*] would become an experience that would give Capra something of a headache, with a long war for film rights, to friction with stars on set creating tensions which undoubtedly led to his decision to call it a day on calling the shots. That unease is very much reflected in the film itself, meaning that Capra's last film is not the capping glory one might expect such a landmark director to have'.[7] While the film was to be his final full-length motion picture, Capra did grace the director's chair one final time a few years later. His final work was to be a short documentary, lasting only 19 minutes, speculating on the future of the exploration of space. *Rendezvous in Space* (1964) was produced by the Martin Marietta Company, and was screened (with much fanfare) at the New York World's Fair. A full half-decade before a human being had set foot on the Moon, *Rendezvous in Space* featured such sequences as space shuttles in Earth orbit, dockable space stations and the challenges of astronauts being sent on long-term space exploration missions. Such was the respect for Capra and his towering reputation, the demand to see the film was so great that once the World's Fair had concluded, it continued to be screened at the New York Hall of Science thereafter.

Irrespective of unfavourable comparisons between the film and *Lady for a Day*, there was certainly no doubting the star power on display in *Pocketful of Miracles*. Star Glenn Ford had established a rock solid reputation as a leading man in the industry thanks to roles in such varied films as *Gilda* (Charles Vidor, 1946), *The Big Heat* (Fritz Lang, 1953), *Blackboard Jungle* (Richard Brooks, 1955), *Ransom!* (Cyril Hume, 1956) and *3:10 to Yuma* (Delmer Daves, 1957). He received three Golden Globe Award nominations throughout his career (winning Best Actor: Motion Picture Musical or Comedy for *Pocketful of Miracles*), was recognised with numerous other industry plaudits, and was named in a star on the famous Hollywood Walk of Fame. Accompanying Ford onscreen was Bette Davis, arguably one of the most instantly recognisable American actresses in history – here very much cast against type, as the epitome of Golden Age Hollywood glamour was remoulded to fit the character of a bedraggled vagrant. Moving from Broadway to Hollywood in 1930, the highly perfectionistic Davis quickly established herself as a major international talent thanks to bravura performances in films such as *Marked Woman* (Lloyd Bacon, 1937), *Now, Voyager* (Irving Rapper, 1942), *All About Eve* (Joseph L. Mankiewicz, 1950), *The Star* (Stuart Heisler, 1952) and *What Ever Happened to Baby Jane?* (Robert Aldrich, 1962). Winning huge critical acclaim for her versatility, Davis was the first individual to amass ten Academy Award acting nominations, and was to win the Best Actress Academy Award on two occasions. Her tremendously successful career saw her not only selected for numerous industry awards such as the Golden Globe Awards and BAFTA Film Awards, but ultimately a staggering lifetime total of 62 nominations and 34 wins. Immensely influential, she made an indelible impact on popular culture which has never truly faded.

Pocketful of Miracles featured many other noteworthy performers, among them the Academy Award-nominated Hope Lange (for Mark Robson's 1957 drama *Peyton Place*) as Queenie Martin and Thomas Mitchell (himself a two-time Academy Award nominee) in the role of Judge Henry G. Blake. While immortalised as Uncle Billy from Capra's earlier *It's a Wonderful Life*, Mitchell led an impressively adaptable performance career which saw him appearing in films as wide-ranging as *Gone with the Wind* (Victor Fleming, 1939), *Stagecoach* (John Ford, 1939) and *High Noon* (Fred Zinnemann, 1952). He famously became the first actor to win an Academy Award, Emmy Award and Tony Award. However, in the eyes of many commentators the film benefited especially from Peter Falk's scene-stealing turn as the marvellously morose, perpetually grumbling Joy Boy, whose magnetic presence and distinctive performance lit up the screen (with even Capra himself openly praising it as the movie's defining bright spot). With a highly decorated career on film and later television, Falk was to become the first performer to be nominated for both an Academy Award and an Emmy Award in the same year – and even more impressively, he managed this on two consecutive years, in 1961 and 1962. He had a hugely prolific career, but is almost certain to be best remembered for his long run as the shrewd detective Frank Columbo in the TV series *Columbo*, which ran from 1968 to 1978, and then from 1989 to 2003.

While there were other reasons to enjoy *Pocketful of Miracles* – from Robert J. Bronner's highly proficient cinematography to Sam Comer and Ray Moyer's inspired set decoration, and the subtle virtuosity of Walter Scharf's original score (complete with many inspired motifs drawn from Pyotr Tchaikovsky's legendary Christmas-situated *The Nutcracker* ballet suite) – the film's response from the critics of the time proved to be decidedly mixed. Some, such as A.H. Weiler of *The New York Times*, lamented the anachronism of the pre-War setting in the fast-moving early 1960s, noting that 'Mr Capra and his energetic troupe manage to get a fair share of laughs from Mr Runyon's oddball guys and dolls, but their lampoon is dated and sometimes uneven and listless. [...] Repetition and a world faced by grimmer problems seem to have been excessively tough competition for this plot'.[8] If critical opinion suggested that the thirties setting had been a gamble that hadn't quite paid off, others instead took issue with the predictability of the plot and the fact that, in comparison to the celebrated original, the film's pace seemed rather limp and its premise largely unfulfilled. *Variety*, for instance, took issue with the fact that 'the picture seems too long, considering that there's never any doubt as to the outcome, and it's also too lethargic, but there are sporadic compensations of line and situation that reward the patience. Fortunately Capra has assembled some of Hollywood's outstanding character players for the chore'.[9]

Later appraisals of the film have remained largely unconvinced of its merits. A general theme has emerged amongst some commentators that the escapist charm of *Pocketful of Miracles* has led to it being considered inoffensive fare if the viewer is in the right mood for its Runyon-esque capers, and are able to subordinate the implausibility of the narrative to the winning charm of the characters. Glenn Erickson is one such exponent of this approach, explaining that '*Pocketful of Miracles* will delight fans of 1930s movies, because it was made by a director whose world view is still back in that era.

Capra handles the delicate, fanciful story well enough but its sheer length frequently bogs it down. Co-producer Glenn Ford cuts a fine figure as Damon Runyon's outdated "good gangster", somehow making Dave the Dude both a tough guy and a creampuff when it comes to his personal sentiments and superstitions. Our dapper hero's ambition is to control all vice rackets in NYC. People talk about bodies ending up in the river, but it's only talk. Nothing that seriously frays the fabric of this sweetness 'n' light fable'.[10] Interestingly, others have instead considered the film specifically through the lens of Christmas cinema, praising it for the fact that it offers up an unconventional and refreshingly inventive take on the festive season. In this context, as Ian Kane argues, the film succeeds as a Christmas feature in ways that transcend its otherwise critically lacklustre reputation: 'There are also a number of other films that may not specifically be Christmas-y films *per se*, but evoke a similar spirit of cheer and goodwill. And that's exactly what I thought about after watching 1961's *Pocketful of Miracles*, directed by Frank Capra. [...] I'd recommend checking this movie out if you're looking for something a little different over the holiday season. It's entertaining and features an interesting storyline, capable acting, and has some good messages'.[11]

Pocketful of Miracles was nominated for three Academy Awards (in the categories of Best Song, Best Costume Design: Color and Best Supporting Actor for Peter Falk), and also four Golden Globe Awards – with the Best Actor in a Motion Picture: Musical or Comedy Award going to Glenn Ford, while Ann-Margret won the Most Promising Newcomer: Female Award. It additionally picked up nominations at a number of other industry awards ceremonies including the Directors Guild of America Awards, Laurel Awards and American Cinema Editors Awards.

Some years later, the film was to be remade as an Iranian production by the name of *Gedayan Tehran* (*Beggars of Tehran*) (Mohamad Ali Fardin, 1967) in Persian, and this in turn provided the inspiration for a subsequent remake, *Elmacı Kadın* (*Apple Woman*) (Feyzi Tuna, 1971), which was a Turkish-dialogue production. Better-known is Jackie Chan's Hong Kong production *Miracles: The Canton Godfather* (1989), which starred Anita Mui, Ah-Lei Gua, and Chan himself in the lead role. Most recently, the story formed the basis of the Indian movie *Singh is Kinng* (*Singh is the King*) (Anees Bazmee, 2008), which starred Katrina Kaif and Akshay Kumar with dialogue in Hindi. Given the film's relatively low-key position within Capra's wider filmography, its influence on international cinema over the decades – with productions taking place across different continents – seems all the more impressive.

In some ways, the uneven tone and critical indifference surrounding *Pocketful of Miracles* reflected a broader uncertainty surrounding the relevance of the Christmas movie in the early 1960s. With the rapidly-shifting social and cultural norms of the era having already been addressed head-on by *The Apartment* (q.v.) the previous year, Capra's cinematic swan-song had likewise proven that the idealised principles and uncomplicated moral lessons of Christmas cinema past were now being vigorously challenged by the demands of complex and fast-evolving contemporary audience attitudes. These changing tastes were already leading to vigorous questioning of traditional values as well as the underlying themes of Christmas cinema – community, family, altruism, and the possibility of greater social harmony. This interrogation of the ongoing significance of the Christmas movie would continue throughout the decade, when it would be subverted, examined, and ultimately would prove to be the grounds for considerable innovation. Capra's film may well have upended expectation of what to anticipate from a feature communicating the tenets and customs of Christmas cinema in the 1960s, but – as we will see – it would certainly not lack competition for consideration as the most surprising festive feature of the decade.

REFERENCES

1. Joseph McBride, *Frank Capra: The Catastrophe of Success* (Jackson: University Press of Mississippi, 2011) [1992], p.635.

2. Dave Kehr, '*Pocketful of Miracles*', in *The Chicago Reader*, 26 October 1985.
   <https://chicagoreader.com/film/pocketful-of-miracles/>

3. James-Masaki Ryan, '*Pocketful of Miracles*', in *DVD Compare*, 20 September 2020.
   <https://www.dvdcompare.net/review.php?rid=6344>

4. Raymond Carney, *American Vision: The Films of Frank Capra* (Cambridge: Cambridge University Press, 1986), p.483.

5. McBride, p.301.

6. Matthew C. Gunter, *The Capra Touch: A Study of the Director's Hollywood Classics and War Documentaries, 1934-1945* (Jefferson: McFarland, 2012), p.205.

7. Andrew Gaudion, 'Capra's Last Laugh: *Pocketful of Miracles*', in *Filmhounds*, 21 September 2020.
   <https://filmhounds.co.uk/2020/09/capras-last-laugh-pocketful-of-miracles-blu-ray-review/>

8. A.H. Weiler, 'Capra's *Pocketful of Miracles* Opens at Two Theaters Here', in *The New York Times*, 19 December 1961, p.39.
   <https://www.nytimes.com/1961/12/19/archives/capras-pocketful-of-miracles-opens-at-two-theatres-here.html>

9. Anon., 'Film Reviews: *Pocketful of Miracles*', in *Variety*, 31 December 1960, p.6.
   <https://variety.com/1960/film/reviews/pocketful-of-miracles-1200419917/>

10. Glenn Erickson, '*Pocketful of Miracles*', in *DVD Savant*, 22 November 2014.
    <https://www.dvdtalk.com/dvdsavant/s4663pock.html>

11. Ian Kane, 'Popcorn and Inspiration: *Pocketful of Miracles*: An Entertaining Comedy for the Holidays', in *The Epoch Times*, 21 December 2022.
    <https://www.theepochtimes.com/bright/popcorn-and-inspiration-pocketful-of-miracles-an-entertaining-comedy-for-the-holidays-4916958>

3

Santa Claus Conquers the Martians (1964)

Jalor Productions

Director: Nicholas Webster
Producer: Paul L. Jacobson
Screenwriter: Glenville Mareth, based on a story by Paul L. Jacobson

THERE are some Christmas films which seem to be perfectly in tune with the cultural zeitgeist of their production; movies which, in their fruitful engagement with the themes and spirit of the festive season, perfectly chime in with the public mood in such a way that they quickly establish a reputation as a holiday favourite amongst audiences. *Santa Claus Conquers the Martians* is, to put it bluntly, not one of those films.

As anyone with even a passing interest in Christmas films is sure to know, *Santa Claus Conquers the Martians* has acquired a reputation as one of the worst festive movies ever committed to celluloid. Although opinions have differed over the years, very few commentators have seen fit to rush to its defence; while some may venture that the film isn't quite as comprehensively awful as urban legend would suggest, virtually no-one has been brave enough to claim it as a must-see cinematic treat. Tim Healey spoke for much of the critical community when he wrote, in *The World's Worst Movies*, 'The film has found few defenders. [...] We will not dwell much longer on an artefact whose chief boast is that it is guaranteed to ruin anyone's Christmas'.[1]

So if *Santa Claus Conquers the Martians* is such a chronically poor example of festive film-making, why should it be included in a history of the genre? The answer, quite simply, is that in spite of the film's relative obscurity, the sheer lack of Christmas films appearing on the big screen in the 1960s has meant that – like it or not – this unremitting kitsch-fest of holiday tackiness has become one of the decade's most prominent exponents of the festive movie. A subgenre of low budget, poor quality Christmas movies had arguably been kick-started by the highly prolific René Cardona's surreal fantasy *Santa Claus* (1959), which had starred José Elías Moreno, Cesáreo Quezadas and José Luis Aguirre. Badly dubbed into English the following year, the film's so-bad-it's-good quality ensured public popularity with several theatrical releases throughout the sixties and seventies, and its unexpected longevity paved the way for other infamous bargain counter Christmas features during this same period.

In all honesty, the real question is not so much why a cinematic disaster like *Santa Claus Conquers the Martians* has come to be remembered all these years down the line, but rather how such a seemingly innocuous family movie could possibly have gone so horribly wrong as to merit its ignominious critical reputation. Even in an era which would spawn numerous poorly-received Christmas movies, this legend of bad film-making bestrides the field like a colossus. With its nonsensical plot, baffling narrative choices, stilted dialogue, questionable performances and substandard production values, its very title has deservedly become synonymous with the concept of low-quality, low-budget Christmas movies. As Alonso Duralde has put it, 'When people talk about bad movies, you hear terms like "cardboard sets", "amateur acting" and "ridiculous concept" thrown around willy-nilly, but few celluloid stinkers reach the depths of *Santa Claus Conquers the Martians*, a movie that combines a loony high-concept plot (it's all there in the title), condescending film-making (there should be a genre called "Make It Really Stupid – It's for Kids"), and a thoroughly pervasive sense of inanity'.[2]

On the planet Mars, two green-skinned alien children – Bomar (Chris Month) and Girmar (Pia Zadora) – are avidly watching a television interview being broadcast direct from Santa Claus's workshop at the North Pole thanks to a team led by a presenter from KID-TV (Ned Wertimer). The reporter, Andy Henderson (though puzzlingly he is also later addressed as Andy Anderson), has been given exclusive access to meet with Santa (John Call) not long before his annual Christmas Eve trip to deliver gifts to children all around the world. Santa explains his busy schedule and emphasises that he and his elves can safely get toys distributed to everyone on time (as always), though he flatly denies any plans to use a rocket-fuelled sled for extra efficiency. After a brief meeting with Mrs Claus (Doris Rich), Santa shows Andy some of the new toys that the elves have been working on. Winky (Ivor Bodin), the space specialist elf at Santa's workshop, has developed a toy rocket, but Andy is most interested in a Martian action figure that has also recently been invented. Andy wonders aloud if there could be children on Mars, and hopes – if this is the case – that they too have their own version of Santa Claus to spread joy and goodwill.

However, unknown to anyone on Earth, all is not well on the Red Planet. Martian patriarch Kimar (Leonard Hicks) is explaining to his goofy servant Dropo (Bill McCutcheon) the concerns he has over the wellbeing of his children. They are so fixated by Earth television programmes that their appetite is suffering, and yet they seem to have no interest in anything else. Unable to fathom their fascination with Earth culture, Kimar sends his son and daughter, Bomar and Girmar, off to bed. He remains troubled, and tells his wife, Momar (Leila Martin), that apparently the problem is the same all across Mars – Martian children have collectively become entranced by the idea of Santa Claus and receiving Christmas presents. Momar suggests that Kimar consults the wisdom of Chochem (Carl Don), an ancient Martian whose many centuries of life have afforded him the intelligence and judgement of the ages.

After confirming his course of action with the Martian ruling council, Kimar makes his way out into a primordial forest to seek out Chochem. The eight-hundred year old sage appears, quite literally in a puff of smoke, and listens patiently to Kimar's concerns. Chochem then explains that although the Martians do not realise it, it is currently early December on Earth and the planet is eagerly anticipating the arrival of Christmas. As Martian children are all technologically augmented from infancy to receive knowledge and understanding, meaning that they learn and mature at a dramatically increased rate, they have forgotten how to play and have fun like human offspring. Chochem urges Kimar that in order to resolve the problem of the children's restlessness, they must rediscover the joy of games and laughter. In short, he says in parting, Mars needs a Santa Claus of its own.

Kimar consults his fellow council members and tells them that Earth has had the monopoly on Santa Claus for long enough — it's time to kidnap Santa and set him to work on Mars instead. Kimar's rival on the council, the obstreperous Voldar (Vincent Beck), is dead against this course of action: he believes that the last thing Mars needs is the distraction of happy, recreation-loving children. But Kimar is resolved on the matter; he orders a spacecraft to be made ready for immediate departure.

Arriving in orbit around Earth, Voldar uses the ship's scanner to home in on New York City. Voldar scoffs that the Martians could lay waste to the surface of the planet easily, though Kimar admonishes him for his bloodthirstiness; they are not there for conquest, but for one reason only — to kidnap Santa Claus. As the scanner's magnification is increased, the Martians are confused when they discover a large number of different men in Santa Claus outfits, most of whom appear to be conducting street collections for charity. Kimar is buoyed by this discovery — surely with so many different Santa Clauses to choose from, the people of the Earth won't notice that one of them has gone missing?

American tracking stations detect the Martian spacecraft in order, causing an alert to be issued. Kimar orders the ship's radar shield to be raised, but is surprised when he is informed that it is malfunctioning. Soon after, it is discovered that Dropo has stowed himself away in the radar control box; the shield begins to function again once he has been extracted. Angrily telling Dropo that he will be dealt with later, Kimar lands the ship near a lake in the United States. There, he meets a couple of American kids named Billy (Victor Stiles) and Betty (Donna Conforti) Foster. At first, the youngsters are shocked at the aliens' unexpected arrival, but quickly recover. Kimar asks why there are so many Santa Clauses spread across the country, and Billy replies that there is only one real Santa Claus – the rest are just his helpers, there only for the holiday season to spread joy and goodwill. Billy also explains that the true Santa will be resident in his workshop at the North Pole, so Kimar determines that they must make haste for that destination at once. Voldar insists on bringing Billy and Betty along with them, to avoid any chance that they might inform the authorities of the Martians' presence before their plans can be carried out.

Once on the ship, the kids are soon befriended by the good-natured Dropo, who takes them on an unofficial guided tour of the control room. However, he is interrupted when Kimar and Voldar return early, and is thus forced to store Billy and Betty in the radar control box to avoid their detection. Kimar manoeuvres the ship to the North Pole, where the Martians – together with their lumbering robot, Torg – set off to bring Santa to Mars by fair means or foul. Before they leave, Voldar suggests that they should now bring the children with them to the Red Planet, leaving the details of Santa's disappearance a mystery as no witnesses will be left to tell of the Martian incursion. Kimar tells Dropo that he must guard the children at all costs until he gets back. But as soon as the Martians have departed from the control room, Billy wastes no time in sabotaging the ship's radar shield, knowing that the Martians will now be tracked whenever they try to leave Earth.

Billy and Betty make a break for freedom, racing into the snowy wastes of the North Pole just before the Martians emerge from the ship. An increasingly insubordinate Voldar has discovered that the children have escaped and, noticing their footprints leading away into the snow, Kimar resolves that they must catch up with the fugitive kids before they have an opportunity to warn Santa of the Martian plans. Betty and Billy prove to be more resourceful than the Martians have given them credit, evading a rampaging polar bear (Gene Lindsey) before eventually being accosted by the hulking Torg. However, the robot ignores Voldar's demand that it should crush the children to death, having been programmed by Kimar to obey only his own commands. The senior Martian safely releases the two Foster kids, but warns them not to attempt another escape – the next time, they may not live to tell the tale.

The Martians move on to Santa's workshop, where Torg storms the building and causes pandemonium among the elf workers. Santa confuses the rampaging robot for a giant clockwork toy, which perplexes the Martians and makes Kimar decide to move his team in on the workshop themselves. Once there, they use a freeze ray to put Mrs Claus and several of the elves into suspended animation. Santa soon realises that if he is to keep everyone safe, he has no choice but to accompany the Martians back to their ship. Kimar is surprised to discover that Torg will no longer obey his voice commands, and so – believing it now to be functionally useless – decides to leave the robot on Earth.

With the eyes of the world firmly on Mars (one newspaper issues a panicked report that Santa has been 'kidnaped' [sic] by the Martians), America's top rocket scientist Dr Werner Von Green (Carl Don again) outlines a plan to send astronauts into space on a rescue mission to bring Old Saint Nick back to Earth in time for Christmas. But as they make their getaway, the Martians are initially oblivious to any attention from the Earth. Santa tries to cheer up Billy and Betty, but they are homesick and worried about what awaits them on Mars. Attempting to buoy their spirits, Santa tells them that he's always wanted to visit Mars and see what the alien world is like, but his attempts at merriment fall on deaf ears. Even the clownish Dropo, who arrives at their cell with some nutritious food pills, is unable to raise a smile.

Back at the control room, the Martians discover that the radar shield is inoperative. Voldar inspects the equipment and ascertains the damage that has been caused by Billy. Kimar is impressed with the boy's inventiveness and orders that the shield be repaired. However, Voldar vows revenge and heads for the cell. There, he offers Santa, Billy and Betty a tour of the ship... and his first destination of choice is the airlock. Voldar secures the oblivious trio into the room and starts the depressurisation countdown; after sixty seconds, Santa and the children will be pulled into the depths of space when the airlock opens. Billy realises what is going to happen and reacts in horror, but Santa manages to keep a cooler head and discovers a nearby ventilation pipe near the main airlock door. In the airlock control area, Kimar is furious to hear of Voldar's nefarious scheme and gets involved in a prolonged fist-fight with him. Just as Kimar gets the upper hand, Santa and the kids arrive out of the blue, having escaped their macabre fate through the air duct. Kimar is amazed that Santa could fit into such a tiny passageway, but Santa replies that all his years of climbing up and down chimneys had come in handy at just the right time.

Determining that Voldar should stand trial for his treachery, Kimar orders the ship to land back on Mars. But before they even have the opportunity to set down on Martian soil, Voldar manages to escape his cell and goes into hiding. Kimar recommends that Santa and the children be given round-the-clock protection, as he is certain that his vengeful adversary will strike again. Santa is introduced to Kimar's family, and – seemingly unfazed by his alien abduction – promises Momar that he will do his best to bring the Christmas spirit to her children, and to all the youngsters of Mars. Kimar encourages Santa to meet his offspring, and in no time the charming Jolly Old Elf effortlessly encourages Bomar and Girmar into a fit of laughter. The Martian children also befriend the two Foster kids, who they discover are the same age as themselves. Kimar, Momar and Dropo are all amazed to hear the guffawing coming from Bomar and Girmar's room, knowing that the young children have never expressed amusement before.

Some time later, Martian operative Shim (Joe Elic) issues a reconnaissance report to Voldar, who is now a fugitive hiding out in a remote Martian cave. He tells Voldar that Santa's new toy factory, which has recently been set up on the surface of Mars, is operating at full capacity. Unlike the North Pole workshop, Kimar has given Santa access to a fully mechanised assembly line, meaning that toys will soon be flowing freely to children all over Mars. Voldar is incensed, believing that Santa and Kimar will sentimentalise Martian life and sabotage their culture's long history of dispassionate efficiency. He decides to hatch a scheme that will derail Santa's seasonal cheer and goodwill once and for all.

At the factory, the Martian conveyor belt is churning out toys faster than Santa's helpers (Bomar, Girmar, Betty and Billy) can possibly handle them. Dropo is particularly impressed by the sheer proficiency of the enterprise. Letters to Santa are flooding in from all over Mars, as the excited alien children each want their own present from Earth's legendary Father Christmas. Santa wistfully considers how, after all his centuries of painstakingly crafting toys for the children of

Earth, he ended up pushing buttons on a control console to produce his gifts. Closing up proceedings for the day, Santa unveils a new suit which has been specially tailored for him by Momar. Dropo is keen to try it on, but Santa tells him that he'd need to dramatically increase his girth before it would even come close to fitting his lithe Martian frame.

Returning to Kimar's home, Santa decides to turn in for the night. Kimar becomes concerned that Billy and Betty seem unhappy and withdrawn; his wife tells him that they are obviously homesick, and that it is imperative that he returns them to their family on Earth. This leaves Kimar with a crisis of conscience – he knows that the children must be returned, but is similarly aware that he can't risk revealing the nature of his kidnap plan to the other humans. Meanwhile, Dropo is gorging on food pills in the hope of being able to fit into Santa's costume. Realising that overeating will take too long to fatten him up, he resorts to using a pillow to increase his waistline. He is elated that he can now fit into the suit (albeit that he has some problems placing Santa's hat over his antennae), and decides to go back to the factory to produce more toys while the real Santa is asleep.

Dropo doesn't realise that someone else is already at the production line – Voldar and his henchmen, attempting to sabotage the conveyor belt's control mechanism. They are interrupted by the sudden appearance of the hapless Dropo and, confusing him for Santa Claus when they see his red suit and false beard, they seize him and take him back to their cave hideout. The next morning, Momar discovers that Dropo is missing. Santa tells her that, as his new suit has also been misplaced, it is likely that Dropo is out having fun pretending to be Santa Claus somewhere. Believing that he has most likely gone to the toy factory, Santa and the children head there in search of their errant Martian friend. However, on arrival they discover that Dropo is nowhere to be found, and that the machine has started producing defective toys.

Santa suggests that Kimar come to the factory and inspect the control box. The Martian father determines that the machine has been deliberately rewired, and he and Santa come to the conclusion that Voldar is responsible for both the sabotage and the abduction of Dropo. Determining to find the renegade and stop his disruption once and for all, Kimar steps out of the factory only to meet none other than his adversary in person. Voldar tells the startled Kimar that he is holding Santa hostage, and will release him only on the condition that the factory be permanently deactivated, the Foster kids returned to Earth, and no further attempt made to transplant Christmas celebrations to Mars. Kimar initially appears to agree, only to then reveal that the real Santa is currently hard at work in the factory. As Voldar exasperatedly realises that he has kidnapped an impostor, Kimar orders that the accomplices be hunted down and a search be conducted to free Dropo. However, neither man realises that Dropo has already made good his escape from the cave and is on his way back.

A struggle breaks out in the storage room where Kimar is holding Voldar. Billy, who is heading for the room to pick up a tin of red paint, overhears Voldar threatening to come after the real Santa. He quickly reports this news, and Santa hatches a plan to throw a spanner in the works. Shortly afterwards, Voldar appears with a ray-gun and tries to intimidate Santa, only to be ambushed by Bomar, Girmar and the Fosters, who attack him with a wide variety of toys from the factory. Santa reacts with hilarity as Voldar is brought down by a nothing more than an avalanche of festive playthings and wind-up models.

The newly-escaped Dropo arrives on the scene only to be held at gunpoint by Voldar's ally Stobo (Al Nesor), but the villain is soon disarmed by the newly-emerged Kimar, who has now regained consciousness. Santa is impressed by the benevolence of the suitably festive Dropo, who has clearly taken the Christmas spirit to heart. As Voldar and his henchmen are taken into custody, Santa suggests to Kimar that Mars doesn't need him at all – it already has a perfectly good Santa Claus of its own in the form of Dropo.

Realising that it's time to leave, Santa bids farewell to Kimar and his family. Billy and Betty exchange gifts with their new friends Bomar and Girmar while Kimar thanks Santa for having brought the Christmas spirit to Mars, changing the planet forever as a result. Even Dropo gets in on the act, now tubbier than ever thanks to some strategically-placed balloons, as the assembled Martians give Santa a heartfelt send-off. The Fosters then head away into space on the Martian ship as Santa assures them that, if they hurry, they should be able to get back to Earth just in time for Christmas Eve.

With some films it can be difficult to find fault with their production, whereas in others a single flaw can fatally undermine a movie's artistic integrity. With *Santa Claus Conquers the Martians*, however, the most difficult issue is to ponder exactly where to start in the veritable catalogue of production gaffes and deficiencies that are so proudly on display. From the badly-animated title sequence (which forthrightly displays crew credits such as the 'custume' designer) to the washed-out colour and jarring edits, the film starts poorly and still manages to go sharply downhill.

Among the many oddities to mull over are the Martians' bizarre, never-explained headgear and their hair-dryer ray-guns (actually re-painted Whammo Air Blasters), to say nothing of their squeezy-bottle spacecraft (complete with a radar control box that looks like it has been made out of balsa wood) and the indigenous Martian forest which appears to be composed of twigs draped in polythene. This is not to say that Earth fares much better, with the North Pole's copious Styrofoam rocks and an actor burdened with arguably the least realistic polar bear costume in film history as he 'terrorises' the region near Santa's workshop. Then there is the unconvincingly-shoehorned, grainy militaristic stock footage scattered around the first act of the film (whether it is required or not), the amazingly bad fight choreography between Voldar and Kimar, and a killer robot which appears to have been constructed almost entirely from cardboard and tinfoil. And this is just for starters.

While the film's title may ostensibly suggest a veritable cornucopia of Christmas tropes, its actual portrayal of traditional holiday celebrations seems oddly muted and largely overshadowed by the campy, low-budget sci-fi elements that are liberally in evidence. Despite the inclusion of Santa Claus as the nominal central character, *Santa Claus Conquers the Martians* perhaps surprisingly seems reluctant to delve too deeply into an exploration of traditional Christmas themes such as friendship, mutual goodwill or the spirit of giving. Instead, it employs Christmas as a gaudy backdrop for its increasingly bizarre and gleefully far-fetched storyline, where themes of community and kindness are subordinated to planet-hopping adventures and implausible plot twists.

That being said, it could conceivably be argued that the film does perhaps indirectly highlight the universal appeal of Christmas and the importance of spreading joy and happiness, even across the vast gulf of space: by kidnapping Santa Claus in a desperate attempt to bring happiness to their children, the Martians demonstrate a desire – even a craving – to experience the same sense of joy and wonder that has long been associated with Christmas on Earth. However, the film's primary focus always remains firmly on its various comedic and fantastical elements rather than any attempt at a meaningful exploration of Christmas themes. As a result, while *Santa Claus Conquers the Martians* may entertain younger audiences with its outlandish premise and decidedly quirky characters, its contribution to a wider understanding of Christmas is invariably more whimsical than it is ever profound.

Although John Call gives an appealingly warm central performance as Santa, unassailably jolly and seemingly unruffled by the prospect of alien abduction from start to finish, his is one of the few displays of acting in the film which can actually be considered watchable for any length of time. Leonard Hicks's Kimar is enjoyably grave and stoical, while a game Bill McCutcheon tries hard – indeed, some might say a little too hard – to wring every ounce of humour out of the never-knowingly-funny Dropo. Otherwise, the overacting ranges from the entertaining (Vincent Beck as Voldar) to the grin-inducing (Al Nesor as Stobo), by way of the downright painful (Doris Rich in her brief appearance as Mrs Claus), whereas Donna Conforti deserves a mention for delivering one of Christmas cinema's single most astonishing displays of wooden acting in the role of Betty.

The plot of Glenville Mareth's gleefully deranged script is peppered with more holes than an entire year's supply of Swiss cheese. Exactly how does a ten-year old boy know how to disable the advanced alien technology of a Martian radar shield? Why does Kimar, so desperate to evade the attention of the Earth authorities that he is willing to kidnap small children in order to conceal his visit to the planet, then decide to leave a massive Martian robot behind (which rather gives the game away about their presence at the North Pole)? For what reason is Dr Von Green's plan to send an astronautic rescue party to Mars given such prominence when, once it has been outlined, it is never mentioned again for the rest of the film? And, perhaps most inexplicably of all, how can Voldar possibly confuse Dropo with Santa Claus when – given that he is bright green, has only half of his body mass and boasts metal antennae protruding from his head – they don't look even remotely alike? These glaring inconsistencies cannot even be excused by the fact that the film is so blatantly aimed at children, given that younger audiences are often the most alert and discerning of all moviegoers.

One of the single most puzzling aspects of *Santa Claus Conquers the Martians* is how the film could have developed into such a nightmare production when so many talented people were involved in its creation. Director Nicholas Webster was a respected and experienced film-maker; initially a film-cutter for Metro-Goldwyn-Mayer, he worked as a cinematographer for the United States Army during World War II and, after the conclusion of the conflict in 1945, was responsible for creating documentaries for the US Department of Agriculture. Webster had previously helmed documentaries and features for television including *The Violent World of Sam Huff* (1960) – which featured the first ever use of a wireless microphone in a TV series – and the Emmy Award-nominated *Walk in My Shoes* (1961). For the cinema, he had been responsible for films such as *Dead to the World* (1961) and *Gone Are the Days!* (1963), before taking a rather more conventional science fiction approach to the exploration of the Red Planet in *Mission Mars* (1968) some years later. His later directorial career, primarily television-based, continued until the early 1980s and included episodes of popular series including *Get Smart* (1970), *Bonanza* (1970 and 1972), and *The Waltons* (1974). It is fair to say that, in spite of the widespread notoriety of *Santa Claus Conquers the Martians*, the film's quality is not representative of Webster's wider career, and nor should it distract commentators from an otherwise skilled and well-crafted body of work.

The genesis of *Santa Claus Conquers the Martians* had come from Paul L. Jacobson, who had spotted a gap in the market for a Christmas science fiction feature. Keen to move into the motion picture industry and with his own production company, Jalor Productions, having been founded from his established work in video production, Webster was appointed to direct the feature with screenwriter Glenville Mareth selected to develop the script from Jacobson's original story. The filming took less than two weeks in the summer of 1964, taking place at Michael Myerberg Studios – a converted aircraft hangar located at Roosevelt Field in Long Island, New York City. (The building's location would later be converted into a shopping mall.) As Duralde notes, 'the film was shot in just ten days on a budget of less than $200,000. And it shows'.[3] Yet by that same token, the straitened financial circumstances of its production – which proudly confronts the viewer with such delights as a polar bear costume that is little more than a shabby headpiece and a bearskin rug wrapped around a hapless actor's frame – can be considered either a shortcoming or part of the film's deeply quirky allure, depending on your point of view. Either way, as Will Knauss remarks, it is difficult not to appreciate the sheer ambition of the production team: 'Another charming part of *Santa Claus Conquers the Martians* is its rock bottom production values. All of the sets have a two-dimensional feel, as if they were once part of a grade school Christmas pageant. [...] It's hard not to admire the filmmaker's can-do attitude'.4

Just as the ill-fated film's crew had the very best of intentions, so too did the cast contain a number of well-established performers. John Call's acting career had included thirty years in Broadway productions and numerous appearances on television and in film (many of them uncredited), including *Hangman's Knot* (Roy Huggins, 1952), *The Kid from Left Field* (Harmon Jones, 1953) and *Happy Anniversary* (David Miller, 1959). Bill McCutcheon likewise enjoyed a long film career, one which extended into the 1990s, and would later win a Tony Award for his performance as Moonface Martin in the Broadway revival of *Anything Goes* in 1988. Perhaps most notably, the film marked the debut appearance of actor Pia Zadora. Active later on stage and in films such as *The Lonely Lady* (Peter Sasdy, 1983) and *Hairspray* (John Waters, 1988), she would win a Golden Globe Award for New Star of the Year in a Motion Picture for her performance in Matt Cimber's *Butterfly* (1982), starring alongside Orson Welles and Stacy Keach.

Santa Claus Conquers the Martians is quite unique in the sense that it doesn't really work as a Christmas film in anything but name, is too dull to be a successful children's film (in spite of its occasional moments of cheery juvenility), and certainly has little currency as a science fiction film. By the time of the 1960s, the age of flying saucers, Martian invasions and ray-guns was starting to give way to a much more sophisticated approach to cinematic sci-fi – lest we forget, this was the same decade which brought audiences features such as Jean-Luc Godard's *Alphaville* (1965), Francois Truffaut's *Fahrenheit 451* (1966), Franklin J. Schaffner's *Planet of the*

Apes (1968) and both Stanley Kubrick's *Dr Strangelove* (1964) and *2001: A Space Odyssey* (1968).

Yet in spite of the fact that the film has more in common with the visual and narrative style of the infamously cheesy *Plan 9 From Outer Space* (Ed Wood, 1959) than the more challenging, thought-provoking movies which were featuring in the sci-fi genre at the time, *Santa Claus Conquers the Martians* was actually treated fairly humanely by critics during the period of its release. As David H. Smith observes, 'It may be difficult for today's jaded readers to believe that, during its initial release, *Santa Claus Conquers the Martians* garnered some pretty good reviews. *The New York Herald-Tribune* found "the children in the film... quite appealing"; across town, Kathleen Carroll of *The New York Daily News* found it "a gay, imaginative Christmas gift for children". It wasn't until the late 1970s that *Santa Claus Conquers the Martians* began to acquire its dubious notoriety'.[5] Indeed, Howard Thompson of *The New York Times* confidently proclaimed the movie to be 'a delightful little film [which] adults will see as naively simple and square as cheese. But let's be honest, from now on until you-know-when, it's the children who count',[6] later observing that the film had 'reaped a box office bonanza in a regular, multi theatre booking'.[7]

Santa Claus Conquers the Martians first appeared in movie theatres just before Christmas 1964 and, following its initial release, it became a favourite festive matinee feature throughout the sixties. It would later vanish into relative obscurity until its somewhat ignominious revival some years later. After being featured in *The Monster Times* and, on television, on *The Canned Film Festival* (1986), the cult reputation of *Santa Claus Conquers the Martians* was firmly cemented into popular culture following its appearance in a special Christmas episode of the offbeat TV series *Mystery Science Theater 3000* which was originally broadcast on 21 December 1991. *MST3K*'s massively entertaining critical demolition of the film was to greatly raise its profile (for better or for worse), and was responsible for bringing it to the attention of a whole new, hitherto-unsuspecting generation of moviegoers. A legend of Christmas pop culture was thus born.

It is difficult to find consensus among commentators as to what exactly makes *Santa Claus Conquers the Martians* such a uniquely bad movie. While its reputation as a stalwart example of chronically maladroit film-making is often mentioned by critics, opinion is divided as to which specific factor was most responsible for its failure. *FilmFanatic*, for instance, noted that: 'Frequently voted as one of the worst "bad" movies ever made, this corny holiday flick boasts laughably cliched alien costumes, unimaginative set design, wooden acting, and Pia Zadora in her screen debut as a Martian child – in other words, just about everything necessary to merit its status as a campy cult classic. With that said, I didn't enjoy *Santa Claus* [...] nearly as much as I wanted to; despite its clever premise, the film's execution lacks bite. Bad movies are a dime a dozen, and the best thing about this one is its promising title'.[8] Some have drawn attention to the laughable production values, whereas others instead pinpoint the exasperatingly hammy performances – usually with the haplessly unamusing Dropo gaining particular mention in this regard. Yet analysis has grown more sympathetic in recent years, with some critics observing that whereas the sheer ineptitude of *Santa Claus Conquers the Martians* could have lent itself quite adequately to an out-and-out parody, the deadly sincerity of the narrative inevitably means that audiences are inevitably laughing at the film rather than with it. Dave Sindelar has been representative of this strain of commentary, enquiring: 'Is this the worst movie ever made? No, it isn't; in fact, it's not even the worst Christmas movie ever made. It is the one, however, which most blatantly calls attention to itself by dint of its title. Yet, I don't have any real problem with the central concept; it's jarring at first, but a movie about Santa Claus or Martians requires a suspension of disbelief anyway. If you buy one, it's not too tough to buy the other. [...] Still, even if it isn't the worst Christmas movie ever made, it's not for lack of trying'.[9]

While it has been noted that the film's sugary sentimentality, which is laid on by the shovel-load, has made it largely unpalatable in the harsh light of the ingrained cynicism of the modern world, some critics have noted that it was also not entirely unaffected by the heightened Cold War tensions of the world which had produced it. As Bill Gordon has sagely observed, in a geopolitical environment still reeling from the Cuban Missile Crisis and the assassination of President John F. Kennedy, some ideological influence seemed virtually inevitable – as does a commentary on the changing nature of how popular culture was being consumed:

> *Santa Claus Conquers the Martians* was made in 1964, as some in-jokes will hint to you. (Santa mistakes one of his reindeer for Nixon and there's a character based off of Wernher von Braun). You might have noticed the metaphor for Martians-as-Communists. Nothing a little Western television can't cure. The best part of this movie is when children everywhere – Earthlings and Martians alike – are shown sitting hypnotized in front of the tube, completely immersed in the television

world. Billy and Betty look at the Martian antennae and think that Martians are TV sets. Of course, why wouldn't they? And you still think Voldar's the bad guy, eh?[10]

Some over the years, particularly in recent times, have voiced the opinion that *Santa Claus Conquers the Martians* has acquired an unfair reputation since its release, and that even although it is far removed from any notion of a cinematic work of genius, it is somewhat undeserving of the universal critical pillorying that it has been subjected to. In its own haphazard way, the movie reflects the universality, the righteousness and the benefits of the Christmas spirit – albeit in an admittedly somewhat low-key manner – and it seems almost unfair to expect too much thematic profundity from a microbudget kids' feature hailing from a more innocent period. Jim Rex has mirrored this sentiment in his appraisal of the film, remarking: 'It's a simple time-waster aimed at the kiddie matinee crowd but in that regard, it may be one of the best. This flick hit screens in 1964. No point playing to the nostalgia of 1964. We're friends, we can be honest. Between race riots and the Boston Strangler, 1964 was as screwed up as any other period in history. But it was a simpler time when a movie like *Santa Claus Conquers the Martians* could entertain its undemanding target audience to maximum effect'.[11] This, perhaps, is the most benevolent thing that can be said about the film: that its heart is always in the right place, even though virtually nothing else is.

Santa Claus Conquers the Martians continues to live on in the popular cultural consciousness, and as long as there are lists of bad movies it is difficult to imagine a time that the film won't be lodged safely at some position in the top ten. Its cult status now assured, it is often shown on alternative TV channels over the holiday season and has been released internationally on DVD and Blu-Ray. It has even proven to be something of a Christmas quiz trivia favourite, given that supporting star Doris Rich appeared in what is thought to be the debut credited motion picture role of Mrs Claus. The notorious theme song 'Hooray for Santa Claus', which plays over the opening and closing credits, has also proven to be surprisingly enduring. Either annoyingly catchy or supremely awful depending on individual opinion, the song was written by Milton DeLugg and Roy Alfred and was released as a single in November 1964 (performed by 'Milton DeLugg and the Little Eskimos') by Four Corners Records. Also that same year, trumpet player Al Hirt also released an instrumental rendition of the theme tune (the B-side bearing a cover version of Irving Berlin's 'White Christmas').

While *Santa Claus Conquers the Martians* inspired a comic book adaptation and read-along version of the film, published by Dell Comics in March 1966, a noteworthy oddity was been the belated release of a novelisation when, in September 2005, author Lou Harry composed a distinctly ironic account of the film's events – abundant with knowing whimsy – which was published by Chamberlain Brothers. Additionally, the movie was adapted for the stage in 1993 as *Santa Claus Conquers the Martians: The Musical*, directed by Sean Abley and taking place at Chicago's famous Factory Theater. This in turn inspired an entirely different stage version, adapted by Brian Newell and Nick McGee, which arrived at the Maverick Theater of Fullerton, California in 2006. A third stage adaptation was to emerge a decade later, in 2016, with this version being directed and written by Nick Poling for The Red Curtain Foundation for the Arts in Marysville, Washington. While talk of a remake of *Santa Claus Conquers the Martians* has surfaced and resurfaced from time to time, though never reaching production, some essence of the film's madcap legacy – albeit in a rather tongue-in-cheek form – has lived on in more recent films such as *Santa Claus Versus the Zombies* (George Bonilla, 2010).

It seems fair to say that *Santa Claus Conquers the Martians* formed something of a nadir for the Christmas movie, and indeed for sixties film-making in general. It marked a decisive break not just from the festive movie's golden age of the forties and fifties, but also the work of other, more celebrated directors earlier in the decade. Whereas Billy Wilder's *The Apartment* and Frank Capra's *Pocketful of Miracles* had both, in their own ways, highlighted aspects of the major social and cultural changes that were sweeping across America and the wider world at the time, *Santa Claus Conquers the Martians* instead sets itself the rather more modest goal of presaging the mass production era of toy-making which had already firmly taken hold of the country. Just as Santa voices regret at the impersonal nature of push-button manufacturing, much preferring the gentle care and attention which goes into the hand-made toys that he constructs at the North Pole, so too are we continually reminded that these technological advancements will never make Santa himself obsolete: the Christmas spirit, after all, is comprised of much more than simply gifts and playthings. But as the world continued to evolve due to the profound changes of one of the most transformative decades of the twentieth century, the innocent artlessness of *Santa Claus Conquers the Martians* and its interplanetary escapades were simply to lay the groundwork for further, critically infamous cinematic adventures that were still to come for the Christmas film genre.

REFERENCES

1. Tim Healey, *The World's Worst Movies* (London: Octopus Books, 1986), p.59.

2. Alonso Duralde, *Have Yourself a Movie Little Christmas* (New York: Limelight Editions, 2010), p.185.

3. ibid.

4. Will Knauss, '*Santa Claus Conquers the Martians*', in *Cool Cinema Trash*, 23 December 2014. <https://jeffandwill.com/willknauss/2014/12/23/cool-cinema-trash-santa-claus-conquers-the-martians-1964/>

5. David H. Smith, '*Santa Claus Conquers the Martians*', in *It's Christmas Time at the Movies*, ed. by Gary J. Svehla and Susan Svehla (Baltimore: Midnight Marquee Press, 1998), 215-19, p.219.

6. Howard Thompson, 'Santa vs Martians', in *The New York Times*, 17 December 1964. <https://www.nytimes.com/1964/12/17/archives/santa-vs-martians.html>

7. Howard Thompson, 'Children's Films Widening Market: Feature Movies at Weekend Matinees are Popular', in *The New York Times*, 13 February 1965, p.10.

8. Anon., '*Santa Claus Conquers the Martians*', in *FilmFanatic.org*, 27 November 2006. <https://filmfanatic.org/?p=1857>

9. Dave Sindelar, '*Santa Claus Conquers the Martians*', in *Fantastic Movie Musings and Ramblings*, 12 June 2005. <https://fantasticmoviemusings.com/2016/09/25/santa-claus-conquers-the-martians-1964/>

10. Bill Gordon, '*Santa Claus Conquers the Martians* – with Pia Zadora', in *Worst Movies Ever Made*, 22 October 2012. <https://worstmoviesevermade.com/santa-claus-conquers-the-martians-with-pia-zadora/>

11. Jim Rex, '*Santa Claus Conquers the Martians*', in *B&S About Movies*, 22 December 2019. <https://bandsaboutmovies.com/2019/12/22/santa-claus-conquers-the-martians-1964/>

4
The Magic Christmas Tree (1964)

Orrin Enterprises

Director: Richard C. Parish
Producers: Jeffrey C. Hogue and Bruce Scott
Screenwriter: Harold Vaughn Taylor

THERE are some Christmas films which, due to their dearth of production values and lack of public profile, may well have disappeared into complete obscurity if not for the sheer lack of festive cinema on offer during the 1960s. Accordingly, *The Magic Christmas Tree* is the kind of motion picture that could really only have been made during this period. A micro-budget curiosity that easily rivals *Santa Claus Conquers the Martians* (q.v.) when it comes to critical drubbing, the movie has arguably only been remembered by Christmas cinema aficionados for reasons far removed from those that the film-makers must have intended.

The sixties was a decade plagued by some of the most ham-fisted Christmas cinema ever to be produced, and *The Magic Christmas Tree* certainly deserves its place within that ignominious pantheon. It was to be the only directorial credit of Richard C. Parish, who also makes an appearance in the film (under the acting pseudonym 'Dick Parish'), and was filmed in La Verne, California, with a cast of unknown actors on the most slender of budgets. In spite of the lack of financial resources, the film certainly didn't lack for ambition: in the time-honoured tradition of the legendary *The Wizard of Oz* (Victor Fleming, 1939), it featured a colour fantasy sequence sandwiched between monochrome scenes intended to represent reality (or what passes for it). Unfortunately for Parish and his production team, the similarities end there, as the film's unhinged narrative and profound deficiencies in quality have led to it becoming one of the Christmas movie genre's most infamous curiosities. As Dennis Schwartz has explained, 'After seeing this mess, you will understand why Parish never directed again. It's a kid Christmas story, that's strictly amateur. It has been rightfully called one of the worst and most depressing holiday films of all time'.[1]

There have been various competing theories as to why the 1960s produced so many low-budget, critically-panned festive movies. While some point to the creative efforts being focused on the Christmas television of the time, helping broader market endeavours to sell colour TV sets to the public, others cite widespread civil unrest and the increasing complexity of post-War geopolitics which presented filmmakers with a creative challenge in making traditional holiday movies appear relevant to contemporary audiences. Whatever the reason, *The Magic Christmas Tree* has certainly not been exempt from criticism that it appears oddly anachronistic and disconcerting amongst theatrical releases of the time; as Dave Sindelar has remarked, 'There must have been something about the sixties to inspire the cornucopia of truly atrocious low-budget Christmas movies that can be found therein. This one has references to Halloween and Thanksgiving as well as Christmas, features a cat and a turtle, has a bizarre mowing scene, has one of the most pathetic comic chase scenes ever committed to celluloid, features a giant named Greed who breaks the fourth wall, and mercifully lasts less than an hour'.[2]

Halloween is being celebrated in an American suburb, and a young boy named Mark (Chris Kroesen), together with two unnamed friends (Bill Willingham and Billy Schaffner), can't wait for their elementary school classes to end so that they can take part in the ghostly celebrations. As they eat lunch, Mark's friends lament that they must babysit or attend parties that evening rather than taking part in more fun activities. Mark triumphantly proclaims that he instead intends to visit the ramshackle old Finch house in the neighbourhood, which is reputed to be haunted. His friends warn him that rather than being abandoned, the house is said to be occupied by a witch, but Mark scoffs at their warning – his father has assured him that she is simply a fearsome-looking elderly woman with no supernatural powers. When they hear of his plans, Mark's friends volunteer to join him on his planned adventure on the way home from school.

Later on, Mark leads his friends to the Finch house, but they begin to lose their nerve on approach. Little do they realise that Miss Finch (Valerie Hobbs) – the old lady that Mark believes to be a witch – is nearby, desperately trying to persuade her cat Lucifer to come down from a tree; her feline companion has become stuck on a high branch. As the three schoolboys reach the house, Mark's friends panic and run off, but Mark is accosted by the elderly woman who asks if he would mind climbing the tree and rescuing her increasingly-distressed cat. Mark is initially reluctant, disinclined to be late for dinner, but eventually agrees to the old lady's request. Upon attempting to scale the tree, however, he slips and falls when Lucifer proves resistant to being rescued. Landing hard on the ground, the young boy is knocked unconscious.

Waking up some time later, Mark is puzzled to discover that he is somewhere different entirely. The old Finch house is gone, now replaced by a traditional fairy-tale cottage. More alarmingly, the old lady is now dressed as a stereotypical witch – complete with dark clothing and a pointed hat. Mark is alarmed, but the witch reassures him that there is no need for concern; after he fell out of the tree, Lucifer the cat was so amused that he decided to climb down of his own accord, so he managed to do as he was asked after all. The witch insists that Mark receive a reward for his efforts, and gifts him an ornate ring bearing the face of Santa Claus. She explains that the ring has magic properties: within it is a hidden compartment containing an enchanted seed. If it is planted in the night under the wishbone of a Thanksgiving turkey, it will grow into a magic tree with the power to grant three wishes. Mark is now thoroughly baffled by this unexpected turn of events, but the witch assures him that there is no need to trouble himself with the fine details: all he needs to do is wear the ring when the seed is planted, turn it three times and speak some magic words, and then everything will be in place for the tree to grow. However, the witch cautions him that he will have only three magic requests in total, so he should consider with great care what they will be.

Mark remains confused, and asks the old lady why she is helping him when he had been led to believe that all witches were wicked and treacherous. She replies that, just like anyone, witches can be either good or bad; some are kind and generous, while others are evil and devious. He is still mystified at why his surroundings look so different, but the witch explains that when he arrived, he expected to see a sinister-looking old house, but now can see it for what it is – a much more welcoming residence. If you think good thoughts, she enlightens him, you will see good things – but the opposite is also true. Billy perplexedly remarks that he feels as though he must be dreaming.

Some weeks later, his family are sharing a Thanksgiving dinner at home. Mark excitedly asks his father (Dick Parish), who is carving the turkey, if he can have the wishbone. His dad finds Mark's single-minded focus confounding, but Mark's mother (Darlene Lohnes) urges him to give their son the requested turkey bone; he has been asking for it since Thanksgiving began. That night, Mark dons his dressing gown, takes the ring and heads for the family garden, stopping only to collect his pet tortoise Ichabod to witness the coming ritual. Following the witch's instructions, he digs a hole under cover of moonlight, retrieves the enchanted seed from the magic ring, plants it beneath the wishbone from the Thanksgiving turkey, and then carries out the incantation. He is shocked when, as he completes the recitation, a bolt of lightning lights up the night sky to the sound of a deafening clap of thunder. Mere seconds later, a full-sized Christmas tree stands where Mark had planted the seed.

The next day, Mark's father is befuddled; there is nothing in his morning newspaper about a freak lightning storm being forecast, and the weather report is for clear weather. He heads out into the garden to mow the lawn – jokingly telling Ichabod the tortoise that he will race him to the finish line – but has great difficulty persuading his temperamental old lawnmower to start up. Once he does manage to get it moving, a madcap race around the garden ensues as he struggles to keep it under control… a skirmish which only ends when the mower collides with the tree that Mark had planted the previous night. Mark's parents look on in shocked surprise; the tree seems to have appeared completely out of nowhere.

Mark's mother reasons that her husband must have planted it earlier and forgotten about it, but he vehemently denies doing so – especially in the middle of the lawn. Instead, he resolves to cut the tree down, but soon discovers that the teeth of his saw are unable to break through its seemingly-impenetrable trunk. He then switches to an axe, only to find that it too is powerless to cut into the bark; no matter how hard Mark's father swings it, the axe-head simply clangs against the tree as though he were hitting a lamp-post. Eventually he gives up, resignedly admitting that it looks as though the tree is there to stay.

With Thanksgiving now having come and gone, the approach to Christmas is soon underway. Mark's mother decides to take her daughter, Diane (Dianne Johnson), out to town for some Christmas Eve shopping. Mark's father, on the other hand, has another mission in mind – in spite of his wife's constant reminders, he is only now getting round to buying the family's Christmas tree. Mark has a different plan, however. With his parents and sister away, he resolves to stay at home and wrap up presents.

In reality, however, Mark has something else to do. Heading for the garden, he regards the mysterious Christmas tree... and is shocked when it suddenly starts talking to him (in a decidedly grumpy tone). The tree asks Mark to turn the magic ring around three times and give the incantation that the witch had taught him back during their Halloween encounter. The young boy does as requested, but is stunned when the tree suddenly disappears, only to rematerialise in the family's living room.

The dumbfounded Mark is hectored by the increasingly-impatient tree, now fully decorated for Christmas, into stating his first wish. Thinking aloud, the boy ventures that he would like to have the same kind of power the tree has – even if only for an hour. Sure enough, the tree grants his wish, and Mark discovers that he can now make items disappear or change their form simply by pointing at them. He heads off to enjoy his new magic powers, but the tree warns him to remember that his supernatural abilities will only last for the next sixty minutes.

Mark bemoans the fact that night has fallen outside, which will restrict his fun, but the tree reminds him that he currently has the power to bring back daylight as he wishes. The youngster is soon out wandering the neighbourhood, abusing his new abilities by startling a delivery driver when he sets his truck in motion while the man is still loading it with boxes of potato chips. This leads to a frantic chase where the driver tries in vain to catch up with his wayward vehicle, while a police patrol car follows closely behind... trailed, in turn, by the hapless officer who wasn't in the car when it took off. Mark instigates other hijinks such as initiating a custard pie fight between a restauranteur and a waitress, and setting a fire truck into motion as its unfortunate driver (Charles Nix) races after it in pursuit. The gleeful boy enjoys causing mayhem, and nobody is harmed by the chaos he has brought about.

After Mark's hour of fun expires, night returns to the town. His family arrive back home after their evening of shopping, though Mark's father bewails the fact that he has been unable to find anywhere still selling Christmas trees. He resolves to again try his hand at chopping down the tree that had mysteriously appeared in the back garden, but is nonplussed when he discovers that it has gone. However, the family are even more amazed when they enter the living room and discover that not only has Mark apparently managed to reposition a seemingly unmoveable tree, but that it is now beautifully decorated.

Later that night, once his family are sleeping, Mark sneaks back downstairs to talk to the tree about his second wish. However, with so many possibilities on offer, he can't decide on what to request. The tree chides him that he had better make his mind up before Santa Claus is due to make his annual Christmas Eve delivery to the house. This then gives Mark an idea – this year, he wants to have Santa all to himself, meaning that the Jolly Old Elf will only visit Mark's home and not those of all the other millions of children across the world. The tree warns that this is a very selfish wish, but Mark is dead set on the idea.

The tree grants the request, meaning that Santa Claus will be unable to return to his workshop at the North Pole without Mark's agreement. Sure enough, a very bewildered Santa (Howard Blevins) materialises next to the tree in the living room, but has no idea how he has got there. Old St Nick is aghast to learn that he is trapped in a chair, and – what's worse – that he can't leave Mark's home. He begs Mark and the tree to let him go, lest children all over the globe will be disappointed to receive no Christmas gifts. However, the boy has other ideas: he will only release Santa if he agrees to give him a seemingly never-ending line-up of presents.

Santa is shocked at being under the tree's spell, as it means that he is not in a position to refuse Mark anything. The young boy heads out into the wilderness with a brand new BB gun, but finds the experience oddly lonely and unfulfilling. As he wanders, he encounters a huge giant named Greed (Robert Maffei), who warns Mark that he fell under his power when he forced Santa to give him so many presents while denying others the joy of receiving Christmas gifts. The giant tells the boy that he is now his slave; he shows him scenes from across the country, where children are distressed at the apparent disappearance of Santa Claus on Christmas Eve. The United States and United Nations commit every resource to tracking Santa down, but there is simply no trace of his famous sleigh anywhere.

Mark is horrified at the effect of his self-centred actions; he has been wallowing in the elation of having an unlimited supply of Christmas gifts while children all over the globe have received nothing. Tearfully, he begs Greed to let him go so that he can make things right again. When the giant realises that the boy's regret is genuine, he releases him, but notes to himself that he will always be able to find another avaricious child to indenture. ('Maybe you!' he cries, pointing directly at the screen as he breaks the fourth wall with a distressingly hearty laugh.)

Racing home, Mark pleads for forgiveness from Santa and asks the magic tree to grant his final wish – he wants to reverse his previous covetous request and release Santa from captivity before he was ever trapped. The tree is pleased that Mark has seen the error of his ways, and brings about his request: Santa is returned to his sleigh, the world's children receive their presents, and everything returns to how it should have been. The tree informs Mark that he must now return to the Land of Magic. The boy is saddened that he must part company with his new friend, but – his three wishes now used up – the tree dissolves into thin air as inexplicably as it first arrived.

To his surprise, Mark wakes up to discover that it is Halloween again. The old lady who lives in the Finch house is gently coaxing him out of unconsciousness, and is relieved to see him recovering from his fall. Miss Finch tells him while it is regrettable that he had taken a tumble from the tree, it had at least scared her cat Lucifer into descending of his own accord. Her animal companion now safe, she tells Mark that he should be rewarded... but is confused when the boy says that he wants nothing to do with a magic ring. Instead, she explains that she had a treat of milk and cookies in mind instead – an offer that Mark gladly accepts. Still dazed, he reflects that the last few weeks had all been nothing more than a dream... until he spots the magic Christmas tree on a hill near the Finch house. Reassuringly, the tree tells him that not everything is always as it seems... and that every Christmas tree contains its very own special amount of magic.

While the plot of *The Magic Christmas Tree* revolves around a mystical Christmas tree, the film's portrayal of Christmas is actually surprisingly minimal, and the themes the film explores are grounded more in the fantastical than they are in the wider conventions of festive traditions as they are usually explored in the cinema of the holiday season. While the movie does feature various elements of whimsical adventure typically associated with some other Christmas-themed stories of the era, its focus is largely concentrated more on the larger-than-life aspects of the narrative rather than on traditional festive themes. The general portrayal of Christmas is thus largely incidental to the storyline, serving as a moral canvas for the dreamlike events that unfold, rather than as a central focus. While some may find a scintilla of entertainment in the presentation of the film's various magical elements, its contribution to our understanding of Christmas cinema is more rooted in fairy-tale quirkiness than in traditional yuletide messages.

While there are some vaguely enjoyable aspects of *The Magic Christmas Tree* – the odd sense of deadly earnestness, the idyllic early sixties suburban interiors, and the waspish testiness of the tree's vocal delivery – the film is essentially one long catalogue of production disasters from start to finish. First and foremost is the awful, wooden acting, which is sub-par even by amateur standards; something that is not helped by the hopelessly stilted dialogue (and even more inexpressive delivery). The film suffers from inconsistent, washed-out colour, with even the monochrome sections being badly in need of proper grading. The egregiously flawed editing (the intercutting proving to be particularly bad), lop-sided pacing and abysmal post-production dialogue dubbing are also major issues, as is the muffled sound quality and constantly uneven volume level of both the dialogue and music. Yet just as debilitating as the film's many production deficiencies are its doomed attempts to generate wit when the screenplay's line in humour is so horribly anachronistic. Consider, for instance, the tortuously laboured humour of the sequence where Mark's father attempts to cut the grass (complete with the cartoon-quality 'comedy' sound effects of his erratic lawnmower), or the domestic cut-and-thrust of the dialogic interplay between Mark's parents, which has all the subtlety and finesse of a flatulent reindeer after a plate of Brussels sprouts.

Harold Vaughn Taylor's screenplay is also riven with gaping logical inconsistencies which stretch credulity beyond breaking point (and considering the fact that the film is centred around a talking Christmas tree, that's bad news). Why does the supposedly 'derelict' Finch house look to be well decorated and in perfect repair? Why does Mark's father expect to read news about a lightning strike which took place mere hours earlier, when the paper would surely have been printed late the previous day so that it was ready for delivery in the morning? If Mark has to turn night into day in order to cause an hour of magic mayhem, why are people wandering around town and doing their jobs in the evening as though it is still daytime? Then there is the fact that Mark's father somehow manages to completely miss the fact that there is a brand new, fully-grown Christmas tree in the middle of his garden while mowing the lawn – which seems all the more bizarre given that he collides with it as though it was hitherto-unnoticed, even though it occupies a central point in the yard. And the least said about the questionable practice of keeping a pet tortoise in the drawer of a bedside cabinet, the better for everyone.

The Magic Christmas Tree was an obscure production even at the time of its release, and the fact that it was overlooked by the critical community (as well as the vast majority of the general public) meant that it soon disappeared into cultural obscurity. However, its sheer clumsiness, tiny budget and plethora of plot illogicalities meant that it nonetheless slowly built a cult following, culminating in its release on VHS video in 1992. Its reputation as one of the worst Christmas movies ever made was finally cemented in December 2011 when it was relentlessly roasted on comedy audio commentary site *Rifftrax* by Mike Nelson, Kevin Murphy and Bill Corbett. The famous trio (headed by Nelson, who had become well-known for his work as head writer on the earlier *Mystery Science Theater 3000*) had developed huge acclaim amongst movie buffs for their entertainingly pithy demolitions of forgotten and unconventional old movies, and their critical annihilation of *The Magic Christmas Tree* ensured that the film came to the attention of a whole new generation who might otherwise have never been aware of its existence.

Modern appraisal of the movie has been unanimously hostile, with it having been critically panned in relation to just about every aspect. As Scott Hamilton and Chris Holland have observed, while the film exhibited abundant ambition, it was very clearly let down by a lack of creative aptitude and resources: '*Magic Christmas Tree* was obviously made by amateur filmmakers working with whatever they had at hand. 〚...〛 The most important element in that situation is talent, and the filmmakers here simply had none. The story doesn't make sense, the comedy style was out of date 20 years before the movie was made, and the acting is bad even when it's dubbed. The greatest Christmas gift we ever got was when this movie was consigned to well deserved obscurity'.[3] Even the film's oft-discussed conceit of reproducing *The Wizard of Oz*'s famous transition between monochrome and colour sequences has been lampooned as pretending to a level of sophistication far beyond its range of capability. This, as Sam Panico has explained, automatically sets *The Magic Christmas Tree* up for a fall by very obviously drawing attention to its own glaring shortcomings: 'Much like *The Wizard of Oz*, *The Magic Christmas Tree* thinks that reality is in black and white while dreams are in color. Both films have a witch. Both movies have wishes. But only one of them had a budget. And only one of them is a classic beloved by families for generations. Sorry Richard C. Parish. Your one and done directorial effort isn't getting a 4K re-release this year. 〚...〛 I would advise you to avoid it and ensure that your Christmas Day isn't filled with relentless horror'.[4]

Other critics have instead drawn attention to *The Magic Christmas Tree*'s overabundance of illogicalities and inconsistencies, such as Alan-Bertaneisson Jones who raises the fact that with a bit of lateral thinking from the characters, the entire central premise of the movie might have been circumvented altogether: 'It is the tale of a cocky youth who is given a magic ring by an old witch for saving her cat from a tree, and the problems the greedy tyke causes when he uses the powers to bring on a magical Christmas and grant himself three more wishes. I am not sure why the witch didn't simply use the ring or her magic power to get the cat down herself!'[5] Perhaps inevitably, the quality (or otherwise) of the acting has also come in for considerable hammering, with some of the critical appraisals – such as that by Charleston Picou – leaving no doubt as to the widespread disdain towards the level of performance talent on offer:

> When discussing this movie, I'd be remiss if I didn't mention the acting. Or better yet, how much I wish actual acting was involved. To say the entire cast was terrible would be an understatement. Everyone showed the emotional range of marionettes. Almost everyone delivered their lines as if they were completely dead inside and all that was left were empty husks of the people they had once been. If you could fill out the cast with the living dead, I'm sure the end results would be similar. I doubt a single one of these people had taken any kind of acting or drama classes. If they had, then the person who taught them should be forced to give these people their money back. I would have felt bad for this cast if not for the fact that after a while of suffering through this film, I began to hate these people. I began to hope that they had

felt the same level of misery making the film that I felt watching the freaking thing.⁶

Ultimately, *The Magic Christmas Tree* is not only the product of its time but also of its highly-restricted budget. Its basic creative intentions are good, even if its execution is far from it. When all is said and done, however, its claim to fame in the modern day is not so much that it is a brave failure, but rather that if the viewer is in the right mood for it, the movie is the very epitome of 'so bad it's good'. *Talk Film Society*'s Sarah Jane perhaps said it best when she remarked: 'Is *The Magic Christmas Tree* any good? Of course not. Should it be watched? Yes, absolutely. In fact, you should watch this with family over the holidays. Subject them to this as well. It's like a Christmas punishment come true'.⁷

For all its manifest failings, *The Magic Christmas Tree* is nonetheless a surprisingly distinctive Christmas offering. For one, it is a fascinating cinematic curio – its director would never helm another movie, its cast was entirely devoid of star power, and with such a miniscule budget it could be considered either audacious or foolhardy to have mounted any kind of film production in the first place. Yet it is when contemplated as a cultural product of the 1960s that the film is perhaps at its most interesting. While its Christmas content is relatively minimal, spreading the action through Halloween and Thanksgiving as it does, the movie often explores the importance of family, generosity and the magical aspects of the holiday season, reinforcing traditional values related to the festive period. While the sixties marked a period of momentous social change, *The Magic Christmas Tree* was almost like a slice of suburban American life pickled in aspic with its perfectly maintained lawns, picket fences and family dinners. The film's idealised depiction of the nuclear family unit, its fresh-faced child protagonists and the unpretentious line in storytelling all mirrored the wider cultural landscape of the early sixties, where family life and childhood innocence were factors which were highly valued.

If anything, the movie's central impulse is one of nostalgia – a yearning to preserve traditional values even in the face of the multiple challenges facing society at the time of production. The linear, child-friendly narrative typifies this era's broader preference for wholesome and innocent entertainment, contrasting with the broader cultural shifts of the decade where themes and subtexts were gradually becoming more complex and even controversial. In this sense, the escapism of *The Magic Christmas Tree* presented a means of diversion for the audiences of the time, giving them the opportunity to temporarily step away from the demanding realities of the rapidly-changing world around them by immersing themselves in a fanciful, romanticised version of Christmas.

The film's diminutive budget and resultingly non-existent production values may often have caused it to be sneered at over the decades, but they also reflected the strength of this era's very diverse range of Christmas films – features ranged from big-budget studio productions to much smaller, independently-produced projects, with the latter being given undue prominence they would not have enjoyed in other eras. This creative diversity underscored the fact that the Christmas movie genre was becoming more accessible to a wider range of film-makers, suggesting its wide-ranging appeal and cultural importance even at a time when the genre's artistic relevance was being interrogated. *The Magic Christmas Tree* thus exemplifies how even the most modest festive movies of the 1960s were used to reinforce traditional moral values, offer innocent family entertainment and provide an escape into a fantastical version of the holiday season. Despite its catalogue of imperfections and relative obscurity, the film remains a helpful artifact for understanding the cultural relevance and characteristics of holiday movies during this turbulent era.

REFERENCES

1. Dennis Schwartz, '*The Magic Christmas Tree*', in *Dennis Schwartz Movie Reviews*, 5 August 2019.
<https://dennisschwartzreviews.com/magicchristmastree/>

2. Dave Sindelar, '*The Magic Christmas Tree*', in *Fantastic Movie Musings and Ramblings*, 18 January 2021.
<https://fantasticmoviemusings.com/2021/06/06/magic-christmas-tree-1964/>

3. Scott Hamilton and Chris Holland, '*The Magic Christmas Tree*', in *Stomp Tokyo*, 25 December 2005.
<http://www.stomptokyo.com/movies/m/magic-xmas-tree.html>

4. Sam Panico, '*The Magic Christmas Tree*', in *B&S About Movies*, 25 December 2019.
<https://bandsaboutmovies.com/2019/12/25/the-magic-christmas-tree-1964/>

5. Alan-Bertaneisson Jones, *I'm Dreaming of a Fright Christmas: A Guide to the Seasonally-Themed Movies of the Macabre and Other Weird and Wacky Tinsel-Tinged Treasures and Turkeys* (Milton Keynes: AuthorHouse, 2010), p.52.

6. Charleston Picou, 'Film Review: *Magic Christmas Tree*', in *HorrorNews.Net*, 19 November 2018.
<https://horrornews.net/147398/film-review-magic-christmas-tree-1964/>

7. Sarah Jane, 'TFS the Season: *The Magic Christmas Tree*', in *Talk Film Society*, 20 December 2017.

<https://talkfilmsociety.com/articles/tfs-the-season-the-magic-christmas-tree-1964>

5

The Christmas That Almost Wasn't (1966)

Bambi Productions / Childhood Productions

Director: Rossano Brazzi
Producer: Barry B. Yellen
Screenwriter: Rossano Brazzi, from a story by Paul Tripp

CONTINUING the theme of low-budget, high-ambition Christmas cinema in the 1960s, *The Christmas that Almost Wasn't* (*Il Natale Che Quasi Non Fu*) is the very epitome of a cult oddity. After all, who could resist a film which has, as its central premise, the idea that Santa Claus is forced to get a job as Santa Claus in order to raise enough money to pay his overdue rent bill on his workshop at the North Pole?

Even aside from its outlandish plot, *The Christmas that Almost Wasn't* was a decidedly offbeat production. Though the film shares its name with a celebrated children's poem by humourist Ogden Nash which had been published nearly a decade earlier in 1957, its story was actually based on a book by Paul Tripp and adapted for the screen by the film's director, Rossano Brazzi.[1] Tripp, who also starred in the movie, had become a prolific screenwriter for children's films, mostly for the TV market throughout the 1950s. However, it was an actor that he came to be most readily recognised by the public, thanks in no small part to appearances in episodes of many high-profile TV series throughout the fifties and sixties including *Lux Video Theater*, *The Goodyear Television Playhouse*, *The Dick Van Dyke Show*, *The Twilight Zone*, *Perry Mason* and many others. He led a life dedicated to creating high-quality youth entertainment, fronting CBS's award-winning *On the Carousel* (1955-59) magazine programme with his wife Ruth Enders Tripp, and presenting WNBC's *Birthday House* (1963-67) with singer Kay Lande. Also an author and musician, his most celebrated composition was almost certainly the song *Tubby the Tuba* (1946), famously performed by Danny Kaye in 1947. The founder of Childhood Productions, a company which produced and distributed films for children's matinees, Tripp had additional duties as the lyricist for *The Christmas That Almost Wasn't*, and had no small amount of experience when it came to this responsibility – amongst his other songs, he had previously penned the lyrics of *Good Night, Dear Lord*, a popular track for Johnny Mathis in 1958.

The film's director, Rossano Brazzi, was considerably better-known in front of the camera as an Italian stage and film actor. He became most immediately familiar to English-speaking audiences thanks to his role as Emile De Becque in the ground-breaking musical *South Pacific* (Joshua Logan, 1958), which was to become one of his defining roles. Though a significant film star in his native Italy, he eventually rose to international prominence thanks to appearances in films as diverse as *Three Coins in the Fountain* (Jean Negulesco, 1954), *The Barefoot Contessa* (Joseph L. Mankiewicz, 1954) and *The Italian Job* (Peter Collinson, 1969). *The Christmas* that *Almost Wasn't* evidenced a broadening of his cinematic career, however, in that it marked the first time that he would act as a screenwriter and director (the latter often under his artistic pseudonym of 'Edward Ross', such as in his 1968 crime comedy *Criminal Symphony*, headlined by Ann-Margret). In appearing as the dour antihero of *The Christmas that Almost Wasn't*, Brazzi very much set out to subvert the expectation of the audiences of the time. As Jessica Pickens notes, 'Italian actor Rossano Brazzi usually played suave, debonair romantic leading men throughout the 1950s and 1960s in films like *South Pacific*, *Summertime* or *Light in the Piazza*. You see Brazzi like you've never seen him in *The Christmas that Almost Wasn't*. In his directorial debut, Brazzi plays completely against his usual type. 〚...〛 Visually, it's really very stunning. It's filled with bright colors, fun Christmas decorations and interesting hair and makeup choices. The beginning of the movie had me shaking my head but I was charmed at the end, and I don't even know why. I really think it was seeing Brazzi in a completely different character than you've ever seen him'.[2]

The Christmas that Almost Wasn't was, like other Childhood Productions, filmed in Europe with an international cast, and then released in the North American market with the dialogue dubbed into American English. In this case, the feature was filmed without live sound recording, with the Italian performers having their lines re-recorded for the American release of the film. Because Brazzi had considerable experience of performing for international audiences, he delivered his own dialogue with his natural accent, whereas his castmates were redubbed to disguise their prominent Italian inflections and intonations. The Italian version of the film had a duration of 93 minutes, whereas the American release was cut down slightly to a running time of 89 minutes.

Following an animated musical overture, the movie opens with the scene of a town square, where excited children are decorating the civic tree under the cheerful supervision of kind-hearted local lawyer Sam Whipple (Paul Tripp). The middle-aged Sam loves the festive season so much, he remarks to the gathered kids that he wishes it could last the whole year round. While his young helpers are disappointed that there has been no snowfall thus far in December, Sam is already equipped with pocketfuls of artificial snow which he tosses around liberally in the hope of encouraging some Christmas spirit.

Indefatigable, Sam continues decorating into the night, but is taken aback when he is approached by a white-whiskered stranger... who turns out to be none other than Santa Claus (Alberto Rabagliati) in disguise. This revelation surprises Sam for two reasons – firstly, it is much too early in December for Santa's annual Christmas visit, and secondly, the Jolly Old Elf looks distinctly lacking in yuletide cheer. Grimly, Santa informs Sam that there will be no Christmas this year, thanks to the unwelcome interference of miserly billionaire Phineas T. Prune. A year ago, Prune had bought the land rights to the entire North Pole, and he is now Santa's *de facto* landlord. But he is demanding a year's rent in full, and Santa doesn't have sufficient cash to pay him. Worse still, the greedy tycoon intends to seize all of the Christmas presents made by Santa at his workshop and take them as payment, meaning that there will be no gifts for the children of the world. The only way to avoid this sad outcome will be if Santa can somehow raise the money necessary for Prune to call off his eviction – though he only has until midnight on Christmas Eve to achieve this ambitious feat.

Sam is puzzled at why Santa should ask him for help, but is told that while millions of children across the world write letters asking for presents, Sam had been the only little boy to send a letter of thanks after Christmas. All those years ago, he had told Santa to call on him if he ever required assistance… and that day has now come. The good-humoured lawyer offers to pay the rent on Santa's behalf, but soon realises that he has inadequate funds to meet the sky-high rate Prune is charging. (He is such a kindly legal representative, he claims that he keeps forgetting to invoice his clients for payment.) However, he is undeterred and tells Santa that he intends to discuss the matter with Prune directly.

Approaching the billionaire's mansion, however, Sam and Santa are accosted by his ferocious guard dog, then curtly told by his chronically glum butler Blossom (John Karlsen) that Prune is not at home. Sam suggests waiting outside the house until the miserly magnate returns, but Santa has another idea – if they head for his workshop at the North Pole, Prune has taken to making an unwelcome appearance there every evening in order to demand that the rent be paid up in full.

Little do they realise that Mrs Claus (Lidia Brazzi) is already waiting for Santa's return at their snowbound abode, apprehensive about the outcome of his journey. The elves, led by their quirky foreman Jonathan (Mischa Auer), have downed tools and refuse to work on the production of any new toys, reasoning that their efforts will inevitably be seized in Prune's confiscation of the property. Mrs Claus cheers them up with a song, and they are soon back at what they do best – creating gifts for children all over the world.

Santa arrives in his sleigh with Sam (slightly disorientated by his fantastical surroundings), and Mrs Claus is immediately buoyed by the news that a skilled lawyer is now on their side. But they have no time to discuss matters before Prune (Rossano Brazzi) arrives, right on time, to request his rental payment. The top-hatted entrepreneur is frozen from having been lingering around in the sub-zero temperatures, but angrily rebuffs any suggestion of hospitality. It quickly emerges that Prune has a pathological phobia of children, whom he irrationally envies for some unknown reason. He believes it is unfair that youngsters get to have fun and enjoy themselves while adults have to work and be responsible.

Prune again demands payment in full for the last year's worth of rent. Santa introduces Sam as his new legal representative, but the posturing skinflint is unimpressed – he knows that the law is on his own side, that he is acting within his rights, and that Sam has no leverage with which to negotiate. In response, the lawyer asks Prune exactly what he expects to achieve by ejecting Santa, Mrs Claus and the elves from their home. It makes no economic sense to evict tenants without someone to replace them, as then he will have no hope of recompense for the unpaid rent or any other income from the property. Prune seems to consider this, and tells Sam that his articulacy has persuaded him to re-evaluate the situation. He is now willing to waive the rental fee for the past year… but only if Santa promises to never again deliver gifts to children anywhere in the world.

Aghast at this ultimatum, Santa tells Prune that gift-giving is essential – he conveys presents to youngsters simply for the love of doing so, and also to know that it will teach them to become kind and generous themselves. Besides, what role will Santa play if he isn't allowed to spread joy and gifts across the globe? But Prune is unmoved by their protests, and is elated by the thought of children everywhere being heartbroken by the unexpected lack of Christmas presents. Reminding Santa of his options – either pay up in full or resign himself to a life without delivering presents – the miserable miser angrily departs.

Mrs Claus reflects that Prune's life must have been visited by some kind of tragedy, given that he despises children to the point that he denies ever having been one himself. Thoughtfully, Sam considers that if they could somehow uncover irrefutable proof that Prune had indeed once been a youngster, they might be able to find the key to his current parsimonious behaviour. Santa thankfully keeps a complete record of every letter he has ever received from the kids of the world, so – enlisting the help of Jonathan and the elves – he resolves to looks back through his records in search of a clue. Realising that this may take some time, Sam suggests that they leave the elves to their research and take slightly more immediate action instead. If they are to have any hope of raising the required funds, Santa is going to need to find a job – and fast. But as Mrs Santa ponders, who in the world will need to employ Santa Claus?

Sam visits the toy section of a department store run by Mr Prim (Sonny Fox), and begs him to find work for Santa. Prim is quite resolved that there are no vacancies available, but when he sees Santa in his customary red and white suit he soon changes his mind. Believing Santa to be an out-of-work actor, albeit a really good one, Prim accedes to Sam's revolutionary idea – that parents can bring their children to the department store to speak with Santa and tell him what presents they would like for Christmas. The manager is over the moon: as no-one has ever thought of such a scheme before, it could make his store stand out from the competition during the festive season.

Santa wonders if the money he earns from this new employment will be sufficient to pay off Prune's rental bill. Sam hopes that as he has also been given a job there – as the store's janitor – that there will be just enough cash between them to cover the costs by the Christmas Eve deadline. Prim wastes no time in publicising his new appointment, and the store goes all-in on their festive decorations to make Santa really look the part. However, Jolly Old St Nick finds himself deeply confused by the situation. Why does Prim want to pay him for simply being himself? And why are the children who want to see him all awake, when he's used to only encountering them when they are fast asleep on Christmas Eve? As he ruminates on these issues, he is unaware that Prune is watching carefully from the street outside the store.

Santa takes cold feet and almost leaves the store due to his nervousness, but Sam convinces him that he need only be himself (quite literally). They run though the procedure, and Santa feels much more confident about encountering the excitable kids. The pair try out some of the display model toys that Prim has on sale, which fascinates the children of shoppers who are passing the store. Seeing customers beginning to queue, the staff members have a mad dash to tidy everything up before Santa can go to work. Thankfully he turns out to be a hit with both kids and parents alike, with everyone captivated by what a realistic appearance he boasts. The novelty of Santa appearing in a department store delights the parents, while the children are stunned at his ability to help them find just the right gift.

Back at Prune's mansion, the tight-fisted billionaire is incensed at Sam's quick thinking – and Santa's subsequent success with festive shoppers. He seems highly anxious about the prospect of their plan being a success, claiming that he will be ruined if they are able to raise enough money to pay off his rental bill. However, Blossom the butler tells him that he has hatched a plan which will derail Sam and Santa's strategy quite comprehensively.

At Prim's department store, the queue of kids waiting to see Santa is growing longer and longer. Little do any of the children suspect that amongst their number is Prune, accompanied by a similarly-hidden Blossom. Growing tired of waiting, the miserable mogul decides to jump the queue and cause some mayhem in the store. Concealing himself away from prying eyes, he sets to work bursting kids' balloons with darts from a blowpipe and targeting them with itching powder. However, when attempting to blow up Santa's throne with a stick of dynamite, one of the queueing children spots Prune in mid-scheme and rumbles his conspiracy before it has the expected explosive effect.

Prune is left with no option but to withdraw, but the ever clear-headed Blossom soon hatches another plot. While Mr Prim looks on approvingly at Santa and Sam charming the children, considering the positive impact all this extra trade is bringing to his shop, he is intercepted by Prune who exchanges a few clandestine words with him. As the store continues to fill with eager youngsters, Santa wonders aloud if Jonathan and the elves have had any success in tracking down details of Prune's childhood. Unknown to him and Sam, the North Pole workforce haven't been able to find a single trace of him, and Mrs Claus has to persuade them to start all over again in the hope that they have simply overlooked a reference to the old miser somewhere in the workshop records.

With the store finally closing for Christmas, Santa and Sam decide to do some tidying up as they wait for Mr Prim to pay their wages. However, they soon find that boxes are being overturned and shelves are mysteriously emptying themselves, leaving the shop floor looking more chaotic than when they started. The culprit is Blossom, quietly choreographing all of the disorder from the shadows. While Sam and Santa react in confusion, Prune appears in the store and reveals that he has bought the entire enterprise from Mr Prim. As their new employer, he announces that they are both fired with immediate effect. After some urging from Sam, he agrees to pay them for their efforts to date... but before Santa can use the funds to cover his rent, Prune informs them that they are financially responsible for all of the broken merchandise (which has only just been damaged by Blossom). Rather conveniently for the dishonest pinchpenny, the value of the spoiled goods comes to almost exactly the amount of money that Santa and Sam have just raised.

Santa is disconsolate at the realisation that Prune has outmanoeuvred them, but Sam is determined that they can use the last few hours of Christmas Eve to turn the tables. The payment isn't due until midnight, and he is resolved to sort things out before then. As families tuck their children into bed with the expectation of Santa's imminent arrival, the pair wander the streets dejectedly in search of inspiration. Santa mentions that the only thing that could help them now is a miracle... at which point, a young boy arrives carrying a Christmas tree for his family. He immediately recognises Santa (who, of course, in turn knows him by name), and is puzzled at why he should be in town so early – his deliveries aren't due until later. When Sam fills him in about Santa's predicament, the boy knows exactly what to do and immediately jumps into action.

Racing around town, the young boy wakes up every child he can and implores them to contribute all they can to help out Santa. Sure enough, the kids obligingly raid their piggy banks and collectively chip in to pay Santa's rent money. Dozens and dozens of them converge on the town square to make their donations in person. Santa is quite overwhelmed by their generosity – for once, it is he who is the recipient of an unexpected Christmas gift. In no time, thanks to the munificence of the children, he has collected more than enough to meet Prune's demands.

At the North Pole, the malign skinflint is already waiting impatiently to evict Santa at midnight. With mere seconds of Christmas Eve left, Prune is ready to declare victory, but Santa and Sam burst into the workshop and present him with the full amount of the rent... in pennies. Prune looks agonised, knowing that it is now his turn to have received an unpleasant surprise: his nefarious scheme has been thwarted. Disgusted by all the festive good cheer surrounding him, Prune makes a decidedly ungracious exit.

Sam urges Santa to get ready for his annual sleigh ride – the children around the world will all be waiting for him. Everyone from Mrs Claus to the elves pitch in to prepare for the departure. Just as the reindeer are heading for lift-off, Jonathan arrives and places a mysterious wrapped present into Sam's hand. With Mrs Claus and Sam on board the sleigh to help out, Santa's deliveries can all be completed on time, and the trio are soon heading back to the North Pole. As they do so, Sam remembers the package given to him by Jonathan, and they realise that it is addressed to none other than Phineas Prune.

Being the early hours of the morning, the stingy businessperson is tucked up asleep in bed (with no obvious explanation of how he has been able to get back to his home town from the North Pole so quickly without the aid of Santa's sleigh). Although Santa intends to simply leave the gift and depart, Mrs Claus accidentally disturbs some dust and causes everyone to sneeze, waking the old miser up. Prune is dumbfounded when Santa offers him a present – especially given his recent actions. Unwrapping it, he is stunned to discover a toy – a simple wooden sailing vessel. Santa apologises, believing that the gifts have been mixed up at the North Pole, but Prune corrects him: the boat was exactly what he wanted. A letter from Jonathan included with the package explains that the elf foreman had found a postcard from a five-year-old Prune which had been lost decades ago, and only now is he being united with his much-wished-for gift from childhood. Deeply emotional, he realises that Santa had never forgotten him in youth – it had all simply been the result of a tragic clerical error.

Prune is visibly moved by the kindness of Santa's generosity, and with an explanation for why he never received presents as a child he is now able to consider things very differently. Seeing a transformation at work in the bothersome billionaire, Santa and Mrs Claus set to work turning his dusty, cheerless abode into the epitome of festive merriment. Prune looks on in stunned silence as his neglected mansion becomes bedecked with colourful decorations. Beguiled, he wishes his guests a sincere Merry Christmas before bursting out of his home onto the snowy streets in his nightgown, issuing heartfelt compliments of the season to everyone he passes. Given his sullen, tight-fisted reputation, none of the townsfolk know quite how to react to his apparent change of heart.

Spotting a shy young boy hiding from him, he offers his treasured wooden sailing ship as a gift – its true worth having been the realisation that even Prune has it in him to treasure the joy of Christmas. He then invites the townspeople into his capacious home so that they can celebrate the holiday together – much to the bewilderment of Blossom. Meanwhile, Santa thanks Sam for his help before returning to the North Pole: the festive season now saved from oblivion by Prune's timely change of heart.

Whether intentionally or unintentionally, there is much to enjoy in *The Christmas that Almost Wasn't* – and not least the fact that the protagonist character sounds like he should be a novelty brand of ice cream. (Interestingly, Paul Tripp had actually portrayed a variation of his Sam Whipple character many years earlier, in two 1952 episodes of ABC's sci-fi anthology series *Tales of Tomorrow*.) Yes, the lip-synch of the dialogue dubbing is often wildly inconsistent. Yes, the quality of the lyrics vary dramatically from song to song. Yes, the miniature modelwork, stop motion photography and fake snow are often far from convincing. And yes, the slapstick comedy (not least Prune's 'hilarious' collapsing office chairs) is generally very laboured. But Tripp makes for an engaging enough lead, being both amiable and exuberant in his performance, and Alberto Rabagliati never gives less than a hundred percent in the role of Santa Claus. Similarly, Rossano Brazzi is clearly enjoying himself as the top hat-wearing, moustache-twirling antagonist Phineas Prune, wielding just the right amount of cartoonish villainy. However, it is the film's idiosyncratic supporting performances which tend to stick around longest in the viewer's memory: Mischa Auer's ingeniously off-kilter turn as Jonathan the elf foreman (he is tall and gangly, while his staff are all diminutive in stature as tradition would suggest), John Karlsen as the highly expressive, cobweb-covered butler Blossom, and especially Lidia Brazzi who brings all of the necessary jollity and motherly concern to Mrs Claus.

Fundamentally, *The Christmas that Almost Wasn't* communicates important messages about the true meaning of Christmas and the significance of generosity, empathy and goodwill towards others. In spite of the film's many eccentric and farcical elements, offering a highly imaginative account of how department store Santa Clauses became a cultural phenomenon, it emphasises the spirit of giving and the joy of spreading happiness to others – both of which are core themes of the festive season. Through the actions of the compassionate Sam Whipple, the film celebrates the virtues of altruism and selflessness as he works tirelessly to ensure that Christmas is not ruined by Phineas Prune's greed. The movie also underscores the idea that Christmas is a time for coming together as a community and helping those in need, rather than focusing solely on materialistic pursuits. Thus it uses its light-hearted and fantastical storyline to convey some timeless lessons about the true spirit of Christmas, reminding the audience of the importance of kindness, generosity and imparting goodwill to friends, family and the wider community during the holiday season.

Overall, however, this low-budget offering suffers more from the derivative qualities of Brazzi's screenplay than it ever does from the budgetary shortcomings of the production. Even younger viewers are likely to ring the changes with other, considerably better-known Christmas films, with the overfamiliarity of the main story beats causing the movie's impact to suffer. With so many obvious influences in play, as William D. Crump observes, the action cannot help but prove to be somewhat predictable as it plays out: 'Prune's mean-spiritedness parallels that of Scrooge in *A Christmas Carol*, and the children's cash-for-Santa scenario parallels that in *It's a Wonderful Life*, when the citizens of Bedford Falls rally to pay George Bailey's debt'.[3]

Central to *The Christmas that Almost Wasn't*, of course, are notes of scepticism about rampant consumerism, the over-commercialisation of Christmas and the need to elevate the needs of the community over the egocentricity of the self. Here, of course, the parallels between Phineas Prune and Ebenezer Scrooge become even more explicit; both characters discover that rejecting the transformative potential of Christmas has made them miserable to the point that mere acquisitive action is no longer adequate to generate any degree of fulfilment or gratification. It is only when they are persuaded of the error of their ways that they are able to fully realise why their attitude, and indeed their worldview in general, requires to be corrected before they are able to achieve redemption and pursue happiness. This has, naturally, become one of the essential themes of Christmas cinema, but one which owes its effectiveness largely to the quality and sincerity of the individual film that is espousing it. As Chandler Swain explains, any hint of cynicism can be enough to undermine the authenticity of this crucial moral message altogether:

> Hollywood (a popular cultural abstract which we use as a convenient shorthand to identify the purely commercial cinema regardless of geographical origin) may be many things, but a reputable harbinger of advancing an unpolluted celebration of Yuletide spiritual innocence is certainly not one of them. [...] How insupportable are these characters

who balk at the very concept of Christmas (and by villainous extension, as shamelessly proffered in every one of these films, the happiness of children), regardless of whether that concept is of the traditionally ecclesiastical variety or of the contemporary sectarian one in which the prominent holy figure is that of the department mall St Nick, the modern symbol of all that is great and good and charitable, yet has been adopted by the purveyors (most especially the media, and most especially the movies) of capitalism, who have effectively converted Luke 2:11 into a mandate asserting that all modern forms of holiday cheer are based upon the fourth quarter retail sales figures (especially to all of those little elves at the annual Macy's stockholders meeting).[4]

Because audience expectation was evolving throughout the course of the sixties, traditional family fare was also gradually becoming more sophisticated and multifaceted, meaning that many festive features struggled to convey long-established Christmas themes in ways that were not immediately disregarded or ridiculed by increasingly urbane critics and audiences. If *The Christmas that Almost Wasn't* succeeds as holiday entertainment, it is as much thanks to the central performance of Brazzi as the over-the-top villain as it is to the proficiency of his screenplay, based on Tripp's earlier story. The movie manages, for the most part, to strike a fine balance between family entertainment and an affecting character study – one which does not tax the patience of the younger audience members, nor strains the fantasy scenario with too much unwelcome verisimilitude. In so doing, however, it does produce a creative melange which proves to be something of an acquired taste, as Dave Sindelar describes: 'The events and revelations that lead up to the redemption of the villain are quite moving in their way. Overall, it's kind of a variation on *How the Grinch Stole Christmas* with dollops of *A Christmas Carol* and *Miracle on 34th Street* in the mix. The songs are still weak, and it remains too glum for most of its running time, but the villain is fun, and his butler (played by John Karlsen) almost steals the movie with his face alone. [[...]] The movie is uneven, and I can equally understand why someone might dislike the movie while another would consider it a classic'.[5]

Sindelar has not been alone in drawing attention to the movie's slightly awkward ambience – Tracy Moore, for instance, has noted that 'It's a wholesome film, though its aesthetic and overall tone are rather maudlin and gothic'.[6] However, this scepticism towards the feature's overall merits was very much mirrored by reviewers at the time of its release, with considerable focus being placed on the unoriginal qualities of its central narrative. Bosley Crowther of *The New York Times* was largely representative of this line of criticism when he wrote: 'The unhappy fact is that Childhood Productions, which has been releasing foreign-made moppet movies such as *Sleeping Beauty*, in making its production debut with *Christmas*, which was filmed in Italy, in English and in uneven color, has turned out a fairly pleasant but highly derivative fable, with some animation and a half-dozen songs that might entrance the younger pre-teens but is likely to bore almost everyone else. With all respect to Paul Tripp, the author, *Christmas* appears to be a direct descendant of Dickens' *A Christmas Carol* and *Miracle on 34th Street*'.[7]

More recent appraisals of *The Christmas that Almost Wasn't* have also reflected similar lack of critical conviction towards many aspects of the production, not least Bruno Nicolai's original musical score (including the title song, which was sung by Glenn Yarbrough). For example, Kevin Matthews has remarked that 'the musical numbers are often a bit clumsy, but there's also fun to be had in their childish simplicity and playfulness. Intentionally or not, the film captures a number of elements that work well in terms of how young children think and play. The acting isn't bad, but it's a film that suffers from some clumsy dubbing, like so many from this era. [...] Nicely mixing a few moments of model work and stop-motion animation with the live-action style that makes up the majority of the film, it feels very much as if anything necessary to get the story told was utilised. The end result is an enjoyable Christmas flight of fancy that deserves to be better known'.[8] Others have been more fulsome in their praise, such as Gordon Maples who has commended the film's guilelessness amongst the more cynical fare beginning to emerge in this era of film-making: 'Not unlike the similarly silly Christmas-themed bad movie classics *Santa Claus Conquers the Martians* and *Santa Claus* (1959), *The Christmas That Almost Wasn't* is mostly ridiculous in how over-the-top its plot is. However, it is also just a goofy, utterly harmless little movie, that is endearing in how simple it is. Its internal logic is wholesome and childlike on a level that few stories can really touch: it sounds and feels like it might have even been written by a child. The odd combination of the whimsy of Santa Claus with the harsh reality of financial inequality and greed is a weird mixture at the core of the movie to be sure, but it always feels grounded on the side of naivete'.[9]

While *The Christmas that Almost Wasn't* drifted into relative obscurity following its initial release in cinemas, it received a new lease of life on television throughout the seventies and eighties, when the film received regular airings on HBO during the festive period.[10] The unedited, full-length 93 minute feature would later receive a DVD release in 2003, and in more recent years has been available for streaming through online services such as Netflix, Amazon Video and Peacock. However, perhaps a greater claim to fame was that it received a comprehensive critical roasting in a 2017 episode of *Mystery Science Theater 3000: The Return*, ensuring that its cult credentials would continue to live on amongst Christmas movie fans – even decades after its initial release.

While it is unlikely to be confused for high art, *The Christmas that Almost Wasn't* still provides some interesting insights into the cultural and commercial significance of festive movies in the 1960s. The film's unrelenting focus on family-friendly content highlights the continuing commercial importance of Christmas movies as a form of wholesome entertainment suitable for viewers of all ages. This reflected the 1960s cultural emphasis – now gradually changing, but still prevalent – on family values and a sense of togetherness during the holiday season. While the conflict between Phineas Prune and Santa Claus touches on themes of commercialism versus the traditional holiday values more generally espoused by Christmas cinema (a conflict which had been revisited many times since the genre's post-War heyday), it also mirrored the continuing and growing commercialisation of the holiday season during the 1960s: a period which was marked by increasing consumerism, and especially by the pervasiveness of the burgeoning advertising industry.

The film's reliance on magical and fantastical elements amply demonstrated the way in which Christmas cinema was still able to tap into a sense of nostalgia and wonder. The audiences of the sixties, witnessing rapid societal changes, had the opportunity to find some kernel of comfort in these escapist narratives, celebrating the enchanted aspects and ingenuous innocence of Christmas even while so much around them proved to be febrile and unpredictable. With its various musical numbers, the film highlighted the role of song in enhancing the festive spirit of Christmas movies and aligned more broadly with a wider 1960s trend of integrating musical elements into films, providing a jubilant and engrossing festive experience for viewers.

Perhaps most prominently of all, *The Christmas that Almost Wasn't* – a production overseen by Italian film-makers and starring a combination of American and European actors – suggested the growing international appeal of Christmas films. This oddly charming cross-cultural production drew attention to the universal themes of Christmas which resonate across different cultures, contributing to the global popularity of the holiday movie genre. Brazzi's film exemplified how the Christmas movies of the sixties could serve as a medium to reinforce customary values like the importance of friendship and philanthropy, address the tension between commercialism and tradition, and provide a compelling means of fantastical escape for audiences during the holiday season.

REFERENCES

1. Terry M. Rowan, *Having a Wonderful Christmas Time Film Guide* (Morrisville: Lulu, 2014), p.54.

2. Jessica Pickens, 'Musical Monday: *The Christmas That Almost Wasn't*', in *Comet Over Hollywood*, 20 December 2021.
<https://cometoverhollywood.com/2021/12/20/musical-monday-the-christmas-that-almost-wasnt-1966/>

3. William D. Crump, *How the Movies Saved Christmas: 228 Rescues from Clausnappers, Sleigh Crashes, Lost Presents and Holiday Disasters* (Jefferson: McFarland, 2017), 58-60, p.59.

4. Chandler Swain, 'Saving Santa: *The Christmas That Almost Wasn't*', in *Chandler Swain Reviews*, 19 December 2018.
<https://chandlerswainreviews.wordpress.com/2018/12/19/saving-santa-the-christmas-that-almost-wasnt-1966/>

5. Dave Sindelar, '*The Christmas that Almost Wasn't*', in *Fantastic Movie Musings and Ramblings*, 11 March 2018.
<https://fantasticmoviemusings.com/2018/03/11/the-christmas-that-almost-wasnt-1966/>

6. Tracy Moore, 'Parents' Guide to *The Christmas That Almost Wasn't*', in *Common Sense Media*, 20 June 2023.
<https://www.commonsensemedia.org/movie-reviews/the-christmas-that-almost-wasnt>

7. Bosley Crowther, 'Screen: Dean Martin in *Texas Across the River*: Weak Western Spoof Has Local Premiere, 2 Other

Movies Open at Theaters Here', in *The New York Times*, 24 November 1966.
<https://www.nytimes.com/1966/11/24/archives/screen-dean-martin-in-texas-across-the-riverweak-western-spoof-has.html>

8. Kevin Matthews, 'The Christmas that Almost Wasn't', in *For It is Man's Number*, 23 December 2023.
<https://foritismansnumber.blogspot.com/2013/12/the-christmas-that-almost-wasnt-1966.html>

9. Gordon Maples, '*The Christmas that Almost Wasn't*', in *Misan[trope]y*, 25 December 2017.
<https://misantropey.com/2017/12/25/the-christmas-that-almost-wasnt/>

10. Rowan, *Motion Pictures from the Fabulous 1960s* (Morrisville: Lulu, 2015), p.39.

6

The Lion in Winter (1968)

Haworth Productions

Director: Anthony Harvey
Producer: Martin Poll
Screenwriter: James Goldman, from a play by James Goldman

FAMILIES at Christmas: surely one of the key themes of festive film-making. Yet for every family that looks forward to spending harmonious time together over the holidays, there are others who consider a week cooped up with their relatives to be nothing less than a yuletide nightmare which must be endured rather than enjoyed. The latter category aptly summarises the experience of one particular family in *The Lion in Winter* – perhaps not the most immediately obvious example of festive film-making, but one which certainly felt as oddly relatable as it was historically evocative.

Primarily set during one particularly fraught Christmas Eve in 1183, *The Lion in Winter* started life as a stage play by James Goldman which premiered at the Ambassador Theatre on Broadway on 3rd March 1966. The initial run of the play starred actors Robert Preston and Rosemary Harris, who won a Tony Award for her performance. While *The Lion in Winter* was to be produced many times over the years, including on London's West End in 2011 (directed by Trevor Nunn) and a prominent Broadway revival in 1999 (directed by Michael Mayer), it is arguably as a film adaptation that it has become most widely known across the world.

Getting *The Lion in Winter* to the big screen turned out to be a matter of good fortune as much as inspired creative intention. The Broadway production had garnered some negative reaction (most conspicuously in *The New York Times*), and had not performed especially well commercially. However, when producer Martin Poll contacted Goldman with a view to optioning his 1965 novel *Waldorf* – a comic espionage tale set in Costa Rica – for a cinematic adaptation, it transpired that he was also familiar with *The Lion in Winter* and had greatly appreciated its intricate character dynamics and twisting, complex storyline. To this end, Poll enlisted Goldman to adapt his stage play for the cinema, and the groundwork was laid for one of the least conventional Christmas movies of the 1960s.

Chosen to helm the cinematic version of *The Lion in Winter* was Anthony Harvey, an actor-turned-film editor who had first moved into a directorial career with *Dutchman* (1966), an adaptation of the Amiri Baraka stage play of the same name. Harvey was ultimately to direct thirteen films (both for TV and the cinema) in his lifetime, and was nominated for numerous awards throughout his career including at the Golden Globe Awards and Directors Guild of America Awards. However, it was almost certainly for *The Lion in Winter* that he became most immediately recognised, and his work on the film earned him the most prestigious plaudits of his career.

Peter O'Toole was chosen to portray the film's lead character, King Henry II. While the 36-year-old O'Toole may have seemed like an unusual choice for the Plantagenet monarch, who is aged 50 during the time of *The Lion in Winter*, the same actor had portrayed the same historical figure as a much younger man in Peter Glenville's *Becket* (1964) to great acclaim some years beforehand. Screen legend Katharine Hepburn was cast as Queen Eleanor of Aquitaine – and, it would later emerge, was actually distantly related to the real Eleanor through a line of descent from the medieval monarch's marriages to Henry II of England and Louis VII of France. The film also featured a very strong line-up of supporting players, including Anthony Hopkins, Timothy Dalton, John Castle, Jane Merrow and Nigel Terry. It was to be the first major film performance from Hopkins, and Dalton's cinematic debut. As Martie Zad has noted, 'Rather than selecting well-known actors for supporting roles, Harvey opted for theater actors – thus Hopkins, Dalton, Terry and Castle. Hopkins was appearing at London's National Theatre and needed the permission of Sir Laurence Olivier to leave and appear in the film. Olivier was reluctant, but finally agreed that Hopkins could make the film during the day if he flew back from Ireland, Wales and France for his evening stage performances in *As You Like It* and *Much Ado About Nothing*'.[1]

The action of *The Lion in Winter* is entirely fictional, and while the characters are based upon real people and refer to historically-accurate events, none of the dialogue has a basis in actual chronicled accounts. While no Christmas Court actually took place at Chinon in the year 1183 (it was actually held at Le Mans, on a much smaller scale than is depicted), the various proceedings which took place prior to the events of the film have a general basis in genuine history. In order to lend a degree of verisimilitude to proceedings, *The Lion in Winter* included extensive location filming in settings which were visually reflective of the scenic historical localities depicted in the screenplay. These included Pembroke Castle, Milford Haven and Marloes Sands in Wales, and in France at the Abbaye de Montmajour, Arles; the Château de Tarascon, Carcassonne; Fontvielle, Bouches-de-Rhône; and Tavasson, Saône-et-Loire. The interiors were filmed at Ardmore Studios in Bray, County Wicklow in the Republic of Ireland.

Set predominantly within the confines of a single day – Christmas Eve – *The Lion in Winter* sets out to depict a family at war during the holiday season, while the veneer of festive celebration partially obscures the manipulations of calculating parents, scheming siblings fighting for influence and attention, treachery and adultery, and the need to weigh family responsibility against duty to the law and the state. This range of themes may have been significant to the machinations of medieval nobility, but they are just as germane to any family that can't live with each other or without each other – which, as David Krauss argues, is exactly why the film's action remained relevant to contemporary audiences even given its early medieval setting:

> Royal families may live in opulent palaces, exude an air of rarefied sophistication, wield considerable power, and command enormous respect, but deep down they're just people... and they're riddled with all the same faults and insecurities that plague the rest of us. That's the idea playwright James Goldman strives to convey in his captivating domestic comedy, *The Lion in Winter*, which bitingly chronicles a fraught family Christmas filled with all the bickering, rivalries, power plays, hurt feelings, tender moments, and rueful recriminations to which all of us can all too well relate.[2]

The year is 1183, and King Henry II of England has reached fifty years of age. With a long, eventful and often tumultuous reign, Henry (Peter O'Toole) finds that his mind has turned to the future. He mock-duels with his youngest son, Prince John (Nigel Terry), whom he bests easily in swordplay. The king remarks to his lover, Alais (Jane Merrow), that he believes that John will be a fine monarch when the time comes for succession. Alais seems unconvinced by this assertion, but Henry is determined: he has spent his life accumulating power, and wants to die knowing that the Angevin Empire will be safe in the hands of his successor. Alais is saddened by his sense of morbidity, fearing that he believes his end to be nearing, but Henry brushes aside her concerns and assures her that of all the many women he has had relationships with, she is the only one he has ever truly loved. She asks if that includes his wife, Eleanor of Acquitaine, but he offers a bitter guarantee that he has not kept her imprisoned for over a decade because of his affection for her, but rather on account of her part in attempting to overthrow him.

Henry orders his man-at-arms Captain William Marshall (Nigel Stock) to prepare his castle in Chinon, Touraine, to hold a Christmas court. All three of his surviving sons are to attend – Richard, Geoffrey and John – and the King of France, Philip II, is also to receive a formal invitation. Henry additionally instructs Marshall to temporarily release Queen Eleanor from captivity for the duration of the holiday. Marshall dutifully informs Prince Richard (Anthony Hopkins) of the summons during a jousting match, and Prince Geoffrey (John Castle) as he co-ordinates an ambush by cavalry officers against a detachment of enemy infantry. Finally, he pays a visit to Wiltshire for an audience with the Queen. On learning of the Christmas court, Eleanor (Katharine Hepburn) does not provide the resistance that Marshall had expected, instead seeming eager to attend – just as Henry had anticipated.

At Chinon Castle on Christmas Eve, Henry wearily but playfully trades barbs with Alais: knowing that he faces non-stop verbal sparring once his belligerent family arrive, he is in no mood to start the arguing this early in the day. The issue of contention is that Alais has been betrothed by treaty to the son that Henry eventually names heir. With his eldest son (also named Henry) having recently died, there is now renewed conflict between the king and Eleanor over whom his successor should be. Eleanor favours Richard, who already has considerable military experience, while Henry prefers the prospect of his young favourite, John, taking the throne. Alais regrets that she will no longer be able to maintain her affair with Henry once she is married to one of his sons, but the King reassures her that she must think about her future: whichever son she marries, she will eventually become the Queen of England... and if they renege on the betrothal, Henry will need to pay back the agreed marriage dowry (a strategically significant French county) to King Philip II.

John spots Alais and Henry in an affectionate embrace, but scarcely has time to take notice before he races into the courtyard to greet the arrival of his brother Geoffrey. The siblings seem to be on relatively good terms, but shortly afterwards Richard arrives and the squabbling between the three begins in earnest. Richard asserts starkly that although he and John are barely acquainted, it is he who will be King when their father's reign ends – his martial reputation demands it. But John is unimpressed, knowing that he is his father's favourite and preferred successor. Henry, of course, knows all too well that his three surviving sons are all competing and plotting against each other to be named his heir. As a huge Christmas tree is hoisted into place, he observes that while his offspring may never truly love him, as long as they conspire and fight amongst one another, he knows they are indeed his true heirs.

Queen Eleanor arrives at the castle via her royal barge, her ladies in waiting by her side. Henry meets her by the shore, and the verbal jousting immediately commences. Eleanor is as sharply observant as her reputation suggests, and she is immediately aware of Alais's affair with her husband. She also notes the fierce rivalry between Richard and John for the throne, though she all but ignores the conniving Geoffrey. There is little time for family reunions, however – Philip II (Timothy Dalton) has arrived with his royal entourage, and Henry demands a short-term secession in family hostilities in order to present the teenaged French King with a united front.

Henry gives Philip a warm welcome, but quickly ushers him into private quarters in order to get down to business. Without preamble, he raises the issue of Alais and the wedding dowry, seeking to address the problem head-on. Philip responds that as an agreement was made for a strategic marriage between England and France, Henry must make good on his promise or return the province he currently occupies. Henry, on the other hand, warns Philip that his troops are already situated in that territory, which would make it difficult to enforce its vacation by any means other than his own personal consent. Philip appears offended by the English King's apparent disrespect, but it becomes clear that he too is adept at the dark arts of international diplomacy. Philip invites Henry to make a counter-offer, but the elder monarch only replies – somewhat unfathomably – that he will think of something eventually.

Richard and John continue their incessant bickering over the succession, but the soft-spoken Geoffrey watches the power struggle with quiet contemplation. Once alone with his parents, he reflects resentfully that his own name is never linked with occupying the throne – merely as chancellor for whomever should be named successor. Yet even when prompted, neither Henry nor Eleanor (whose contempt for him is palpable) can give voice to the reason why he is always overlooked. As Geoffrey departs, Eleanor remarks that she cares little for any of her sons, but has a soft spot for Alais whom she raised through childhood. Yet even this observation is merely an opportunity to taunt Henry about his many extramarital affairs over the years. Realising that Eleanor means to attack her with a seemingly-serene series of taunts, Alais too decides to evacuate the royal quarters.

Now finally alone, Henry and Eleanor take stock of their situation. After more than thirty years of marriage, and innumerable children, she is embittered about her situation yet seemingly accepting of her fate. They adore each other and yet they hate each other – when did it all go wrong? They again discuss the succession, and she notes that it must be difficult for him to contemplate losing Alais if he is to make good on his treaty obligations and marry her to one of his sons. Henry, on the other hand, has grown cynical and listless; there is an uneasy peace with France, and while the calculating Eleanor remains incarcerated there is an end to the civil wars that had rocked the kingdom in years past. He finds himself at an impasse: domestic politics bore him, and yet he has also grown tired of the prospect of endless warfare.

The royal couple enter the castle's banquet hall to a chorus of cheers from the assembled nobility. Once again, Henry has succeeded in presenting an image of royal unity to his barons and aristocracy. Quietly, Eleanor reveals that she actually has little interest in which son ascends the throne after Henry dies – the only reason she favours Richard is to thwart her husband, who clearly prefers John. Likewise, knowing his determination to hold on at any cost to the county of Vexin – the territory in France granted as the marriage dowry for Alais, which is within striking distance of Paris – Eleanor tells him that she will happily frustrate his plans simply out of spite.

Later that day, Richard visits his mother as she prepares wrapped Christmas gifts. She has summoned him for a reunion, but Richard – knowing all too well her reputation for scheming – is naturally wary. He rebuffs her understated protestations of maternal affection and tells her that he is all too aware that all she wants from him is Aquitaine – the wealthy Duchy of which she was once part of the ruling family, but which will come under Richard's administration if he is to become king. Their fraught get-together is interrupted by John, who bursts in to inform her that Henry has just completed his draft of the terms of treaty with Philip. The shrewd Geoffrey looks on silently.

When Eleanor and her sons encounter Henry, he makes a startling revelation: he has changed his mind, and decided to name Richard as his successor after all – meaning that Alais will also become his wife. John is outraged, feeling betrayed by the sudden turnaround in fortunes, but neither Richard nor Eleanor believe that Henry has really had a change of heart. The king retorts that as Richard is the proven military leader, he would simply seize the throne from John if it was not willingly offered to him, but Richard is unconvinced: surely Henry would enjoy the prospect of provoking further sibling rivalry rather than seek to avoid it? The answer, the monarch claims, is obvious – only Richard has the leadership qualities necessary to keep England and its territories safe from conquest. Alais is devastated by this surprising development, but John can only vainly wallow in his own self-pity.

Seeing an opportunity, Geoffrey suggests to his mother that he act as her proxy and become Richard's chancellor instead of John's. However, Eleanor sees too many of her own manipulative, unscrupulous qualities in her son and distrusts his motives. He replies that he only seeks to protect his own position, irrespective of who becomes king, but Eleanor warns him that Henry is playing a complex game and in no way has given up on the prospect of John taking the throne. However, she knows that Geoffrey serves only himself and cannot be depended upon; she recognises the burning animosity and hunger for power in his heart, because she shares it herself.

Richard tells Eleanor that he has no illusions about her support. He knows that she only desires him to become king in order to frustrate Henry's plans. However, she assures Richard that her endorsement of him as the successor to the throne has cost her dearly on a personal level – not least in terms of her long-term imprisonment. All she desires in return is to regain control of Aquitaine, a condition upon which all of her schemes are contingent. Richard refuses to give the territory up, knowing that his self-regarding, venal mother is hatching plans within plans. To his surprise, however, she launches into a shockingly sincere protestation of maternal affection for him which squarely puts him on the back foot.

Enjoying some yuletide entertainment in the form of a troupe of clowning jesters, Henry unobtrusively orders Captain Marshall to set up a secret meeting between himself and King Philip in the castle parlour within half an hour. Philip is informed of the invitation as he plays a game of chess with

Geoffrey, who in turn tells him that Henry's terms – when they are presented – cannot in any way be trusted. The prince makes clear to the French King his own ambitions to become Henry's successor, then pays a visit to John to seek his support. Geoffrey explains that if he, John and Philip join forces, they can collectively thwart Richard's claim to the throne and end Eleanor's influence at the same time. John is unconvinced, but Geoffrey and Philip together assure him that the ultimate victory will be theirs.

Alais confronts Henry, still infuriated at being betrothed to Richard, but the king is baffled at her naivete. He reveals that he has no intention of formally naming Richard his successor, and continues to support John's claim to the throne instead. Henry knows that in addition to seeking to undermine him, Eleanor's steadfast support for Richard is primarily driven by her determination to regain control of Aquitaine. He doesn't realise that the Queen is eavesdropping on the conversation, and is momentarily taken aback when she enters the room with the subterfuge of delivering Christmas gifts. Knowing now that she is truly little more than a hostage to fortune in Henry's endless political games, Alais leaves him and Eleanor to their latest round of verbal fencing.

Henry is unsurprised that Richard has refused to give up his claim to Aquitaine in favour of Eleanor, and presents a counter-proposal. If she will relinquish her entitlement to the province in favour of John – which, as the wealthiest territory in Europe, Henry hopes will act as a kind of compensatory concession to his youngest son when Richard takes the throne – then he will guarantee her freedom. This offer comes as a shock to the usually-unflappable Eleanor. As someone who treasures her liberty and has travelled widely, the past decade in captivity has been a nightmare for her. She congratulates

Henry on his strategic prowess: he is offering her the one thing she wants, in exchange for the one thing she has been plotting for. The prospect of emancipation proves to be too tempting to refuse, but Eleanor's agreement to Henry's terms comes with one condition: the marriage between Richard and Alais must take place immediately, which will fulfil the requirements of the treaty with France.

The family assembles at the castle chapel, where Hugh de Puiset, the Bishop of Durham (O.Z. Whitehead), readies for the wedding ceremony. Alais is enraged at Henry's apparent disinterest, denying his professed love for her in order to arrange her marriage of convenience to his son. However, when the king reveals that the wedding is a condition for the governance of Aquitaine to be transferred from Richard to John, the would-be wedding groom promptly realises that he has been manipulated and refuses Alais's hand in marriage. This in turn outrages Philip, who believes that Henry is reneging on the betrothal and their long-held territorial pact. Infuriated at having been misdirected, Richard threatens retribution and storms out. Eleanor claims to be unsurprised at having been outmanoeuvred by her husband, seeing it as simply one more round of their continual interpersonal competitions, but becomes visibly upset when she witnesses the genuine affection that he obviously has for Alais and realises that the princess is not simply another of Henry's conquests – he genuinely seems to have a true emotional connection with her.

That night, as everyone prepares for the arrival of Christmas Day, Eleanor is feeling dejected. In the privacy of her royal quarters, she quietly reflects that it looks as though her schemes have been outmanoeuvred. Her gloominess is interrupted by the arrival of Geoffrey, who has come to keep her company. He wishes her the compliments of the season, but before long his hurt and acrimony becomes apparent when he asks her why neither she nor Henry have ever shown him anything other than apathy and disinterest. Not for the first time, she struggles to formulate a sincere and coherent answer, but before Geoffrey can press the matter he is joined by John and Richard – both still sniping at each other. John gloats at the apparent defeat of his mother's plans, while Richard is enraged at having been outwitted. Eleanor, however, has had enough. She tells Richard that there will always be other Christmas courts to offer future opportunities for political machinations, and implores her children to seek unity for once rather than being constantly at odds. The dim-witted John suddenly remembers aloud the terms of his military pact with King Philip, which will no longer be required now that he has been named successor to the crown, and races off. Realising the opportunity this presents, Eleanor tells Geoffrey to divert John while Richard meets with Philip instead with an aim to forge a different, more favourable agreement. If Henry discovers the conspiracy, Eleanor surmises, he will punish John for his treachery and transfer his allegiance to Richard instead.

Geoffrey manages to get to Philip before Richard's arrival, and strikes a bargain with him – if the French King will support Geoffrey's claim to the throne, he will guarantee him all English territories in France. They are interrupted by John, hiding behind a tapestry in Philip's quarters, who is infuriated at being outfoxed by his brother. Before their quarrel can begin in earnest, they are forced into hiding when Richard knocks on the door. Rather awkwardly, he and Philip enter into yet another negotiation, and it becomes obvious that they have shared history together. Richard petitions Philip for military support in exchange for the return of some (but not all) English lands on the continent. However, Philip has heard all this before. Instead, he is more intent on learning why Richard broke off a romantic relationship the pair had shared some years ago. Richard replies that he had thought any attempt to rekindle their affection would have been doomed, but Philip disagrees with his appraisal of the situation.

Before they can achieve rapprochement, however, a further knock on the door sends Richard scurrying into hiding too. It is Henry, who has come to resume negotiations in a rather less formal environment. The English King offers the chance of peace, but Philip is unconvinced. By his reckoning, Henry's advancing years mean that Philip need only wait; even if he can't outthink or outfight his rival, he can outlive him and then wage war on his (presumably less capable) successor instead. Henry knows all too well that, sensing the conflict within his family, Philip need not attack him when the three royal heirs are perfectly capable of doing so themselves. Gleefully, Henry then informs Philip that their exchange has revealed to him not only how his teenage French adversary thinks, but also the extent of his strategic prowess... and has found both to be wanting. Yet even Henry is lost for words when Philip unexpectedly reveals his romantic relationship with Richard – only to then claim that it was all simply an act of political subterfuge, so that he could one day reveal the private details of Richard's liaison with him directly to his father, along with his plotting against the crown.

Furious, Richard bursts out of hiding, claiming that the love he shared with Philip was genuine. The French monarch, however, aloofly dismisses his affections and reaffirms that their romantic bond was actually nothing more than a feint.

Henry's response, however, suggests that he is more concerned about his fragile strategic hold over French interests being compromised than he is with the details of his son's private life. Realising that Richard's very presence means that he has already been scheming with Philip, Henry apprehends that Eleanor's intrigues continue. Geoffrey also emerges and protests that he too has a right to the throne, but is coldly disregarded by his father who reveals that he has never wasted any time even recognising his son's presence, much less his ambitions. Finally, John is also revealed in his hiding place, but Henry tricks him into showing his true colours as he eventually divulges that he too can't stand his father's complicated schemes and cold-blooded machinations.

For once, Henry feels that circumstances have spiralled out of his control. None of his sons are who he thought they were – and each are less than the sum of their parts. He now considers the warmongering Richard to be politically inept and truly little more than Eleanor's puppet, the intellectually agile Geoffrey to be an amoral, opportunistic conniver, and John – his favourite – to be a self-serving dullard. Unfeelingly, he tells them that history will record that King Henry II had no male children: he disowns them all. Storming from Philip's guest quarters, however, the depth of the monarch's despair becomes apparent. How can he plan for the end of his life when he regards none of his sons to be a suitable successor who is deserving of the right to inherit his towering legacy?

Distraught, Henry can find solace nowhere. He paces the length and breadth of the palace, but his mind is in turmoil – and certainly anything but festive in mood. Meanwhile, Eleanor pays Alais a visit in the royal quarters. Eleanor resents the strength of feeling that her husband has for the French princess, but Alais knows that their situations are not comparable. She points out that Eleanor sees in Henry a means of power and influence, whereas she is interested only in the man himself. As they reminisce, Henry returns, reflecting on the Nativity story – in one way, an account of a family succeeding and surviving against the odds. Sending Alais away, he attempts to ascertain Eleanor's true intentions. The Queen responds that she is aware of the explosive revelations made in Philip's chambers, and wonders at how serious Henry is about disinheriting his sons. Eleanor claims to be tired of all the plotting and counter-plotting, and no longer cares about who ends up ruling any kingdom – she seeks only peace and seclusion. Henry, of course, doesn't believe a word she says. As a symbol of her sincerity, the Queen offers to sign away any future rulership of Aquitaine to John, but – to her surprise – Henry won't agree to her proposal. Instead, he seeks a divorce... though this revelation comes as a genuine shock to her. Henry plans to petition the Pope for an annulment of their marriage so that he can wed Alais and have new sons with her. Finally he will have a new, more worthy heir to take control of his kingdom.

Eleanor is stunned at his latest proposal. Though they clearly still love each other, they know they can't live either together or apart. Henry explains that he feels as though they have failed at parenthood – Richard was predominantly led by her tutelage and John by his own, but neither has emerged as a suitable inheritor of the throne, while they consider the ever-neglected Geoffrey to be closer to an emotionless machine than a human being. Wearily, they agree that while they may excel at statecraft, when it comes to family matters they have been dismal disappointments. However, Eleanor is aghast at the prospect of being sidelined while Henry produces a new heir, and warns that his existing sons – even if divested of their inheritance – would surely usurp any pretender to the throne while he was defenceless in the cradle. The king rebuffs her pleas to abandon his plans, so Eleanor threatens to incite an uprising against him when he rides to Rome for an audience with the Pope. This, Henry ripostes, is easily remedied: if she, Richard, Geoffrey and John cannot be trusted in his absence, he will have them all incarcerated at the Chinon Castle until his return.

Henry wakes Marshall in the dead of night, and they assemble troops who are ordered to take the princes into custody. All three brothers are seized from their rooms in the early hours of Christmas morning and are thrown into the castle dungeon. The siblings regard each other in disbelief, none quite believing that Henry has gone through with his threat. The king then wakes the multitude of royal servants, and orders Marshall to prepare Eleanor for her departure back to captivity in England the next day. Arranging an entourage to convey him to Rome, Henry explains his plans to Alais. While she is initially shocked at the audacity of his scheme to have the Pope marry them, she warns him that any children they have would be in immediate danger – any one of his existing sons would be an obvious threat to what they see as a pretender to the throne. Henry is conflicted, but decides that she is right: if his plan is to work, he will have no choice but to execute all three of his perfidious offspring.

Still in the early hours of Christmas morning, before dawn has broken, Eleanor takes advantage of the upheaval as the servants plan the royal departure from the castle. Unseen, she descends into the dungeons, has her guard overpower Henry's sentry, and tracks down Richard, Geoffrey and John. Presenting them with a dagger each, she informs them that she will soon be departing and wanted to bid them farewell in a way only she could – by presenting the means of their vengeance. Richard favours fighting their way out of the castle, raising an army and attacking Henry head-on. The cool-headed Geoffrey, on the other hand, favours hiding the daggers, waiting for Henry's inevitable arrival, and then murdering him before he can execute them – a plan which has a three-to-one chance of success.

Unfortunately for them, they quarrel for so long that Henry arrives with Alais before they can agree on a definitive plan of action. He claims to have come to bring a fresh supply of candles, but he knows what Richard suspects: his plan to have new heirs can't possibly work if any of his existing sons survive. A fight breaks out between them, but Henry easily disarms John and holds a dagger to his throat. Eleanor goads her husband to end John's life, thus repaying his treason with justice. But the king instead draws his sword and solemnly sentences all three sons to death. He swings the blade at an impassive Richard... but at the last second, he realises that he can't go through with the execution. Emotionally drained, he watches as all three sons escape from captivity.

Henry is crushed by the way that events have played out. Chagrined, he sends Alais away from the dungeon – only Eleanor truly understands what he is feeling. Knowing that he was unable to murder his own sons, Henry appreciates that even he has limits – though Eleanor points out that only he seemed to think himself capable of carrying the executions out. For once, they seem to share a moment of emotional honesty. It becomes clear that Eleanor genuinely loves Henry, but knows with agonising clarity that the life they could have had is gone forever. Henry, for his part, recognises that he shares that love, but acknowledges that he can never trust Eleanor –

even in the short term. They are fated to forever live apart, though their hearts seem eternally entwined.

As the sun rises on Christmas morning, Henry escorts Eleanor back to her royal barge, where she will be conveyed back to her gilded cage in Wiltshire. Wistfully, they recognise that they will not be reunited until the next Christmas court takes place. Absolutely nothing has been resolved as regards the royal succession, but Henry and Eleanor seem to have a new lease of life. The barbs and schemes will resume again in a year's time. For now, Henry reflects that he hopes that the pair will live forever – even if that means their mental and emotional skirmishes must go on eternally, too.

Far from a traditional yuletide treat, *The Lion in Winter* offered audiences an uncompromisingly complex and multidimensional exploration of power, family dynamics and betrayal. While Christmas served as the backdrop for much of the film's action, its portrayal was far from the customary depiction of festive cheer so often associated with the holiday. Harvey presents a world of shadows, where no-one is sincere and absolutely nothing can be trusted. Yet while Christmas becomes the stage for political intrigue and familial conflict rather than a period of joy and celebration, *The Lion in Winter* still creates a highly distinctive and very different style of festive atmosphere with its medieval banquets and torchlit chivalric entertainments. The highly dysfunctional Plantagenet family may well have ostensibly been gathered at King Henry II's castle in Chinon to celebrate the holiday, but tensions quickly boil over as the various members constantly vie for power and control over the throne. The film brilliantly highlights the juxtaposition between the good-humoured public façade of holiday festivities and the private struggles of the respective characters playing out behind their public personas.

In the shadows, Henry and his estranged wife, Queen Eleanor, engage in a battle of wits and manipulation, using their children as proxies in their quest for dominance over the family's future. Their sons, by contrast, must deal with differing levels of parental neglect and a gnawing sense that each of them are little more than pawns in the schemes of the royal court. There is much to enjoy in the terse interplay between the melancholic, mercurial Richard; the charmingly calculating Geoffrey; and the sulkily buffoonish John.

The film delves – subtly yet highly effectively – into themes of betrayal and mistrust, which are only heightened on account of the festive season setting. As the family members scheme and plot against each other, the sense of treachery and deception permeates the atmosphere, casting a dark shadow over the supposed merriment of the holiday. *The Lion in Winter* thus portrays Christmas as a time of amplified tension and conflict, rather than focusing on the expected unity and harmony that audiences may otherwise have anticipated. The holiday is deliberately used, to great effect, to create an environment of febrile celebration against which the characters' inner turmoil and power struggles are gradually brought to the forefront, offering a stark contrast to the predominant traditional portrayal of a peaceful, harmonious family Christmas in popular culture.

The film did generate a certain amount of controversy amongst historians at the time of release, largely due to the anachronistic presentation of some characters and locations. There was no Christmas court held by Henry II in Chinon in 1183, for instance, though there had been one in Caen the previous year. The large family get-together depicted in the film wouldn't happen until 1184, and that would take place at Windsor Castle. There were also numerous dialogue inaccuracies which piqued some eagle-eyed history enthusiasts. Eleanor mentions syphilis, in spite of the condition not being termed as such until 1530 by Italian physician Girolamo Fracastoro. Henry also speaks of Poison Oak, which is native to North America and remained undiscovered by Europeans at the time of the film's events. (Captain John Smith is thought to be the first person to write about its presence in the New World in 1624.) Likewise, pineapples appear at Henry's banquet in spite of never reaching Europe until some point in the late 15th century, once Christopher Columbus returned to Spain with them following an expedition to Guadeloupe in 1493. Even Christmas trees, seen being used as a means of festive decoration, wouldn't be introduced to the celebrations of the British Royal family until the time of Queen Charlotte (Charlotte of Mecklenburg-Strelitz), who was married to King George III between 1761 and 1818. Her first recorded use of a Christmas tree as a festive decoration was in 1800, when it was bedecked with sweets and candles.

In spite of these minor pedantic quibbles, the film did link seamlessly with other historical events, both prior to and following its proceedings. The Revolt of 1173-74, where Eleanor had persuaded her sons to rebel against Henry II, is what led to her imprisonment at Old Sarum Castle in Wiltshire (an incarceration which endured until Henry's death in 1189, when Richard released her from captivity). Their firstborn, William, is not mentioned in the film as he had died in infancy back in 1156. There was a second Revolt in 1183, following which Henry II's second son (also named Henry) died of illness, but it took a third and final rebellion in 1189 before the combined efforts of Richard and Philip successfully deposed the King. While Geoffrey had died in 1186 as a result of a jousting accident, aged only 27, King Richard the Lionheart famously went on to become a central military commander in the Third Crusade. He died from an infected shoulder wound that had been inflicted on him during a siege. Following the end of Richard's reign, John took the throne in 1199, but would become one of England's least popular monarchs in all of history. Most immediately recognised as the key villain in many variations of the Robin Hood tales, John was the subject of a revolt by his own barons, who managed to pressurise him into accepting the *Magna Carta Libertatum* ('Great Charter of Freedoms') at Runnymede in June 1215. Having lost many of his father's lands, he died of dysentery at Newark Castle in Nottinghamshire the following year.

The Lion in Winter provided a skilfully-produced and highly unconventional take on the Christmas movie genre which was a perfect fit for the pioneering 1960s, reflecting wide-ranging trends and themes relevant to the decade at large. Unlike traditional Christmas movies that often focus on themes of shared joy, family unity and redemption, *The Lion in Winter* instead explored themes of power, betrayal and familial conflict set against a deceptively merry yuletide milieu. This shift in viewer tastes indicated a growing appetite for more complex and sophisticated narratives among 1960s audiences – one which would become even more pronounced with the arrival of the following decade. As Kevin J. Harty has described it, 'From James Goldman's 1966 play *The Lion in Winter*, this film allowed Hepburn and O'Toole, who had played a younger Henry in the 1964 film *Becket*, the opportunity to deliver bravura performances (Hepburn earned her third Oscar as Best Actress). While the film takes liberties with historical fact, it is a feast for the eyes – and ears'.[3] Indeed, the famous interplay between the two leads is the highlight of a film that is filled with intriguing interpersonal chemistry, relational conflicts and rewarding plot connections. The warring spouses, set against the ostensible jollity of Christmas, made for one of the most memorable cinematic pairings of the decade. This is relatable precisely because, as Ted Byfield suggests, it presents a prism of emotional consequence through which even the motivations of historical nobility can become perceptible and tangible to the contemporary general public: 'The couple often spent Christmas together, providing a plot for the delightful 1968 film *The Lion in Winter*. [...] It portrays that species of dysfunctional marriage where the couple cannot live together and cannot live apart either'.[4]

Interestingly, Harvey's film adaptation of *The Lion in Winter* succeeded – both critically and commercially – where the original New York run of the stage play had not. This was not only due to the greater accessibility to the story that was made possible by a worldwide cinematic release, but also the fact that augmenting its dramatic possibilities through location filming and sumptuous set design unfetters its action and allows it to extend far beyond its stage-bound origins. As David Krauss has noted, '*The Lion in Winter* did not take Broadway by storm when it premiered in 1966 (it ran for only 92 performances), but director Anthony Harvey's 1968 film version, brilliantly adapted by Goldman, won far more success and acclaim. Opening up the drama broadens its scope, while filming in medieval castles in Wales and the South of France brings welcome authenticity to the tale, which is distinguished by innumerable brisk, poetic exchanges that cleverly blend a Shakespearean rhythm and formality with contemporary turns of phrase'.[5] This acknowledgement of the striking contrast between historical dialogue and present-day discourse also combines with the festive setting to create a highly distinctive milieu which allows the film to transcend audience anticipation and subvert expectations both in regard to its style and content. Similarly, Harvey's highly effective use of both wide open spaces and grand interiors help greatly in obscuring the stage-based origins of the action. This, as Kimberley Jones observes, gives *The Lion in Winter* the capacity to toy with its audience just as it presents a pressure cooker of familial conflict that would seem instantly recognisable to anyone who has ever faced close-quarter squabbles with their relatives over the festive season:

> Eleanor of Aquitaine, greeting her estranged husband, King Henry II: 'How dear of you to let me out of jail.' Henry: 'It's only for the holidays.' That's no metaphorical jail. For some, closed quarters with the family at Christmas can feel like a prison sentence. Quite the opposite for Eleanor of Aquitaine (Katharine Hepburn), enjoying time off for good behavior. [...] The children are all monsters, and their parents – alternately smothering and withholding – aren't much better, distracted by their own battle of wits and wounded pride, a screwball comedy curdled. With all this nastiness gathered under one roof, forget 'deck the halls'.[6]

If there was one aspect of *The Lion of Winter* which marked it out for special praise, it was the impeccable quality of the cast, most prominently its high-profile pairing of Peter O'Toole and Katharine Hepburn. Though still only in this thirties at the time of filming (albeit visually aged up to appear closer to Henry II's fifty years of age during the events of the film), O'Toole had enjoyed a stellar acting career by the late 1960s. Having made an acclaimed start on stage and television, he received a nomination for the Academy Award for Best Actor following his performance in the title role of *Lawrence of Arabia* (David Lean, 1962), marking the beginning of huge screen stardom thereafter. He received nominations for the Best Actor Academy Award on no less than eight occasions throughout his lifetime, and received four Golden Globe Awards, a BAFTA Award for Best British Actor and a Primetime Emmy Award. Among his best-known performances were the musical *Goodbye, Mr Chips* (Herbert Ross, 1969), dark social satire *The Ruling Class* (Peter Medak, 1972) and comedy *My Favorite Year* (Richard Benjamin, 1982), alongside innumerable others over the decades. He was awarded the prestigious Academy Honorary Award in 2002.

With an acting career that spanned six decades, Katharine Hepburn is arguably one of the most famous and instantly-recognisable performers in Hollywood history. Having commenced her acting career on Broadway, by the 1930s she was achieving great critical success on the big screen, with high-profile appearances in films such as *Bringing Up Baby* (Howard Hawks, 1938) and *The Philadelphia Story* (George Cukor, 1940). Usually playing sophisticated and highly intelligent characters, she performed to great success in a very wide variety of genres throughout the decades, with appearances in films such as *State of the Union* (Frank Capra, 1948), *The African Queen* (John Huston, 1951), *Desk Set* (Walter Lang, 1957) and *Long Day's Journey into Night* (Sidney Lumet, 1962). From the 1970s onwards, she also became increasingly active in television and continued to win widespread critical praise for her performances. Her final performance was to be in the festively-themed TV movie *One Christmas* (Tony Bill, 1994), for which she was nominated for a Screen Actors

Guild Award at the age of 87. She remains the only person ever to win four Academy Awards for acting, having won in the Best Actress category for *Morning Glory* (Lowell Sherman, 1933), *Guess Who's Coming to Dinner?* (Stanley Kramer, 1967), *The Lion in Winter* and *On Golden Pond* (Mark Rydell, 1981). She received an incredible eight further nominations for Academy Awards in her lifetime, and was also the recipient of numerous awards and nominations at the BAFTA Awards, the Golden Globe Awards, the Emmy Awards and the Tony Awards, amongst many others.

Similarly impressive was the acting pedigree of the supporting cast. Anthony Hopkins had been best-known for his work in theatre and in the short film *Changes* (Drewe Henley, 1964) before his breakthrough role in *The Lion in Winter*. He later went on to major success on television and in cinema as well as on stage, achieving huge acclaim in all three media. Gaining massive public recognition as a result of his performances in films such as *The Silence of the Lambs* (Jonathan Demme, 1991), *The Remains of the Day* (James Ivory, 1993) and *Shadowlands* (Richard Attenborough, 1993), he has been the recipient of two Academy Awards, four BAFTA Awards, two Primetime Emmy Awards and nominations for eight Golden Globe Awards, as well as many other industry plaudits throughout his long and illustrious career. John Castle, though perhaps better-known as a stage actor of great acclaim, was at the time most instantly recognisable to cinemagoers for his appearance in *Blowup* (Michelangelo Antonioni, 1966), though he would go on to many other roles including *Man of La Mancha* (Arthur Hiller, 1972) and, on television, as Postumus in the BBC's star-studded Robert Graves adaptation, *I Claudius* (1976). He has been especially noted by critics for his work with the Royal Shakespeare

Company. Nigel Terry also enjoyed success on film, television and on stage, and of the three was most active in theatre. While he achieved numerous film and TV credits throughout his career, he was perhaps best-known for his starring role as King Arthur in the fantasy epic *Excalibur* (John Boorman, 1981).

Thanks to the astonishingly mature performance of the enigmatically saturnine Timothy Dalton, even the lesser-known figure of King Philip II of France is brought to life with much gusto and panache. As Sean McGlynn has remarked, Philip's depiction in cinema, in general, 'is hardly the stuff of vibrant, thrusting chivalry. The image has been enduring. Philip hardly ever makes an appearance in British popular culture, but when he does it is never flattering. In *The Lion in Winter*, a film about Henry II of England's dysfunctional family, Philip is portrayed as a calculating, devious Machiavellian figure with no suggestion of martial prowess'.[7] Producers of the James Bond film series, Albert R. Broccoli and Harry Saltzman, were so impressed by Dalton's debut performance in *The Lion in Winter* that they offered him the starring role in *On Her Majesty's Secret Service* (Peter Hunt, 1969) as a successor to the internationally-recognised Sean Connery. Dalton decided to turn down their offer, believing himself to be too young for the role (he was aged only 22 at the time, while Ian Fleming's literary Bond was generally accepted to be in his mid-to-late thirties), and it instead went to Australian actor George Lazenby. However, so swayed were the producers by the charismatic Dalton, the actor was later to be cast as the world's most famous secret agent many years later in *The Living Daylights* (John Glen, 1987) and *Licence to Kill* (John Glen, 1989) to much critical acclaim, when he had reached his early forties.

The Lion in Winter had much to recommend it beyond its towering array of performances, from John Barry's stirring original score to Douglas Slocombe's dexterous cinematography and Lee Poll's masterful set design. It is interesting, therefore, to note that contemporary reviews of the film were decidedly mixed at the time of its release. *The New York Times*'s Renata Adler, for instance, found the film to be a qualified success where nostalgia was the most obvious winning factor: 'The dialogue of *The Lion in Winter*, taken from James Goldman's Broadway play, is witty and dated in a twenties way – as all wit from drawing room and insult comedy seems dated now. At moments, the parents, sons and visiting royalty at Chinon in 1183 talk so nastily that they seem like a whole household full of men who came to dinner. But the movie, which opened last night at the Lincoln Art Theater is, for the most part, outdoorsy and fun, full of the kind of plotting and action people used to go to just plain movies for'.[8] At the other end of the critical spectrum, Pauline Kael of *The New Yorker* famously disliked the film, opining that Harvey had miscalculated in attempting to elevate the melodramatic plot 'with serious emotions, more or less authentic costumes and settings, pseudo-Stravinsky music, and historical pomp. And it just won't do to have actors carrying on as if this were a genuine, "deep" historical play on the order of [Robert Bolt's drama] *A Man for All Seasons...* They're playing a camp historical play as if it were the real thing – delivering commercial near-poetry as if it were Shakespeare'.[9] Overall, however, *The Chicago Sun-Times*'s Roger Ebert provided an appraisal which was much more in tune with the film's lasting critical legacy:

One of the joys which movies provide too rarely is the opportunity to see a literate script handled intelligently. *The Lion in Winter* triumphs at that difficult task; not since *A Man for All Seasons* have we had such capable handling of a story about ideas. But *The Lion in Winter* also functions at an emotional level, and is the better film, I think. [...] I imagine *The Lion in Winter* will be a leading contender for this year's Academy Award. I'm not convinced it's the best picture of the year, but I think Peter O'Toole's performance is of Oscar quality, and Anthony Hopkins and Timothy Dalton deserve nominations for their supporting roles as Richard and Philip. As for Katharine Hepburn, she is magnificent; what other actress could have played this role?[10]

Ebert was correct in his prediction about awards success, as *The Lion in Winter* went on to perform strongly at industry awards ceremonies following its release. The film garnered seven nominations at the Academy Awards, including the coveted Best Picture and Best Director Awards, but only won in three categories: Best Actress for Katharine Hepburn, Best Screenplay for James Goldman and Best Original Score for John Barry. It also did well at the British Academy Film Awards, scoring eight nominations with wins for Katharine Hepburn as Best Actress and John Barry for Best Film Music, and there were a similarly impressive seven nominations at the Golden Globe Awards, with the film winning Best Motion Picture (Drama) and Peter O'Toole receiving the Best Actor in a Motion Picture (Drama) Award.

In spite of this huge array of achievements, however, later reviews of the film have continued to be diverse in their criticism. Gil Jawetz, for example, has noted that part of the success enjoyed by *The Lion in Winter* was on account of its gradual but powerful subversion of expectation: 'The story itself is familiar from Shakespeare and other sources: The aging king plans his successor's coronation, but choosing between his pathetic trio of sons causes a great deal of conflict. [...] *The Lion in Winter* seems initially to draw itself from innumerable costume dramas but through the energy, intensity, and humor of the script and cast it turns out to be quite a unique experience'.[11] Not everyone has been quite as convinced of the film's merits, however, with Don Druker offering a rather contentious dissenting view of its famous duelling dialogue: 'This 1968 historical drama is a disaster. [...] James Goldman's screenplay, so chic and sophisticated to the ears of suburbanites, is chock-full of the worst kind of sophomoric fiddling with what Goldman takes to be genuine highfalutin lingo'.[12] In the final analysis, though, Chuck Wilson speaks for many critics in his acknowledgement that irrespective of one's appreciation (or otherwise) for any aspect of the production, it is the central pairing of O'Toole and Hepburn that has made the film so enduringly memorable:

> *The Lion in Winter* is a classic film, but not a great one. It's clunky and overlong, as costume dramas with Shakespearean pretensions tend to be, especially back in the day. Some of the dialogue, by screenwriter James Goldman, adapting his 1966 play, strains for poetic profundity, but that too, was the way of things (then and now). No matter. The movies we take to our hearts are usually im-

perfect, and all that's ever mattered about *The Lion in Winter* are Hepburn and O'Toole, and the pleasure we take from watching two masters inspire each other to greatness. Scenery chewing has rarely been so artful. [...] But we're ultimately here for Eleanor and Henry and the mighty duo playing them, the likes of whom we'll never see again.[13]

For its significance to cinema, the Academy Film Archive formally preserved *The Lion in Winter* in 2000. A few decades later, the film was remade for television in 2003 by Andrei Konchalovsky for Showtime. The cast included Patrick Stewart as Henry II and Glenn Close as Eleanor of Aquitaine, with the three Plantagenet sons portrayed by Andrew Howard as Richard, John Light as Geoffrey and Rafe Spall as John. King Philip II of France was played by Jonathan Rhys Meyers. As befitted the film's Christmas setting, it premiered on 26 December 2003 in the UK, later appearing in America on 26 May 2004. There was some critical scepticism at the time over the wisdom of attempting to recreate such a renowned classic, especially given its extended running time – a comparatively unwieldy 167 minutes, in comparison to the 134 minutes of the 1968 version. While Konchalovsky's remake has never seriously challenged the reputation of Harvey's original film, its performances won praise and it did very well at awards ceremonies of the time, with numerous nominations at the Primetime Emmy Awards, Golden Globe Awards, Costume Designers Guild Awards and Producers Guild of America Awards. Glenn Close was to win Best Actress (Miniseries or Television Film) at the Golden Globes and Outstanding Female Actor (Television Movie or Miniseries) at the Screen Actors Guild Awards, and the film also won in the Outstanding Costumes for a Miniseries, Movie or a Special category at the Primetime Emmy Awards.

The sixties were marked by significant political and social upheaval, and films such as *The Lion in Winter* resonated with contemporary viewers by portraying historical power struggles that paralleled modern concerns which were arising in relation to authority, rebellion and change. The movie's focus on character dynamics rather than festive cheer reflected a broader trend in 1960s cinema towards more character-driven and psychologically nuanced storytelling; this era of film-making had witnessed an increasing emphasis on the complexities of human relationships, even in the context of holiday settings. By presenting a story of intense personal and political conflict as taking place during Christmas, the film challenged the traditional portrayal of the holiday as a time of unalloyed happiness and goodwill. This aligned with the broader sixties counterculture movement, which often sought to question and subvert established norms and conventions.

Thanks to the powerful performances of its actors, led by Peter O'Toole and Katharine Hepburn, the movie's emphasis on strong character development indicated a shift in audience preferences towards quality performances and intricate character studies, even in films associated with the festive season, which would continue to resonate throughout the decades to come. *The Lion in Winter* exemplified how the Christmas movie genre in the 1960s could be used to explore darker and more complex themes, reflecting the broader cultural and cinematic trends of the era. It suggested that audiences were open to the prospect of more challenging and thought-provoking content, even in the context of traditionally festive settings, which efficiently laid the groundwork for the arrival of the 1970s and its enthusiastic embrace of the experimental and inventive.

REFERENCES

1. Martie Zad, '*The Lion in Winter*', in *The Washington Post*, 27 March 1994.
   <https://www.washingtonpost.com/wp-srv/style/longterm/movies/videos/thelioninwinterpgzad_a09eof.htm>

2. David Krauss, '*The Lion in Winter*: 50th Anniversary Edition' in *High-Def Digest*, 13 March 2018.
   <https://bluray.highdefdigest.com/45804/thelioninwinter.html>

3. Kevin J. Harty, *The Reel Middle Ages: American, Western and Eastern European, Middle Eastern and Asian Films about Medieval Europe* (Jefferson: McFarland, 2015), p.313.

4. Ted Byfield, ed., *A Glorious Disaster: A.D. 1100 to 1300: The Crusades: Blood, Valor, Iniquity, Reason, Faith, The Christians: Their First Two Thousand Years*, Vol. 7 (Edmonton: The Christian History Project, 2008) p.73.

5. David Krauss, '*The Lion in Winter*: 50th Anniversary Edition' in *High-Def Digest*, 13 March 2018.
   <https://bluray.highdefdigest.com/45804/thelioninwinter.html>

6. Kimberley Jones, 'Holiday Viewing: *The Lion in Winter*', in *The Austin Chronicle*, 6 December 2017.
   <https://www.austinchronicle.com/daily/screens/2017-12-06/holiday-viewing-the-lion-in-winter/>

7. Sean McGlynn, 'Fighting the Image of the Reluctant Warrior: Philip Augustus as Rex-not-quite-so-bellicosus', in *The Image and Perception of Monarchy in Medieval and Early Modern Europe*, ed. by Sean McGlynn and Elena Woodacre (Newcastle: Cambridge Scholars Publishing, 2014), 148-167, p.151.

8. Renata Adler, 'Screen: James Goldman's *Lion in Winter* Arrives: O'Toole and Katharine Hepburn Starred, Story of Mideast War Also Makes Bow', in *The New York Times*, 31 October 1968.
<https://www.nytimes.com/1968/10/31/archives/screen-james-goldmans-lion-in-winter-arrivesotoole-and-katharine.html>

9. Pauline Kael, 'The Current Cinema' in *The New Yorker*, 9 November 1968, p.189.

10. Roger Ebert, '*The Lion in Winter*', in *The Chicago Sun-Times*, 4 November 1968.
<https://www.rogerebert.com/reviews/the-lion-in-winter-1968>

11. Gil Jawetz, '*The Lion in Winter*', in *DVD Talk*, 19 June 2001.
<https://www.dvdtalk.com/reviews/2383/lion-in-winter-the/>

12. Don Druker, '*The Lion in Winter*', in *The Chicago Reader*, 26 October 1985.
<https://chicagoreader.com/film/the-lion-in-winter-3/>

13. Chuck Wilson, 'Hepburn and O'Toole Roar Again in *The Lion in Winter*', in *The Village Voice*, 12 December 2016.
<https://www.villagevoice.com/hepburn-and-otoole-roar-again-in-the-lion-in-winter/>

7

Scrooge (1970)

Waterbury Films / Cinema Center Films

Director: Ronald Neame
Producer: Robert H. Solo
Screenwriter: Leslie Bricusse,
from a story by Charles Dickens

WHILE the sixties had exhibited an unusual creative balance of the traditional and the inventive, perhaps reflecting some aspect of the unsettled geopolitical milieu of that tempestuous decade, its peculiar blend of the conventional and the experimental was set to continue for some years to come – only more so. The 1970s would witness a perpetuation of Christmas cinema's long wilderness period, where fewer well-known movies in the genre would appear on the big screen during the course of the decade. Those features that did make it into theatres, however, would mark some of the boldest departures from the styles and themes of the genre's golden age that it had witnessed since its zenith in the 1940s.

The musical *Scrooge* arrived at the very beginning of this new decade, and in creative terms the film was to face an uphill struggle on two fronts. Firstly, the shadow of Alastair Sim's exceptional portrayal of the central character – considered by many to be the definitive cinematic Ebenezer Scrooge – in Brian Desmond Hurst's 1951 version of the story continued to loom large in the public consciousness. Any new interpretation of Charles Dickens's story would therefore need to break entirely new ground for itself in order to justify its existence when the seemingly-authoritative 1950s adaptation still remained a firm favourite amongst moviegoers, particularly in Britain. Secondly, because the new production was to be a musical version of Dickens's tale, the film would need to raise the bar considerably in order to meet the requirements of public expectation. The 1960s had seen a very large number of incredibly popular screen musicals, many of which had performed impressively both at the box-office and with the critics. These films had included *West Side Story* (Jerome Robbins and Robert Wise, 1961), *My Fair Lady* (George Cukor, 1964), *The Sound of Music* (Robert Wise, 1965), *A Funny Thing Happened on the Way to the Forum* (Richard Lester, 1966), *Camelot* (Joshua Logan, 1967), *Thoroughly Modern Millie* (George Roy Hill, 1967) and *Doctor Dolittle* (Richard Fleischer, 1967), to name only a few of the most prominent in the genre.

However, most relevant to the production of *Scrooge* was the massive acclaim that had been afforded to Carol Reed's *Oliver!* (1968) a few years earlier, which had starred Mark Lester as the eponymous Oliver Twist and Ron Moody in the role of Fagin. With a plethora of memorable songs penned by Lionel Bart, *Oliver!* had proven without doubt that while Dickens was a novelist who had engaged with the most weighty of social issues during his lifetime, his unique skill in creating memorable characters and his gift for spellbinding dialogue continued to lend his work perfectly to adaptation for the big screen. The result, as Grace Moore would put it, was 'a musical adaptation of the novel, which remarkably manages to convey some of the terror of Dickens' original writing'.[1]

Helming this new version of *Scrooge* was director Ronald Neame. Also a film producer, director, cinematographer and screenwriter, he was nominated three times for Academy Awards in his lifetime and was a true stalwart of British cinema by the time of *Scrooge*'s production. Active in the film industry from the late 1920s, he became a cinematographer in the thirties and made his debut as a director with *Take My Life* (1947). Occasionally an actor alongside his many other talents, the many films that he directed included *The Million Pound Note* (1954), *The Chalk Garden* (1964), *The Prime of Miss Jean Brodie* (1969) and, following the release of *Scrooge*, *The Odessa File* (1974), *Meteor* (1979) and *First Monday in October* (1981). He will of course always be fondly remembered amongst cineastes for popularising the disaster movie genre with his hugely successful *The Poseidon Adventure* (1972), produced by Irwin Allen. For his lifetime of contributions to the international film industry, he was presented with the highly-esteemed BAFTA Academy Fellowship Award in 1996 – the same year that he was appointed a Commander of the Order of the British Empire (CBE).

Contributing *Scrooge*'s screenplay, as well as its all-important lyrics, was composer Leslie Bricusse. While Bricusse was to compose the score of the film, the music was arranged and conducted by Ian Fraser. Also an established producer as well as a screenwriter, Bricusse was nominated for Academy Awards on no less than eight occasions, and won twice (in the Best Music, Original Song Score category for Richard Fleischer's *Doctor Dolittle*, 1967, and Blake Edwards's *Vic-*

tor/Victoria, 1982). At the time, Bricusse had become especially well-known for the lyrics that he had provided for Herbert Ross's *Goodbye, Mr Chips* (1969), a musical remake of Sam Wood's 1939 classic of the same name. In 1971, he would write the lyrics for the Anthony Newley-composed score for Mel Stuart's wildly successful *Willy Wonka and the Chocolate Factory*, starring Gene Wilder in the title role as Roald Dahl's famously eccentric confectionery maker. Bricusse had also composed the lyrics for many stage musicals, and his Dickensian credentials were especially apparent from his work on *Pickwick* in 1963, which he had written in collaboration with Cyril Ornadel.

Scrooge was filmed at Shepperton Studios in Surrey, which had been the same location where *Oliver!* had been directed by Carol Reed two years beforehand. The choice of site was not coincidental: Neame's production was able to reuse many of the Victorian-era sets from the earlier film, which had been safely retained in storage. Further underscoring their visual commonality, both *Oliver!* and *Scrooge* were photographed by cinematographer Oswald Morris, who would go on to win the Academy Award for Best Cinematography for his work on *Fiddler on the Roof* (Norman Jewison, 1971) the following year.

It's Christmas Eve in Victorian London, and notorious merchant banker and money-lender Ebenezer Scrooge (Albert Finney) is not having a good day. Repulsed by the festivities, he is first faced by an unwelcome throng of youthful carol singers – which he quickly disperses from his office – followed by his ever-cheerful nephew, Harry (Michael Medwin). As is his annual tradition, Harry invites Scrooge to Christmas dinner with him and his wife the following day… and in turn, his uncle rebuffs the invitation with the observation that

Christmas is only for the foolish and sentimental. Refusing to allow his seasonal cheer to be diminished, Harry leaves with the assurance that his offer will always stand – cheered on by Scrooge's harried clerk, Bob Cratchit (David Collings).

The miserly Scrooge makes clear his total disdain for Christmas and everything associated with it. He cares only for the acquisition and retention of money, and perceives all human kindness as insincere and duplicitous. Seven o'clock arrives, and – with the day's business now well and truly over – Cratchit readies himself to leave the office. Scrooge grudgingly parts with his administrator's meagre wages, but warns him ominously that Christmas is nothing more than a superficial indulgence: if he is to expect a break from work on Christmas Day, he should expect to be back at the office all the earlier on Boxing Day morning.

Leaving his tight-fisted employer to his own personal gloom, Cratchit heads off into the evening of Christmas Eve and finds a general air of goodwill amongst his fellow Londoners. He soon discovers two of his young children, Kathy (Karen Scargill) and the crutch-bearing Tiny Tim (Richard Beaumont), staring beguiled at the opulent display in a toy shop window. Smiling ecstatically, Bob promises them the best Christmas he can muster with fifteen shillings. With much gusto, he takes his youngsters on a whirlwind tour of old London town as he stocks up on modest presents, treats and food in preparation for the big day. He arrives home to the delight of his other three children and his doting wife (Frances Cuka), and they ready themselves for a well-earned holiday from the usual daily grind of work.

Back at Scrooge's office, the skinflint businessman is just in the process of locking up when he is intercepted by two well-meaning charity representatives (Derek Francis and Roy

Kinnear). The gentlemen implore Scrooge to consider donating to a good cause – the alleviation of the suffering encountered by the impoverished. But the money-lender is perplexed by their charitable aims: surely, he argues, he is already paying taxes to keep the prisons and work-houses operating? Undeterred, the two gentlemen explain that they are determined to do what they can to provide any comfort and support possible for the less fortunate, but Scrooge is incensed as he perceives their altruism to be shallow and inconsequential. As far as he is concerned, the poor are insignificant and should not be indulged. He may hate people in general, but he cares nothing if they despise him in return. To make himself feel better after this unwelcome exposure to the charity collectors' compassion, Scrooge decides to track down some of his clients to demand they pay up their regular instalments on debts they have accrued with his company. Two of the debtors (Molly Weir and Helena Gloag) beg him to consider the circumstances – no-one has excess funds at Christmas, especially those who are already in financial difficulty. But Scrooge is adamant: they must either pay up, accrue an eye-watering amount of interest on a delayed payment, or have their street market stall confiscated.

Scrooge works his way through the Christmas market, attempting to extract repayment from everyone ranging from Punch and Judy puppeteer Mr Miller (Reg Lever) to fast-talking Cockney broth seller Tom Jenkins (Anton Rodgers). He barely slows down even when his hat is temporarily stolen by the vengeful carol singers he had dispersed earlier. Things seem considerably quieter, however, when he finally puts away his pocketbook and heads home through the winding, gaslit streets. Unlocking the front door of his town house, Scrooge is startled when he momentarily encounters the spectral face of his old, long-deceased business partner, Jacob Marley (Alec Guinness), in the brass door-knocker. Shaken, he makes his way into the cold, dark and neglected interior, but is further taken aback when he encounters a ghostly horse and carriage which appears (and then disappears) seemingly out of nowhere.

Scrooge retreats into his living quarters, his nerves shredded, but even there he can achieve no respite. First he hears his name being called from within an ethereal mist, yet shrugs it off as a figment of his imagination. Then the house's servant bells start ringing, soon accompanied by a deafening cacophony of church bells... only for them all to suddenly fall back into silence. Finally, his candle blows itself out, and his parlour door abruptly loosens its bolts and unlocks itself. Striding through the door is the supernatural form of the late Jacob Marley, bedecked in heavy metal chains. Even meeting his old partner face-to-face, Scrooge is reluctant to believe that his presence is real. He asserts that Marley is nothing more than an hallucination, but the ghost has other plans – with an otherworldly scream, his chains flail around the room, finally convincing Scrooge that he can no longer deny the unearthly reality that faces him.

Marley informs Scrooge that the heavy chains he wears are representative of his greed and disregard for his fellow human being; they were forged by his deeds in life, and now must be endured for eternity. Scrooge is baffled; surely Marley had been just as successful and wealthy a businessman as he is, so how can he count himself a failure? But his one-time associate is determined to make Scrooge see that real success comes from empathy and compassion, not money and property. He spirits the miser out of his house and into the skies, where they encounter a multitude of wailing spectres – all of them tormented by the wrongful actions of their mortal lives, knowing that they can never make amends for their transgressions.

Scrooge is shocked by this supernatural horror-show, but – before he can begin to process its full implications – he finds himself back next to his fireplace. Baffled, he questions whether anything that he has just witnessed actually took place at all, but is again accosted by Marley. In deadly earnestness, the spirit warns Scrooge that he will be visited by three Ghosts over the coming hours. If the miser is fortunate, there is the most slender of chances that he might still manage to avoid the eternal fate that has befallen Marley. His erstwhile business colleague then departs as he first emerged, confounding Scrooge as he discovers that the parlour door is now relocked and firmly bolted.

Still attempting to convince himself that nothing he has seen or heard has been real, Scrooge prepares for bed. He settles himself down for the night, but – just as Marley warned – at the stroke of one o'clock, he is visited by a spirit. The Ghost of Christmas Past (Edith Evans) appears to him in the form of a well-dressed woman in late middle age, and seems to manifest herself in his bedchamber without warning. Scrooge is mystified by her purpose – what is it about the past that should concern him, when it is already unchangeable history? However, the spectre replies that she is concerned specifically with *his* past... and the chance of his redemption.

Scrooge is invited to take the ghost's hand, and is instantly transported back to his childhood. They watch as a cavalcade of costumed children in horse-drawn carriages thunder through the countryside, singing merrily about the festive season as they speed away from school to their family homes. Scrooge spots his sister, Fan, but is puzzled when she doesn't respond to his greeting. The spirit explains that what they are witnessing are the events of the past which have now been and gone; they cannot be influenced or changed. Scrooge, however, is not to be found amongst the excited youngsters. His younger self is left alone in the cheerless, empty school building, neglected by his own family. Events skip forward a few years, and an older Fan enters the empty classroom with jubilant news; their obstinate father is now no longer in quite so strict a frame of mind, and young Ebenezer is to be allowed home for the holidays. The ghost reflects on the sad fact that Fan, in spite of being so full of joy and life, would not survive long into adulthood – but that she did, at least, give birth to one child: Scrooge's jocular nephew, Harry.

Further years pass, and suddenly Scrooge finds himself in the offices of his old employer Fezziwig (Laurence Naismith), a merchant whom he once served as a young clerk. Quite in contrast to his own grim offices in the present day, however, Fezziwig's business is bright and welcoming. He is clearly a kind and cheerful man who loves the holidays. On Christmas Eve, Fezziwig finishes business early so that his commercial premises can accommodate an exuberant festive party. There is merry dancing, led by the proprietor's wife (Kay Walsh), accompanied by up-tempo fiddle music and plenty of opportunity for yuletide socialising. Young Scrooge refuses to get into the spirit of the lively dance, however, as he doesn't know the steps and is reluctant to make a fool of himself (thus missing the entire point of the party, which is simply to have fun with friends). The ghost asks the older Scrooge why he admires his long-departed old employer so much, and the old penny-pincher realises that it was because while Fezziwig had the same power as any employer to make his personnel miserable and beleaguered, he consciously chose to value his staff and create a happy workplace. The acquisition of money was an entirely secondary consideration to him.

Later in the party, Scrooge watches as his younger self enters into conversation with Fezziwig's affable, outgoing daughter Isabel (Suzanne Neve). There is obvious attraction between them, and the pair start to dance. The older Scrooge witnesses their eventual courtship with a mixture of wistfulness and remorse. Isabel is as cheerful and exuberant as Scrooge is reticent and reserved. The present-day skinflint looks on with genuine sadness as the relationship sours before his eyes; the covetousness of his earlier self, spurred on by a fixation on business matters, caused him to grow emotionally cold and thus to neglect his only true love. Realising that she cannot compete with monetary wealth when it comes to Scrooge's life priorities, Isabel returns her engagement ring and tells him that she has chosen to set him free from romantic ties. The younger businessman, intently absorbed by company concerns, watches her go without protest... but the elder Scrooge desperately beseeches her to stay, and berates the obstinacy and short-sightedness of his youthful self. However, what has been done is now part of his past, and no amount of regret can change it.

Suddenly, Scrooge is back in his bedchamber in the present day. Still moved by the whirlwind tour of his past, he berates himself for his emotional response and attempts (somewhat desperately) to rationalise the experience as nothing more than a dream. The clock then chimes two o'clock, and in an instant the room's door begins to glow with an ethereal light. A deep, booming voice demands that Scrooge enter his living room, and in doing so he is met with a bizarre sight. The bearded, Bacchanalian figure of the Ghost of Christmas Present (Kenneth More) is seated above a prodigious mountain of Christmas treats, gifts and decorations, all illuminated by a multitude of candles. The bright and joyful sight seems all the more astonishing in the environs of Scrooge's run-down, ramshackle house. This rambunctious, outsized spirit cautions the miser that he has thus far managed to live while ignoring the joy and happiness of Christmas, but that this neglect will now change. He offers Scrooge a gigantic goblet and demands that he drink from it; totally bewildered by the taste of its contents, which he claims to have never sampled before, the ghost tells him that it contains the milk of human kindness.

The jocund spectre tells Scrooge that he is on a mission to endorse all the positive aspects of the festive season, and as such he will demonstrate why Christmas is so important. Smashing through the window of Scrooge's living area, they fly off together into the night, darting across the London skyline until they land next to the home of Bob Cratchit in Camden Town. The thrifty businessman watches in bewilderment as his employee and his family, in spite of their obvious poverty, enjoy a wonderful celebration together. They relish preparing themselves for a meal of roast goose and cheap punch, and Tiny Tim and Kathy rejoice in raising tenpence from their carol-singing efforts. It is clear that it is the loving company of family, not the opulence of the festivities on offer, that is the real source of happiness. Bob proposes a toast to Ebenezer Scrooge, his employer, but neither his wife nor his children will join him in it. As Mrs Cratchit points out, while Scrooge may have paid the fifteen shillings necessary for their Christmas revelries, Bob most certainly earned it – at a rate of threepence per hour, and with no increase in salary for almost a decade. Scrooge is chastened by the family's reaction, but is also surprised to see a fun-loving side to

Cratchit that he had never suspected. Concerned by Tiny Tim's ailing health, Scrooge asks the ghost if the young boy will survive for much longer, but his earlier disdain for the poor is thrown back at him: does he really care whether an ill child lives or not? Seeing Tim's plight within the context of his warm and adoring family, Scrooge is no longer quite so sure of the answer to that question.

The next destination is the well-appointed home of Harry, Scrooge's nephew, and his wife (Mary Peach). While the surroundings are markedly less modest than those of the Cratchit family home, the atmosphere is similarly convivial. The drawing room is crammed full of friends and well-wishers, all full of festive cheer. As he always does every Christmas Eve, Harry toasts the good health of his uncle… a gesture which meets with universal contempt. One guest, Tom (Gordon Jackson), enquires why Harry insists on going through with this thankless ritual every year when it is plain that no-one in London can stand the tight-fisted old moneylender. But Scrooge's nephew replies that while he can't deny that his uncle is a rude, unbearable, greedy skinflint, he still lives in the vain hope that he will one day have a change of heart and embrace the season of goodwill. (As the ghost remarks, if this is what Harry says when he actually likes and cares about Scrooge, he can only imagine what he might choose to remark if he didn't.) Thus with every passing year, Harry continues to hold on to the forlorn belief that a better man might yet emerge from the unscrupulous exterior of the old – or that at the very least, the festive benevolence of Christmas might eventually persuade his uncle to finally give the long-suffering Bob Cratchit a well-deserved wage increase.

Unwilling to give Scrooge the oxygen of attention, even in his (presumed) absence, Harry's wife calls on her many guests to take part in some Christmas Eve parlour games. In spite of his initial contempt for the frivolity of proceedings, Scrooge is soon getting into the spirit of the gathering and finds himself getting involved – even if no-one there can see or hear him. By the time the event is over, Scrooge feels as though he is the life and soul of the party, but the ghost is starting to have difficulty staying awake as Christmas Present slowly begins to turn into Christmas Past. The miser reflects sadly on how the party reminded him of his good times with Fezziwig, which in turn brings back his crushing regret over his separation from Isabel all those years beforehand.

The spirit returns Scrooge to his home, but before they part he issues a stern warning: life is short, and it is important that it is enjoyed and lived to the full. Live a life of melancholy and regret, however, and prepare to lament the experience. With those sage words, the spectral form has gone, and Scrooge once again finds himself in the shadowy confines of his bedchamber. Realising that no trace of the giant ghost's banquet remains in his living room, Scrooge again tries to assert that these supernatural encounters are nothing more than bad dreams... but he finds it difficult to convince himself of this claim when the cloaked, Grim Reaper-like Ghost of Christmas Yet to Come (Paddy Stone) manifests itself at the stroke of three o'clock. Terrified at the portentous sight of the menacing, ominous spirit, Scrooge beseeches it to explain its purpose. However, unable or unwilling to speak, the spectre instead decides that visions will speak louder than words.

In an instant, Scrooge finds himself transported to an indeterminate date in the near future. Tom Jenkins, the broth-seller who is one of Scrooge's debtors, can be seen gleefully polishing the plaque to the old miser's offices. With a surprising degree of merriment, he loudly informs the vast crowd that has assembled in the street that they are all present for one common purpose: a sense of gratitude towards Mr Ebenezer Scrooge. Looking on in puzzlement, the penny-pinching money-lender can't understand why there is such an outpouring of affection for him when everyone in the crowd owes him money. But as he tries and fails to address the multitude of people drawn from right across the length and breadth of London life, given that they are unaware of his presence, Scrooge himself is oblivious to the fact that pall-bearers are removing his coffin from the interior of his office. He similarly has his back turned as Jenkins can be seen tearing up the office debt collection book, and thus is ignorant to the fact that the reason for the crowd's celebration is his own future demise.

Bowled over by the goodwill of the huge gathering, Scrooge finds himself joining in with their triumphant song, never realising that he is following his own funeral procession. Just as the one-time debtors are now rejoicing in the fact that a new life awaits them, given that their arrears have now lapsed, Scrooge also feels that he too has the ability to feel optimistic for the future – he has now been given proof that he can make people feel happy and contented (even if he is unaware of exactly why this is). However, his delight soon turns to concern when the procession runs through Camden Town, and the spirit instructs him to take note of the situation in the Cratchits' home.

Once again peering through the family's front window, Scrooge sees Mrs Cratchit and four of her children in mourning and obvious lamentation. Suddenly apprehensive, Scrooge asks the spirit to take him to Tiny Tim's current whereabouts. Instantly, they are transported to a church cemetery, where

Bob Cratchit is tending to a small and simple grave. It is obvious that this visit is a daily occurrence for the tearful clerk. Realising only now what has happened, Scrooge asks the spirit if these events are still malleable, and indeed what part he plays in this gloomy future. At this point, the spirit reveals its true and horrifying skeletal form, sending a panicked Scrooge tumbling down through his own grave into the depths of the earth. He passes out during the long descent, but awakens in a infernal, cavernous landscape of stalactites and stalagmites. There, the disoriented skinflint discovers that every surface is blisteringly hot, and the air is full of the sound of agonised screams.

Scrooge meets with a morbidly amused Marley, who has come to greet him upon his arrival in hell (as no-one else wanted to). The miser is bemused, having thought that he would end up in heaven after death, but Marley assures him that quite the opposite is true – Scrooge's actions on earth were so pleasing to the Devil, he has decided to appoint him as his personal clerk in the underworld. Horrified, Scrooge discovers that a perfect replica of his offices has been constructed in hell, but that – unlike the rest of its surroundings – it is freezing cold. (The Devil decided that the heat might make his new clerk indolent, thus condemning him to become the only person in the netherworld who is chilled to the bone.) Worse yet, Scrooge's chains – forged by his wicked deeds on Earth – are so long and so massive, they have required extra demons to forge them. As he is swathed in the metal bonds, he finds himself barely able to speak, let alone move. Marley looks on impassively as his old business partner is swamped by link after link of huge metal chains, but ignores his desperate pleas for aid. After all, who did Scrooge ever seek to help when he was alive?

Just as all hope seems lost, the shocked skinflint suddenly finds himself once again in his bedchamber, all vestiges of hell abruptly gone. Stunned by the emotional impact of the evening's events, Scrooge is overcome by euphoria at being given a second chance to make things right – even with a last-minute reprieve. He throws open the curtains of his home and sees that morning has at last dawned in London. Rushing out of his front door, still in his nightgown, he meets a young boy and gives him money to purchase the prize turkey from a nearby butcher's shop. Then, pausing only to get dressed, he heads for the toy shop of Mr Pringle (Geoffrey Bayldon), where he proceeds to buy just about everything in the store. Pringle is staggered by the transformation in the notorious miser's outlook, but Scrooge happily tells him – as the Ghost of Christmas Present had taught him – it turns out that he really does like life after all.

Hiring the service of a legion of small children to help him transport his many Christmas gifts, Scrooge procures several bottles of wine and distributes them freely amongst surprised passers-by. He even joins in with the jolly dance of some costumed street performers... which meets with the amazement of Harry and his wife, who happen to be walking nearby. The couple are staggered by the miraculous alteration in Scrooge's attitude, and once again invite him to Christmas lunch – an offer which, for the first time, he happily accepts. Then, the reformed businessman acquires a Father Christmas outfit from a shop window and merrily starts distributing toys to children near and far.

Eventually, Scrooge reaches the home of Bob Cratchit, where he enters and starts distributing lavish gifts to the couple and their children – culminating in the present of a beautiful mechanised merry-go-round for Tiny Tim. Bob is befuddled at the sight of Father Christmas in his home, until Scrooge reveals his true identity... leading the Cratchits to believe that he must have taken leave of his senses. Scrooge assures them not only that he is entirely sane, but also that he intends to double his downtrodden clerk's salary as soon as he gets back to work. What's more, he promises to find the best doctors to take care of the infirm Tiny Tim, and to cover the expenses until such time as he is well again. He then leaves them (in a state of shock) with the prize turkey, which looks larger than Tim himself.

Tom Jenkins and Scrooge's various other debtors are watching this scene play out with a mixture of astonishment and perplexity. But the money-lender assures them that all of their debts are cancelled – tearing up his pocket book, he emphasises that it really is time to turn over a new leaf. Spotting the charity collectors from Christmas Eve, he also offers to donate a small fortune to good causes not just on this occasion, but in every December yet to come. The assembled Londoners erupt in celebration at Scrooge's new-found generosity. As the singing and dancing continues, the rehabilitated money-lender slips away from the crowd in order to return home and get changed for his Christmas meal with Harry and his wife. Scrooge pauses only to address the unseen Jacob Marley via his door-knocker: he'll never truly know whether his supernatural encounters really happened or if he simply dreamed them, but all that really matters is the fact that he can now see life in a more positive and constructive way. Thus while it is Christmas that has transformed him, the impact of this change will continue to touch other lives right throughout the rest of the year.

At its core, just like its influential Dickensian source material, *Scrooge* emphasises the perennial themes of redemption, compassion and the power of human connection, all of which are central to the festive season. Through Ebenezer Scrooge's well-known journey of self-discovery and redemption at Christmas, the film reminds viewers of the importance of generosity, empathy and kindness towards others, especially during the holidays. The film also highlighted the story's timeless contrast between Scrooge's initial indifference to Christmas and the joyous spirit of the festivities celebrated by those around him. Scenes depicting Christmas festivities, such as carol-singing, seasonal feasting and gift-giving, all serve as a stark contrast to Scrooge's depressing and insular personal existence, underscoring the potential transformative nature of the holiday season.

Beyond this, as had been the case with so many previous adaptations of the stalwart Dickens tale, *Scrooge* portrays Christmas as a time of reconciliation and forgiveness. We see Scrooge realising the need to mend his broken relationships and make amends for his many past mistakes – a development made all the more profound due to the musical interpretation of his character's evolution. The film's emphasis on absolution and second chances resonated with audiences, just as it had when Dickens first released the original novella to his readership in 1843, serving as a powerful reminder of the importance of reconciliation and healing during the festive period. Through its portrayal of redemption, compassion and the transformative power of love, Neame's film celebrates the spirit of generosity and goodwill that defines Christmas, inspiring audiences to embrace the values of kindness and empathy in their own lives.

Neame was to court some degree of controversy in his casting of his protagonist; the ageing miser Ebenezer Scrooge was to be played by accomplished actor Albert Finney, a performer who was only in his early thirties at the time of filming. Rather than allowing his comparatively young age to be a hindrance, however, Finney actually made for a highly effective and very distinctive Scrooge. Though make-up was carefully applied to make him appear much older than his 33 years (the painstaking process would take more than three hours per day to apply the required prosthetics and cosmetics), he wisely avoided any caricature of Alastair Sim's earlier performance – or, indeed, any other cinematic Scrooge which had come before him. Though his bitter, snappish miser makes for a compelling central character throughout, it is in the film's closing stages – where Ebenezer takes on a youthful energy and vigour as he realises that he has quite literally been given a fresh lease of life – that Finney's portrayal really shines. There was a further benefit to Neame having cast such a comparatively young actor in the role, in that Finney could also play Scrooge in his youth without the need to cast an additional performer. As John Simon reflected, 'Finney's interpretation of the role is novel: no creaking ancient he, but a relatively young, dirty-handed, droop-mouthed, near-hunched miser with the very few gray hairs that are the mark of the unloving'.[2]

An actor of considerable distinction, Finney had been active in television and theatre, including the Royal Shakespeare Company, from the mid-1950s. He made his cinematic debut as Mick Rice in Tony Richardson's *The Entertainer* (1960), and soon after was to enjoy many high-profile, critically successful roles in films such as *Saturday Night and Sunday Morning* (Karel Reisz, 1960), *Tom Jones* (Tony Richardson, 1963), *The Victors* (Carl Foreman, 1963), *Two for the Road* (Stanley Donen, 1967), and *Charlie Bubbles* (1967), which Finney was also to direct. He was nominated for Academy

Awards on five occasions, and also received three Golden Globe Awards (Most Promising Newcomer: Male, for *Tom Jones*; Best Motion Picture Actor in a Musical or Comedy for *Scrooge*, and Best Performance by an Actor in a Mini-Series or a Motion Picture Made for Television for Richard Loncraine's *The Gathering Storm*, 2002), as well as nominations for six other Golden Globes during his long career. At the BAFTA Awards he was nominated for twelve awards over the years, winning two of them (Most Promising Newcomer to Leading Film Roles for *Saturday Night and Sunday Morning*, and Best Actor for *The Gathering Storm*), as well as receiving the prestigious BAFTA Academy Fellowship Award in 2001 in recognition of his outstanding achievement in cinematic productions.

Fundamental to the success of any musical, of course, is the quality of its songs, and Leslie Bricusse was to pepper *Scrooge* with a wide variety of different forms and styles which suited the diverse group of performers well. Finney impresses with his delivery of pieces such as 'I Hate People' (the unreformed Scrooge's misanthropic anthem, more or less), 'You... You...' (as he voices his heartbreak over the loss of his one true love), and the concluding 'I'll Begin Again'. But there are many other enjoyable songs which were as entertaining as they were powerful, including Suzanne Neve's performance of 'Happiness', as Isabel rejoices in her ill-starred love for the young Scrooge, and 'The Beautiful Day', delivered by Richard Beaumont's Tiny Tim. Arguably the most well-known of them all, of course, was 'Thank You Very Much', the lively ensemble piece near the film's conclusion led by Anton Rodgers which was nominated for Best Original Song at the Academy Awards.

As had been the case with Brian Desmond Hurst's 1951 adaptation, there were a number of variations between the narrative of *Scrooge* and the original source material. Some are fairly innocuous, such as Scrooge's nephew now being named 'Harry' rather than the traditional 'Fred', or the revelation that Scrooge's one-time fiancée ('Isabel' here, instead of the previous version's less formal 'Belle') had been the daughter of his old employer Fezziwig. But other differences are much more pronounced, such as the extended sequence in hell where Scrooge is forced to face the grim consequences of his life's self-serving choices, and also in the film's closing musical number where the rehabilitated penny-pincher famously dresses in a Father Christmas outfit to accentuate the profound transformation of his character.

Like the Alastair Sim film before it, Neame's *Scrooge* was to form an impressive who's-who of British acting luminaries. Though many are obvious, such as stage legend Dame Edith Evans and *Reach for the Sky*'s Kenneth More, one of Britain's most popular screen performers at the time, the film also featured a great many experienced character actors who were familiar to UK film and television audiences. These included Roy Kinnear, Gordon Jackson, Molly Weir, Anton Rogers, David Collings, Kay Walsh, Derek Francis, Laurence Naismith and – in a particularly entertaining cameo appearance – Geoffrey Bayldon, who will forever be remembered by a whole generation of children as London Weekend International's eccentric mediaeval wizard *Catweazle* (1970-71).

Foremost among this extensive list of performance talent was none other than Alec Guinness, a man often regarded as one of the greatest British acting talents of the twentieth century. A multiple winner and nominee at the Academy Awards, Golden Globes, BAFTAs and Emmy Awards, amongst many others, by the time of *Scrooge* he was already a towering figure in British cinema, known to the viewing public for his many roles which had included David Lean's films *Great Expectations* (1946), *The Bridge on the River Kwai* (1957), *Doctor Zhivago* (1965) and *Lawrence of Arabia* (1962); Robert Hamer's *Kind Hearts and Coronets* (1949); Charles Crichton's *The Lavender Hill Mob* (1951); Alexander Mackendrick's *The Ladykillers* (1955); Anthony Mann's *The Fall of the Roman Empire* (1964), Ken Hughes's *Cromwell* (1970) and, with Ronald Neame, *The Card* (1952), *The Horse's Mouth* (1958) and *Tunes of Glory* (1960). And all this before the world had even heard the name Obi-Wan Kenobi.

Guinness makes for an unforgettable Jacob Marley; ironically flippant at times and yet implacably serious at others, he brings a simultaneous sense of both wrath and pity to the role, along with an almost painful sense of compassion that has arrived tragically too late. It is no surprise, then, that – as Kate Carnell Watt and Kathleen C. Lonsdale have observed – his portrayal is so memorable, this adaptation is as noteworthy 'for Finney's "euphoric" turn as Scrooge [as it is for] Guinness's "spooky" Marley'.[3] When the spectral Marley says that he has not a single word of comfort to bring Scrooge, it seems impossible to doubt him, and Guinness makes full use of the film's supplementary scenes in hell to flesh out the character, making him seem much more than the wailing spectre of foreboding that audiences had come to expect from some previous screen versions of the tale. The result, as Fred Guida notes in his pioneering study of adaptations of *A Christmas Carol*, this innovative and exceptional rendering of Marley's character is just one of the reasons why Neame's *Scrooge* has been one of the most remarkable adaptations of the Dickensian tale to have appeared on cinema screens thus far: 'All in all, this *Carol* is one of those wondrous collaborative efforts that proves that "big" films can work. Along with Bricusse's songs (and screenplay) the work of veteran director Ronald Neame, who was co-producer and co-scenarist of the classic 1946 British version of *Great Expectations*, cannot be faulted. Ronald Searle's wonderfully evocative titles at the beginning, and Oswald Morris's outstanding cinematography throughout, also contribute greatly to what must be judged one of the two or three best looking *Carols*'.[4]

Fundamental to the success of any new version of *A Christmas Carol* is the extent to which the film presents a new and inventive angle on Dickens's often-told story, and additionally the way in which it makes itself relevant to its contemporary audience. In the case of *Scrooge*, Neame and Bricusse work hard – just as Finney does – to represent a different take on the well-established tale by emphasising the aspects of Ebenezer's psychology which have been affected by the protagonist's shifting goals and renewed sense of self-worth. This was a particularly challenging remit, given that the earlier Hurst version of the film had been so widely praised for the manner in which it had sketched out the dark foundations of Scrooge's later self-interest and material avarice. However, Bricusse's script is effective in the way that it subtly shifts the emphasis onto the young Ebenezer's comprehensive betrayal of his benefactor Fezziwig, first rejecting the older man's philosophy of compassion and benevolence, and then callously breaking the heart of his daughter Isabel into the bargain. Finney very effectively conveys the bitterness of Scrooge over both his lost love and his missed opportunities in life, giving a restrained but telling glimpse into the emotional turmoil that is fuelling Ebenezer's angry, objectionable exterior. Like the earlier version of *Scrooge*, the production benefits from some lavish period costumes,[5] courtesy of Margaret Furse, and also Terry Marsh's skilled costume design – along with Bob Cartwright's art direction – which creates a suitably distinctive Dickensian London, albeit one which sometimes seems darker and slightly more foreboding than the version which had been offered up by Hurst back in the early fifties.

Neame's film received an uneven response from reviewers at the time of its release. Some, such as *Life*'s Richard Schickel, were sceptical of the need to revive the Dickens tale at all after so many previous cinematic outings, even if there was concession that it still retained something of the emotional power of the original novella: 'There was certainly no pressing need for yet another remake of the piece, and the attempts of Songwriter Leslie Bricusse and Director Ronald Neame to re-create the spirit of the recently successful *Oliver!* strike me as very weak indeed. [...] Even in this basically uninspired version of an excessively familiar work, the lumps form in the throat at all the right times'.[6] Others, including Roger Ebert of *The Chicago Sun-Times*, took a contrary view, opining that the story's timeless quality provided it with a degree of public acceptance that lent itself to revision and updating: 'Why does *Scrooge* work? Because it's a universal story, I guess, and we like to see it told again. Ronald Neame's direction tells it well this time, and the film has lots of special effects that were lacking in the 1935 and 1951 versions. I was less than convinced by Scrooge's visit to a *papier-mâché* hell, but the appearance of Christmas Present (Kenneth More) surmounting a mountain of cakes and candies was appropriately marvelous'.[7]

An interesting divergence became apparent amongst the reviewers of the time, with some praising the quality of

Scrooge's production values at exactly the same time as others were berating them from looking substandard and unconvincing. Vincent Canby of *The New York Times*, for example, considered the film's visual distinctiveness to be one of its most creditable qualities: '*Scrooge* has something of the freewheeling quality of one of those London pantomimes. It is absurd, sentimental, pretty, never quite as funny as it intends to be, but quite acceptable, if only as a seasonal ritual. [...] Mr Neame has directed the movie with all of the delicacy possible after a small story has been turned into a comparatively large, conventional musical. The settings – London streets and interiors, circa 1860 (updated from the original 1843) – are very attractive, somewhat spruced-up variations on the original John Leech illustrations'.[8] Conversely, *New York Magazine*'s John Simon took the view that the production had a rather cut-price quality – even as he conceded that this was unlikely to matter to anyone other than the hardened Dickens aficionado: 'Although *Scrooge* is spectacular, complete with special effects and replete with scads of Dickensian types (and nauseating kiddies), there's a sense of skimping and making do. But that's for the connoisseur's eye'.[9] Ultimately, however, it was Finney's central performance which came in for the most recurrent praise, with critics such as *The Pittsburgh Press*'s Thomas Blakley remarking that the actor appeared to have harnessed the *zeitgeist* in a highly effective manner: 'For a modern version, Albert Finney is probably the outstanding Scrooge of all time; a little young and round-faced, perhaps, compared to the image from the old days, but then these are changing times and anyway he's such a fine actor and his performance is superb'.[10]

No matter how divergent critical opinion had proven to be over the perceived merits of *Scrooge*, there was no doubting its achievement at awards ceremonies. The film received four Academy Award nominations in 1971: for Terence Marsh, Robert Cartwright and Pamela Cornell in the Best Art Direction/Set Decoration category; for Margaret Furse's costume design; for Leslie Bricusse's song 'Thank You Very Much' in the Best Music: Original Song category, and for Leslie Bricusse, Ian Fraser and Herbert W. Spencer in the Best Music: Original Song Score category. Additionally, Albert Finney was to win a Golden Globe Award for Best Motion Picture Actor (Musical/Comedy) for his performance as Scrooge, with further nominations for Leslie Bricusse (for Best Screenplay as well as Best Original Song), and Ian Fraser, Herbert W. Spencer and Leslie Bricusse for Best Original Score. His work on the film was also to see Terence Marsh nominated for the Best Art Direction Award at the 1971 BAFTA Awards Ceremony.

Recent critical responses to *Scrooge* have continued to be diverse, with commentators continuing to disagree over the film's merits. Reviewers such as Dave Sindelar, for instance, have noted that Dickens's common themes of personal redemption and the reforming power of Christmas have remained so persuasive that *Scrooge* was enhanced by their articulation: 'That Dickens's Christmas classic would be converted into a musical is no real surprise, especially after the success of *Oliver!* But in its own way, the original story is just fine the way it is, and it simply doesn't need the spectacle-heavy retooling it's been given here. It's far from a bad movie, though; the songs are decent, the performances are solid, and there are some great moments here. [[...]] But I miss the simpler and more compelling charms of the story that have been set aside to make way for the songs and dances which often tend to distract rather than enhance'.[11] This observation has also been reflected by advocates of the film's effective expression of individual responsibility and the value of community spirit, even amongst those who believed that Finney was miscast as the film's protagonist, such as Jessica Pickens: 'This 1970 film comes at the tail end of the musical era, which began to die in the mid-1960s. There are a few show-stopping numbers, such as "Thank You Very Much" while everyone is dancing down the street and a finale that recaps most of the songs. [...] While this isn't my favorite *Christmas Carol* adaptation, it had some interesting points. I do just wish Richard Harris had been Scrooge'.[12] Overall, however, there have been a considerable number of critics – such as David Krauss – who have praised the central performance and considered the music and lyrics to be enjoyable to the point that they have made *Scrooge* one of the most successful and well-rounded cinematic versions of *A Christmas Carol* to date:

> Although some purists may find the idea of a song-filled *Christmas Carol* distasteful, even blasphemous, I am constantly struck by how well Dickens' classic works as a musical. The slow ballads add extra poignancy and emotion to the tale, while the rousing ensemble pieces lend the film a festive, exhilarating flavor that eclipses other versions. [...] Unfortunately, the film stumbles at times, taking a few unnecessary liberties with the material. Whenever *Scrooge* strays too far from Dickens' novel, it loses credibility.[13]

One indication of *Scrooge*'s enduring popularity has been the success of its stage version, featuring Bricusse's songs from the film, which premiered in November 1992. Originally starring Anthony Newley in the title role, *Scrooge: The Musical* was first staged at the Alexandra Theatre in Birmingham. It continued to be well-attended by audiences, being revived for a British national tour with Tommy Steele in 2003 and, in the United States, opening in Chicago in October 2004 with Richard Chamberlain as Scrooge. Steele reprised the role at the London Palladium in 2004, and again for a lengthy run between October 2012 and January 2013. Actor Shane Richie also played the title role when the musical was staged at the Manchester Palace in 2007, while an Australian run of the play took place in Melbourne in 1993 starring Keith Michell.

The Neame film was remade, in animated form, as *Scrooge: A Christmas Carol* in 2022. Written and directed by Stephen Donnelly, the remake had a limited run in American theatres in November of that year before being released via Netflix in the December. Starring the voices of Luke Evans as Scrooge and Jonathan Pryce as Jacob Marley, the film retained a number of Leslie Bricusse songs from the original but otherwise featured an updated, original screenplay.

Although *Scrooge* has generally not been regarded as the most prominent entry in Neame's filmography, it was commercially successful and has remained popular amongst audiences since the time of its release. It has also, as Terry Rowan has noted, enjoyed another type of accomplishment in the sense that 'the film received four Academy Award nomination⟦s⟧ and is the only live-action version of this story to be nominated for Oscars'.[14] Just as importantly, it had proved that it was entirely possible to create new and accomplished iterations of *A Christmas Carol* even when the fond memories of Alastair Sim's authoritative performance continued to set a particularly high watermark for any subsequent adaptation to meet.

Neame's version of *Scrooge* was to shed light on several aspects of the cultural relevance of Christmas movies in the 1970s. The adaptation of Dickens' tale into a musical reflected a desire to reconnect audiences with classic, familiar stories. This suggests that even given the general tide of experimental and trail-blazing cinema at the time, audiences in the 1970s had a strong appreciation for traditional holiday narratives that evoked a sense of nostalgia and reinforced timeless values. The film's strident emphasis on family-friendly entertainment aligned with a continued trend of creating holiday content that could be enjoyed by viewers of all ages, reinforcing the idea of Christmas as a time for family bonding and shared experiences.

This being said, the 1970s were marked by various profound socio-political challenges, including major economic struggles and global tensions. A feel-good, uplifting Christmas movie like *Scrooge* helped to provide a temporary escape from these difficulties, offering audiences a hopeful and redemptive story that emphasised the power of personal transformation and the spirit of generosity. As we have seen, film musicals remained popular during this era, both on stage and in film, and the decision to adapt *A Christmas Carol* into a musical format took advantage of this trend, wagering that audiences would still be drawn to the lively, engaging and often emotionally resonant experience that screen musicals can provide.

The film's themes of deliverance, moral renewal, empathy and the importance of community reflected wider cultural concerns of the time as much as it did the classic themes of festive cinema. The seventies, despite its many pressing challenges, witnessed a growing awareness of social issues and a yearning for positive change, which is obliquely mirrored in the redemptive arc of Ebenezer Scrooge. *Scrooge* highlighted how Christmas movies in the 1970s, even at the beginning of the decade, served as a vehicle for nostalgia, family entertainment and escapism, while also reflecting the cultural values and technological advancements of the period. Although it was imparting one of the most traditional of all Christmas tales, *Scrooge* had nonetheless demonstrated that the cinema of the festive season still had room for innovation and creative ingenuity. And yet, as we shall soon see, this only marked the start of the inventiveness at work in the genre that was to come later in the decade.

REFERENCES

1. Grace Moore, *Insight Text Guides: Charles Dickens' A Christmas Carol* (St Kilda: Insight Publications, 2012) [2004], p.67.

2. John Simon, 'Divine Didactics', in *New York Magazine*, 23 November 1970, p.77.

3. Kate Carnell Watt and Kathleen C. Lonsdale, 'Dickens Composed: Film and Television Adaptations, 1897-2001', in *Dickens on Screen*, ed. by John Glavin (Cambridge: Cambridge University Press, 2003), 199-207, p.206.

4. Fred Guida, *'A Christmas Carol' and Its Adaptations: A Critical Examination of Dickens' Story and Its Productions on Stage, Screen and Television* (Jefferson: McFarland, 2000), 110-15, pp.114-15.

5. *Life* Magazine ran a photographic showcase of some of the film's costumes just prior to the time of its release: Marie Cosindas, 'Gallery', in *Life*, 27 November 1970, pp.8-11.

6. Richard Schickel, 'Critic's Roundup', in *Life*, 18 December 1970, p.6.

7. Roger Ebert, '*Scrooge*', in *The Chicago Sun-Times*, 20 November 1970.
<https://www.rogerebert.com/reviews/scrooge-1970>

8. Vincent Canby, '*Scrooge* Varies Ritual in Version at Music Hall', in *The New York Times*, 20 November 1970.

    <https://www.nytimes.com/1970/11/20/archives/scrooge-varies-ritual-in-version-at-music-hall.html>

9. Simon, p.77.

10. Thomas Blakley, '*Scrooge* Musical Slant of Dickens' *Christmas Carol*', in *The Pittsburgh Press*, 4 December 1970, p.35.

11. Dave Sindelar, '*Scrooge*', in *Fantastic Movie Musings and Ramblings*, 19 November 2008.
    <https://fantasticmoviemusings.com/2018/06/19/scrooge-1970/>

12. Jessica Pickens, 'Musical Monday: *Scrooge*', in *Comet Over Hollywood*, 5 December 2016.
    <https://cometoverhollywood.com/2016/12/05/musical-monday-scrooge-1970/>

13. David Krauss, '*Scrooge*', in *High-Def Digest*, 11 October 2011.
    <https://bluray.highdefdigest.com/5705/scrooge_70.html>

14. Terry Rowan, *Motion Pictures from the Fabulous 1970s* (Morrisville: Lulu, 2015), p.109.

8

Whoever Slew Auntie Roo? (1971)

American International Pictures / Hemdale

Director: Curtis Harrington
Producers: Samuel Z. Arkoff and James H. Nicholson
Screenwriter: Robert Blees and James Sangster,
from an original screen story by David Osborn,
with additional dialogue by Gavin Lambert

ONE of the most idiosyncratic of all 1970s Christmas movies, *Whoever Slew Auntie Roo?* perfectly typified the decade's strange melange of the traditional and the experimental. About as far from a customary Christmas movie as it is possible to imagine, it was to become known as one of the earliest horror-thrillers to employ the holiday season as a backdrop for its chilling events, thus laying the groundwork for a whole new subgenre of festive cinema which would eventually include other films of the time such as *Tales from the Crypt* (Freddie Francis, 1972) and *The Legend of Hell House* (John Hough, 1973).

Part modern fairy-tale, part horror and part period Christmas fable, *Whoever Slew Auntie Roo?* (retitled *Who Slew Auntie Roo?* for the North American market) was never going to be in danger of being mistaken for conventional festive fare. A co-production between the United Kingdom and the United States, the movie (which had the working title of *The Gingerbread House*) was filmed at the famous Shepperton Studios near London. Though both the star and director were American, the famous British taste for the darkly amusing and the drolly macabre was very much in evidence in this eccentric parable, based loosely on the German folktale of *Hansel and Gretel* which had been popularised by the Brothers Grimm in the 19th century. Far from the medieval setting of the original legend, however, *Whoever Slew Auntie Roo?* instead centres on an inter-war setting where a psychologically unbalanced widow becomes fixated on an orphan girl, mirroring the obsession of the cannibalistic witch in the Jacob and Wilhelm Grimm tale. The end result may have distantly reflected its origins in the enchanted and mythological, but suitable for young children it definitely was not.

The film was a somewhat unlikely star vehicle for Shelley Winters, an actress who had achieved huge success over the course of a long career with Academy Award wins for her appearances in *The Diary of Anne Frank* (George Stevens, 1959) and *A Patch of Blue* (Guy Green, 1965). Winters was nominated for many awards over the course of several decades, including Golden Globe Awards, Primetime Emmy Awards and BAFTA Awards, and was active on television and the stage as well as in cinema. Her diverse performance career spanned films such as *A Double Life* (George Cukor, 1947), *The Night of the Hunter* (Charles Laughton, 1955) and *Alfie* (Lewis Gilbert, 1966), while she gained further Academy Award nominations for *A Place in the Sun* (George Stevens, 1951) and *The Poseidon Adventure* (Ronald Neame, 1972). Just prior to the production of *Whoever Slew Auntie Roo?*, Winters had appeared in Curtis Harrington's unorthodox horror feature *What's the Matter with Helen?* (1971)

alongside Debbie Reynolds, and her experience on that film encouraged her to recommend Harrington for the later movie as it entered production.

Curtis Harrington was an American director active in both cinema and television, who became especially well-known for his work on experimental films and in the horror genre. His career began in the 1940s as a film critic, but he soon moved into directing short films and, from there, would helm several feature-length movies which included *Voyage to the Prehistoric Planet* (1965), *Queen of Blood* (1966), *Games* (1967) and the aforementioned *What's the Matter with Helen?* (1971). He also directed TV movies and individual episodes of long-running TV series, and was even an occasional actor. His critical works included a pioneering early analysis of classic horror cinema, and informed many of his works which toyed with audience expectation, explored both the morbid and the nostalgic, and which would flesh out the horror of personality subgenre. The Academy Film Archive was to preserve a number of his films as culturally significant, and he established a reputation as a cult visionary with a truly individual creative apparatus.

It was Harrington who made the creative decision to situate *Whoever Slew Auntie Roo?* in an often claustrophobic period festive setting, thus adding to the film's discomfiting ambience. As he explained in an interview a few years after the time of release, 'The first draft of the script was laid in the present day, and it was my idea to place it in the early '20s. I have a great fondness for all the imagery and quality of the traditional Victorian Christmas celebration. I tried to put as much as I could of that in the film. I added a great deal to it. [...] There are an awful lot of moments in it that are purely filmic, that I did on the set'.[1] While the heady mix of fairy-tale whimsy and suspense horror would not lend itself to every taste, there was little doubt of the artistic inventiveness and distinctive narrative playfulness that was presented to audiences.

The place is rural England, and the time is the 1920s. Mrs Rosie Forrest (Shelley Winters), affectionately known as 'Auntie Roo', is an American widow living in a country mansion house named Forrest Grange. She has converted her attic into a nursery festooned with dolls and toys, and sings softly to her young daughter Katharine (Charlotte Sayce) who is nestled in a crib. While Auntie Roo sees a healthy girl, however, the camera reveals that the cot actually contains the mummified remains of a long-dead corpse.

One evening, psychic medium Mr Benton (Ralph Richardson) pays a visit to Auntie Roo's fairy-tale mansion. A storm is brewing as the butler, Albie (Michael Gothard), takes the guest's coat. Auntie Roo has summoned Benton in the expectation of communicating with her daughter via a séance, and she hopes that the charged atmosphere will increase the chances of success. Together with Albie, they join hands around a table, and Benton calls out into the afterlife in the hope of hearing from Katharine. Soon enough, a faint knocking sound can soon be heard, followed by a childlike voice which identifies itself as Auntie Roo's long-departed child. The interaction is only brief, however, and reveals little. Auntie Roo becomes hysterical as the little voice falls silent, as she begs the ghost of her daughter to remain for longer. It is obvious that she somehow blames herself for Katharine's death all those years beforehand.

At a grim orphanage, foundling children Christopher (Mark Lester) and Katy Coombs (Chloe Franks) have been ordered to attend the building's dispensary. There, a young boy named Peter Brookshire (Richard Beaumont) has just been declared fit and healthy, and asks whether he will be allowed to attend the Christmas party being held at the 'Gingerbread House'. The stern supervisor, Miss Henley (Rosalie Crutchley), explains that an appearance at the annual festive gathering is a privilege, and that only a select number of students will be nominated – though she admonishes him that he should really be referring to the building by its proper title: Forrest Grange. Miss Henley tells Matron Wilcox (Marianne Stone) that she is concerned about the behaviour of Christopher and Katy. Since escaping from the orphanage and being recovered, they have both refused to speak a word to the staff. Christopher has also been banned from reading books by the probation department, as his keen imagination and love of folktales has been the source of much distress amongst the infant children at the institution, who have been frightened by his tall tales.

Back at the Grange, local butcher and poulterer Mr Harrison (Hugh Griffith), known colloquially as 'The Pigman', brings a prize turkey to be prepared for the Christmas party. It seems that every year, Auntie Roo holds a festive celebration for the children of the orphanage, which is even now being prepared. Albie is accompanied in the mansion's expansive kitchen by Clarine (Judy Cornwell), Auntie Roo's maid. Harrison argues over late payment for the previous month's meat, but eventually agrees to Albie's assurances that he will reimburse the butcher within the next two days. As Harrison departs, he eyes up Clarine lasciviously – much to Albie's obvious distaste.

Auntie Roo has had difficulty sleeping, but Albie convinces her that her issues are likely to be explained by the strong emotions stirred by Mr Benton's séance the previous evening. She is concerned to have heard nothing from the orphanage about the Christmas party. The butler offers to check in with Miss Henley that afternoon, and collects Mr Harrison's outstanding fees from his employer at the same time. (While Albie grossly overstates the amount owed, it is unclear whether he is including the newly-arrived turkey with the total or is intending to dishonestly pocket the difference himself.)

At the orphanage, the children assemble excitedly as Miss Henley makes the long-awaited announcement about Auntie Roo's Christmas party. Only ten children are selected to attend the event, and Christopher and Katy are not among their number. While they are visibly disappointed, Miss Henley mentions the conciliatory fact that those who will be remaining at the orphanage are to be allowed to stay up a full hour later than usual to play games, and that there will be treats. Compared with the prospect of Christmas at a mansion house, however, this is met with muted enthusiasm at best amongst those who have not been chosen to go to the party.

As the jubilant children are ferried to Forrest Grange by car, the adults discuss the enigmatic woman who owns the mansion, of whom little is known. The driver, Police Inspector Willoughby (Lionel Jeffries), remarks that while Auntie Roo's husband was the greatest stage magician he had ever seen in his life, next to nothing is known about his reclusive American widow. The children soon arrive at the Grange, and Auntie Roo warmly welcomes them – and their adult guardians – to her home. None of the party suspects that Christopher and Katy have stowed away in one of the cars, and make a break for the house's expansive grounds as soon as they can do so unnoticed.

While Auntie Roo gets the children settled in, the orphanage's medical officer Dr Mason (Pat Heywood) guardedly asks Willoughby what the circumstances of the late Colonel Forrest's death had been. The honest answer, the Inspector explains, is that even the police don't know for certain how he died; all that can be ascertained for certain is that the couple's daughter, Katharine, had mysteriously disappeared several years ago and has never reappeared, which has been the source of much consternation amongst the constabulary.

Auntie Roo wastes no time in offering her young guests endless sweet treats, much to their delight. The strict Miss Henley is disdainful of her host's indulgence, but the householder objects: she explains that childhood should be cherished, as youngsters have only a very short period before they are corrupted and demoralised by the troubles and iniquities of the world. Before the authoritarian supervisor can respond, there are gasps around the room as Albie arrives with Christopher and Katie, whom he has discovered trying to break into the kitchen via the back door. Miss Henley is mortified at having been disobeyed so flagrantly, but Auntie Roo refuses to see them disciplined. It is Christmas, after all: there is ample food for everyone, and she insists that they be allowed to join the other guests. In response, Christopher offers his heartfelt thanks on behalf of his sister and himself, causing surprise amongst the orphanage staff as he finally recovers the use of his voice. The adults are nonplussed by the arrival of the Coombs children; how did they manage to get to the countryside mansion when it is located over three miles away from the orphanage? Miss Henley is clearly furious by their unabashed disregard of her instructions, but is in no position to vent her frustrations without the risk of upsetting their ebullient host.

Later, Auntie Roo treats the children to a reading of Clement Clarke Moore's classic poem, 'A Visit from St Nicholas'. The children ask her about her past, and she replies that she had originally been a successful dancer in Paris before falling in love with Colonel Forrest, who would in time become her husband. One of the youngsters asks her if her spouse is now dead, but strangely she seems momentarily unsure. Eventually, she responds that the notion of death is relative; he may no longer be among the living, but that does not necessarily mean that he is unreachable. This inscrutable response seems to mystify the orphans. Promising a pantomime the next day, she sends the children off to bed with the requisite Christmas Eve observation that Santa Claus may visit them with presents during the night – if they have been good.

As the clock strikes eleven, Auntie Roo spots a Christmas bauble trundling down her main stairway and smiles, supposing it to be a message from her long-departed daughter. (In reality, one of the children has taken it from Katy and thrown it down the stairs.) She looks up in horror to see young Katy about to slide down the banister, and reacts with hysterical shock. Her response seems completely out of proportion to the situation... until, through a flashback, we see her own little girl Katharine in an identical position years earlier, just before she accidentally plummeted to her death. Back in the present, Clarine comes racing into the hallway, alarmed by the commotion. However, Katy has slid down the banister safely, with no repeat of Katharine's grisly fate.

Auntie Roo asks Clarine if she would like to join the séance circle later that evening, but the maid politely declines due to her household duties. Drained by the trauma of reliving her bad memories, Roo tells Clarine to have Albie escort Mr Benton into the study as soon as he arrives. Upstairs, Christopher and Katy excitedly discuss their good fortune in a guest bedroom. They wish that they could be adopted by Auntie Roo and thus avoid the gloomy environment of the orphanage. Katy is too excited to sleep, and pleads with Christopher to tell her a bedtime story. Not wishing to disappoint, the boy launches into a heartfelt rendition of the morbid fairy-tale of *Hansel and Gretel.*

In the study, Mr Benton has arrived and is already preparing for the next séance. Auntie Roo is insistent that they must get a message through to Katharine at any cost. Benton seems optimistic of their chances, and calls out to the young girl to make contact with her mother. With the house otherwise in silence, Katy is awakened by the distant sound of Benton's stentorian pronouncements and – confused by the unfamiliar voice – gets out of bed to investigate. Using Katharine's teddy bear for its psychometric properties, the medium continues to cry out to the other side, little realising that his voice is actually drawing Katy closer instead. Christopher wakes up and follows his sister, but instead finds himself attracted to the source of what appears to be Katharine speaking. Far from the result of the séance, however, he quietly watches as he sees Clarine in the service room using a childlike tone of voice to impersonate the long-dead young girl. Silently, he realises that the voices Auntie Roo presumes to be from the afterlife are actually being mimicked by a source that is all too alive. Back in the study, Auntie Roo's impassioned pleas for Katharine to stay for longer fall into silence when the door swings open to reveal young Katy. Benton reacts with genuine surprise at the girl's arrival, but Auntie Roo immediately mistakes her for Katharine – in spite of Albie's reassurance to the contrary.

While Auntie Roo finds it increasingly difficult to convince herself that Katy and Katharine are not one in the same, the young girl focuses on the old teddy bear, further deepening Roo's confusion. Realising that there is little point in continuing the ritual, Benton asks for his payment and is richly rewarded. He apologises that his spiritual efforts have not been as successful as he might have liked, but Auntie Roo declares puzzlingly that his labours might have been more fruitful than he realises. Once she has left the room, the increasingly shifty Benton promptly pays a cut of his imbursement to Albie. It is becoming ever more obvious that the so-called psychic medium is actually a charlatan, and that the butler is in the know about his schemes. While this is happening, Auntie Roo discovers Christopher in the hallway as she returns Katy to the guest room and is confused by his presence. The young boy explains that he had heard a voice coming from the service room, but as the door was locked he was unable to pinpoint the source of the unidentified speech by looking through the keyhole. Auntie Roo throws open the door, which is now unlocked, and reveals an empty space filled with cleaning equipment and other household utensils. The source of the mysterious voice appears to have vanished without a trace.

In the dead of night, Auntie Roo – now becoming increasingly unbalanced – sneaks into the guest room and retrieves her daughter's teddy bear from a sleeping Katy. As dawn breaks, Roo bursts back into the room, declares that it is snowing outside, and tells the children that Santa Claus has been to visit. Somewhat out of the blue, Auntie Roo asks Katy if she would like to be adopted by her and live at Forrest

Grange permanently. The young girl seems happy with the idea, but it is less well-received by Christopher who rejects the very notion of being separated from his sister when they have been through so much together. It is obvious, however, that Roo's plans do not involve him, which leads to his hostility to the proposal. As she departs, Auntie Roo makes the throwaway remark that as Katy is so slight, she will need to fatten her up with Christmas goodies. This causes Christopher to remember the macabre narrative of the *Hansel and Gretel* story he had related as a bedtime story the previous evening.

Downstairs, the children excitedly open their presents under Auntie Roo's lavishly-decorated Christmas tree as she watches them benevolently. She tells them to wrap up and have fun in the snow outside while it lasts, following which they will all share Christmas dinner together. Before they depart, Auntie Roo tells Katy that she has a special gift just for her: a brand new teddy bear. However, Katy seems oddly disappointed; she didn't want just any toy bear, but rather the one which had once belonged to Katharine. Roo watches her reaction with a mixture of disenchantment and curiosity.

The children make the most of the thin covering of snow to enjoy themselves in the winter cold and play games. Christopher and Katy seem rather more contemplative, but their mood changes when they discover an outhouse which contains the late Colonel Forrest's illusionist stage props. They look in awe at the assembled costumes, marionettes and paraphernalia, and soon find a brightly-coloured magic cabinet which Christopher uses to 'disappear' and substitute himself with a plastic skeleton – much to Katy's amazement. When they spot a collection of fake jewellery, the young girl remarks that she has seen a drawer with a hidden interior in Auntie

Roo's study which is stuffed with real gems and money. Her brother notes this information carefully.

Katy asks Christopher to demonstrate the operation of a guillotine which had once belonged to the Colonel, and – believing it to be a stage replica – he asks her to place her head on the block while he puts it through its paces. However, at the last second she loses her nerve and substitutes her head for that of her new teddy bear... which is just as well, as the guillotine's blade turns out to be real and promptly decapitates the toy. Christopher is shocked at how close they came to tragic disaster. At that point, a number of masks and puppets start to flail around, following which a fearsome cowled figure emerges and races after the children. This causes them to flee the outhouse in terror. Little do they realise that the mysterious pursuer is actually Albie in disguise, keen to remove the pair from the building – but also revelling in their alarm and discomfort.

Back in the safety of the mansion, Auntie Roo has returned to her professional roots as a stage entertainer to perform a surprisingly ghoulish song and dance act for her orphan guests. The children look more bewildered than amused, while Albie and Clarine both struggle to conceal their disinterest. During the recital, Katy uses the distraction to slip away to the study and retrieve Katharine's teddy bear. Roo notices her absence and intercepts her, indignant that she should be so stubborn. Having just gifted her a brand new teddy bear, she is confused as to why Katy should be so persistent in wanting Katharine's old, beloved toy. The young girl explains that before being orphaned, she had once been gifted a bear which looked just like Katharine's cherished plaything. This causes Auntie Roo to enter a state of mental conflict, where she reasons that she is unable to part with such an adored memory of her daughter... until she suddenly rationalises Katy's attachment to the toy as proof that she is actually some kind of physical reincarnation of Katharine. With this in mind, Roo finally agrees to let Katy keep the treasured teddy bear. In response, the girl tells Auntie Roo that she loves her, further reinforcing her delusion that Katy is somehow Katharine reborn.

In the dead of night, Christopher is awakened to the sound of a woman singing. Confused by the origin of the voice, he creeps downstairs undetected and makes his way to the service room. Inside, he discovers a dumb waiter and realises that sound echoes eerily along its shaft. He thus is able to determine that the singing is actually coming from Auntie Roo, present elsewhere in the house. Because he is small enough to fit into the tiny freight elevator, he decides to ascend the shaft to find out where it leads. Eventually, he discovers that it terminates in the mansion's attic... where, peering through the dumb waiter's doorway unseen, he witnesses Auntie Roo in the morbid nursery as she moves Katharine's shrivelled corpse from her cot into a coffin. Stunned by this gruesome sight, Christopher attempts a descent but is detected by Roo. Seeing the tiny elevator moving down, she emerges from the attic (which, it is revealed, can only be accessed via a wardrobe with a fake rear panel in her bedroom) and heads down to the service room to intercept whoever is responsible for the intrusion. However, Christopher is long gone by the time she gets there. Suspecting his involvement, Auntie Roo heads for the guest room, but by now he is back in bed and convincingly feigning sleep. Before she leaves the room, Roo addresses the slumbering Katy with motherly affection as she sees her hugging Katharine's teddy bear, which gives Christopher further cause for alarm.

Boxing Day morning arrives, and the children are leaving to return to the orphanage. As Auntie Roo assures Miss Henley that they have all been well-behaved, but Christopher interrupts the fond farewells to report that Katy is missing. Everyone seems mystified by her absence; as Roo heads for the hallway to call for her, Christopher tries to convince Miss Henley of the widow's febrile mental state, but she is unwilling to believe a word he says as she has convinced herself that he is a compulsive liar. Christopher makes a break for the mansion in an attempt to find his sister, but is caught by Albie and promptly returned. Auntie Roo wishes all of the children a happy New Year, and assures Christopher that wherever Katy might be, she is sure that she will be safe and well. As the cars depart, the young boy is again reminded of the witch in the *Hansel and Gretel* story kidnapping unsuspecting children.

In the drawing room, Albie becomes uncharacteristically straight-talking and abruptly tells Auntie Roo that he will be leaving her service – as will Clarine. Assertively, he demands that she write them a cheque for £2,000 before they part company. Confused by his curt attitude, she can't understand why he would want to resign so suddenly after having been in her service for so long, but he reiterates that if she doesn't pay up, he will report her to the police for kidnapping Katy, who he knows to be trapped in the attic nursery. Realising that she is being blackmailed, she grudgingly signs the requested cheque. Albie contemptuously tells her that all of the séances had been nothing more than a fantasy; Mr Benton was simply a confidence trickster, while the supposed voice of Katharine had been (as Christopher had suspected) merely Clarine calling down the dumb waiter shaft with a disguised voice.

Dissatisfied by the glib and unsatisfactory explanations he has been offered about Katy's disappearance, Christopher escapes from the orphanage, purloins a bicycle and travels the three miles back to Forrest Grange. On arrival, he breaks into the mansion through the study window, finds the trick drawer that Katy had spotted earlier, and loads his pockets with stolen jewellery and other personal effects. Although the Christmas celebrations had only taken place the day before, the rambling old house already looks shadowy and solitary – a world away from its earlier festive décor. Checking the guest bedroom, he can find no trace of Katy anywhere, and thus decides to try ascending to the attic in the dumb waiter. When he reaches the nursery, it initially seems deserted, but he soon discovers his sister hiding behind an elaborate doll's house.

Katy appears quite content to be Auntie Roo's new ward, and regales Christopher about the lavish dinner they had just shared. Her brother is baffled by her sense of satisfaction, pointing out that she hasn't been formally adopted – merely abducted. He worries that if the authorities find out about what has happened, they will both be sent to a reform school and thus will have no chance of being adopted by a family. Christopher points out that Auntie Roo has been behaving exactly like the witch in the *Hansel and Gretel* legend, but Katy doesn't care: she is happy to be treated kindly, fed well and clearly valued in ways that she never was when in the care of the orphanage. Exasperated, Christopher explains that she is being trapped in a gilded cage – no matter how opulent her surroundings, Auntie Roo has taken away her right to freedom. Katy finally starts to see her brother's point.

Discovering that there isn't enough room to fit both of them into the dumb waiter, Christopher worries about making their escape undetected, but Katy demonstrates that there is another way out of the room via the hidden entranceway in Auntie Roo's wardrobe. They emerge into Roo's bedroom, where she is sleeping fitfully, and silently make good their escape. Neither of them realise that she has climbed out of bed in order to intercept them at the mansion's main doorway. Cheerfully, but with more than a hint of manic hysteria, she tells them that they can't possibly want to leave: after all, why would they, when this is now their home? Before the children can protest, she corrals them back into the hallway and locks the front door.

Some time later, Inspector Willoughby visits Forrest Grange to enquire about the whereabouts of the children. Auntie Roo feigns ignorance of Katy's location, and similarly affects shock when she hears that Christopher has also disappeared from the orphanage. Disingenuously, she points out that the pair appeared to be dead set on escaping from the institution on Christmas Eve, when they first arrived at the mansion... so who is to say that they hadn't planned to use Christmas as a distraction to cover their getaway from the beginning? The Inspector is unconvinced by her theory and asks permission to search the house, but ultimately finds no trace of the siblings. Eventually, Auntie Roo breaks into an agitated panic and tells the senior policeman that she feels persecuted: how could he possibly suspect her of kidnapping children when all she has ever had is their best interests at heart? (In reality, the outburst is simply a feint to avoid him discovering the secret entrance to the attic.) Remarking that he has no official warrant to search the property, she ejects him from the mansion, but the Inspector warns her that the Chief Constable is insistent that he search the grounds and leave no stone unturned.

Sure enough, a couple of policemen with bloodhounds are soon combing the gardens, and the outhouse full of magician's props is also investigated. Nothing turns up the faintest trace of the missing children, however. When the woods and the garden pond are also examined without any results, the Inspector's suspicions remain well and truly provoked – but with not even a hint of evidence, there is nothing else that he can do. Little do the police officers realise that up in the concealed nursery, Christopher is busily stuffing Katy's beloved teddy bear with the stolen jewellery to conceal it from prying eyes. Auntie Roo arrives with dinner, and the young boy asks her how long she expects to hold them in the attic against their will. Now clearly unhinged, she explains that the situation will only last until the New Year, and frenziedly cuts the rope supporting the dumb waiter to prevent their escape.

Seeing one last chance to get away, Christopher makes a break for the nursery door, but Auntie Roo catches him before he can leave and drags him away, locking Katy in the attic behind her. As she pulls the boy into the hallway, however, she is distracted by a loud knock at the front door. Christopher lunges for the doorhandle, hoping against hope that the police have returned, only to find Mr Benton instead. The young boy blurts out that he and his sister have been abducted, but the semi-inebriated fake psychic clearly doesn't believe a word of it. Auntie Roo, on the other hand, reveals that she is now all too aware of Benton's ruses and will not tolerate any further deceit. With the pretence of being scandalised by her accusations of wrongdoing, the phoney medium takes his leave.

Auntie Roo takes Christopher to the kitchen and sets him to work on domestic tasks – with the warning that if he should try to escape again, he should remember that she has

Katy in her clutches. Thus when she orders him to collect wood for the fire, he does so without being tempted to leave the grounds and seek help. Brandishing a sharp knife and later a cleaver, she explains that they will all enjoy a dinner of turkey with stuffing. With Albie and Clarine now both long gone, Auntie Roo transforms herself into the acme of domesticity, setting herself to work in the kitchen while Christopher continues to gather fuel. It is clear from her odd outbursts of mania, however, that she is now far from psychologically stable.

Christopher hatches a plan and sneaks around to the front door of the mansion, ringing its bell. Believing that she has company, Auntie Roo heads off to answer the door, little realising that Christopher has double-backed on himself and is frantically trying to retrieve the nursery key from a board in the kitchen… which is infuriatingly just out of his reach. He only just manages to grab it mere seconds before Roo returns, still confused by the fact that there was nobody to be found at the front door. She orders Christopher to collect more wood for the fire, but he manages to evade her gaze as she collects supplies from the larder. Unseen, he races back to the nursery to free Katy.

Unfortunately for the increasingly frantic young boy, his sister doesn't quite grasp the severity of their situation. First he has to persuade her to go, and then she forgets her teddy bear and insists on going back to the attic to collect it. The delays give Auntie Roo the opportunity to realise what is going on, leading to her intercepting them both in the act of absconding. Knowing the front door to be locked, Christopher leads Katy down into the kitchen… where they realise that the back door has also been secured. Resignedly, they can only watch as an increasingly disturbed Roo entreats them to behave and stop trying to break out of the mansion. Christopher picks up a carving knife to defend himself, but the irrational widow quickly disarms him and manages to trap both children in the larder, which she then securely locks up.

Now utterly insane, Auntie Roo reasons that due to her continual disobedience, Katy can't be the reincarnation of her angelic Katharine after all, and thus she retrieves her daughter's coffin and attempts to return her body to the crib in the nursery. However, the desiccated remains have grown brittle from all the recent handling, causing the corpse's skull to collapse. Roo recoils in horror at the baleful sight and rushes out of the attic. Now, she comprehends, she has nothing that she wished for: Katharine is reduced to dust, and Katy is a mere impostor. Much to her distress, her worst fears have been realised – she is completely alone.

Dissociating herself from this moment of pure panic, she decides to return to the kitchen and finish preparing dinner. As she starts cutting potatoes with a meat cleaver, distant voices can be heard calling to her from the larder door. Deducing her fragile mental state, Christopher and Katy use emotional manipulation to make Auntie Roo feel as though they have finally accepted her as their surrogate mother. Suddenly overjoyed, she unlocks the door and rushes into the larder, but it has all been a ruse. Christopher attacks her from above, then he and Katy race into the kitchen and bolt the door behind them. Hysterical, Roo starts trying to break down the door with her cleaver, but Christopher has had enough of the cat-and-mouse game. He stacks a pile of wood against the door and promptly sets fire to it. Auntie Roo reacts in alarm, knowing that she has been condemned to a fiery death from which there is no escape. Pausing only to recover the teddy bear stuffed with Roo's jewellery, the children finally manage to take flight through the front door just as the mansion is engulfed in flames. Just as they reach the courtyard, Mr Harrison unexpectedly arrives with a promised delivery of butcher's meat – a prize roasting pig. Realising with shock that Forrest Grange is on fire, but unsuspecting of the cause, he tells Christopher and Katy to stay clear of the building while he goes to summon the Fire Brigade. Katy is confused: if Auntie Roo had ordered fresh meat, why was Christopher worried about the widow eating children? Her brother grimly replies that given the chance, she would have consumed them eventually – one way or another.

By the time the Fire Brigade has arrived, the mansion has been gutted by flames. Inspector Willoughby is on the scene, along with the sympathetic Dr Mason from the orphanage, and they promise to take the children back to the safety of the institution. The firemen note that the blaze seems to have started in the kitchen, and the children voice their disappointment that they were unable to save Auntie Roo due to the heat of the inferno. Ominously, the veteran policeman mumbles that the two children will probably be psychologically scarred for life by the trauma of what they have witnessed. But Christopher and Katy exchange an unseen smile, feeling that Auntie Roo had received the fate she deserved. Whether she really was a witch, as in the *Hansel and Gretel* fable, or simply someone who wanted to imprison them against their will, the children know that what remains of her wealth will one day give them financial security when they come of age – but until then, the jewels will remain safely hidden inside Katy's beloved teddy bear.

In *Whoever Slew Auntie Roo?*, the supposedly jubilant Christmas ambience of the film's setting serves as a stark contrast to the sinister and disturbed actions of the mysterious, larger-than-life protagonist — and the calculating strategies of her would-be wards. While the holiday season typically evokes feelings of joy, warmth and family togetherness, Auntie Roo's descent into madness and obsession deftly subverts all of these traditional notions. The cheerful decorations, festive music and jovial atmosphere of Christmas all combine to provide an eerie backdrop to the sense of horror that slowly reveals itself, emphasising the juxtaposition between the surface appearances of holiday cheer and the underlying darkness of Auntie Roo's subsequent actions.

The film explores weighty themes of loss, grief and mental instability, suggesting that the holiday season can exacerbate feelings of loneliness and isolation for those who are struggling on an emotional level. Auntie Roo's fixation on Katy and her increasingly desperate attempts to fill the void left by her deceased daughter reflect the complexities of grief and the lengths to which people will go to attempt to find solace and meaning, even at the expense of others' wellbeing. *Whoever Slew Auntie Roo?* thus offers a chilling and often unsettling exploration of the darker aspects of human nature, set against the superficially ebullient environment of the holiday season. While not a traditional Christmas movie by any means, Harrington uses an inspired concatenation of Christmas imagery and themes to enhance the atmosphere of suspense and horror, creating a unique, memorable and generally disturbing viewing experience.

It is intriguing, in spite of the fact that the film bears so many of Harrington's highly distinctive creative touches, that he was not in favour of the producer's lurid choice of title, explaining that 'the film, while in production, was called *The Gingerbread House*. This was an appropriate title and it was the title I gave the script. *Who Slew Auntie Roo?* was the producer's idea of a commercial title. It is my opinion that it harmed the commercial chances of the film'.[2] That Harrington's preferred option for the title suggests a closer association with the movie's folktale origins is interesting, as it brings into closer focus his thematic aims to use the fantastical and the illusory as a lens through which to view the psychological horror that is on display.

While it is certainly easy to see Harrington's point – doesn't the film's title rather give the game away about its conclusion before the action even begins? – there were other fairly major issues with the film's fairy-tale pastiche. Christopher reading *Hansel and Gretel* as a bedtime story lacks subtlety: not least as it is hardly the kind of folktale that is likely to soothe an infant to sleep, but also because it presages his preoccupation with Auntie Roo supposedly being (or behaving in the same manner as) the witch antagonist of the old fable with all the subtlety of a sledgehammer. Thus, as Peter Shelley has observed, 'Christopher telling Katy the *Hansel and Gretel* tale seems an odd choice to help her sleep, though its children-triumphing-over-wicked-adult theme offers a form of empowerment. The tale will be further used by Harrington throughout the film in voice-over [...] as the narrative matches the succession of predicaments faced by both pairs of children. As a literary device, the use of the tale reads as somewhat obvious; it would have been preferable had the audience been allowed to make the connection rather than having it literally told to us'.[3]

There are also, of course, major moral implications in the way that the narrative plays out. Auntie Roo's precarious mental state is gradually revealed throughout the film, starting with the pre-title sequence and the shock disclosure of Katharine's current mummified state in the present day, but it is difficult to know whether the audience is supposed to feel some degree of sympathy for the widows' condition (her terror of being left alone, the false friendship of her unscrupulous employees, and her manipulation by malign third parties) or simply revulsion at her selfishness and possessiveness (the kidnapping of Katy, the real and implied danger signalled towards Christopher, and blatantly lying to the authorities in order to cover her tracks). James Morrison has described the contradiction thus:

> In *Whoever Slew Auntie Roo?*, comedy and horror collapse into one another, exchanging places in syncopation with sudden, inexplicable shifts among expressions of love, hostility, and aggression between generations. [...] In the film's last third, Winters shuttles between enacting avuncular tenderness and shrewish malevolence, both in registers of muffled hilarity, with no framing perspective to explain these starting alternations or to ground the shifting attitudes. The ending refuses to establish whether Auntie Roo's death is a form of justice or an unspeakable cruelty, the murderous outcome of the children's malicious delusions.[4]

Harrington had previously dealt with themes of psychological instability, legerdemain and insanity in his earlier films *Games* and *What's the Matter with Helen?*, and his refusal to conclude the film with any easy ethical answers is brave — not least as the audience is forced to decide for themselves which of the characters has been the most self-serving: Christopher, who robs a mentally unsound widow and then murders her by destroying her home to cover his escape, or

Auntie Roo herself, who is willing to risk everything to satisfy her maternal instincts by resorting to kidnapping minors against their will. These may seem like weighty issues of principle for a film that is set over the course of the customarily easy-going holiday period, but their import is blunted by the over-the-top hysteria of Winters's central performance, which is as uneven as it is poorly restrained. As Jack Zipes has put it, 'Winters is so ridiculous and comical as a would-be witch that the film becomes more camp than horrific',[5] and it is true that there are points where it can be difficult to know when Robert Blees and James Sangster's screenplay is building a sense of horror or offering a knowing wink to the audience. While there is much on display here that carefully constructs a discomfiting atmosphere, to say nothing of an adroit subversion of the traditional Christmas ambience, it is difficult – as Gary A. Smith has argued – to consider *Whoever Slew Auntie Roo?* anything other than a qualified success when the subtlety of its narrative and thematic nuances are so comprehensively overshadowed by the frenzied hysteria of the film's central performance: 'This *Hansel and Gretel* takeoff is an entertaining but ultimately sick affair, with Winters giving yet another of the shrill and overwrought performances that have plagued her later career'.[6]

While the premise of Mr Benton's séance con trick is ingeniously played – largely thanks to the skill of Ralph Richardson's knowing performance as the drunken old swindler – there are numerous other aspects of the film which make less sense. Given that the character comes from a professional live performance background and was married to a stage illusionist, would the depth of Auntie Roo's gnawing grief and personal guilt really be enough to distract her from the sleight of hand being performed by Benton, Albie and Clarine? Similarly, in spite of much groundwork being laid, the audience never does discover what happened to the long-departed Colonel Granger or why his widow treats the matter of his assumed death so perplexingly. In spite of Inspector Willoughby's ominous pronouncements that the strange case of Granger's disappearance is still open, many years after he was last seen – thus emphasising that even the police have no idea what fate may have befallen him – there is never even an implied resolution to the mystery by the end of the film. (Certainly, given Auntie Roo's terror at the prospect of being alone and her obsession with being a caring and attentive mother, her singular disinterest in remarrying and thus recreating an idealised, traditional family unit may be intended in some way to cast suspicion on her own part in her late husband's unexplained departure – especially given her comparative reluctance to discuss him or his fate in any detail.) Another peculiarity is the fact that while the orphans revel at the chance to play in the Christmas snow, there is actually little more than a minor scattering on the ground, while the trees and bushes are all clearly still in leaf. This was because, while the film is set in late December, it was actually filmed in the spring of 1971 and thus fake snow had to be brought in for the purposes of presenting a wintry environment. The vast majority of these exterior shots, as was the case with the interiors, were filmed at Shepperton Studios in Shepperton, near London.

The film benefited from a variety of admirable production aspects, not least the entertainment provided by Kenneth V. Jones's marvellously overdramatic original score and the eye-catching art direction by George Provis. However, the greatest strength of *Whoever Slew Auntie Roo?* was arguably in its remarkable cast of supporting character actors, led first and foremost by Ralph Richardson – the world-famous star of stage and screen who had already made his mark on Christmas cinema thanks to his performance as the Reverend Martin Gregory in *The Holly and the Ivy* (George More O'Ferrall, 1952), an adaptation of Wynyard Browne's 1950 stage play. Richardson and then-child actor Chloe Franks would both appear the following year in Freddie Francis's *Tales from the Crypt*, an anthology movie which contained its own tribute to the festive season in the form of the '...And All Through the House' section of the film, which starred Joan Collins. Mark Lester had famously starred in the title role of *Oliver!* (Carol Reed, 1968), a period musical drama adapted from Lionel Bart's 1960 stage play of the same name. Lionel Jeffries, a screenwriter and director as well as a prolific actor, was a much-admired mainstay of British cinema who had been nominated for a Golden Globe Award for his performance as Stanley Farquhar in *The Spy with a Cold Nose* (Daniel Petrie, 1966). Hugh Griffith had won much acclaim for a varied career on screen and the stage, winning an Academy Award for Best Supporting Actor in *Ben-Hur* (William Wyler, 1959) as well as great acclaim for his work with the Royal Shakespeare Company. Judy Cornwell, who would later play Mrs Claus in pop culture titan *Santa Claus: The Movie* (Jeannot Szwarc, 1985), was also to become well-known for her role in the BBC's long-running situation comedy *Keeping Up Appearances* (1990-95), while Michael Gothard would find fame as the sinister villain Emile Locque when pitched against Roger Moore's James Bond in *For Your Eyes Only* (John Glen, 1981).

Perhaps unsurprisingly given its iconoclastic nature, many reviewers of the time seemed unsure quite what to make of *Whoever Slew Auntie Roo?*, leading to a decidedly indeterminate critical reception. Roger Greenspun of *The New York Times* led the charge against Shelley Winters's performance, opining that the film was 'an Edwardian horror movie that opens up the full scope of Miss Winters's acting talent, which is insufficient reason for making a movie'.[7] This line of assessment was also evident in Bernard Drew's review for *The Evening News*, which offered criticism of the so-called 'psycho-biddy' horror subgenre more broadly: '*Who Slew Auntie Roo?* continues the camp horror cavalcade begun with the now classic *What Ever Happened to Baby Jane?* It may be called a series – though the pictures are unrelated, have been made by different directors for different companies, and have different casts. They certainly have gotten progressively worse. [[...]] The picture falls utterly to pieces after a quite chilling first hour. Miss Winters, who previously played Ma Barker for American-International, producers of this, is in danger of becoming the company hag. Her Auntie Roo begins outrageously and ends inexcusably'.[8] Not all commentary was uniformly unenthusiastic, however, as some media outlets – such as *Variety* magazine – did take note of the technical competency of Harrington and his production team: 'Sort of a grim, modern-day fairy tale based loosely – very loosely – upon the *Hansel & Gretel* theme of the witch and the two tots, [[the]] script is overly-contrived, but carries certain [[a]] certain element of interest that may see it through selected bookings. [[...]] Curtis Harrington's direction is sound and has the benefit of expert technical talent in every direction'.[9]

Upon fast-forwarding to the present day, critical opinion of the film has continued to remain deeply divided. Some, such as Glenn Erickson, have offered moderate praise of the production while also highlighting its drawbacks: '*Whoever Slew Auntie Roo?* is a fairly tame retelling of *Hansel and*

Gretel with Shelley Winters getting a nice opportunity to play a monstrous mother desperate not to be left alone. [...] But there are a lot of uneven elements in the mix of this nicely-produced melodrama. Ralph Richardson's mountebank is colorful, and Lionel Jeffries and Hugh Griffith are perfectly fine in bits, but none of them are central to the core story'.[10] Others, such as Peter Hanson, have drawn more attention to the movie's shortcomings and reiterated scepticism over Shelley Winters's exaggerated approach to the title role: 'An attempt at translating a classic fairy tale into a (somewhat) modern horror picture, the US/UK coproduction *Whoever Slew Auntie Roo?* falls considerably short of its ambitions, thanks in part to flat cinematography that robs the piece of necessary atmosphere but thanks mostly to an embarrassing star turn by Shelley Winters. With her bulging eyes, flailing movements, and shrill vocalizations, Winters exudes cartoonishness, and not in a good way. [...] While the sets are relatively lavish, shooting the whole picture on soundstages with harsh high-key lighting makes everything feel fake and unthreatening'.[11] One other note of criticism, as exemplified by Dave Sindelar's review, is that the film is difficult to categorise: neither explicitly fantasy or horror, nor unambiguously comic or dramatic, it is difficult to know exactly how to respond to it: 'I think the problem is that it never really becomes either a full-blooded horror movie or an effective variation on the fairy tale. The scare scenes would be more effective if they didn't seem so arbitrary, and the last third of the movie fails to build up the necessary tension or suspense. As it is, what I most enjoy in the movie is seeing some familiar faces such as Ralph Richardson, Hugh Griffith and Lionel Jeffries, all who are quite entertaining in their roles and severely underused. It's a curiosity, but little more'.[12]

Whoever Slew Auntie Roo? is a fascinating example of how the Christmas movie genre continued to evolve during the 1970s. While Christmas films are typically associated with themes of joy, family and togetherness, this peculiar feature instead combines the holiday setting with elements of horror and suspense – and often to striking effect. This blending of genres was reflective of several wider trends in cinema during that period. The seventies were a time of significant social and cultural upheaval, and many films from that era manifested a sense of growing cynicism or desire to challenge established norms. *Whoever Slew Auntie Roo?* takes the traditional warm and familial setting of Christmas and subverts it by progressively introducing numerous dark, macabre elements which challenge expectations of what a festive season narrative might offer. This contrast amplifies the horror elements, as the film plays on the anticipation of safety and comfort associated with Christmas only to then gradually replace it with a growing atmosphere of fear and danger.

The 1970s saw the inexorable rise of horror as a mainstream genre, with films like *The Exorcist* (William Friedkin, 1973), *The Texas Chain Saw Massacre* (Tobe Hooper, 1974), *Suspiria* (Dario Argento, 1977) and *Halloween* (John Carpenter, 1978) all pushing boundaries in comparison to what had gone before. *Whoever Slew Auntie Roo?* was a modest part of this wider trend as it merged horror with a yuletide setting, creating an early niche within the broader category of Christmas film in doing so. This also echoed the era's fascination with psychological horror: particularly stories involving unstable characters and creepy, atmospheric settings deliberately cast against the relative mundanity of the everyday. Additionally, the film touched on the darker aspects of family life, which was similarly a recurring theme to be explored by

1970s cinema. The film delves into themes of loss, obsession and the breakdown of traditional family structures, reflecting a more extensive societal questioning of the idealised family unit during this eventful decade.

Just as significantly, *Whoever Slew Auntie Roo?* contributed to a more wide-ranging definition of what could be considered a Christmas movie. It demonstrated that a holiday setting can be used to tell a variety of stories – not just those that are specifically focused on happiness and goodwill, or which reinforce traditional themes. This idea has continued to evolve, with films in subsequent decades exploring the extremities of the genus even further as more distinctive subgenres began to establish themselves under the umbrella of Christmas cinema. Thus *Whoever Slew Auntie Roo?* reflected the distinctive seventies trend of blending horror with other genres, subverting traditional themes and expanding the concept of what a Christmas narrative was capable of presenting. While very much a product of its time, capturing the era's shifting attitudes toward both cinema and societal norms, Harrington's movie would lay the groundwork for many further Christmas horror features in the years that were to come.

REFERENCES

1. Curtis Harrington, in Dale Winagura, 'Harrington: Curtis Harrington discusses *Games, What's the Matter with Helen?* and *Who Slew Auntie Roo?*', in *Cinefantastique*, Fall 1974, p.23.

2. Harrington, in Charles Derry, *Dark Dreams 2.0: A Psychological History of the Modern Horror Film from the 1950s to the 21st Century* (Jefferson: McFarland, 2009), p.358.

3. Peter Shelley, *Grande Dame Guignol Cinema: A History of Hag Horror from Baby Jane to Mother* (Jefferson: McFarland, 2009), p.183.

4. James Morrison, 'Shelley Winters: Camp, Abjection, and the Aging Star', in *Hollywood Reborn: Movie Stars of the 1970s*, ed. by James Morrison (Piscataway: Rutgers University Press, 2010), 120-37, pp.134-35.

5. Jack Zipes, *The Enchanted Screen: The Unknown History of Fairy-Tale Films* (New York: Routledge, 2011), p.200.

6. Gary A. Smith, *Uneasy Dreams: The Golden Age of British Horror Films, 1956-1976* (Jefferson: McFarland, 2006), p.237.

7. Roger Greenspun, '*Who Slew Auntie Roo?*' in *The New York Times*, 16 March 1972, p.59.
   <https://www.nytimes.com/1972/03/16/archives/by-roger-greenspun.html>

8. Bernard Drew, '*Who Slew Auntie Roo?* Continues Camp Horror', in *The Evening News*, 8 April 1972, p.7.

9. Anon., '*Whoever Slew Auntie Roo?*', in *Variety Reviews 1971-74* (New York: R.R. Bowker, 1983), pp.176-77.

10. Glenn Erickson, '*Whoever Slew Auntie Roo?*', in *DVD Savant*, 5 September 2002.
    <https://www.dvdtalk.com/dvdsavant/s586roo.html>

11. Peter Hanson, '*Whoever Slew Auntie Roo?*', in *Every '70s Movie*, 16 January 2023.
    <https://every70smovie.blogspot.com/2023/01/whoever-slew-auntie-roo-1972.html>

12. Dave Sindelar, '*Whoever Slew Auntie Roo?*', in *Fantastic Movie Musings and Ramblings*, 30 December 2015.
    <https://fantasticmoviemusings.com/2015/12/30/whoever-slew-auntie-roo-1971/>

9

Santa and the Ice Cream Bunny (1972)

R & S Film Enterprises

Directors: R. Winer and Barry Mahon
Producer: Barry Mahon
Screenwriter: Richard Winer and Barry Mahon,
from stories by Hans Christian Andersen
and Benjamin Tabart

WHEN it comes to Christmas cinema, there are inevitably some features which defy easy categorisation. Like any other genre of film, there will be movies which are popular and well-received, some which are critically derided, and a select few which are so overwhelmingly and comprehensively demolished by reviewers, they almost immediately fade from view never to be seen again. But scrape below the bottom of even that barrel, and there is another substrata of cinematic detritus that is even more obscure. Films which were so bad, they were almost completely ignored by critics and audiences at the time of release, and whose reputations live on only as a result of widespread incredulity at just how singularly awful they actually are.

Santa and the Ice Cream Bunny is an excruciatingly low-budget Christmas-themed film which was first released in 1972. It is now often regarded as one of the worst films ever to be made in any genre, and has gained a cult following for its sheer absurdity and bizarrely convoluted plot. The narrative is nonsensical, featuring random musical numbers, awkwardly-integrated stock footage and abysmally-executed attempts at comedy. The production values are extremely low, with very noticeable continuity errors and special effects that border on the pathetic. Yet despite its many shortcomings, *Santa and the Ice Cream Bunny* has become something of a Holy Grail amongst fans of 'so-bad-it's-good' cinema. The infamy it has gained on account of its absurd storyline, crushingly low production values and the unintentional hilarity caused by its attempts to achieve even basic competence has led to annual screenings at festively-themed bad movie nights across the world, and its notoriety has gone on to become the stuff of legend in cult movie circles.

Santa and the Ice Cream Bunny is ostensibly a musical fantasy film which was written and directed by film-maker Richard Winer in order to frame some of director Barry Mahon's earlier (decidedly non-festive) children's films for a Christmas release. The movie was filmed at Pirates World in Dania, Florida – an amusement park once located to the south of Fort Lauderdale, which was founded by entrepreneur Nate Ullman in 1967. As its name suggests, the park had a nautical adventure theme, offering rollercoasters, thrill rides and live performances (many of them from high-profile acts). It initially achieved solid financial results, but eventually began to suffer from fiscal challenges – largely due to dwindling visitor numbers. When Walt Disney World opened in Orlando in October 1971, it heralded a whole new era in American theme parks and established Florida as a major location of international significance for such resorts. However, the slick marketing and vast popularity of Disney's new park also provided overpowering competition for its rivals elsewhere in the State: as William D. Crump observes, 'Opening in 1967 in Dania, Florida, Pirates World was a buccaneer theme park that was developed by Recreation Corporation of America. It did well until Walt Disney World opened in 1971, and by 1973, Pirates World was bankrupt; it did not operate beyond 1975'.[1] Nothing now remains of the theme park in Dania; its site has long since been redeveloped for residential and commercial usage, meaning that only memories of it persist.

Part of Pirates World's marketing strategy was the production of a number of ultra-low-budget movies filmed on location at the park, with the intention of showcasing it as an attractive vacation destination to the general public. Three initial features were all directed by Barry Mahon in 1970, and included *Thumbelina*, an adaptation of the Hans Christian Andersen tale; *Jack and the Beanstalk*, a musical retelling of the well-known fairy-tale story; and *Musical Mutiny*, a psychedelic concert movie featuring rock band Iron Butterfly. *Santa Meets the Ice Cream Bunny* was to be the final feature shot at the park prior to its closure, and was also the only one of the films with a Christmas theme. Additionally, it was the only movie to be produced at Pirates World which was directed not by Barry Mahon, but rather by Richard Winer, whose other work behind the camera had included adventure mystery *Mr Angel* (1966) and Bermuda Triangle documentary *The Devil's Triangle* (1971), which was narrated by none other than horror legend Vincent Price. The plan, as mentioned earlier, had been for Winer's film to make use of Mahon's earlier work by situating it within a festive framing story, thus repackaging these features for potential new audiences. As Sam Panico has explained, the story behind the genesis of *Santa and the Ice Cream Bunny* is arguably even more remarkable than the film itself:

> The director Barry Mahon, who created the films for the park, lived an insane life that inspired the film *The Great Escape*. During World War II, Mahon escaped Stalag Luft III only to be captured on the Czechoslovakian border. He escaped again, was recaptured again, and was finally saved by Patton's 3rd Army in 1945. So what did he do when he got back to the USA? He became Errol Flynn's personal pilot and manager. His directorial credits alternate between children's fare, like *Santa's Christmas Elf (Named Calvin)* and *The Wonderful Land of Oz*. [...] No one is really sure who R. Winer is, but some think he was Richard Winer, a cinematographer and director whose entire [Internet Movie Database] page is devoted to films he either created or appeared in that were all about the Bermuda Triangle and UFOs. Of course.[2]

The main issue with the approach favoured by the filmmakers (aside from the very obvious lack of production values due to the razor-thin budget) was the fact that – as we will see – shoehorning a completely different film into the main narrative invariably means that a substantial section of the movie is completely superfluous to the events of the central storyline... such as it was. Further complicating matters, two entirely different prints of the movie have been circulated over the years; while both feature the same framing story, they each include one of two entirely different movies implanted within the main narrative. They are (depending on the particular version) either Mahon's earlier adaptation of *Thumbelina*, or his production of Benjamin Tabart's story *Jack and the Beanstalk*. To this end, the following synopsis takes into account the different extant versions of the film by indicating the differences between the two disparate cuts.

Framing Story (Part 1): At Santa Claus's workshop at the North Pole, a happy group of elves sing as they lovingly prepare toys for delivery on Christmas Eve. One of the group peeks through the building's doorway and spots (via a very obviously-inserted piece of stock footage) a herd of reindeer wandering in the wilderness. This leads to profound puzzlement amongst the elves: why would Santa's reindeer have returned home when the Jolly Old Elf is nowhere to be seen?

The answer, an unseen narrator helpfully informs us, is that Santa's sleigh has become stuck in the fine sand of a Floridian beach. The reindeer having grown too hot in the sunshine, they had decided to fly back to the North Pole to avoid sunstroke, even though this has left poor Santa (Jay Clark) trapped. Sweltering in the heat, he breaks into a tuneless lament bemoaning his predicament (in spite of the fact that the rails of the sleigh are very obviously only covered by an inch or so of sand). He reflects that if his friends back at the workshop knew of his dilemma, they would immediately take action to free him, but as it stands he must find an alternative means of escape.

Little does Santa know that nearby, a group of children (performers from Ruth Foreman's Pied Piper Playhouse) are happily playing outdoors in the Florida sunshine, oblivious that he and his sleigh are trapped nearby. Exhausted by the exertion of his singalong in the intense heat, Santa falls asleep, but in his unconscious state he issues a telepathic summons to the proximate kids – all of whom he knows, having delivered gifts to them every year. Made aware of the sleigh's location, the group of concerned children converge on the beach along with Rebel, their friendly dog. From a distance, literary characters Tom Sawyer and Huckleberry Finn (along with a raccoon on a leash) watch Santa's helpers racing to his aid. They are traversing the water on a makeshift wooden raft, and decide to come closer to the shore to find out more about what's going on.

Reaching Santa's sleigh, the children are nonplussed at his presence. Santa explains that every year he takes an early flight around the world to get a better idea of who has been naughty and nice, but on this occasion he has accidentally become stuck – and in spite of the best efforts of his now-disappeared reindeer, he can't get his sleigh free. One of the kids suggests that he book a flight on a plane back to the North Pole, but Santa replies that he can't possibly leave his sleigh unattended. There is considerable debate between the various gathered helpers before they suddenly hit on a solution and collectively scramble away into the distance. Some time later, a girl returns with a gorilla, which she encourages to pull the sleigh. However, in spite of its great strength, the huge primate is unable to dislodge Santa's flying vehicle from the sand.

Over time, the kids bring a variety of different animals onto the beach with the hope of pulling the sleigh. These include a donkey, a pig, a sheep, a cow and a horse... but none of them have enough pulling power to help free Santa's famous flying means of transport. Desperate not to lose hope, and all too aware that children all over the planet will be counting on him, Santa tries to manually dig the sleigh out of the sand but is defeated by the effort. As the children reassemble on the beach, now seemingly out of options, Santa encourages them to keep believing that everything will turn out fine in the end. To buoy their spirits, he decides to tell them a story about having faith in achieving success against all odds.

Version A: At the Pirates World theme park in Dania, Florida, a fashionably-dressed young woman (Shay Garner) is wandering around the various attractions when she discovers a Hans Christian Andersen fairy-tale exhibition. After trying many of the park's other rides first, she decides to attend a presentation based on Andersen's tale of *Thumbelina*. Listening to a piped-in commentary retelling the Andersen story, the woman looks at miniature models which have been constructed to demonstrate the world as it looked to Thumbelina during her adventures.

The narrator explains that an ageing spinster (Ruth McMahon) – tired of living alone – once decided to visit a witch (Heather Grinter) who is resident in a nearby cave, in the hope of enlisting her help in finding a companion. Thankfully for the woman making the request, the witch only used her powers for good and was amenable to providing aid. She is initially sceptical about the woman's request for a daughter, but the older lady protests that her inability to find a partner is what lies behind her loneliness; she would gladly have had children by more conventional means if the opportunity had been available. Hearing the woman's sincere pleas that she promises to be a kind and attentive mother, the witch relents and agrees to help her – but only in exchange for twelve pennies, and the assurance that she will treat her new daughter well. When the woman agrees to the conditions, the witch rummages around her collection of bizarre ingredients, finds a magic seed, and asks the woman to plant it and tend to its development carefully. If she does so, she will have the daughter her heart desires – but, the witch warns, it is very important that she looks after her new child kindly, as one day she will become a princess.

The woman returns home and, mindful of the witch's instructions, plants the seed in her modest garden. She watches in incredulity as a flower grows instantly, and its petals open to reveal a fully-clothed girl in her teens (Shay Garner)... who stands only two inches tall. To the good fortune of the new mother, the recent arrival also speaks perfect English. The woman decides to name her Thumbelina on account of her stature. Unprepared for a daughter quite so diminutive in size, she has to improvise and gives her a walnut shell as a bed so that she has somewhere to rest.

Though her life is largely confined to a tabletop, Thumbelina enjoys her new existence and revels in being so obviously adored by her mother. Unfortunately her good fortune doesn't last for long, as the tiny girl is kidnapped (offscreen) by a frog who intends to marry Thumbelina to her son. This comes as a shock to Thumbelina's mother, who has no idea of the girl's whereabouts and fears that she has run away from home. In a stroke of luck, a fish takes pity on Thumbelina and breaks free the lily-pad where she is being held captive. She thus makes her escape through a forest, but is frightened by the unfamiliar landscape and its many hazards. Shortly afterwards, she is intercepted by a trio of birds, who regard her with confusion – as they know human beings to be large creatures, they presume that she must be some kind of insect. Thumbelina evades the would-be predators while they argue over what she actually is.

As time passes, she becomes accustomed to her new woodland environment and learns to take care of herself with whatever items nature makes available to her. With her naturally cheerful temperament, she is determined to make the most of her situation even if she misses her home. However, the seasons soon change, and the warm sunshine soon turns to snow and frost. Realising that she can't survive the perpetual cold, she decides to follow the example of other forest creatures and heads underground to stay warm. Finding the warm burrow of Mrs Mole (Pat Morrell), Thumbelina asks for sanctuary from the freezing temperatures. The friendly subterranean mammal agrees, also offering her some food. She relates her story to Mrs Mole, who is sympathetic to her predicament and agrees that marriage is something to be considered carefully – not decided by an outside influence like the scheming frog who kidnapped her.

Thumbelina is invited to stay at the mole's cosy home over the long winter months, though she longs for the sunshine of summer to come again. Once spring arrives, Mrs Mole's den is visited by her old friend Mr Digger (Bob O'Connell), another mole who lives nearby. The elderly tunnelling gent has travelled widely, and offers to show Thumbelina his extensive collection of artefacts he has gained on his journeys. Ushering her through a maze of tunnels, Mr Digger encounters the body of a bird which has frozen solid from the cold; it had obviously been too late in gaining access to the underground from the freezing environment above. Eventually, the distinguished mole welcomes Thumbelina to his home: another comfortable subterranean lair, but one which is full of fine furniture and decorations gathered from all over the world. However, he reveals, in spite of all the wealth he has acquired over the years, he feels sad and unfulfilled; he worked so hard in his youth to achieve success, he is now lonely because he never set aside time to find a wife. While he has many friends, he feels that they would soon desert him if they thought he had lost his financial holdings, but true love is a different matter. Thumbelina can identify with his situation; she too feels unhappy and despondent, but for entirely different reasons. Having lost her home, she has no possessions and is living from day to day with an uncertain future ahead of her.

Perceiving that he can offer her safety and security, Mr Digger proposes marriage. Thumbelina is surprised at his suggestion – not least given that they have only known each other for a matter of hours. In response, he explains that while he is much older than she is, he has wealth and resources that will support her through the rest of her life. He suggests that she speak with Mrs Mole and consider the offer carefully before making a decision. Realising that he has only the best of intentions at heart, Thumbelina agrees to think about the matter seriously.

Back at Mrs Mole's home, the friendly old creature urges Thumbelina to accept Mr Digger's hand in marriage. She assures her that the elderly gent is wise and kind as well as prosperous, and it is important to consider her future security. Thumbelina is happy to remain as Mrs Mole's guest instead, but it transpires that her host's supply of food – stored by her late husband – is starting to run low due to it now having to support two people rather than one. The young woman feels guilty at having imposed on Mrs Mole's hospitality for so long, but is disappointed at the prospect of exchanging a marriage based on love and romance with one which is essentially little more than a transactional agreement. However, the old mole urges her to think about the practical benefits of comfort and prosperity, seeking to keep her safe in an otherwise threatening world.

While Thumbelina can sense the judiciousness in Mrs Mole's advice, she yearns to see the sunshine again. Remembering the frozen bird from earlier, she decides to revisit its location and take a blanket to cover its icy form. Filled with compassion for its fate, she hugs its petrified body... and detects a faint heartbeat. Realising that it can still be saved, she clings on to the bird and eventually manages to warm its frame until it is revived. The hapless avian is grateful for Thumbelina's assistance in saving its life, not realising that she is thankful too – for the chance to take her mind off the prospect of a marriage of convenience.

Some weeks later, Mrs Mole has tailored a wedding dress for Thumbelina, but is saddened that the young woman seems so gloomy about the notion of matrimony with Mr Digger. If only he was younger, more handsome, and indeed a human being, Thumbelina reflects, she might be more enthusiastic about the wedding. But Mrs Mole impresses on her that it's too late for misgivings at this stage; she felt certain that her young guest had already resigned herself to the fact that the marriage would be the best option for her future. But Thumbelina knows that a marital match means more than money and security – it has to be a bond of love, mutual support and shared affection.

Mrs Mole suggests that Thumbelina make the most of her remaining time as an unmarried woman and enjoy a walk outside. Changing back into her everyday clothes, the young woman explains that she would rather visit her friend the bird and see how his recovery is progressing. Mrs Mole has little time for the flying foe, considering it to be a natural predator. But Thumbelina feels a certain emotional commonality with her new acquaintance, as he seeks to see the blue skies and feel the warmth of the sun again – just as she does. On returning to the tunnel, however, she is crestfallen to discover that the bird has already recovered enough strength to fly away... without saying goodbye.

In his opulent den, Mr Digger feels elated. While he accepts that he is too old to offer Thumbelina much in the way of exciting, whirlwind romance, he resolves to ensure that she will always feel comfortable and secure. Little does he realise that his bride-to-be is currently saddened by the unexpected departure of the bird she had nursed back to health, and marriage is the last thing on her mind. Mrs Mole suggests that Thumbelina take a walk outside to restore her spirits. There, she is elated to be suddenly reunited with the bird, who has been testing his wings in an attempt to restore their strength after a long period of inactivity. Thumbelina is delighted to see how well his health is improving, but cannot hide her own unhappiness over the prospect of her wedding to Mr Digger the next day. Dismayed, she tells the bird that she must now face the prospect of perpetual life underground with no hope of seeing the world above ever again. The bird suggests that if she does not love Mr Digger, and is unwilling to accept Mrs Mole's hospitality any longer on account of the stress it is putting on her resources, it is time for her to depart and find a new future. He tells her that it would be better for her in the long term if she found another human being to marry instead, and offers to fly her south in the hope of better prospects. She is reluctant to cause undue distress to Mrs Mole and Mr Digger with a sudden departure, but the bird promises to return and explain to them what has happened.

True to his word, the bird flies Thumbelina south to the Kingdom of the Flower Children. There, she finds a whole society of diminutive humans who have emerged from within flowers – just as she once did. She is welcomed by a Flower Girl (Sue Cable), who takes her to meet with their ruler, the Flower Prince (Mike Yuenger). To her surprise, the prince has been expecting her arrival; prophecies from their ancient texts had foretold that a woman named Thumbelina would one day come to their realm and become its rightful queen. When she realises that this will mean marrying the prince, she feels disinclined: after all, she has only just arrived, and has met this royal suitor mere minutes beforehand. She suggests that she find out what life is like in the kingdom first and get to know the prince better before making any decisions. Seeing the wisdom of her words, he agrees. Sure enough, Thumbelina finally feels as though she has found a community where she feels integrated and at home, and in time she agrees to marry the prince. The bird, witnessing the wedding, flies back to the forest to tell Mrs Mole and Mr Digger the news as promised. Thus the witch's foretelling has finally come true, and Thumbelina was to become a princess after all.

As the tour narrator reveals that Mr Digger also found companionship in the end – by marrying the widowed Mrs Mole, thus ensuring a happy ending for everyone – the young woman visiting Pirates World returns to exploring the theme park and unites with her boyfriend. The story of Thumbelina thus concludes with a montage of shots from different attractions around the park, including water-slides, rollercoasters and merry-go-rounds.

Version B: In a modest suburban living room, Jack (Mitchell Poulos) and his sister Rosemary (uncredited) reminisce wistfully about their happy lives in the time before their father had died. It feels so long ago for them, it now seems like an eternity since their family was affluent and influential. Their mother (Dorothy Stokes) chides them for their longing nostalgia; they can only deal with the situation they have in the here and now, where the family's 'enchanted possessions' have been stolen and they live in straitened circumstances. Jack asks his mother if it is true that the family once owned a hen that could lay golden eggs and a harp that was capable of playing itself. She replies that rather than magic items, these were complex mechanical contraptions created by her husband – but when they were stolen, he found himself unable to recreate them in spite of his best efforts. Jack laments that once the family had enough wealth to share with the poor, but now they are impoverished themselves. Rosemary points out that the situation is even more grim for her, as she wants to get married but has no way of raising a wedding dowry.

Jack's mother decides that as the family's circumstances have become so distressed, they will have no choice but to sell their only cow at market. Their bovine companion produces very little in the way of milk, and it is now prohibitively expensive to feed her. Rosemary and Jack are both deflated, having become attached to the animal over the years, but their mother is insistent – the only way to raise some much-needed funds will be to trade the cow at the local town square.

The next day, Jack takes the family's cow to the market, where he encounters Honest John, a 'used cow salesman'. Honest John (Christopher Brooks) is harangued by unsatisfied customers who pillory him for mendacious trading. (Unlike the other townsfolk, all of whom are dressed appropriately for the 1970s, John's clothing seems better suited to the early 17th century.) Jack explains that he needs to sell his cow to raise funds for the family to live on. John agrees to the trade, but not for money – instead, he offers three magic beans. Sensing a swindle, Jack is reluctant to agree, but the fast-talking salesman assures him that if the beans don't exhibit magic powers then he will exchange them later for an unspecified amount of money. As soon as Jack has departed, however, he promptly sells the cow to one of the townsfolk for a tidy profit and then removes the sign from his shop, obviously intending to make a quick getaway.

Back home, Rosemary continues to fret that the family's poverty will continue to impact on her inability to find a husband. Jack arrives and proudly exclaims that their worries are over – with the three magic beans, they will all know good fortune again. His mother and sister are less convinced, however, and scorn his gullibility. They insist that he and Rosemary return to Honest John's shop and renegotiate... but, of course, on arriving at the town they discover that he has gone. The pair decide to head into the forest to see if they can find him, but the stealthy John – realising that they are in pursuit – easily manages to evade them.

The following morning, Jack and Rosemary explain to their mother that the cow salesman has gone out of business – or, at least, is nowhere to be found. Frustrated that they have no way of being reimbursed, their mother throws the beans out of the living room window. The family then watch in incredulity as a massive beanstalk immediately grows out of the ground, extending up into the sky. Reasoning that its magic origin presumably means that the beanstalk leads somewhere, Jack decides to climb it. His mother is concerned for his well-being, but Rosemary is beginning to believe that this might just be the turnaround in fortune that the family needs.

Jack makes his way up the beanstalk, amazed at how high it reaches. Eventually, after much effort he makes his way through the clouds and discovers an enchanted castle suspended in the air. Curious, he decides to explore the impossible building, and only just manages to creep inside its mist-enshrouded main gate. In the castle interior, he is stunned to discover a giant woman (Sami Sims) working at a table. Shortly after, she is joined by her similarly massive husband (John Loomis), who has returned home for lunch. Before he can eat, however, he pauses to declare that he can smell the blood of a human being and goes in search of the interloper. However, he is unable to find anything to confirm his suspicions. His wife has prepared food, and the giant asks her to bring him his hen that lays golden eggs – which he promptly instructs to produce fresh eggs on demand. She enquires whether he will also require his self-playing harp, but for the moment he replies in the negative. From a tiny crack in the wall, Jack watches this interaction play out with astonished disbelief.

The giant's wife announces that she is heading for the market. As she departs, the giant falls fast asleep. Spotting that the golden egg-laying hen has been left unattended on the tabletop, Jack sneaks over and snatches it (not noticing that, for some reason, the hen has now reduced in mass and dimensions sufficiently for a tiny human to carry it). He then races out of the castle and descends the beanstalk, leaving the puzzled giant at the absence of his magic hen. Now convinced that an intruder has infiltrated his castle, the giant angrily vows vengeance.

After a careful return to the surface, Jack proudly announces to his mother and sister that he has brought back his father's hen – which immediately produces a golden egg. He explains that as the giant also had the self-playing harp and a huge bag of golden eggs in his possession, it seems clear that he must have been the one responsible for stealing them from the family in the first place. However, as he had no way of carrying more than one item and still have the ability to descend the beanstalk, the other goods are still languishing in the giant's castle.

Later, Rosemary is making her way through the forest to meet her boyfriend when she meets Honest John, who is hard at work changing his shop sign. Apparently he now sells magic beans for a living. John explains that given Jack's good luck, he has decided to undergo a change of business, though he still has to find a new source of magic beans in order to sell them in greater quantities. Returning to his shop, he explains to passing customers that he is willing to sell the beans for $10 each, but he has underestimated the level of publicity Jack's story has created – nobody will believe that a genuine magic item is selling so cheaply. Purchasing a fresh supply of beans from a local boy for a dollar, he then goes on to sell them to Jack's neighbours for $100 each. The customers still feel that this price is too low for an item that really has magic qualities, but Honest John explains that he has to remain competitive; while he could charge vast sums, he wants the beans to remain accessible to the general public. On learning that the customers don't have a hundred dollars to spend, he reveals his easy payment plan that will let them pay up in monthly instalments; if, like Jack, they are able to access a source of wealth in the magic kingdom at the end of the beanstalk, surely the beans will quickly pay for themselves? Reluctantly, the couple agrees to sign a contract with him.

As they depart, Rosemary and her boyfriend (Renato Boracherro) arrive in the town square. She repeats her desire to get married, and her betrothed agrees. However, he is nonplussed by her insistence on her family providing a substantial dowry; he believes that a marriage should be based on love and mutual support, not financial agreements. Rosemary explains that as the hen is a delicate mechanism which they have no way of repairing if it should break, the family are only using its powers to produce enough eggs to keep their finances modestly solvent. Their days of fantastic wealth are long gone. Her boyfriend says that without a dowry, he will need to learn a trade – and ensure that no-one else in the town beats him to it and takes up his intended role before he can. Knowing that this will mean having to wait for months or even years before they can have a wedding, Rosemary tells him that she will try to encourage an increase in the hen's egg production so that they will have a suitable dowry.

At his family home, Jack tells his mother that he has decided to return to the castle in the sky. The giant still has possession of many items that are rightfully theirs, and it seems only fair that he gets them back. His mother is reluctant, however, knowing how much he had risked just to return the golden egg-laying hen. Rosemary and her boyfriend arrive and explain their need for a dowry; she explains to her mother that if they had sufficient funds, they would purchase an inn near a local crossroads which would generate the means to support themselves in married life. However, Rosemary's mother is unwilling to allow the risk; if the hen's delicate mechanism should break through overuse, they will again be penniless. Jack tells them that as the giant has a huge bag of accumulated golden eggs in his castle, he is willing to retrieve them for the family, which will give Rosemary and her husband-to-be the best possible start to their life as newlyweds.

Heading back up the beanstalk, Jack heads directly for the giant's castle and again sneaks inside. As it happens, the gluttonous giant is once more finishing off a meal, and he asks his wife to bring his magic harp and bag of golden eggs. Sure enough, as she clears the table her husband closely inspects the tiny gold eggs while the harp accompanies the action with music. Jack watches carefully as the giant's wife heads into the cellar to complete some household tasks while the giant himself dozes off to the soothing tones of the harp. But before Jack can seize his chance, the giant again smells the blood of a human being and launches into another search of the castle. Now wide awake, he makes it clear that he still hasn't forgiven the intruder for the theft of his magic hen, causing Jack to cower into a crack in the wall. However, unable to track down the diminutive trespasser once again, the giant decides that he must have been mistaken and falls asleep at the table.

Jack finally senses that his opportunity has come, and he emerges from the wall to scale the table. Knowing that he can only carry one of the available items, Jack leaves the magic harp behind and snatches the bag of golden eggs (which, once again, has dramatically shifted proportions between shots). He then escapes via the window, flees the castle and returns to the beanstalk. Upon awakening, the giant is enraged to find that his golden eggs have gone, and he again swears vengeance on the thief who has had the audacity to take them.

Back on the surface, Jack's mother has prepared the house for the wedding reception of Rosemary and her new husband, who reflect wistfully that they should perhaps have considered waiting until after Jack's return before they tied the knot – just in case his mission to recover the golden eggs should be unsuccessful. But their concerns are misplaced: Jack races into the living room with the bag of gold, which he proudly presents to Rosemary's new husband as their dowry. The couple are delighted to see him back, and are also elated by his success. Little do any of them suspect that up in the sky, the giant is preparing a trap if Jack should dare to return – a suspended 500lb weight is being set up over his table, meaning a deadly surprise for any repeat visit from the diminutive interloper.

The wedding party at Jack's house is now in full swing, with accordion music complementing the guests' dancing. The newlyweds cut their wedding cake, and everyone joins in the celebration. Shortly afterwards, however, there is a difficult conversation to be had between Rosemary and her husband. They have used up all of the golden eggs from the giant's bag to fund the celebrations, and now have nothing left as a reserve for operating the inn. Her new partner suggests that they cook the meals and serve at the bar themselves, avoiding the need to hire additional staff and thus cutting costs. Rosemary bemoans the fact that running the inn is proving to be no fun at all: the work is hard, and she and her husband barely have time to see each other. He assures her that, in time, it will all become second nature for both of them.

Some time later, Honest John is alarmed when he overhears dissatisfied customers complaining that the supposedly magic beans he had supplied were worthless. Furious at having paid over the odds for useless goods, they resolve to run him out of town. Knowing that his time is up, John surreptitiously removes the sign from his shop and makes a quiet getaway. Meanwhile, Rosemary and her husband return to the town square and start arguing. A new and significantly more successful inn has opened on the other side of the crossroads, which has led to a catastrophic plunge in their business fortunes. Realising that they can't compete with the new company as things stand, her husband decides that they need an edge that their rivals can't replicate. He suggests using the magic harp that can play music by itself, but Rosemary reminds him that the giant still has it. She is unwilling to risk Jack's safety on yet another expedition to the castle, but her new spouse protests: surely one last trip to retrieve the harp wouldn't hurt anyone?

The couple don't realise that Jack has already convinced himself to make a final ascent of the beanstalk. The fact that his father's mechanical harp is still in the possession of the giant rankles him, as he knows that his family should rightfully have it back. Leaving a note for his mother, he begins to climb the beanstalk. Seconds later, Rosemary and her husband arrive and realise that Jack has already gone. They hope desperately for his safe return, knowing that if he returns the harp it could mean the revival of their fledgling business.

In the woods, a fugitive Honest John is becoming increasingly desperate. Having only just managed to escape being tarred and feathered by the townsfolk, he can't survive for much longer on nature's bounty of berries and other woodland foods. Sensing that he has nothing further to lose, he resolves to head for Jack's home to ask for his help; after all, if he hadn't traded the magic beans for their family cow in the first place, Jack would never have been able to recover his family's stolen artefacts from the clouds.

Jack once again creeps into the castle just as the giant is starting lunch. The oversized layabout tucks in, satisfied that his deadly trap will deter any further burglary. However, he soon scents Jack's presence and is enraged, but his wife manages to calm him down. She heads off to visit friends, and the giant orders the harp to play soothing music as he once more drifts into a sound sleep. Oblivious to the danger above him, Jack slinks his way onto the tabletop and grabs the harp. The giant is immediately alert to his presence, but in his zeal to pursue Jack he hits his head on the suspended weight, temporarily dazing himself in the process.

Heavily encumbered by the magic harp, Jack makes his way back down the beanstalk. Little does he realise, however, that the furious giant is close behind him in pursuit. Back at Jack's home, his family fret over his safety, but are relieved when he arrives back with the harp. At last he feels the satisfaction of knowing that all of the items stolen from his father have been returned. However, the sense of fulfilment soon turns to trepidation when they realise that the giant is heading down the beanstalk in search of Jack. This could cause disaster not just for the family, but for the town in general. Thinking quickly, he decides to chop the beanstalk down, which rapidly causes it to collapse... and the giant to plummet to the ground as a result. Jack feels sorry for the giant's wife, who will never know her husband's fate, but the family celebrates that their fortunes have been restored and they are now safe. Their friends join them for a closing musical number, and Jack even invites Honest John into their company, proving that there are no hard feelings for his earlier underhand dealings. The film ends (naturally) with a short but suitably incongruous montage of various rides available at Pirates World.

Framing Story (Part 2): Back on the beach, Santa concludes his story with a comforting reminder that the kids need never be discouraged: if you can maintain hope, anything is possible. As he reiterates the need to keep believing in good outcomes, a girl named Robin – the owner of Rebel the dog – tells Santa that he needs to have faith in his own advice. Santa is puzzled: how can a small dog possibly pull his sleigh when much bigger animals have failed? But Robin explains that Rebel can do anything... just not necessarily the way anyone expects. The children race off again, leaving Santa alone in his sleigh – and more stumped than ever by his situation.

Santa dozes off in the sun, but is re-awakened by the sound of an air raid siren accompanying the approach of a vintage fire truck. At the wheel is a giant white rabbit, with all of the kids along for the ride. The antique fire engine cruises at a leisurely pace through the Pirates World theme park before eventually reaching the beach. From his sleigh, Santa reacts in bafflement: he can hear sirens, but sees no smoke or fire that would indicate an emergency. Then, shortly after, he realises to his delight that his old friend, the Ice Cream Bunny, has come to his aid. Santa thanks Rebel the dog, who knows the huge rabbit and had persuaded him to bring his fire engine to save the day. The non-speaking Ice Cream Bunny agrees to drive Santa back to his North Pole workshop – and, as Santa points out, they have only a few days to make the journey if Christmas is to be saved. Clambering onto the fire truck, he again impresses upon the kids the need to keep believing in happy consequences. The group of children wave as Santa departs, but then wonder what will happen to the unattended sleigh now that he is returning to the North Pole. As it happens, they have no need for concern – on heading back to the beach, they watch in incredulity as the sleigh disappears into thin air. The narrator explains that by the time Santa has returned to his workshop, the sleigh will be there waiting for his arrival.

Despite its title and nominal festive setting, *Santa and the Ice Cream Bunny* exhibits only a loose relationship with the traditional themes of Christmas cinema. While the film takes place during the holiday season and features Santa Claus as a central character, it deviates significantly from what might be considered a typical festive narrative. Instead of focusing on themes of generosity, goodwill and the spirit of giving, the film primarily serves as a vehicle for bizarre and preposterous storytelling, where any entertainment value that can be garnered from the experience largely comes from the production's sheer ineptitude which makes the action (and its execution) an unintentional source of hilarity.

Conventional Christmas themes such as celebrations of the family unit, altruism and redemption are largely absent from the film's events. Instead, *Santa and the Ice Cream Bunny* openly embraces arbitrary absurdity and general haphazardness, making it more of a cinematic curiosity than any kind of meaningful exploration of yuletide themes. In essence, with its relationship to traditional festive tropes being minimal at best, the film's reputation has become primarily established amongst Christmas movie aficionados for its outlandish narrative and rock-bottom production values rather than its adherence to holiday traditions or messages, meaning that it has been pilloried by near-universal ridicule from critics and viewers alike.

The film's rambling and oddly disconnected storyline, punctuated by the inserted film-within-a-film which serves only to make the narrative even more diffuse and incoherent, offers no layers of meaning, consequential parallels, metanarrative content or indeed any kind of commentary on the main plot. The framing story itself pads out the action to such an extent that the momentum draws to a near-standstill at times, while the entire storyline is riven with contradictions and inexplicable happenings. Not only do the inserts run twice as long as the main framing section, but neither of them have anything remotely to do with Christmas whatsoever. This, as

Tim Brayton has noted, makes the film surprisingly difficult to categorise amongst Christmas movie subgenres: '*Santa and the Ice Cream Bunny* isn't an inexplicable movie. [...] But it's exactly the kind of movie that *feels* inexplicable, colliding random nonsense in a matrix that we're obliged to call a narrative more out of habit than accuracy. The plot more resembles a transcription of a bad peyote experience than a motion picture, and its execution is at places so determinedly bereft of even the most limited, accidental filmmaking talent that it doesn't seem right to call the resultant object an actual work of cinema'.[3]

As might be expected given the film's reputation, there are many strange inconsistencies, continuity errors and production gaffes on display which have contributed to its standing as one of the worst Christmas movies ever made. Among them is the inexplicable cameo appearance by Tom Sawyer and Huckleberry Finn, whose presence was only possible on account of Mahon having once mounted (and then promptly abandoned) an earlier, short-lived attempt to adapt Mark Twain's 1876 novel *The Adventures of Tom Sawyer*, and thus the meagre amount of extant footage was later used to embellish *Santa and the Ice Cream Bunny* instead. The pair's arrival on a makeshift raft is never explained (or even acknowledged by the other characters), but the closest access point to the Mississippi River in the State of Mississippi – which the two characters traditionally call home – is located around 150 miles from the closest beach on the Florida panhandle, meaning that they would have had to endure a very long journey with no obvious provisions for the voyage.

Then there is Santa Claus himself, who seemed oddly slender and youthful: in this film, he is portrayed by actor Jay Clark (more commonly billed as Jay Ripley or Jay Ripley

Clark), who – according to various sources – was reputedly aged anywhere between his late teens and early thirties at the time of production. (A scattering of unconfirmed references have even suggested that he was as young as nineteen during filming.) This particular Santa has an unusual quality in that he is able to communicate mentally with those around him; as Lauren Rosewarne comments, 'Telepathy is also a brief theme in *Santa and the Ice Cream Bunny*: when Santa's [...] sleigh gets stuck, local children telepathically hear him calling for help'.[4] Yet sadly, Jolly Old Saint Nick's perceptual powers stop short of offering him an easy answer to his unfathomable predicament. If his sleigh is only trapped by an inch or so of sand on the Florida beach where it becomes grounded, why can't it be pulled by any of the various animals that are volunteered by the kids to help? If Santa refuses to be separated from the sleigh long enough to travel home to his North Pole workshop in a plane, why does he later approve of the plan to join the Ice Cream Bunny to get there on a vintage fire engine – which is essentially the same idea but with a different mode of transport? And, perhaps most pressingly, if the sleigh could be recalled to the North Pole via teleportation at any time, why does he need to physically free it from the sand on the beach in the first place? As Panico clarifies, 'Rebel the dog knows the Ice Cream Bunny, who drives Santa to the North Pole, leaving behind the sled, ruining the main conceit that Santa had brought up before, that he would never leave his sled behind. The children wonder what to do and then the sled disappears. The conflict that has driven this movie was all a lie. Why did we sit through all of the animals trying to pull the sled? Why did we have to watch the movie within a movie? Why were Tom Sawyer and Huck Finn in this film?'[5]

This, inevitably, leads us to the enigmatic and oddly sinister figure of the Ice Cream Bunny himself – not least the question of why he is so named when he doesn't eat ice cream, sell ice cream, give away ice cream or seemingly have anything whatsoever to do with gelatos of any kind. It is never made clear why the bunny is so famous that all of the kids and Santa seem to know him by reputation, when this appears to have been his one and only outing: according to anecdotal accounts, the character was never even used as an attraction at Pirates World during the park's heyday, so he seems to have been conceived solely for the events of the movie. Likewise, there is never an explanation for why he drives around in an antique fire truck – though what *is* glaringly obvious is the ill-starred individual who was responsible for pushing the truck around while the bunny is at the wheel, as they are very clearly noticeable in shot at the rear of the vehicle. Indeed, at one point Rebel the dog can be seen running directly into the path of the fire engine, leading the production team to halt the shot to ensure his wellbeing; there is an excruciatingly observable editing jump where he is taken to safety during the break in filming. Far from being an uplifting and reassuring presence, the bunny's off-putting appearance and creepily silent nature has become one of the film's most unintentionally enduring features: as Brayton notes, 'Eventually, the Ice Cream Bunny arrives, and it is an eldritch abomination; there's a long shot of a dog jumping and barking at it frantically, and I think we're meant to take it as "Oh, the happy dog, it wants to jump up and lick the Ice Cream Bunny!", but anyone who knows dogs will immediately understand it as the natural response of canine fury to something horrifying and wrong that needs to barked all the way back to hell. And it's not just the freaky design of the thing, though its coal-black eyes, the right one of which sags in a sorry approximation of a wink, would cause any dog or man to feel the chill grip of the abyss'.[6]

The plot inconsistencies (and there are many of them) are only one reason behind *Santa and the Ice Cream Bunny*'s infamy, however. Appalling musical numbers, dreadful performances (the actor in the gorilla suit is almost as unconvincing as the eponymous Ice Cream Bunny himself), agonisingly bad dubbing, and sound quality which is so muddy that the dialogue is often close to inaudible, all combine to make for a less than optimal viewing experience. (As for the lyrics, the least said the better – when Santa repeatedly sings 'Oh woe is me!' he speaks for the audience at large.) Perhaps wisely, the film was all but completely ignored by media commentators at the time of release, but over the years it has since gone on to generate significant critical incredulity amongst reviewers. Some, such as Peter Hanson, have alluded to the fact that the entertainment value of the film's many faults have made it a firm favourite amongst a certain stratum of the viewing public:

> The whole concept of so-bad-it's-good cinema is something of a wormhole. To enter this realm, a movie must be so spectacularly misguided that viewers can see past the onscreen content in order to marvel at the deranged decision-making that brought the flick into existence. On the other side of the wormhole are the true cinematic dregs, movies so inept and pointless that only the most masochistic of viewers can find any pleasure watching them. That brings us to *Santa and the Ice Cream Bunny*, which has more than a few devo-

tees among the Psychotronic set. [...] Winer prudently left filmmaking behind after this disastrous debut, which survives as the ultimate lump of coal in the stocking that is holiday-themed cinema.[7]

While the sheer panoply of production drawbacks and odd creative choices have made *Santa and the Ice Cream Bunny* a challenging film to analyse – where does a critic even begin to start? – many reviewers have flagged up particular attributes for special consideration. Dave Sindelar, for instance, draws attention to the abysmal quality of the musical content, stating: 'Let's face facts. This movie [[...]] is almost unwatchable. In fact, I don't think most people will make it through the opening song by the elves; and I will gladly proclaim this moment to be the single worst musical moment in the history of cinema'.[8] On the other hand, commentators such as Alonso Duralde have instead focused on the threadbare and ridiculous plot which is stretched agonisingly thin for the purposes of reaching a feature length duration: 'There's maybe five minutes of actual story here, but director Winer (Mahon did the *Thumbelina* section) pads out every individual moment past its breaking point. [[...]] One can only imagine the scarring effects this movie must have had on the poor kids who actually suffered through it in the theater – Santa looks drunk and overheated, and the Ice Cream Bunny (whose name is never explained) sports an animal costume which, according to the website *The Agony Booth*, resembles "a ratty, torn-up bunny suit that the filmmakers probably found in a dumpster behind a shopping mall".'[9] In the final analysis, however, the cineastes who have managed to glean the greatest amount of entertainment value from *Santa and the Ice Cream Bunny* are those who have been able to take it at face value and revel in its procession of flaws and unrelenting level of brazen cheapness. Mitch Lovell perceives this strange phenomenon perfectly:

> *Santa and the Ice Cream Bunny* is one of the worst Christmas movies I've ever seen, which is to say I'm sure it'll become a yearly yuletide tradition in my home. There are so many WTF moments here that your brain will have trouble cataloguing it all. [...] Then there's the Ice Cream Bunny. Never mind that he never brings anyone any ice cream. I can handle that. It's the fact that he looks so damned creepy that I can't get over. The scene where the Bunny slowly approaches the beach in his jalopy accompanied by the sound of air raid sirens is the stuff of nightmares, and when he slowly winks at the kids, it's nothing short of horrifying.[10]

In spite of the film's lack of recognition at the time of its release, its profile has risen amongst cult movie enthusiasts in more recent years on account of being championed by movie commentary website *RiffTrax*. In December 2010, the company launched a downloadable commentary for *Santa and the Ice Cream Bunny* which proved to be so popular, it was later made available on DVD and as a streaming video title. Some years later, in December 2015, *RiffTrax* was also to release a live airing of the film in select American cinemas (using the somewhat rarer *Jack and the Beanstalk* version of the film rather than the more commonly-available *Thumbelina* variant), which has further raised awareness of Winer's movie. Over the years, variations of *Santa and the Ice Cream Bunny* have been released on VHS and DVD, and it is now also widely available via streaming video sites.

Santa and the Ice Cream Bunny provides a unique (if admittedly incongruous) lens through which to examine the significance of Christmas movies in the 1970s. As we have seen, the seventies were a time of considerable experimentation in filmmaking, and festive cinema was no different in this regard. *Santa and the Ice Cream Bunny* is a prime example of this development, as it combined a whimsical, almost surreal narrative with highly unusual characters and outlandish settings. While most of its creative choices were undoubtedly dictated by the ultra-low budget and the necessity to make use of whatever was available, the film did undeniably reflect a wider trend in 1970s cinema where film-makers often took artistic risks and explored unconventional storytelling.

Despite its highly irregular approach, the film still managed to tap into a handful traditional Christmas themes – if only fleetingly – such as the gift-giving of Santa Claus and the indefinable magic of the holiday season. This indicated that, even in the exploratory creative environment of the seventies, there remained a strong desire to maintain a connection to nostalgic and conventional elements of Christmas, reflecting the festive period's enduring cultural significance. The film's very-low-budget nature highlighted a broader trend of independent and inexpensive productions emerging throughout the 1970s, which often found niche audiences. This welcome democratization of film-making allowed for the arrival of a variety of new voices and narratives, even in the realm of Christmas movies. *Santa and the Ice Cream Bunny*, being produced in Florida, was just about as far away from the traditional Hollywood film-making hubs as could possibly be imagined. This pointed to the growing significance of regional film production over the course of the decade, where local production companies could increasingly contribute to the national film landscape, offering diverse and localised perspectives – even on universally celebrated holidays such as Christmas.

The film's eventual cult status underscores how seventies festive film-making, regardless of the initial reception of many of these obscure movies, could eventually gain a dedicated audience over time. This phenomenon reflected how certain features, through their sense of uniqueness or just their sheer, unadulterated weirdness, could carve out a lasting place for themselves in popular culture. In that sense, *Santa and the Ice Cream Bunny* – for all its many faults – did illustrate the diverse and evolving nature of Christmas films in the 1970s, for it exemplified the ways in which film-makers were willing to push creative boundaries and consider new approaches while still drawing on the timeless, universal appeal of traditional Christmas themes.

REFERENCES

1. William D. Crump, *How the Movies Saved Christmas: 228 Rescues from Clausnappers, Sleigh Crashes, Lost Presents and Holiday Disasters* (Jefferson: McFarland, 2017), p.212.

2. Sam Panico, 'Christmas Cinema: *Santa and the Ice Cream Bunny*', in *B&S About Movies*, 24 December 2017. <https://bandsaboutmovies.com/2017/12/24/christmas-cinema-santa-and-the-ice-cream-bunny-1972/>

3. Tim Brayton, '*Santa and the Ice Cream Bunny*', in *Alternate Ending*, 6 April 2015. <https://www.alternateending.com/2015/04/santa-on-the-beach.html>

4. Lauren Rosewarne, *Analysing Christmas in Film: Santa to the Supernatural* (Lanham: Lexington Books, 2018), p.388.

5. Panico.

6. Brayton.

7. Peter Hanson, '*Santa and the Ice Cream Bunny*', in *Every '70s Movie*, 25 December 2015. <https://every70smovie.blogspot.com/2015/12/santa-and-ice-cream-bunny-1972.html>

8. Dave Sindelar, '*Santa and the Ice Cream Bunny*', in *Fantastic Movie Musings and Ramblings*, 6 June 2017. <https://fantasticmoviemusings.com/2021/02/21/santa-and-the-ice-cream-bunny-1972/>

9. Alonso Duralde, *Have Yourself a Movie Little Christmas* (New York: Limelight Editions, 2010), p.181.

10. Mitch Lovell, '*Santa and the Ice Cream Bunny*', in *The Video Vacuum*, 19 November 2018.
    <*https://thevideovacuum.blogspot.com/2018/11/santa-and-ice-cream-bunny-1972.html*>

10

Silent Night, Bloody Night (1972)

Armor Films Inc. / Cannon Productions / Jeffrey Konvitz Productions / Zora Investments Associates

Director: Theodore Gershuny
Producers: Ami Artzi and Jeffrey Konvitz
Screenwriters: Theodore Gershuny, Jeffrey Konvitz and Ira Teller, from a story by Jeffrey Konvitz and Ira Teller

AS we have seen, the seventies were something of a boom period for experimental festive cinema, and for innovative horror films in particular. Some of these films were to perform better with critics and audiences than others, but many would capture imaginations and prove to be influential even years after their date of release. *Silent Night, Bloody Night* (not to be confused with Charles E. Sellier Jr.'s significantly better-known and considerably more controversial 1984 film *Silent Night, Deadly Night*) is set within the claustrophobic confines of a small American town during Christmas time, providing a new spin on the 'haunted house' subgenre by following the sinister events which surround a series of brutal murders that occur in an old mansion. As the mystery unfolds, dark secrets about the town's history and the house's past are revealed, leading to a chilling conclusion. *Silent Night, Bloody Night* was to use Christmas imagery and themes to enhance the film's shadowy atmosphere of suspense and horror. While certainly not a conventional Christmas movie, as was the case for so many other festive features of the decade, it offered a chilling exploration of the darker aspects of human nature set against the seemingly-cheerful backdrop of the holiday season.

The film was directed by Theodore 'Ted' Gershuny, and was an excellent example of why a low-budget production need not suggest a lack of creative quality. Working from a budget of less than $300,000, Gershuny – with a screenplay developed by himself, Jeffrey Konvitz and Ira Teller – was to deliver a feature which not only transcended the constraints of its limited production values, but which presented a genuinely innovative take on the nascent Christmas horror subgenre. Gershuny was, at the time, predominantly known as the writer-director of short film *American Roulette* (1966) and thriller *Kemek* (1970), for which he was nominated for the Gold Hugo Award at the Chicago International Film Festival in 1971. He had also acted as the narrator in unconventional drama *The Battle of Love's Return* (Lloyd Kaufman, 1971) and was later to perform as the character Saul in political thriller *Rosebud* (Otto Preminger, 1975), further emphasising the versatility of his talent on both sides of the camera. Gershuny would later achieve further recognition as a director after moving into the world of television, where he helmed episodes of various anthology series including *Stephen King's Golden Tales* (1985), *Tales from the Darkside* (1983-88) and *Monsters* (1988-90).

Part of the reason for *Silent Night, Bloody Night*'s relative obscurity amongst other Christmas-themed horror features of the time can be traced to complications surrounding its release. The movie was filmed in atmospheric Oyster

Bay in Long Island, New York in 1970, but it would not reach cinemas until November 1972 – and then, only as a limited American release under the title *Night of the Dark Full Moon*. It would not be known as *Silent Night, Bloody Night* until it was released more widely the following year. Further confusing matters, Cannon Films would re-release the film in 1981 with the title *Death House* (which was sometimes stylised, including in the opening credits, as *Deathouse*). Thus with so many alternative titles, the film's reputation struggled to gain traction amongst horror enthusiasts over the years since its release, leading to a subsequently deleterious (if unfair) impact on its critical standing. It also, as Alan-Bertaneisson Jones has observed, been unjustly overlooked as an influential early exponent of its subgenre: 'This 88-minute film had apparently been shelved by its producers for a couple of years (so it too might have something of a case to lay claim to being of one of the first-made of the Christmas Horror Movies proper and a progenitor of the "slasher" sub-genre!). Co-written and directed by Ted Gershuny, the fairly obscure, low budget *Silent Night, Bloody Night* (a.k.a. *Death House*, *Night of the Dark Full Moon* and *Zora*) is a little seen, but actually reasonably effective little horror film whose main action occurs at Christmastime in two separate eras'.[1]

On a cold and gloomy winter's day, a young woman named Diane Adams (Mary Woronov) wanders the expansive grounds of an old house in the small town of East Willard, Massachusetts, determined to see it one last time. Through narration, she explains that she grew up near the house's location, the daughter of the town's mayor. The highly distinctive building had once been the home of Wilfred Butler, a recluse who rarely stayed at the house. However, on the Christmas Eve of 1950, he came to visit his property...

only to be mysteriously burned to death there. The general opinion of the townsfolk was that he had perished as the result of a tragic accident, but none of them suspect that a rather more sinister explanation was behind his grisly end. In a flashback, a mysterious figure can be seen playing the house's organ as the autopsy report is read out; the official verdict confirms that Butler's death was formally recorded as accidental and self-inflicted.

Wilfred Butler's funeral takes place a week later, but no mourners are there to grieve his passing. The voice-over relates the reading of the late householder's Last Will and Testament, which confirms that all of his property and possessions are bequeathed to his only surviving relative – his grandson, Jeffrey Butler. However, there is an addendum to the Will: Wilfred requests that Jeffrey leave the house exactly as it is, so that it will stand as a monument rather than being an active residence. Jeffrey accedes to his grandfather's final command, and the house lies empty for the next twenty years.

By the time Christmas comes around in the year 1970, word begins to spread that Jeffrey has put the house on the market. The news eventually reaches a nearby institute for the criminally insane, where – upon hearing of the intended property sale – one of the inmates violently escapes and commandeers a car parked outside. Unseen, the patient manages to evade the authorities and heads for an unspecified location. Meanwhile, city lawyer John Carter (Patrick O'Neal) has come to East Willard on the request of his client, Jeffrey Butler. Accompanied by his personal assistant (and lover) Ingrid (Astrid Heeren), Carter has been instructed to sell the property on Butler's behalf. The house's exterior looks neglected after twenty years of abandonment, and the lawyer seems keen to conclude his business promptly.

Diane Adams is on the road when she hears a radio report that the escaped mental hospital inmate is still at large. She spots a broken-down car at the side of the road, but decides to drive on rather than risk any danger in answering its driver's request for help. Indignant with her unwillingness to stop, the sinister-looking driver (James Patterson) smashes his car's windshield with a tyre iron in a fit of pique. While this is happening, Carter arrives at a meeting with East Willard's civic leader, Mayor Adams (Walter Abel), and the town's sheriff, Bill Mason (Walter Klavun). He is also introduced to the non-speaking local newspaper owner Charlie Towman (John Carradine) and town communications director (and telephone switchboard operator) Tess Howard (Fran Stevens). Carter explains his professional duties to agree the sale of the Butler house, and the sheriff explains that he has spent years defending the abandoned property from burglars, intruders and inquisitive kids who are fascinated by its gruesome past. Tess suggests that Butler had been a hateful man, and that his misanthropy has continued to permeate the property even long after his death. None of them realise that as they speak, a prowler at the Butler mansion has stabbed a guard dog to death and has forced entry into the building. They make their way around the abandoned interior, still full of Wilfred's personal effects and furniture, as though they are already familiar with the place.

Back at the meeting, Carter enquires whether the townsfolk intend to go through with their plan to purchase the house from Jeffrey Butler. The mayor and his colleagues are suspicious – they have been trying to buy the property for years, so they are puzzled at why Jeffrey should suddenly be amenable to the sale after having ignored them for so long. Dodging the question, Carter responds that Jeffrey is now willing to sell the house for $50,000 – a huge reduction on its true value – provided that he receives the full amount in cash the next day. As the assembled delegates argue over the matter, the lawyer explains that he will remain in town overnight and receive their answer the next day. The mayor suggests that Carter and his assistant stay at the local motel, but the attorney instead replies that they will sleep at the Butler house and return the following morning. Tess offers to reconnect the mansion's long-dormant phone line, just to ensure that there will be an active line of communication if it is needed. Mayor Adams asks if Carter knows Jeffrey Butler well, to which the lawyer replies that they have never actually met – all of their interactions have been by telephone. However, they are due to convene face-to-face soon to discuss some personal items at the house.

Carter departs to call his wife on a public payphone; while she is presumably unaware of his affair with Ingrid, he still finds her cold and distant in conversation. Back at the mayor's office, Adams suggests that he go to the county bank and collect the cash in full. Though it is a substantial amount to consider for a town that is not exactly affluent, the unanimous opinion seems to be that the payment will be worth it just to get the Butler house into public hands. The mayor wonders aloud what they should do with the place once they have access to it, to which Towman instantly rasps that they should 'tear it down'.

Carter and Ingrid return to the abandoned mansion to spend the night. Neither realises that the building is no longer uninhabited, however; an unseen figure on the premises has become very aware that they suddenly have company. Ingrid remarks on how unspoilt the house's interior seems, and Carter replies that a caretaker ensures the property is constantly maintained, in order to fulfil Wilfred Butler's desire for it to become a monument rather than a residence. This explains why the clocks are still ticking, and the furniture is so immaculately preserved. Jeffrey spots the house's organ and the fact that it still has sheet music in place; he plays and sings along to the old hymn he sees there, remarking that it is a song he associates with funerals from his childhood. As he and Ingrid embrace, they are oblivious to the fact that the mysterious figure is scuttling around the house's upper landing, carefully staying out of view.

Carter lights the fire, causing smoke to rise from the chimney just as it had done back in the fateful Christmas of 1950. The couple sit down to dinner in the dining room, and Ingrid observes that the family who lived in the house must have had a happy existence in such opulent surroundings. Carter admits surprise that Jeffrey Butler should consider selling the property for $50,000 when it is worth five times that at the very least. However, he assumes that Butler simply needs the money quickly. The lawyer points out that the house is extremely well-built and that if it should be demolished to make way for a new housing development, it will be difficult and time-consuming to bulldoze it.

As Carter and Ingrid prepare to go to bed, the sheriff asks Tess Howard to check the phone line to the Butler house. Sure enough, the lawyer hears the phone ringing and answers it, assuring Tess that the line is working perfectly. He goes to his car to retrieve a Christmas package for Ingrid, but tells her not to open it for another two days; their Christmas celebrations won't take place until the property sale is complete and they are safely back home. Their intimate situation is soon violently interrupted when the prowler bursts in and massacres the pair with an axe. The master bedroom now drenched in their blood, the unseen murderer leaves a copy of the Bible in the room and places a crucifix in the palm of Ingrid's hand.

The phone rings in the sheriff's office. Mason is bewildered when he hears a whispering, grating voice on the other end of the line. The mystery caller explains that he is the house's owner, but denies being Jeffrey Butler. Instead, he requests that the sheriff come to the Butler mansion as quickly as possible in order to investigate the unexplained disappearance of John Carter. Tess, who has connected the call on the switchboard, speaks to the secretive caller, who remembers her by name. The voice explains that they have returned to their father's house, have found it to be lonely there, and identifies themselves as 'Marianne'. The switchboard operator is disturbed by the rambling monologue as the caller finally hangs up, but the unidentified figure refuses to answer the phone when she attempts to ring back.

Trying to relate what she has learned, Tess calls the sheriff's office, but Mason has already left for the mansion. Distressed, she then calls her colleague Maggie Daly (Lisa Blake Richards) and requests that she come in to work early. It is still only eight o'clock in the evening. At the Butler house, the man with the broken-down vehicle from earlier can be seen gaining access to Carter's car and driving it away from the property. He eventually arrives at the mayor's home, where his daughter Diane is wrapping Christmas gifts. Recognising the man as the would-be hitch-hiker from the previous day, she arms herself and holds him at gunpoint when he enters the house. The stranger insists that he is simply searching for the mayor, as he has just come from the sheriff's office and found it to be deserted. Nonplussed, Diane asks him who he is, to which the man replies that his name is Jeffrey Butler.

Still concerned about the escaped mental inmate from the nearby institute, Diane checks Butler's driver's licence and discovers sheepishly that he is telling the truth. Lowering her gun, she explains that her father is currently in transit with the cash necessary for the purchase of the Butler house. Jeffrey has reason to be confused himself; having already been to the mansion, he can find no trace of Carter and is unable to enter the property. Diane suggests that he contact the sheriff's deputy and try to collect a key from there.

Maggie has arrived at the town's switchboard, rather confounded by Tess's heightened state of agitation. Tess warns her that if there are any further strange calls from the Butler house, she should call either the mayor, the sheriff or Charlie Towman immediately – but no-one else. Neither are aware that the sheriff is already approaching the mansion, but he spots a strange light nearby and decides to investigate. This turns out to be a lamp that is being used by the murderer for unknown purposes in the local cemetery. There, the sheriff is horrified to discover that Wilfred Butler's grave has been disturbed, and that a copy of the dead man's diary has been placed next to the gravestone. However, he has little time to process these details before he is brutally murdered by a shadowy figure with a shovel.

Jeffrey returns to the mayor's house and tells Diane that there is no sign of either the sheriff or his deputy. When she asks if he has had any luck contacting Carter, he replies that only his car was at the house – which he has had no choice but to borrow, given the impracticable state of his own vehicle. They share a drink, and Diane asks why he has suddenly decided to sell the property after so many years of refusal. Jeffrey responds that he simply needed access to the money quickly, and thus had no choice. He also reveals that he has never even seen the house until today, so its interior is a mystery to him. Diane mentions that someone keeps calling on the phone, keen to speak with her father the mayor, but that all they will say is that they are waiting in the reception room of the Butler house. Curious, Jeffrey decides to check it out for himself, and Diane decides to join him.

On the way to the mansion, Diane asks Jeffrey if he intends to return home to California after selling the property, but he inscrutably replies that he intends to travel instead. They spot the sheriff's car parked at the side of the road and investigate, but Mason is nowhere to be seen. They then see the disturbed grave of Wilfred Butler, and discover the sheriff's sunglasses lying discarded in the snow nearby. Sensing that nothing there seems quite right, they decide to get back on the road and report what they have seen. Meanwhile, the mayor is now heading back to East Willard, having withdrawn the funds necessary to purchase the Butler house.

Jeffrey and Diane decide to pay a visit to Charlie Towman, the owner of the town's newspaper. While Towman has no power of speech, he uses a series of written notes to inform the pair that Tess has gone to the mansion – though no-one can work out why she would do so, as she famously can't stand the place. Jeffrey offers to accompany Towman there to intercept Tess, while Diane locks herself into the newspaper office for safety. Towman appears to recognise Jeffrey somehow, but does not divulge why this might be.

To Jeffrey's surprise, Towman drives not to the Butler house but instead to Tess's home. There is no sign of the communications director there, which perplexes Towman. However, when Jeffrey mentions the unexplained phone calls coming from the mansion, the silent journalist becomes alarmed and rapidly drives off in his car, leaving a mystified Jeffrey in his wake. While this is happening, Diane receives a phone call from the mystery individual while she waits at the newspaper office. The caller again identifies themselves as 'Marianne', and tells Diane that her father must visit the Butler house as soon as possible. They claim to have 'the diary', and forebodingly tells her that the mayor will remember the Christmas Eve of 1935.

Elsewhere, the shadowy figure stores an unseen load in the trunk of the sheriff's car and turns off the vehicle's radio. The car is later discovered by Tess near the Butler house as she approaches the front door. Finding the mansion's entrance unlocked, she walks into the main hallway and looks for Bill Mason, who she assumes to be alive and continuing his investigations. Instead, she spots movement from behind a partition doorway, following which the room is plunged into darkness. The whispering voice, which she recognises from the phone calls, tells Tess that he knows her and asks her to take his hand. When she does so, however, she realises that the offered appendage has actually been severed. Screaming in horror, she is promptly bludgeoned to death with an axe.

Back at the newspaper office, Diane has decided to do some research into the history of the Butler house. Looking through the archives, she discovers that Wilfred Butler restored the building back in 1927, but three years later his wife Katherine died from tuberculosis. Then, in 1933, Butler's daughter Marianne is attacked and sexually assaulted at the age of fifteen. The following year, she gives birth to a son named Jeffrey; the infant is sent to be cared for in California. By 1935, Butler had given over the house to the care of a psychiatrist named Dr Robinson (Michael Pendrey), who converted the property into a mental hospital. Diane is stunned to discover that Wilfred Butler had committed his own daughter Marianne into the care of this institution, but she is unable to discern the reason why because Towman has carefully redacted the various articles in the archives to obscure the facts.

Out on the road, the mystery figure has discovered Towman's now-abandoned car and is attacking it vigorously with an axe, following which it is set on fire. Jeffrey arrives at the newspaper office and explains that Towman had curiously decided to drive off without him. Diane asks him about his mother, to which he casually replies that she had died in childbirth – an account which contradicts the newspaper reports, much to his shock. He is reluctant to learn more about his family history for fear of what he might discover, but Diane suggests that he review her findings. Based on what she has discovered, Diane posits that the 'Marianne' making the phone calls may well be Jeffrey's mother – not dead at all, but waiting for him back at the Butler house. With new-found conviction, Jeffrey decides that it is finally time to find out what is going on once and for all. He and Diane get into Carter's car and head for the mansion.

While they are driving, Diane spots the burning wreck of Towman's car and identifies it, though with the relieved caveat that it is empty. They get back on the road, but they have barely resumed their journey before Towman himself jumps out of the undergrowth into the path of the car. Jeffrey has no time to react, and the vehicle strikes the elderly journalist at speed, sending him tumbling over a steep incline. Concerned, Jeffrey brings the car to a standstill and races down the slope, but it is too late – Towman is dead. Diane is aghast that Jeffrey has ended the older man's life, even accidentally, but Jeffrey has entirely separate cause to be shaken: he can see that before Towman had been struck by the car, someone had amputated both of his hands.

The pair finally arrive at the Butler house, and Jeffrey spots the sheriff's car – still left deserted near the front door. With trepidation, he makes his way into the hall, while Diane remains alone in the automobile outside. She realises that Jeffrey has taken the vehicle's keys, leaving her trapped in the house's grounds without him, and then spots an unidentified figure moving around in one of the building's upstairs windows. Meanwhile, Mayor Adams has just returned home when his phone rings. It is the mystery caller, who identifies themselves as 'Marianne Butler' and requests that he come to the mansion as quickly as possible. The voice curiously tells him that they have organised a reunion, and everyone is invited – even his daughter Diane. He pauses to collect a shotgun before he departs.

Jeffrey explores the seemingly-empty Butler house, but can find no trace of life. He discovers Wilfred Butler's diary on the house's organ, and with some apprehension decides to read it. Horrified, he learns that it was Wilfred who had subjected his own daughter Marianne to incestuous rape and impregnated her as a result. Thus Wilfred is both Jeffrey's father and grandfather. The diary explains that Wilfred had placed Marianne into the care of psychiatrists in the hope that they could 'cure' her (presumably helping her to cope psychologically with the dreadful ramifications of her father's unspeakably evil actions), but results were slow in developing. Eventually Wilfred came to consider the doctors and nurses to be self-satisfied and ineffectual, and grew frustrated at the pace of their results. At a Christmas Eve party in 1935, he decides to secretly liberate all of the patients in the care of the mental hospital, leading to the slaughter of the entire medical staff. With the medics inebriated and the patients armed with tools, gardening equipment and any other weapons they could find around the house, a blood-soaked massacre took place, but – unintended by Wilfred – Marianne was accidentally caught up in the carnage and died as a result of it. He thus swore vengeance on the inmates who murdered her, but as they had escaped the Butler house after the bloodbath, he was never able to make good his retribution on them.

Jeffrey learns that Wilfred decided to fake his own demise on the Christmas Eve of 1950 by immolating a squatter he had found on the premises of his house. Far from having burned to death, Wilfred lived anonymously in a mental institution near the town as a form of self-inflicted penance. However, upon learning that his grandson/son intended to sell the Butler house, he decided to escape and take his long-delayed revenge on the townsfolk. No longer content to remain outside, Diane resolves to enter the mansion, and Jeffrey explains that Wilfred's wrath can now be explained. Sheriff Mason, Charlie Towman and Tess Howard had all once been inmates of the asylum back in the 1930s... as had her father, Mayor Adams. The escaped Wilfred has been systematically murdering every person he holds responsible for his daughter's death. The mayor arrives at the mansion and enters, his shotgun at the ready. He mistakes Jeffrey, who has never met, for Wilfred and shoots him – at the exact second that Jeffrey takes aim and fires at the intruder. Both men thus simultaneously murder each other, much to the horror of Diane who watches the split-second homicide from nearby. She has little time to process this before the aged Wilfred Butler (Grant Code) emerges, dishevelled and unkempt, his visage pale and cadaverous. Mistaking Diane for his long-departed daughter

Marianne in his mania, he tries to grab her. In response, she grabs Jeffrey's handgun and fires multiple times at the elder Butler, instantly killing him.

Hysterical with grief and terror, Diane runs from the room and suffers a breakdown due to the horror she has witnessed. However, when Christmas morning arrives, she has psychologically taken stock of the situation and realised that her father and Jeffrey were simply the last of many victims claimed by the accursed house over the decades. A year later, a demolition team have arrived on the grounds to finally bulldoze the property, paving the way for a new beginning for the community. However, Diane melancholically reflects that while the old house may be torn down at last, she can never forget the terror that played out there – or the indelible shadow that the mansion had cast over the community.

Silent Night, Bloody Night was, as its title suggests, nothing close to a traditional Christmas movie; rather than a festive feature with horror elements, it would instead prove itself to be a psychological thriller that used the festive season as an effective setting for its eerie, horrifying story of insanity and obsession. Here, Christmas served as a purposeful counterpoint to the film's sinister and foreboding atmosphere rather than as its central purpose. While the holiday season customarily symbolises peace, joy, and a sense of togetherness with friends, family and the wider community, in this movie it was instead marked by tension, fear and paranoia. The festive decorations and cheerful music provided a stark contrast to the underlying sense of dread and menace that so skilfully permeates the narrative throughout.

The movie craftily but effectively subverts the traditional Christmas promotion of domestic devotedness to explore more complex themes of family secrets, mental illness and the consequences of long-buried past actions, suggesting that the festive season can serve as a catalyst for uncovering suppressed truths and confronting unresolved trauma. As the characters grapple with their own demons and the legacy of the town's dark and hidden history, the holidays soon become little more than a veneer for their descent into madness and violence. Here there was no family reconciliation and celebration of community: instead, we see the joy of Christmas inverted into a parody of itself, with abuse and violence replacing comfort and friendship in a disturbing but highly effective way.

The action benefits immeasurably from Gershon Kingsley's unnerving original score, which not only augments the film's disconcerting atmosphere but also manages to turn even the sound of well-known Christmas carols – a source of reassuring nostalgia for most of us – into something which seems dark and foreboding. As Dave Sindelar has observed, 'What is it about the song *Silent Night* that seems to inspire the titles for Christmas-themed horror movies? I fully anticipated that I was about to watch another of those killer-Santa Claus movies, and I wasn't expecting much. Such is not the case, though – there are no killer Santas to be found here. Instead, I found myself sucked in by this one. It's not a great movie, but it is surprisingly suspenseful at times, largely due to the fact that a certain amount of creative style went into it, and the central mystery/backstory is truly intriguing. [...] At other times, the editing is fascinating, and the use of Christmas music on occasion is unexpectedly haunting'.[2]

With bright Christmas decorations strung around deliberately gloomy sets, dark and often disorienting location filming (at time of writing, the grand property used to represent the Butler house still exists at Mill Neck in Long Island,

New York) and a genuine, building sense of menace, *Silent Night, Bloody Night* was never short on distinctiveness, though the convolutions of its plot (not least the fact that the disconsolate history of the Butler house plays out diffusely over not one but three Christmas periods – in 1935, 1950 and 1970) did garner it criticism from the few critics of the time who took notice of its release. As Matthew C. DuPée explains, however, the movie was so much more than a triumph of style over substance:

> A stylish and moody early American slasher film set around Christmas, *Silent Night, Bloody Night* effectively uses handheld point-of-view shots from the killer's perspective and frightening, harassing phone calls that predated similar techniques and attributes found in the Christmas horror masterpiece *Black Christmas* (1974). The story is a slow burn, but it intimately examines abuse, victimization, madness and perversion of justice. [...] Critics panned the film for its convoluted plot and gritty cinematography, but the film is propped up by a fascinating location, strong acting and a visceral story. The Christmas carol *Silent Night, Holy Night* plays as a musical motif throughout, adding a layer of acoustic eeriness to an already atmospheric haunted house tale.[3]

Undoubtedly, the screenplay by Gershuny, Jeffrey Konvitz and Ira Teller contains plenty of recognisable horror tropes, from classic misdirection (the red herring of Jeffrey's black gloves matching those of the serial killer) through to sly plot diversions (the fact that Charlie Towman's laryngectomy initially seems to be set up as a plot point, but in the end its cause is never explained). Even the antagonist, Wilfred Butler, is revealed to be not a supernatural peril but is instead simply a damaged human being capable of great evil; having committed unspeakable acts against his own daughter, his inability to rationalise or resolve the consequences of his wickedness leads again and again to a cascade of deadly violence over the decades. His orchestrated murder of the mental health staff seems predicated first and foremost by their inability to help conceal his repellent actions through 'curing' his daughter Marianne of her psychological trauma quickly enough, again showing his egregiously self-serving nature, whereas his later mass slaughter of the various townsfolk who had once been patients themselves seems almost like a series of vengeance killings intended to salve his conscience for his daughter's death – even though he is himself indirectly responsible for it. The presence of his diary at the end of the film almost seems to represent a confession of his crimes – and his culpability for them – that he was unable to bring himself to make in life.

Yet it was in its sporadic Christmas-themed flourishes that the film seemed most interesting – Diane wrapping presents in the comfort of her festively-decorated living room mere hours before her father's violent demise, or Carter and Ingrid planning to exchange Christmas gifts but never getting the opportunity to unwrap them when their extramarital love tryst is cut short by the murderer's axe. In this sense, as Gordon Maples notes, the feature may well have been more significant as a horror movie – set at the festive season or otherwise – than it had initially seemed: '*Silent Night, Bloody Night* was clearly ahead of its time as a slasher movie, predating movies like *Halloween* and *Friday the 13th* by the better part of a decade. It is hard to say whether it had any influence on the genre, given how obscure of a release it was until it was dug up again in the early 1980s. Regardless, it is a prescient feature in a number of ways, and is interesting to watch as a harbinger of what would become the dominant sub-genre of horror for many years'.[4]

While many of the cast were relative unknowns, there were plenty of effective performances on display here, not least in the memorable meeting between Patrick O'Neal's slick city lawyer John Carter and the town's most influential citizens, which grows incrementally more discomfiting as it becomes increasingly clear that they are hiding something – a triumph of character acting by the cast. James Patterson (who had won a Tony Award in 1968 for his appearance in Harold Pinter's stage play *The Birthday Party*) impresses as the sinister, mercurial Jeffrey Butler, who – right until the end – always manages to appear to be something other than he seems. Similarly, Mary Woronov's Diane – the lynchpin of the film, whose monologue opens and closes the action – is memorably glacial and serene; this strong and confident figure steadfastly refuses to allow the unfolding horror to disturb her composure (thus making her eventual breakdown seem all the more alarming). Woronov collaborated on numerous occasions with cult movie legend Roger Corman, and later became an author and painter. John Carradine was also noteworthy in his brief, largely non-speaking role as Charlie Towman; using a small reception bell in exchange for conventional dialogue, the enigmatic newspaperman grows ever more desperate as it becomes clear that his efforts to sanitise the town's dark past have not been sufficient to prevent the re-emergence of alarming truths. Carradine remains one of the most prolific character actors in history, with over 350 credits to his name across film and television at the time of his death in 1988. In his long career, he worked with major industry figures ranging from Cecil B. DeMille to John Ford, with performances in films across genres including Westerns, dramas and horror movies.

However, for all the individual acting talent on display in the main roles, *Silent Night, Bloody Night* would become especially well-known amongst cult movie fans for the brief inclusion of many performers who had once worked in creative collaboration with Andy Warhol. As Bill van Heerden remarks: 'The history of the asylum in the film is told using flashbacks, and all of the inmates of the asylum are played by New York City underground movie veterans. They include Ondine [Robert Olivo], Jack Smith, Tally Brown (*Night of the Juggler*, 1980) and female impersonator Candy Darling, who died two years after making this movie'.[5]

The movie failed to make much impact with commentators at the time of its release, largely due to its low public profile, and it rapidly fell into obscurity before finding a cultural resurrection in the most unlikely of places. While the film's ownership is recognised as belonging to Zora Investments Associates in the credits, in reality the film was never formally registered with the United States Copyright Office. This meant that it actually fell into the public domain after its initial run in cinemas, which soon led to its lack of recognition amongst all but the most die-hard of cult horror fans. However, as Michael Verrati has stated, the story of the film's eventual renaissance was almost as remarkable as its fictional events themselves:

> Perhaps one of the biggest hurdles in *Silent Night, Bloody Night*'s strange trajectory were the circumstances of its release and subsequent rediscovery.

Finally given the title by which it's known today, the film was distributed to the drive-in circuit in the spring of 1973 and made the rounds until December of that year. Unfortunately, due to a failure to register the film for copyright, *Silent Night, Bloody Night* fell into the public domain shortly after its drive-in run and, outside of a few festival screenings, slipped into relative obscurity as a result. Enter: Elvira, Mistress of the Dark. In 1981, as part of her first season of *Movie Macabre*, Elvira aired *Silent Night, Bloody Night* (Oct. 3, 1981 – the show's second episode) and in the process, helped kickstart a new chapter of the film's history. Initially acquired due to its public domain status and as admitted counter-programming to family-friendly holiday fare, *Silent Night, Bloody Night*'s re-emergence on late-night cable helped introduce it to a whole new audience and cemented the film's status as a horror host staple. For the next several decades, *Silent Night, Bloody Night* found a comfortable seasonal home on hosted programs such as *Miss Misery's Movie Massacre* and *After Hours Cinema*.[6]

Following its revival on late night TV, *Silent Night, Bloody Night* soon started to grow a solid cult following that only gained further longevity when it was released on VHS video. Later, it would be issued multiple times on DVD. As a result, the movie has been revisited by numerous reviewers in recent years, though critical response has proven to be uneven. Some commentators, such as Ian Sedensky, were to praise the film's distinctive sense of atmosphere while issuing a note of caution about its highly convoluted storyline: '*Silent Night, Bloody Night* is an unusual mix of old dark house thriller, small town secret mystery, and ax-murdering mania from a time in slasher history when dramatic theatricality went beyond snarky one-liners and creative kills. It is continually engaging as a gradually unfolding horror whodunit, though it surely fails to grab some viewers because of that slow pace, and because its plot is probably more complicated than it needs to be. 〚...〛 Changing directions almost as much as it changes scenes, *SNBN* has a lot of story on the table, though not all of it adds up to a meaningful payoff in the end'.[7] Others, such as Peter Hanson, have taken issue with the film's creative approach, considering its sinister ambience to be cynically constructed rather than artistically crafted: 'Despite a few creepy flourishes and the presence of horror-cinema icon John Carradine in a minor role, *Silent Night, Bloody Night* is more like a lump of coal than a brightly wrapped Christmas present. 〚...〛 If there's anything genuinely interesting or unique about *Silent Night, Bloody Night*, it's buried beneath lots of superficial atmospherics, and obscured by needlessly befuddling plot machinations'.[8]

Overall, however, the film's critical legacy has generally been perceived to have been elevated by the skill of its director Theodore Gershuny over the challenging budget and restricted production values, creating a striking feature even in spite of the convolutions of its narrative. As Kevin Burns and William Tuttle have put it, '*Silent Night, Bloody Night* is an example of a script being produced by a director whose technical grasp of the medium is far greater than the material deserves. A strange, unsettling business meeting, anonymous phone calls, an extended sequence in a mental hospital – the film's core setpieces are all perfectly chilling in a (dare I say it?) elegant way'.⁹ Similarly, Sam Panico has praised the film for the way that it provided a refreshingly different creative approach to the festivities, neatly upending expectations of what a truly experimental Christmas film can offer audiences: 'There are some really interesting techniques here, especially in the flashback sequences, which feel like tinted photographs come to life with the saddest version of *Silent Night* ever playing behind the action. I love how experimental and dark these sequences look – they remind me a little of the [1989 E. Elias Merhige] film *Begotten*. This is a dark film for your holiday viewing, so if you want to chase away the family for a while, this is the one to do it'.¹⁰

Due to its resurgent profile, it seemed inevitable that *Silent Night, Bloody Night* would eventually be revisited, and – sure enough – a late-in-the-day British remake of the film was produced by North Bank Entertainment in 2013, entitled *Silent Night, Bloody Night: The Homecoming*. (It would later reach the North American market by way of a DVD release the following year.) Starring Alan Humphreys as Jeffrey Butler and Mel Stevens as Diane Adams, the remake was directed by James Plumb and loosely followed the premise of the original film – a man inherits a seemingly-abandoned mansion from his late grandfather, only to run into unexpected and decidedly gory events as he attempts to negotiate the sale of the property.

Shortly afterwards, a completely unrelated production was to provide a direct sequel to the original movie. *Silent Night, Bloody Night 2: Revival* was directed by Dustin Ferguson and released by New Wave Independent Pictures in 2015. Picking up the action some four decades after the Gershuny film, the sequel focused on siblings Angelica and James Zacherly (Julia Farrell and Luc Bernier) as they visit

East Willard following the death of a relative. Arriving at Christmas, they discover Jeffrey Butler's long-lost journal and soon learn that Santa Claus appears to have a chilling alter-ego who intends to spread anything but joy and goodwill. But, as they soon discover, nothing in the town is quite as they expect. The sequel featured no recasting of characters from the original movie, though some footage from the Gershuny feature was repurposed in the form of flashbacks.

Silent Night, Bloody Night has also been produced as a stage play. One and Done Productions painstakingly adapted the drama for a one-off performance at The Hive in Brooklyn, New York in December 2016. It was scripted by Sean Pollock and Drew Weinstein, with a seven-person cast which included actors Hannah Allen, Darby Harmon, Carl Hsu, Claire Hsu, Suzie Leger, Clinton Powell and Roberto Tolentino.

For all its restrictive budget, *Silent Night, Bloody Night* was a horror film with genuine ambition that reflected well the shifting cultural landscape of the 1970s – especially in terms of how Christmas movies were being actively reimagined to meet modern tastes, and the growing appetite of audiences for horror narratives that challenged and defied traditional narratives. The film considered the customary, seemingly-serene themes of Christmas – peace, family, community and goodwill – and then progressively subverted them with horror, violence, discomfiture and madness. In so doing, it was to tap into a growing trend throughout the seventies where filmmakers were beginning to explore the darker sides of American life, including the ways in which the holidays – often seen as peaceful and idyllic – can demonstrate underlying tensions and traumas. This reworking of Christmas themes was a reflection of a broader cultural shift during the decade, where there was a growing disillusionment with traditional values – partly as a result of phenomena such as the long-running Vietnam War, the Watergate scandal and numerous other major societal disruptions.

Silent Night, Bloody Night has also become significant for its influence on the slasher genre, which would become more prominent later in the decade and also in the early years of the 1980s. It features many elements that would become long-held staples of this category of film, such as a mysterious unidentified killer, gruesome deaths and a narrative focused on past traumas coming back to revisit characters in the present. With its focus on a sinister or haunted house, it also riffed on a theme that would lay the groundwork for many other horror films later in the decade (and into the eighties) including *Burnt Offerings* (Dan Curtis, 1976), *The Amityville Horror* (Stuart Rosenberg, 1979) and *The Changeling* (Peter Medak, 1980). The movie demonstrated the ways in which Christmas, customarily associated with joy and celebration, could be narratively repurposed in cinema to create tension and fear, thus contributing to the development of horror as a genre that could transform even the most benevolent settings into places of terror and uncertainty.

The film's moody tone and dark themes are reflective of the wider cultural mood of the 1970s: a decade which was marked by uncertainty, mistrust in institutions and a vigorous questioning and re-evaluation of the American Dream. The horror genre during this period often dealt with these anxieties, and *Silent Night, Bloody Night* was no exception. By setting its horror narrative during the festive season, the film emphasised the contrast between the surface appearance of normality and the darkness which lurked beneath: a theme that resonated with audiences of the time. The feature illustrated the significance of Christmas movies in the seventies by showing how the holiday could be used to explore darker, more complex themes that resonated with the cultural and societal shifts of the era. Its approach to Christmas as a thematic apparatus for horror reflected wider trends in 1970s cinema, where once-traditional genres and themes were being re-examined and reinterpreted to reflect contemporary anxieties and aid in artistic experimentation.

REFERENCES

1. Alan-Bertaneisson Jones, *I'm Dreaming of a Fright Christmas: A Guide to Seasonally-Themed Movies of the Macabre and Other Weird and Wacky Tinsel-Tinged Treasures and Turkeys* (Milton Keynes: AuthorHouse, 2010), p.89.

2. Dave Sindelar, '*Silent Night, Bloody Night*', in *Fantastic Movie Musings and Ramblings*, 30 June 2006.
   <https://fantasticmoviemusings.com/2017/03/19/silent-night-bloody-night-1974/>

3. Matthew C. DuPée, *A Scary Little Christmas: A History of Yuletide Horror Films, 1972-2020* (Jefferson: McFarland, 2022), p.73.

4. Gordon Maples, '*Silent Night, Bloody Night*', in *Misan[trope]ly*, 10 December 2015.
   <https://misantropey.com/2015/12/10/silent-night-bloody-night/>

5. Bill van Heerden, *Film and Television In-Jokes: Nearly 2,000 Intentional References, Parodies, Allusions, Personal Touches, Cameos, Spoofs and Homages* (Jefferson: McFarland, 2008), p.121.

6. Michael Verrati, '*Silent Night, Bloody Night* at 50: Reflecting on Five Decades of Festive Fright', in *Fangoria*, 16 December 2022.
   <https://www.fangoria.com/silent-night-bloody-night-at-50-reflecting-on-five-decades-of-festive-fright/>

7. Ian Sedensky, '*Silent Night, Bloody Night*', in *Culture Crypt*, 11 February 2014.
   <https://culturecrypt.com/movie-reviews/silent-night-bloody-night-1972>

8. Peter Hanson, '*Silent Night, Bloody Night*', in *Every '70s Movie*, 28 March 2015.
   <https://every70smovie.blogspot.com/2015/03/silent-night-bloody-night-1972.html>

9. Kevin Burns and William Tuttle, 'Greetings from Spider Island: Mill Creek's *Chilling Classics* 50-Movie Collection', in *The Video Basement*, 17 November 2014.
   <https://videobasement.wordpress.com/2014/11/17/greetings-from-spider-island-mill-creeks-chilling-classics-50-movie-collection/>

10. Sam Panico, 'Christmas Cinema: *Silent Night, Bloody Night*', in *B&S About Movies*, 18 December 2017.
    <https://bandsaboutmovies.com/2017/12/18/christmas-cinema-silent-night-bloody-night-1972/>

11

Black Christmas (1974)

Film Funding/Vision IV

Director: Bob Clark
Producer: Bob Clark
Screenwriter: Roy Moore

IF the 1970s can be considered one of the most innovative periods for festive cinema, *Black Christmas* stands as one of the bravest experiments with the genre of its time. As its title so aptly suggests, the film is a clever and effective inversion of everything that had come to be associated with the Christmas movie thus far: the warm celebration of the family unit was replaced by the pain of dysfunctional relationships, comfort and joy were substituted with fear and suspense, and there was most certainly no happy ending on offer. In short, *Black Christmas* is one of the darkest representations of the festive period ever to be presented on the big screen, and a landmark feature for the Christmas horror subgenre.

Black Christmas has become significant for two reasons. Firstly, it was almost certainly the most famous Christmas horror movie even amongst other emergent features of the era, bringing this category of film to the attention of the general public as never before. Secondly, it was a seminal entry in the field of 'slasher' horror films – some commentators have even come to consider it the first of its kind, though (as we will see) there has been some contention amongst critics on this point. One thing remains certain, however: *Black Christmas* was a mould-breaking, highly original piece of film-making, and one which has garnered a considerable cult following since the time of its release.

An inventive director, Bob Clark was also a producer, actor and an accomplished screenwriter. By the time of *Black Christmas*, he had helmed various films including fantasy *The Emperor's New Clothes* (1966), light-hearted horror *Children Shouldn't Play with Dead Things* (1973) and the dark suspense movie *Dead of Night* (1974). His prior experience in the horror genre was to serve him well in the production of *Black Christmas*: not only has it come to be considered one of the best-regarded of his early films, but it was ultimately to establish itself as among the most prominent of his entire filmography. Clark would, of course, later revisit the festive season some years later with his warmly nostalgic family classic *A Christmas Story* (1983), and while it is difficult to imagine a more profound tonal shift than the one which exists between these two films, there were also common touches which continue to fascinate commentators. As Noel Murray suggests, 'In less than 10 years, Bob Clark went from codifying the slasher film genre in 1974's *Black Christmas* to making a different kind of holiday movie in *A Christmas Story*. But the two films aren't too far apart, at least in terms of their settings: Both take place in big, lit-up, snowbound houses. In *A Christmas Story*, it's a suburban nuclear family home preparing for the holidays; in *Black Christmas*, it's a sorority house being stalked by a serial killer. Both look so warm, inviting, and communal that it's hard to imagine how anything really awful could happen there. In *Black Christmas*, Clark cracks the happy façade quickly'.[1]

The genus of *Black Christmas* stemmed from a screenplay entitled *Stop Me* which had been penned by Canadian writer Roy Moore. The original script was heavily inspired by a chain of real-life murders which had been committed over the Christmas of 1943 in Montreal, Quebec, in which a fourteen-year-old boy was found guilty of brutally murdering members of his family during the holiday season. As the script was developed, the film's fictional setting shifted to a sorority house on a university campus, and Clark was determined to reflect the serious-mindedness, individuality and personal responsibility of modern students rather than having them depicted as stereotypically vapid and shallow (as many other movies of the time had been guilty of portraying them). Clark also asked Moore to tone down the interpretation of the murders which appeared throughout the film, believing that the film would be much more effective if the violence was portentously suggested rather than brutally represented. Moore agreed to restrain the violence in comparison to earlier drafts of the screenplay, leading to a much greater level of suspense as a result. The movie was filmed in and around the Toronto area of Ontario, including on the campus of the University of Toronto, and was produced on a budget estimated at around $686,000.

Black Christmas opens with a shot of a festively-decorated sorority house at night. The building, with its brightly lit windows, looks warm and inviting while the song 'Silent Night' plays through the opening credits. But as students are making themselves comfortable inside, the camera switches to a subjective viewpoint: an unknown figure is watching the house's inhabitants from the cold outdoors. Barbara 'Barb' Coard (Margot Kidder), one of the students inside, seems surprised that the front door has been left open and promptly closes it to keep in the heat. The mysterious prowler, still unseen, backs off momentarily. After a few moments he then begins trying to find another way of gaining entry to the building.

A low-key Christmas party is taking place in the sorority house. Arrangements are being made for hosting a children's party on campus the next day. The telephone rings and student Jessica 'Jess' Bradford (Olivia Hussey) answers it. Discovering that it is a long-distance call for Barb, she passes on the message, causing Barb to withdraw from the room in order to take the call on another line. Meanwhile, the prowler has succeeded in gaining access to the house via an open window, clambering into a darkened attic. Downstairs, Barb is trying hard to have a conversation with her mother on the phone, in spite of interference on the line and the noise of the party in the next room. She is completely oblivious to the fact that she is now being closely watched by the silent stalker.

Another student, Clare Harrison (Lynne Griffin), arrives at the house just as Barb is ringing off. They begin to chat in the main room when the telephone rings once again. Jess picks up the receiver and hears heavy breathing on the other end. As this has become a regular occurrence, the others come through to hear what 'the moaner' has to say for himself this time. What follows is a bizarre collection of animalistic noises, screams and yelps, peppered with graphic profanity. As the caller's taunts become more obscene in nature, Barb takes the receiver from Jess and derides the anonymous pervert for his unwanted verbal perversity and suggestive deviance. Apparently angered at being insulted, the voice on the other end of the line states matter-of-factly that Barb will soon be dead... and then immediately hangs up.

Barb seems unaffected by this mysterious threat, shrugging it off as a random crank, but the others are rattled by the menacing call. Barb assures them that she has received several such calls while living in the city, and that the threats are nothing to worry about – they are merely the delusional fantasies of a sick mind. Clare warns her that another student was violently raped recently, and that she cannot be too careful when it comes to the viciousness of strangers, but Barb casually brushes off her words of caution. Upset by her friend's cavalier attitude, Clare withdraws to pack up her belongings before she leaves for the holidays. As Jess chides Barb for having been so blunt with Clare, brassy house mother Mrs Barbara 'Mrs Mac' MacHenry (Marian Waldman) arrives at the door with a bundle of presents. Though Barb is unimpressed by her appearance, the other students are pleased to see the matriarchal figure and are quick to usher her into the warmth of the lounge.

Upstairs, Clare is packing in her room. She is happy to be reunited with Claude, the house cat who has been missing for the past few days but who has now taken up residence on her bed. Clare removes some neatly-stored clothes from her closet to put them in her suitcase, completely oblivious to the fact that the prowler is watching her through a sheet of dress protection plastic at the back of the cupboard. When she hears the cat mewling in distress, Clare heads back to the closet and is shocked to see a vague figure there. Before she has any time to react, the plastic sheeting is forced over her face, suffocating her.

Clare's screams cannot be heard downstairs, however, where the students are persuading a reluctant Mrs Mac to try on a floral night-dress that they have bought her as a Christmas present. In the hallway, the shadow of a misshapen profile can be seen shuffling away; the sound of bestial grunting can be heard in the figure's wake. As the party is winding down, the telephone rings once again – in spite of some trepidation, it turns out to be Jess's musician boyfriend Peter Smythe (Keir Dullea). Jess is keen to talk to Peter face-to-face about a matter that she considers to be of the utmost importance. But Peter has been practicing a piece of music around the clock for the past three days, hence his absence from the party, and is reluctant to come over so late at night when he has a pending examination. Obviously anxious to speak with him, yet bristling at his lack of enthusiasm to discuss things, Jess arranges to meet with Peter the following afternoon instead.

While the eccentric Mrs Mac becomes ever more inebriated, thanks to a variety of carefully-concealed bottles of alcohol, Jess knocks on the door of Clare's room and is surprised when her friend doesn't answer. Unknown to her or any of the other students, however, Clare's body has been chillingly deposited on a rocking chair in the attic, the plastic sheet still wrapped around her now-lifeless face.

The next day, Clare's father Mr Harrison (James Edmond) is becoming worried; he had arranged to meet his daughter at a quadrangle on the university grounds but is concerned that she hasn't appeared on schedule. He meets the inscrutable Peter, who directs him to the sorority house, but after enquiring with Mrs Mac it becomes clear that she hasn't seen Clare recently either. The house mother suggests that they try the common area where the children's Christmas party is being held.

Over at the main campus, Jess explains to Peter that she is pregnant with their child. Peter is delighted to hear the news, but Jess makes it plain that she wants to have an abortion; indeed, she hadn't initially intended to tell Peter of the conception at all, and has only recently decided to inform him. Troubled by her apparent disregard for his own feelings on the matter, Peter asks her if she has entirely thought through all of the ramifications of such a monumental decision. However, Jess has her own reasons and doesn't want to discuss the issue any further: she emphasises to Peter that he has no chance of changing her mind. Dismayed at how aloof and clinical she seems over this most emotional of matters, he sends her away, but relents before she leaves the room and asks if she will meet him that night to talk further about the situation.

Mr Harrison is still drawing a blank with regard to Clare's whereabouts. When it becomes apparent that none of the other students have seen her, he heads to the police station and reports her missing. The desk sergeant, Nash (Douglas McGrath), tells Harrison that he is probably worrying over nothing; there's a good chance that there is an innocent explanation, such as Clare having a secret tryst with a suitor no-one else knows about.

Back at the sorority house, Jess takes another call from the prowler. It is even stranger than his previous one, with a woman's voice calling for someone named Billy followed by sundry brutish grunting noises. Jess is shaken up by this most unusual of communications, though she can make no sense of it. Later, she heads for an ice hockey arena where Clare's boyfriend Chris Hayden (Art Hindle) is practicing with his team. She explains about Clare's disappearance, and together they head for the police station where he demands an explanation from Lieutenant Kenneth Fuller (John Saxon) as to why Clare's case is not being taken seriously.

At night, Mr Harrison remains at the sorority house, where Mrs Mac continues to reassure him that his daughter is probably safe... wherever she might be. But he remains troubled by the out-of-character lack of communication, to say nothing of being perplexed by the off-the-wall ramblings of Barb, who has become seriously drunk after the children's party. The increasingly paranoid Barb begins ranting that because she had upset Clare the night before, everyone is certain to blame her if her sorority sister is later discovered to have fled the house and has somehow been murdered as a result. Phyllis 'Phyl' Carlson (Andrea Martin), one of her sorority sisters, eventually manages to persuade Barb to retire to bed before she can upset the already-anxious Mr Harrison any further. As soon as Barb has departed, however, Jess and Chris arrive and tell Mr Harrison that the police have now finally instigated a search for the missing Clare. Together with Phyl, they depart to assist in the hunt, leaving Mrs Mac alone in the building with Barb.

The search party is gathered at a local park, where a young schoolgirl named Janice Quaife had gone missing earlier that day. Lieutenant Fuller explains the procedures to the assembled crowd; they are to spread out and comb the area for any evidence that may lead to the young woman's discovery. It is hoped that anything which can pinpoint Janice's location may also assist in finding Clare. However, Mr Harrison and Janice's mother, Mrs Quaife (Martha Gibson), seem to be losing hope of finding either of their respective daughters alive.

Mrs Mac is busy getting packed to leave for the holidays, little realising that the prowler remains focused on the sorority house. Her taxi waits outside, the driver blowing his horn impatiently. Almost ready to leave, Mrs Mac hears the distressed meowing of Claude the cat and decides to check on him before she heads off. Tracing the cat to the attic, she is horrified when she discovers Clare's suffocated corpse, but has little time to ponder the situation before she, too, is killed by the prowler. The taxi driver (Gerry Arbeid) grows increasingly intolerant at the fact that his fare still hasn't shown up, unaware that she has been throttled to death inside the house. The mysterious figure watches as the taxi eventually drives away and then becomes caught up in a frenzied tantrum, throwing a random selection of objects around the cluttered loft space in an inexplicable fit of rage.

Back at the park, a grisly discovery is made when Janice's body is finally found in the undergrowth. The assembled searchers are horrified with what has been uncovered – all, that is, apart from Jess, who has returned to the sorority house for her scheduled meeting with Peter. As soon as she has entered, however, the telephone rings. Upon answering it, she encounters more strangulated yelps and the usual range of discordant voices, only this time crying for help... and repeatedly calling for Billy. Jess pleads with the menacing caller to stop ringing the house, but eventually is left with no choice but to hang up. She searches for Mrs Mac but, knowing that she intended to leave for Christmas, finds nothing unusual in her absence.

Jess rings the police to report the string of obscene phone calls, and is shocked to discover that Peter is in the sorority house with her; when she was late for their rendezvous, he let himself in to wait for her return. The volatile Peter is not in the best of moods, however: distracted by her news earlier in the day, his recital had gone badly with his examiners, later causing him to destroy his Steinway piano in an outburst of fury. He tells Jess that he intends to leave the university's conservatory and asks her to marry him. Jess is startled by the offer but is resolute: she tells Peter that she still has many ambitions that she intends to fulfil, and that it is unreasonable of him to expect her to abandon them in order to get married, even if his own vision of the future happens to have changed. Disappointed, but willing to accept that his proposal has been snubbed, Peter then presses Jess further on the issue of the abortion. He remains resentful over both her dispassionate detachment from the issue and her reluctance to involve him in the decision. Peter insists that she reconsider, but Jess will not be dictated to – especially on matters of her own body – and demands that he leave. He does so, though he is insistent that if she has an abortion she will regret the consequences. The threatening tone of his parting words is not lost on Jess.

At the police station, Fuller discovers the report about the obscene phone calls and puts two and two together – the address is the same one where Clare is resident during termtime. Fuller heads to the sorority house with Phyl and a technical specialist, Bill Graham (Les Carlson), arriving at the building just as the agitated Peter is leaving. Graham puts a tap on the phone line in an attempt to trace the mystery caller, while Fuller heads for Clare's room to search it for any hint as to her whereabouts. Fuller's low-key interrogation of Jess and Phyl turns up nothing new, but he gives the remaining sorority sisters the reassurance that an unmarked police car is waiting outside; the officers inside are ready to act at a moment's notice. As Fuller and Graham leave the house, however, Peter can be seen waiting among the trees nearby, his expression intense.

Back inside the house, Phyl becomes upset as the events of the day start to catch up with her. She is certain that Clare is dead, but Jess reassures her that they shouldn't jump to conclusions. Tired out by everything that has happened, an exhausted Phyl retires to bed, leaving Jess alone downstairs. Neither of them are aware that the muttering, increasingly deranged killer is still in the attic, gently swinging Clare's dead body back and forth on the rocking chair.

Apprehensive, Jess waits by the phone for the next call to come. But the prowler is on the move once again, descending from the loft. He makes his way into Barb's darkened room, where she lies sleeping. A few moments later, Jess hears Barb making sounds of distress and rushes to her aid. She discovers that Barb is having an asthma attack, and quickly gives her access to an inhaler. Barb quickly recovers and puts her symptoms down to a nightmare she was having – she had merely dreamed that the intruder was coming for her. Neither of them notices that the actual prowler is silently backing away from the room and retreating into the hallway.

The sound of carol singers can be heard from outside the building, and Jess withdraws from Barb's room to investigate. Still drowsy from her earlier heavy drinking, Barb appears to fall back into slumber. Jess opens the front door and discovers the child choir to be an oddly emotionless collection of carollers, technically proficient but singularly lacking in seasonal spirit. While they sing (rather soullessly), the murderer sees his chance and returns to Barb's room. Telling the sleeping Barb 'It's me, Billy,' he grabs a large glass ornament of a unicorn from a nearby table and repeatedly stabs her with its protruding horn. Barb only recovers consciousness as the attack is delivered, and is thus too shocked to cry out as she is brutally killed by the unseen assailant.

As soon as their carol is over, the children are shooed away from the door by an attendant, who informs Jess that due to the murder of Janice Quaife earlier in the day they are unwilling to risk the safety of the carollers by leaving them unsupervised. Their conversation is interrupted when the house's phone rings. Full of trepidation, Jess heads back to answer it, while Graham and Fuller wait patiently to track the call. Lifting the receiver, Jess is met with another bizarre exchange, with a child's voice crying out to 'Billy' in pleading tones to cease attacking, while adult voices respond cryptically. With a woman's assurance that something will be 'just like having a wart removed', which reminds Jess of the exact words used by Peter during their earlier argument about her forthcoming abortion, the line goes dead. Jess is once again disturbed by the alarming concatenation of exclamations from the phone, but is especially worried about the caller having used the exact same expression as Peter had spoken.

A few moments later, Fuller rings Jess to tell her that Graham was unable to trace the call – the next time the prowler phones the house, he reiterates the fact that she will have to keep him on the line for longer. Puzzled at the discomfiting way that the mystery caller is apparently able to shift between different voices, Fuller asks Jess about Peter, who he saw leaving the house. Before he is able to continue the conversation, an unexpected disturbance in the police station causes him to ring off abruptly, but he promises to call her back soon.

Phyl has awakened due to all the commotion of Barb's asthma attack, and discusses with Jess the possibility that Peter may have been the one involved in Clare's disappearance. The unseen prowler is watching them from a crack in a nearby doorway. Phyl is unconvinced that Peter would be capable of such a sadistic act, but Jess is not so sure: the caller's precise selection of words seem to be too much of a coincidence. Almost on cue, the phone rings; this time it's Peter, sobbing uncontrollably. His words almost unintelligible due to his distress, Peter desperately begs Jess once again to reconsider aborting the baby. Jess pleads with him to calm down and discuss things rationally, but Peter proves to be anything but coherent. Before the police can get a trace on his location, he hangs up.

Now highly suspicious at Peter's distraught state of mind, Fuller calls up Jess and demands to know what the conversation was about. Reluctantly, Jess explains about her abortion plans, leading Fuller to suspect that Peter could indeed be the same person who is behind the obscene calls. However, Jess remembers that Peter had been present in the house earlier in the evening when one of the calls was made, which appears to exonerate him. Unconvinced, Fuller resolves to question Peter and asks about his likely whereabouts. Thinking ahead, he also requests Peter's administrative records from the university's dean of admissions.

One of Fuller's aides explains that a full search of the campus has revealed no trace of Clare. Left with little option, Fuller instructs him to start a house-to-house search of all residences in the adjacent area. A couple of socially inept search party members (Jack Van Evera and Les Rubie) arrive at the sorority house and scare Phyl and Jess with their unforeseen appearance. They urge the two students to keep the house securely locked to avoid encountering the abductor, which Jess assures them that they will. She and Phyl laugh at the searchers' apparent incompetence as they leave, but Jess seems less amused when she suddenly realises that the back door is currently the only entrance to the house that is actually locked. They quickly set about securing all of the windows (pointedly neglecting to visit the attic) when Phyl enters Barb's room to check on its safety. Just as soon as she has stepped into the darkened area, however, the door slams closed behind her.

Downstairs, Jess has finished a sweep of the doors and windows and is confused when Phyl doesn't respond to her repeated calls. She is cut short when the phone rings. Answering it with customary trepidation, she is met with a succession of wailing animal noises, more fevered pleas to 'Billy', and another barrage of sinister grunting. This time, however, the conversation is intercut with shots of another room in the sorority house, making it clear that the obscene caller is ringing from the same location as Jess. The exchange becomes more and more heated, with an agitated adult male demanding to know 'where the baby is'. Jess seems as baffled as she is uneasy by this chaotic and disturbing commotion.

Fuller is examining the wreckage of Peter's piano at the conservatory, noting that the troubled musician is not present in the building, when one of his officers informs the lieutenant that a trace has finally been made on the mystery caller. Returning to his car, he contacts Nash at the station only to be told the one thing that he didn't expect to hear: the prowler is calling from the very same building that his victims are located in. Frantically, he radios Jennings (Julian Reed), the detective that he had positioned on a stakeout near the sorority house. Fuller is frustrated when he doesn't respond, unaware that his colleague is slumped dead in his car, his throat slashed.

Realising that it is imperative he reach the sorority house as quickly as possible, Fuller orders Nash to call Jess and persuade her to leave the building as quickly as possible. However, the tactless Nash lets slip that the prowler is likely in the same building as Jess, making her unwilling to leave without her friends Phyl and Barb. Retrieving a poker from the common room's coal fire, she creeps upstairs to Barb's room. Finding that the door is trapped shut, Jess forces it open, only to be met with the sight of Barb and Phyl's bloodied corpses. Shocked by this horrific scene, she notices the killer's eye peeking through a gap in Barb's closet. 'It's me, Billy,' he whispers dolefully, beseeching her to keep quiet about what he has done. Jess slams the door against him, causing the prowler to cry out in uncontrollable rage. Racing downstairs, she almost reaches the front door when the prowler grips her, dragging her backwards. Narrowly escaping his grasp, she hides in a nearby room as he yells furiously and flails around like a trapped animal. Then, suddenly, he stops. Jess listens as his footsteps fade away into the distance, a door closing behind him.

Still armed with the poker, Jess silently stalks through the house and eventually descends into the basement in search of safety – and possible escape. Hearing some muttering and scuffling noises accompanied by the dark profile of a shadow, she locks herself in and withdraws into the darkness just as Peter arrives at the external door. Calling out for Jess, Peter breaks the door's glass pane and gains entry to the basement. Searching through the darkness, Peter appears relieved when he finally finds her hiding against a wall, gripping the poker tightly. Calmly, Peter asks her why she didn't respond to his calls, but Jess offers no answer.

Outside the house, Fuller arrives with backup and discovers Jennings's dead body. A sudden scream from the building causes the officers to come running to its source. Heading down into the basement, the police discover Jess pinned under Peter's corpse; it is obvious from his injuries that she has attacked him with the poker. Jess is clearly in shock, so the officers sedate her and return her to her room. Fuller is keen to question her, but the medical specialist on site explains that due to her condition she will most likely be unresponsive to conversation until the next day. The bodies are removed from the premises, and Fuller is keen to deflect the sudden press and media interest away from the sorority house over to the police station, which will give the soon-to-arrive State Police forensic teams some breathing room. Believing that Jess will be safe asleep in her bed now that Peter has been dealt with, the police withdraw from the house, leaving her asleep.

But Jess is far from safe, and certainly not alone. Panning through the empty house, including views of Barb's blood-spattered mattress and Clare's poignantly half-packed suitcase, the camera centres on the accessway into the attic where ominous humming can be heard. 'Agnes? It's me, Billy,' says the baleful voice, as the viewpoint edges away from the still-undiscovered corpses of Mrs Mac and Clare to leave the house through the loft window. Pulling out to a wider shot of the house, an unsuspecting police officer stands guard at the sorority house's doorway as, eerily breaking the silence, the telephone begins to ring for one last time as the end credits roll.

Black Christmas boldly subverts traditional notions of festive cheer and safety, presenting a dark and ominous portrayal of the holiday season. While Christmas is the setting for the film's events, it serves predominantly as a framework for terror rather than an uplifting, celebratory environment. The juxtaposition of violence and horror cast against the festive decorations and comforting carols creates a profound sense of dissonance and unease throughout the film. Furthermore, the movie explores themes of isolation, fear and vulnerability, which are deliberately heightened by the Christmas Eve setting. The sorority house, typically a place of camaraderie and sisterhood, now becomes a claustrophobic and ominous space as the characters are terrorised and gradually eliminated by the unseen killer. The sense of isolation and helplessness experienced by the protagonists reflects the darker side of the holiday season, where loneliness and despair can be amplified amidst the persistent, customary expectation of joy and togetherness.

In addition, *Black Christmas* touched on themes of family dysfunction and societal pressure, as the characters grappled with personal demons and external expectations during what was traditionally anticipated to be a time of warmth and connection. The movie thus offered a chilling and unsettling perspective on the holiday season, challenging traditional notions of Christmas cheer and safety and revealing the darker undercurrents of the festive season, leaving viewers with a sense of intense unease long after the calculatingly abstruse conclusion. Yet as Kim Newman has observed, the film would likely have been considerably less effective (or memorable) without its yuletide setting:

> Like *Halloween*, *Black Christmas* uses a holiday as a backdrop: the end-of-term setting excuses the characters' failure to notice that the people around them are disappearing one by one, and also provides a logical reason why the old dark house should be empty. Whereas [John] Carpenter uses *Halloween* to epitomise his childlike bogeyman, Clark plays with the contrast between Christmas and the horrors, intercutting a Dario Argento-style

murder (Kidder stabbed with a crystal ornament) with an angelic troupe of carol singers. The most heavily criticised aspect of *Black Christmas* – the transformation of its unknown psycho villain into a quasi-supernatural presence – would be seen as *Halloween*'s strongest suit.[2]

Black Christmas is a film which has few pretensions beyond telling a suspenseful story well, and in that it exceeds brilliantly. To his credit, Clark makes a laudable artistic decision to limit the amount of blood and gore on display in favour of building an atmosphere of tangible foreboding, and both he and screenwriter Roy Moore are highly successful in ratcheting up the tension and air of apprehension as the film progresses. As Peter Hanson has put it, 'Somewhat interesting as a footnote in the history of horror films because it bridges the suspenseful storytelling of Hitchcock thrillers and the gruesome excesses of slasher flicks, *Black Christmas* is a low-budget Canadian flick about a psychopath stalking the residents of a sorority house. Oddly, however, the film isn't as lurid as the premise might suggest, because there's very little gore and almost zero sexual content; instead, director Bob Clark focuses on colorful character details'.[3]

Yet while it can seem easy to forget the fact that this is also a Christmas film, in spite of its title, in many ways it almost feels like an anti-Christmas feature at times. Clark and Moore create a sly subversion of many traditional Christmas themes as the foundation of the movie's sinister ambience. Bright fairy-lights and festive decorations adorn the sorority house all the way throughout the evening's butchery – it is heavily implied that the massacre takes place on Christmas Eve – while church bells ring out traditional carols at the same time as Peter and Jess are discussing the implications of her pending abortion. This latter point is particularly noteworthy, for the central religious significance of Christmas – namely the Virgin Birth – is here being juxtaposed with an unwanted pregnancy which is almost certainly going to end with a termination (presuming that the foetus survived the violent struggle between Peter and Jess in the basement). With the US Supreme Court decision on the landmark Roe vs Wade abortion case having taken place just a year beforehand, in 1973, the independently-minded Jess's resolve to determine what happens with her unborn child was a noteworthy development for a film of the time. Yet in spite of the spiritual iconography, adherence to traditional Judeo-Christian ethical traditions prove to be neither a help nor a hindrance in the ensuing slaughter: the staid, morally-upright Clare is dealt with by the killer just as decisively as the hard-nosed, foul-mouthed Barb is.

The effectiveness of the prowler and their indeterminate identity is a vital ingredient of the film's success and, as some commentators have noted, it should not be forgotten that *Black Christmas* was one of the very first slasher horrors to use subjective camera angles to articulate the murderer's first-person viewpoint. As Andrew Patrick Nelson explains, 'Although comparatively neglected in scholarship, *Black Christmas* is considered by some to be the first slasher film. Interestingly, it anticipates *Halloween* in a number of ways. For example, the movie makes extensive use of a mobile camera – here using a wide-angle lens, which creates a distorting effect – accompanied by heavy breathing to represent the killer's subjective point of view'.[4] Indeed, the creative decision to follow the murderer's covert actions while refusing to reveal their identity has become one of the most prominent hallmarks of *Black Christmas*'s highly inventive approach. Nina Nesseth has also emphasised just how innovative this technique actually was, to say nothing of how influential it would become: '*Black Christmas* put us as the audience into the killer's shoes. The perspective was filmed with a head-mounted camera setup created by camera operator Bert Dunk specifically for the film; the Steadicam wouldn't be introduced until 1975. You can see the genetic connection between *Black Christmas* and the slashers that would follow'.[5]

Director Bob Clark himself was one of the anonymous figures behind the prowler's shadow, and also one of the uncredited voices who took part in the character's unfathomable but deeply disturbing phone calls. (The actual dialogue and incidental sound of the calls to be heard in the movie were only inserted during the post-production phase, with Clark performing the menacing and obscene discourse off-camera during filming so that the actors had a prompt to respond to.) The evolution of the phone conversations' mounting danger, beginning with random obscene abuse and then edging towards a very real sense of imminent peril, manages to be genuinely disturbing: not least as every call accompanies another murder being committed by the unseen felon.

For all the violent depravity that is in evidence, Clark infuses his film with a very wry sense of humour which is obvious from the ironically cosy opening sequence: a scene that – with its picture-book decorated house and comforting carols – is evocative of much more traditional family Christmas fare. To the eyes of modern audiences, the movie no doubt appears strangely bloodless in comparison to later entries in the genre, with Clark allowing suspense and dramatic tension to triumph over superfluous gore, while an effective measure of macabre humour is injected into the narrative without the dark wit ever seeming strained or jarring. This is particularly true of the dim-witted Sergeant Nash's incessant bumbling, and also the guilty secret of Mrs Mac's many hidden bottles of booze (they are found, throughout the film, in locations which include toilet cisterns, shoeboxes and hollowed-out books). Clark was said to have been determined to introduce a greater degree of humour to the film in order to flesh out its characters, thus heightening the audience's emotional investment in them, and he had a hand in dialogue changes which included enhancing Barb's sharp-tongued drunken diatribes and Mrs Mac's various eccentricities (which he had reportedly based on one of his own aunts). But there was also a more subtle type of drollness in evidence throughout the film, such as the eerie concurrence of a (more than slightly creepy) children's choir singing 'O Come All Ye Faithful' with Barb's brutal murder, and the revelation (from the police cars' bodywork decals) that the murders are taking place in the fictional university town of Bedford: surely a dark subversion of the security and contentment brought to mind by *It's a Wonderful Life*'s inviting community of Bedford Falls.

One of the most mysterious aspects of the film – or unsatisfying, depending on one's point of view – is the ambiguous question of the identity of *Black Christmas*'s murderer and what his motivations actually were. Certainly Peter appears to be a plausible culprit for at least some of the killings, and it is easy to see why Jess and the police are highly suspicious of his lack of emotional self-control. Unusually for films of this type, Peter is not simply employed as a diversion from the true killer: such are his actions, many may well interpret the character as actually being responsible for some of the evening's carnage. His early displays of violent temper, destroying his eye-wateringly expensive piano in reaction to

Jess's pregnancy revelation and his subsequent poor performance at the recital, coupled with his surprise early appearance at the house when Jess returns from the search party at the park, initially makes him appear to be little more than a red herring: his likely culpability seems to be too heavily emphasised to be plausible. Yet there is no logical reason that he could not have been responsible for some (or even most) of the obscene phone calls – not least given the deranged caller's intimate knowledge of Peter's heated arguments with Jess over her abortion plans – with the singular exception of the one which takes place following his death.

Although Peter does make an appearance in person when Jess is on the phone, which seems to exonerate him, at the time of his emergence she is actually calling the police to report the calls after they have taken place, leaving Peter ample time to have rung her anonymously from an extension line before coming downstairs. It even appears to be Peter (or someone with a very similar physical frame) who drags Jess away from the front door when she is frantically trying to escape the house after discovering Phyl and Barb's butchered bodies, and yet the wild animal noises seem to be coming from upstairs at the same time as Peter is struggling with her downstairs. And perhaps most tellingly of all, after Peter's emotional, grief-choked phone conversation (quite different from the obscene calls that have been plaguing Jess), his cold, distant mode of address in the basement – followed by the manner and distribution of his wounds when the police discover his body – make it appear that Jess has acted in self-defence rather than attacking him pre-emptively. The sense of equivocality, and the growing plausibility of Peter's involvement in any number of the crimes in some unspecified capacity, only adds to the gripping sense of narrative tautness.

Yet for some commentators, such as John Kenneth Muir, this element of the film was eventually overplayed: 'There's ⟦...⟧ a problem with the last portion of the film, the portion that sets up Peter as the (false) culprit. Misdirection is one thing, but it strains believability that Jess (Hussey) would kill her boyfriend without at least some kind of pretty solid confirmation that he is, in fact, the killer. Worse, after she murders Peter, the police sedate Jess and then leave her alone in the house! *At a crime scene!* Again, the behaviour doesn't ring true. When the phone blares again, revealing that the killer is still at large, the audience thus feels cheated. It wants to get to the same point of horror the movie does, but it wants that to happen in a believable, honest fashion'.[6]

The closing shots, which suggest that the deranged, muttering prowler has both the means and ability to escape the house (unseen by the police) from his attic lair after the evening's massacre, raises profound questions. Is the phone ringing one last time to herald the unseen murder of Jess – the film's sole survivor (until that point)? Could Peter really have been responsible for any of the deaths – even Detective Jennings – prior to his own demise? The deranged eye peeking at Jess through the crack in Barb's closet door doesn't appear to match Peter's features, and the prowler's wild commotion appears to be independent of Peter's endgame attack on Jess while occurring simultaneously with it. But did Peter act alone, with another murderer working in the house autonomously, or were they somehow both involved in the carnage together? Is Peter in fact entirely innocent of criminality (as most commentators assume), with the mysterious unknown figure being solely responsible for all of the killings? Were either of them responsible for the murder of Janice, the schoolgirl found dead in the park nearby, or was that tragedy simply coincidental and the work of another killer altogether?

Many theories have been advanced relating to the central question of who exactly Agnes and Billy really are. Some have suggested, based on the incidental dialogue present during the obscene phone calls, that Billy (the caller) has a multiple personality disorder which was either initiated or exacerbated by his murder of Agnes in childhood, and that his subsequent guilt is expressed through the adult voices which manifest themselves throughout his ranting monologues. Was Agnes's killing accidental or premeditated – and does the solution to that unanswered question underpin his motivation for the subsequent bloodbath which later ensues years later? Does Billy's involvement in the demise of an infant child later connect to his unhealthy interest in the intense debate between Jess and Peter over the issue of the abortion of an unborn foetus – and if so, whose side does he take in this provocative dispute? His opinion never seems clear one way or the other, but his obsession with the abortion (typified by his repetition of Peter's exact expressions to unsettle Jess) further heightens the controversial nature of the contentious argument between the two opposing partners, just as it augments the prowler's unbalanced tendency to superimpose tragedies of the past onto seemingly-unrelated events in the present. Others have posited that the reason why Billy takes up residence in the sorority house's attic was because he had once lived in the property in youth, and has returned there in an attempt to revisit and address the tragic outcomes of his past actions (hence the brutal murders as he ends up recreating the original homicide over and over again). Unquestionably, the fact that the loft space is crammed full of incongruous belongings and personal effects which would seem out of place in student accommodation adds credence to this theory, suggesting that these items are in storage from an earlier time when the multiple-occupancy building had once been a family home. Or perhaps it is simply the comforting evocation of family life that has attracted the killer, stimulating memories of a now-irretrievable past.

Whatever the truth behind the killer's identity, Clark and Moore were dogged in their determination to present no easy answers – either in the film or in the years which followed its release – leading many commentators to note that the audience is left with little choice but to accept that the killer may well have no logical purpose behind their actions at all: he is, quite simply, insane. As Jeff Kuykendall has noted, the lack of a conclusive resolution has become one of the movie's defining qualities: 'Clark keeps the film's story as simple as possible, so that it plays like a dark fable for the holidays. There's an admirable purity at work. [...] You expect a neat resolution – even the *giallos* solved their twisted mysteries – and you don't get one. Those calls, so strange and inexplicable (who's Agnes, anyway?), never receive a clinical explanation from *Psycho*'s psychiatrist. This is how you do it'.[7] While this refusal to provide definitive answers now seems like a brave decision, especially given the seminal nature of the film, it also confounded some audiences of the time and proved to be a contentious creative choice. In some ways, as Bartlomiej Paszylk has argued, Clark's courageous artistic choices may have led to its cult longevity, but they have similarly unfairly distanced *Black Christmas* from many later discussions of horror cinema: 'Perhaps the main reason for the movie being perpetually overlooked by genre historians is that it lacks the suspense, swift pacing and payoff characteristic of mystery, fleshes out several interesting characters (the one played by

Kidder being a standout), and leaves us puzzled with its bold, vague ending. [...] In effect, *Black Christmas* is a movie at the same time surprisingly restrained and shockingly perverse'.[8]

The film's central performances were strong, with the actors appearing to fit in seamlessly with the authentic seventies pop art and student paraphernalia of the sorority house just as effectively as they were to blend into the ominous darkness of the house's shadowy interiors. As Jess, Olivia Hussey presents an unconventional heroine for the time; this resilient character's absolute sense of independence and self-determination makes her very different from the 'scream queens' of horror movies past. Hussey had been active on television since the mid-sixties, appearing in the cinema in films such as *The Battle of the Villa Fiorita* (Delmer Daves, 1965) and *Cup Fever* (David Bracknell, 1965). Her big break came when Franco Zeffirelli cast her as Juliet in his beautifully-composed cinematic adaptation of William Shakespeare's *Romeo and Juliet* (1968). Her performance in Zeffirelli's film was to win her the Most Promising Newcomer (Female) Award at the Golden Globes in 1969. Following that, her profile as an actress continued to remain prominent with the public due to appearances in a variety of features such as domestic drama *All the Right Noises* (Gerry O'Hara, 1971), crime thriller *Summertime Killer* (Antonio Isasi-Isasmendi, 1972), and *Lost Horizon* (1973), Charles Jarrott's adaptation of the James Hilton novel.

Keir Dullea is both chilling and enigmatic as Peter, the temperamental musician who appears glacially cool one moment and uncontrollably emotionally charged the next. His performance excels in presenting a disturbed and troubled character whose actions, in spite of screen time which is actually quite brief, manage to instil the film's third act with genuine menace. Dullea was a well-established film star by the time of his appearance in *Black Christmas*. He had performed regularly on television and on the big screen since the early sixties, with prominent roles in *Hoodlum Priest* (Irvin Kershner, 1961) and also *David and Lisa* (Frank Perry, 1962), for which he received a BAFTA Film Award Nomination for Most Promising Newcomer to Leading Film Roles. Having also won the Golden Globe for Most Promising Newcomer (Male) in 1963, Dullea's career grew in stature with a continued and prolific television career interspersed with performances in films ranging from *Le Ore Nude* (Marco Vicario, 1964), an adaptation of Alberto Moravia's novel *Appuntamento al Mare*; Old West comedy *West of Montana* (Burt Kennedy, 1964); war drama *The Thin Red Line* (Andrew Marton, 1964); and thriller *Madame X* (David Lowell Rich, 1966). He then was to take up what has become, in the eyes of many critics, his most famous role in the form of Dr David Bowman, the central character in Stanley Kubrick's ground-breaking science fiction drama *2001: A Space Odyssey* (1968). (He would brilliantly reprise this role many years later, in Peter Hyams's *2010: The Year We Made Contact*, 1984, which was similarly based upon an Arthur C. Clarke novel.) He then continued to alternate between challenging film roles, starring in *De Sade* (Cy Endfield, 1969) and *Paul and Michelle* (Lewis Gilbert, 1974), as well as television features such as *Black Water Gold* (Alan Landsburg, 1970) and *Montserrat* (David Friedkin, 1971).

The film also benefits from a wide and rather diverse range of solid supporting performances, many of them highly memorable. James Edmond's dignified but increasingly traumatised Mr Harrison, Marian Waldman's coarsely amusing Mrs Mac, John Saxon's stoically professional Lieutenant

Fuller and Andrea Martin's sweet-natured Phyl are all impressively-drawn characters. But Margot Kidder's larger-than-life appearance as the hard-drinking, always-outspoken Barb made her the standout supporting actor in the views of many reviewers. Kidder had been active on television since the late sixties, making her film debut in *Chicago, Chicago* (Norman Jewison, 1969). In the 1970s she continued to develop her television career while also starring in cinematic releases including *Quackser Fortune Has a Cousin in the Bronx* (Waris Hussein, 1970), *Blood Sisters* (Brian De Palma, 1973) and *The Gravy Train* (Jack Starrett, 1974). She would, of course, become instantly recognisable soon after for her performance as award-winning journalist Lois Lane in Richard Donner's celebrated comic-book adaptation *Superman: The Movie* (1978), a role that she was to reprise in the film's three sequels throughout the eighties.

Black Christmas received a rather muted response from the critical community at the time of release, heightening later notions that the film was somewhat ahead of its time in its approach. *Variety*, for instance, considered the film to be both unimaginative and formulaic: '*Black Christmas*, a bloody, senseless kill-for-kicks feature, exploits unnecessary violence in a university sorority house operated by an implausibly alcoholic ex-hoofer. Its slow-paced, murky tale involves an obscene telephone caller who apparently delights in killing the girls off one by one, even the hapless house-mother. The plot has the usual abundant cliches'.[9] It fared little better in *The New York Times*, with critic A.H. Weiler finding fault in the movie's underlit presentation and what he considered to be lacklustre dialogue and characterisation: '*Black Christmas*, which landed on local screens a year after its release in Canada where it was produced, is a whodunit that begs the question of why it was made. The answer is hard to come by. This moody depiction of the Christmas slayings of university sorority sisters and their housemother, among others, is as murky as the script, which dotes largely on obscenities that are no more pointed than the violence, dull direction and pedestrian performances'.[10] The movie was, however, more warmly received by *The Los Angeles Times*, with its reviewer Kevin Thomas appreciating how Clark's meticulous craft had led to the presentation of an absorbing narrative: 'Before it maddeningly overreaches in a gratuitously evasive ending, *Black Christmas* [...] is a smart, stylish Canadian-made little horror picture that is completely diverting'.[11]

However, *Black Christmas*'s pioneering inventiveness within the genre to which it belongs, and an almost-immediate cult following which has only developed with the passing years, has seen its reputation grow considerably. This has led to an extensive critical re-evaluation of the film, which has taken into account its wide-ranging influence on later features in both the slasher horror and Christmas-based thriller categories of cinema. As a result of its trailblazing approach, a great many critics have cited John Carpenter's famous cult hit *Halloween* (1978) as being stylistically influenced to a degree by the format and conventions established by *Black Christmas* – not least in the gruesome action being set during an annual holiday. As Mike Long remarks: 'If *Black Christmas* can be acknowledged for anything, it's its vision. The movie employs shots from the killer's point-of-view whenever he is on the prowl. This use of P.O.V. (as it's known) would become a staple of the genre and most would assume that it was Carpenter's idea. But, *Black Christmas* used it first and the film is very ambitious in this regard, especially when we watch the killer climb a trellis. [...] It seems that with every re-release, a new audience discovers *Black Christmas*. Despite the slow pacing and a questionable plot, the movie serves as a nice transition piece between the *gialli* which were coming out of Italy at the time and the slasher films which would overtake America. If those unfamiliar with the film can make their way through the movie's problems, they will no doubt see why fans consider the movie to be so influential'.[12] Not everyone has been convinced of the merits of Clark's movie, however. Gary Panton is among some critics who have derided the narrative obscurity and suspense of *Black Christmas* as ultimately unconvincing: 'If you're after an alternative to the tinsel-draped merriment normally to be found in films associated with this time of year, you might think *Black Christmas* as good a choice as any. [...] There's only really one way to describe *Black Christmas*, and that's silly. The story makes no sense, we're always far too aware of the killer's presence for there to be any proper shocks, and the ending has none of the impact it should'.[13] In the final assessment, though, more reviewers in the present day have been appreciative of the film's merits than not, with some – such as Anthony Arrigo – even drawing attention to its unlikely celebrity proponents:

> For the uninitiated [...] let me say that I cannot overstate how exceptional Clark's film is – never giving the killer an identity, an entire subplot concerning abortion, a palpable sense of grief for Claire's father, a cast of interesting, unique people who don't ever feel like archetypes, and a potential downer of an ending. Some of his moviemaking tricks are brilliant, like the decision to create Billy's voice from a combination of three different people (one a woman) and using inter-

changeable actors to portray the killer so you're never quite sure who is in the attic. Carl Zittrer's score is disorienting and minimal, making use of odd instrumentation to add extra unease; it also appears infrequently, giving the movie more of a real life quality. *Black Christmas* was a reasonable success upon release, more so commercially than critically, but time has been kind to this old gem and many now view it as an outright horror classic. Hell, it was Elvis' favorite Christmas movie.[14]

Black Christmas was nominated for the Golden Scroll Award for Best Horror Film at the 1976 Academy of Science Fiction, Fantasy and Horror Films Awards, and Roy Moore's screenplay was also nominated for an Edgar Award for Best Motion Picture at the Edgar Allan Poe Awards the same year. Additionally, Margot Kidder won the Best Performance by a Lead Actress Award at the 1975 Canadian Film Awards, while Kenneth Heeley-Ray won the Best Sound Editing (Feature) Award at the same ceremony.

The film was remade in 2006 by director Glen Wong. Also entitled *Black Christmas* (though abbreviated to *Black X-Mas* in the film's publicity posters), Wong's movie took a dramatically different approach to Clark's original, not only identifying the killer but giving him a detailed (and somewhat convoluted) backstory in order to more fully explain Billy's crimes. The film also beefed up the Christmas connection to the murders; in Wong's remake, the festive season is not simply the backdrop to the killings, but actually responsible (in a roundabout way) for the prowler's motivation. Andrea Martin – who played Phyl in the earlier movie – is recast as house mother Mrs Mac, but otherwise the remake featured an entirely new cast of actors (and characters) which included Michelle Trachtenberg, Katie Cassidy, Lacey Chabert and Oliver Hudson. The remake did, however, also raise the unavoidable question as to whether it may have been better for Billy and Agnes's identities to have remained an inexplicable mystery: the additional information about the killer's *modus operandi* seemed to greatly lessen the impact of the film's suspense rather than enhancing it. Reviews of the remake were very uneven at the time of its release, ranging from the lukewarm to the decidedly unsympathetic.

Following the success of the new film, another sequel was released in 2019. Also entitled *Black Christmas*, this movie was helmed by director Sophia Takal and starred Imogen Poots, Aleyse Shannon and Brittany O'Grady, along with Cary Elwes in the role of Professor Gelson. This second sequel was to completely abandon the original film's premise, instead focusing on a new cast of characters and a serial killer that was entirely unrelated to Billy from the Bob Clark feature. It also contained a more stridently feminist subtext which updated and built on some of the themes from the 1974 film. Like Glen Wong's earlier sequel, the 2019 version of *Black Christmas* was a commercial success, but it similarly met with mixed reviews from critics.

For an overwhelming majority of viewers, however, Bob Clark's original *Black Christmas* is forever likely to be the definitive version of the story, due to the movie's firmly-held popularity amongst cult horror fans and the continuing interest being generated via repeat viewings and releases on home video formats. Today the film's significance to the slasher horror subgenre cannot be overstated, and it is viewed by many commentators as an important evolutionary link between proto-slasher films such as *Peeping Tom* (Michael Powell, 1959),

Psycho (Alfred Hitchcock, 1960) and *Bay of Blood* (Mario Bava, 1971) and the many later entries in this category of movie including *Friday the 13th* (Sean S. Cunningham, 1980), *Prom Night* (Paul Lynch, 1980), and *A Nightmare on Elm Street* (Wes Craven, 1984). As Jeffrey M. Anderson has observed, the film succeeds largely because, far from being content to exist merely as an excellent exponent of nascent slasher suspense, it seems determined to carve its own niche in cult Christmas cinema as much as it does in the horror genre: 'This dark holiday classic ranks as one of the screen's very first slasher flicks. I love it because it understands the concept of maneuvering between relaxing scenes and frightening scenes, and what better time to relax than at Christmas (in a sorority house, with lots of booze)? [...] In spite of itself, it has become a holiday favorite of mine'.[15] Naturally, the film's impact was even more profound in terms of the less-well-populated Christmas horror movie subgenre. *Black Christmas* has had a major impact in this field, its profile firmly eclipsing other early Christmas horror features of the same decade and subsequently influencing many later films such as *Christmas Evil* (Lewis Jackson, 1980), *To All a Good Night* (David Hess, 1980), *Silent Night, Deadly Night* (Charles E. Sellier Jr., 1984) and *Don't Open Till Christmas* (Edmund Purdom, 1984).

There is no doubting that *Black Christmas* is a film that demands attention. The iconic poster image of the suffocated Clare, a sheet of transparent plastic wrapped around her face as she lies slumped in a rocking chair, was a striking precursor to later horror imagery such as the blood-stained hockey mask of *Friday the 13th* and Freddy Kreuger's infamously lethal bladed metal glove in *A Nightmare on Elm Street*. Not only was the film to spawn dozens of imitations and spark inspiration for many other directors and screenwriters in the coming years, but it had proven to be among the most ingenious and influential Christmas films of the 1970s.

Black Christmas offered a unique perspective on the relevance of Christmas cinema in the seventies, illustrating with great creative verve how the genre could be subverted to explore darker themes. The movie deviated from the traditional, heart-warming Christmas narratives that had become firmly established in popular cinema. Instead of celebrating family, friendship and communal companionship, it instead employs the holiday setting to heighten its horror elements, suggesting that not all Christmas stories needed to be cheerful and light-hearted. This subversion reflected a more widespread trend throughout 1970s cinema, where filmmakers often explored more mature and complex themes. The film tapped into the anxieties and fears prevalent right across the seventies, including distrust in authority figures, the threat of violence and the breakdown of the previously-sacrosanct nuclear family unit. By setting the horror within the familiar and supposedly safe context of a Christmas celebration, the film reflected and emphasised these societal concerns, making them more palpable and relatable to the audience.

Because *Black Christmas* has come to be considered one of the earliest examples of the slasher genre, predating more famous entries like *Halloween*, its success demonstrated that horror could be effectively combined with other genres, and this of course included Christmas films. This experimental innovation opened the door for future films to blend horror with other genres and settings, greatly expanding the possibilities of horror cinema. The film's critical success and longevity amongst cult movie aficionados indicated a cultural shift in how Christmas media was being perceived; while traditional

Christmas movies focused on joy, companionship and miracles, *Black Christmas* showed that audiences were also interested in stories that used a festive milieu to propagate suspense and horror. This shift paved the way for more diverse and unconventional Christmas-themed movies in the future, and highlighted a significant moment in the evolution of Christmas cinema during the 1970s. More than most films of the period, it showcased very clearly how the holiday season could be used as a setting for a wide range of narratives, including those that challenged traditional expectations and contemplated contemporary societal issues.

REFERENCES

1. Noel Murray, '*Black Christmas*', in *The Onion A.V. Club*, 13 December 2006.
   <https://www.avclub.com/black-christmas-1798202200>

2. Kim Newman, *Nightmare Movies: Horror on Screen Since the 1960s*, rev. edn (London: Bloomsbury, 2011), p.200.

3. Peter Hanson, '*Black Christmas*', in *Every '70s Movie*, 6 March 2011.
   <https://every70smovie.blogspot.com/2011/03/black-christmas-1974.html>

4. Andrew Patrick Nelson, 'Traumatic Childhood Now Included: Todorov's Fantastic and the Uncanny Slasher Remake', in *American Horror Film: The Genre at the Turn of the Millennium*, ed. by Steffen Hantke (Jackson: University Press of Mississippi, 2010), 103-118, p.111.

5. Nina Nesseth, *Nightmare Fuel: The Science of Horror Films* (New York: Tor Publishing Group, 2022), p.72.

6. John Kenneth Muir, *Horror Films of the 1970s* (Jefferson: McFarland, 2012), p.315.

7. Jeff Kuykendall, '*Black Christmas*', in *Midnight Only*, 17 December 2016.
   <https://www.midnightonly.com/2016/12/17/black-christmas-1974/>

8. Bartlomiej Paszylk, *The Pleasure and Pain of Cult Horror Films: An Historical Survey* (Jefferson: McFarland, 2009), pp.135-36.

9. Anon., '*Black Christmas*', in *Variety*, 31 December 1974.
   <https://variety.com/1973/film/reviews/black-christmas-1200423278/>

10. A.H. Weiler, 'Screen: Murky Whodunit: *Black Christmas* is at Local Theaters', in *The New York Times*, 20 October 1975.
    <https://www.nytimes.com/1975/10/20/archives/screen-murky-whodunitblack-christmas-is-at-local-theaters.html>

11. Kevin Thomas, 'Gothic Tale of a *Black Christmas*', in *The Los Angeles Times*, 6 August 1975, p.12.

12. Mike Long, '*Black Christmas*', in *DVD Sleuth*, 12 November 2008.
    <https://www.dvdsleuth.com/BlackChristmasReivew/>

13. Gary Panton, '*Black Christmas*', in *Movie Gazette*, 30 December 2003.
    <https://movie-gazette.com/577>

14. Anthony Arrigo, '*Black Christmas*: Collector's Edition', in *DVD Compare*, 9 January 2017.
    <https://dvdcompare.net/review.php?rid=4557>

15. Jeffrey M. Anderson, '*Black Christmas*: Slay Bells', in *Combustible Celluloid*, 2006.
    <https://www.combustiblecelluloid.com/classic/blackxmas.shtml>

12

The Silent Partner (1978)

Carolco Pictures

Director: Daryl Duke
Producers: Joel B. Michaels and Stephen Young
Screenwriter: Curtis Hanson,
from a novel by Anders Bodelsen

THE seventies was a decade which saw something of a boom period for the thriller movie genre. Boasting unforgettable suspense classics such as *The Parallax View* (Alan J. Pakula, 1974), *The Conversation* (Francis Ford Coppola, 1974), *Chinatown* (Roman Polanski, 1974), *Dog Day Afternoon* (Sidney Lumet, 1975) and *Taxi Driver* (Martin Scorsese, 1976), it was a period that truly raised the bar when it came to the quality and depth of the features being presented by the studios of the time. These films explored diverse topics ranging from media exploitation to psychological breakdown, by way of complex subtexts including the power dynamics of law enforcement and the differing social causes of criminality. However, what has been less discussed is how many excellent thrillers of the 1970s featured sequences which depicted the atmosphere and iconography of the festive season. Prominent movies including *The French Connection* (William Friedkin, 1971) and *Eyes of Laura Mars* (Irvin

Kershner, 1978) would draw upon wintery environments and/or yuletide elements, sometimes in a low-key manner, to contrast the holiday spirit with dark, suspenseful plots. This often succeeded in creating an unsettling atmosphere, typical of the wider thriller genre, or to provide a layer of irony or tension to already suspenseful plots. Key to this strategy were films such as *Three Days of the Condor* (Sydney Pollack, 1975), which combined a highly intricate conspiracy plot with a frosty, holiday season ambience that greatly enhanced its extensive filming around famous New York and Washington D.C. locations. The film's insightful and deviously paranoid narrative is only heightened by being set against the deceptively comforting backdrop of Christmas in these iconic American cities, deliberately contrasting the season of joy and goodwill with suspicion, threats and mistrust to striking effect.

One of the most prominent Christmas-set thrillers of the decade, and certainly one of the most memorable, was Daryl Duke's *The Silent Partner* (1978). Though set over the holiday season, the film was most certainly no conventional slice of festive cinema, and its content was far more likely to evoke nail-biting suspense than a sense of warm goodwill. (As Alan-Bertaneisson Jones has remarked so accurately, while *The Silent Partner* 'was not a Christmas Horror Movie; it did feature one of the nastiest realistic characters in a Santa suit you are ever likely to see'.[1]) *The Silent Partner*'s story was based upon a 1969 novel entitled *Think of a Number* (*Tænk på et tal*) by Danish author Anders Bodelsen, which had already been adapted for the big screen as the Denmark-based production *Tænk på et tal* (Palle Kjærulff-Schmidt, 1970), starring Henning Moritzen, Bibi Andersson and Peter Ronild, and then as a West German TV movie entitled *Der Amateur*

(Rainer Erler, 1972) which had featured Klaus Herm, Edith Schultze-Westrum and Will Danin. Some years later, the American film-maker Curtis Hanson wrote his own English language screenplay based on the events of Bodelsen's novel, transferring the action to contemporary North America. His hope had been to find a production deal to helm the screenplay himself, but in the end directorial duties were assigned to experienced Canadian film-maker Daryl Duke.

By the late seventies, Duke had enjoyed a long-established career in the director's chair, being most prolific in the television industry where he had skippered episodes of series such as *Wojeck* (1966), *Night Gallery* (1970) and *Banacek* (1972), in addition to well-regarded TV movies including *I Heard the Owl Call My Name* (1973) and *The President's Plane Is Missing* (1973). He would later go on to global acclaim thanks to his critically-acclaimed work on famed drama miniseries *The Thorn Birds* (1983), starring Richard Chamberlain and Rachel Ward. In cinema, he had directed country music drama *Payday* (1973), written by Don Carpenter and featuring Rip Torn, and in later years would helm high school tale *Hard Feelings* (1982) and James Clavell novel adaptation *Tai-Pan* (1986).

There was to be some creative turbulence behind the scenes of *The Silent Partner*, where Duke found himself in artistic disagreement with the producers over certain more extreme sequences of violence which he refused to film near the end of the production. As Sam Panico has observed, the resulting disharmony ultimately led to a change in the occupant of the director's chair late in the production's lifespan: 'Based on the Anders Bodelsen novel *Think of a Number*, this Daryl Duke-directed (*The Thorn Birds*) and Curtis Hanson-written [feature] was an early Carolco film and also one of the earliest films to take advantage of Canada's Capital Cost Allowance incentive plan, which gave production companies tax inducements to make commercial films in Canada. It's probably the best-regarded film to ever take advantage of that tax shelter, as most are the slashers that we love. [...] Duke walked off the film due to creative differences and Hanson, who had originally wanted to direct the film, took over the remainder of the shoot and handled all the post-production on the film'.[2] Though *The Silent Partner* took place early in his career, Hanson had already gained considerable writing and directorial experience at the time of the film's production. He had been the co-writer (along with Henry Rosenbaum and Ronald Silkosky) of Lovecraftian horror movie *The Dunwich Horror* (Daniel Haller, 1970), and would later write, produce and direct the garish thriller *Sweet Kill* (1973). However, in later years he would go on to far greater success as a result of directing high-profile features including *The Hand that Rocks the Cradle* (1992), *The River Wild* (1994) and *L.A. Confidential* (1997). During his illustrious career, he was conferred the Academy Award for Best Writing: Screenplay Based on Material Previously Produced or Published (for *L.A. Confidential*), in addition to nominations for the BAFTA Film Awards, Golden Globe Awards, Primetime Emmy Awards, and the Palme d'Or Award at the Cannes Film Festival. As a result of Duke's late-in-the-day departure from the production of *The Silent Partner*, Hanson was asked to take the directorial reins of the remainder of the movie, including the pick-up shots and supervising all of the post-production process.

The Silent Partner was one of the first features to be produced by Carolco Pictures, and was also a production which would make use of the tax shelter potential of filming in Canada under the auspices of the Capital Cost Allowance

(CCA) incentive plan – an arrangement which was to make the country a popular destination for film-makers from the 1970s onwards. The film was also noteworthy for featuring a very early appearance by popular Canadian actor-comedian John Candy (only 28 years old at the time of the movie's release) and for featuring music by Oscar Peterson, a giant of the jazz music world. While Peterson is credited as the composer of the feature's original score, however, there has been disagreement over the full extent of his involvement, with Derrick Bang noting that '*The Silent Partner* (1978) is an ingeniously twisty crime thriller: a rare case where Curtis Hanson's script is vastly superior to *Think of a Number*, the 1968 Anders Bodelsen novel on which the film is based. It's also the only feature film scored by famed jazz pianist Oscar Peterson... except that he *didn't* score it, contrary to the on-screen credits and every reference source from IMDB downward. He wrote several key themes, but the actual score was composed by Ken Wannberg, misleadingly credited as conductor and music arranger'.[3]

The Christmas shopping season is well underway at the bustling Eaton Centre shopping mall in Toronto. Various costumed Santa Clauses, collecting for charity, can be seen in abundance as customers mill around in search of festive purchases. One particularly intense Santa (Christopher Plummer) has taken up a position outside the branch of a bank, deep within the mall, and seems to be watching the comings and goings of consumers very carefully. Inside, the staff busy themselves as they work their way through the seemingly-endless queue of clients. Among the bank's clerks is industrious administrator Miles Cullen (Elliott Gould), the branch's vault teller. After business is over, Miles asks his similarly-fatigued colleague Julie Carver (Susannah York) if she would like to join him for a drink, but his advances are politely rebuffed. As he laments his lack of good fortune on the dating front, Miles notices – with some alarm – a note written on a discarded bank deposit slip which demands the staff's compliance in an armed hold-up. As there is obviously no such crime in progress, he deduces that the note was intended to be presented to a clerk to ensure their acquiescence, but for some reason had been abandoned before the offence had actually taken place.

Before Miles can ruminate any further on what this might mean, the bank's self-important manager, Charles Packard (Michael Kirby), tells him that he must make an unexpected visit home, and asks if he will take Julie to nearby hotel and keep her company until Packard is able to join her. Miles thus unavoidably deduces that Julie and the branch manager are having an affair. He and Julie pay a brief visit to an aquarium, where Miles reveals his interest in keeping fish and fulfils a personal ambition by purchasing an graceful angel fish, before they head on to the hotel bar. There, they have an awkward conversation about the affair between Packard and Julie, and the latter more fully determines that Miles has an interest in her. She reveals that the relationship between her and their branch manager is not long established, and questions whether his interest in the topic is driven by ethical objections or the fact that she is romancing their boss and not Miles himself. Teasingly, Julie points out that an element of risk is what drives life – while she admittedly can't be certain of where this relationship will take her (emotionally or professionally), she considers the insecurity and excitement preferable to Miles's unadventurous existence looking after pet fish. This makes him think, and – just as soon as Packard arrives – Miles respectfully excuses himself to leave the pair alone.

The contemplative clerk takes the subway home, but can't put his concerns to rest about the discarded hold-up note that he accidentally discovered at the branch. The next morning, Packard admonishes Miles for the amount of cash that is being held on the bank floor – even given the increased demand given the approach to Christmas, around $35,000 had been present in the branch the previous day, which the manager feels should have been more efficiently and adequately secured. As an afterthought, Packard explains that he and his wife will be holding a Christmas party at the weekend, and that he would like to invite all of the staff members. However, he requests that Julie accompany Miles to the event in order to avoid raising any suspicion with Packard's wife. Meekly, the clerk agrees to aid in the subterfuge.

Later, as Miles talks with his colleague Simonson (John Candy), Julie surreptitiously discusses the vault teller with newly-arrived fellow clerk Louise (Gail Dahms). The latter woman expresses a vague interest in him, believing the tall, stoic Miles to be dapper and enigmatic. However, Julie wards her off the idea, explaining that he is actually more dull and pedestrian than he appears. Still feeling despondent over his lack of a love life, Miles takes a short break and wanders the mall near the bank. There, he spots the suspicious Santa Claus collecting for charity next to the branch and immediately notices that he has a sign encouraging donations which has been inscribed in handwriting that exactly matches the hold-up note Miles discovered the previous day. Miles also notices that this mysterious Santa is still keeping a very close watch on the movements of the bank's clientele.

Spotting the arrival of local business owner Mr Fogelman (Jack Duffy), Miles rapidly returns to the branch to take deposit of his $4,206 in revenue. Immediately afterwards, the secretive man in the Santa Claus enters the branch and writes an ominous-looking note on a bank deposit slip. Before he can approach the bank counter, however, he is intercepted by an excitable young boy (Jimmy Davidson) who insistently tells him about the gifts he wants for Christmas. Clearly irritated, the sinister Santa realises that he has attracted too much attention to carry out the crime, and he rapidly departs the branch. Miles, realising exactly what has happened, watches this interaction very closely.

Later, once he has returned home, Miles plays a game of chess against himself (as damning an allegory for personal loneliness as it is possible to imagine). Unable to shake his worries about the disturbing behaviour of the sham Santa Claus, he phones Julie to discuss the matter but discovers that she is with Packard, making discussion impossible. Frustrated, he knocks the pieces from his chessboard in anger... but on replacing them, he realises that he has unwittingly become a pawn rather than a major character in the game. Determined to change that fact, he digs out an old metal lunchbox and discovers that it has capacity to fit a precise number of banknotes. He then covertly stashes it away in his business briefcase.

The next morning, before the bank opens, Miles manages to secretly stuff the lunchbox full of cash from various previous deposits that have not yet been placed in the branch's vault. He manages to achieve this with no-one noticing, even though he is interrupted by Julie's unexpected request for a seasonal kiss beneath a sprig of mistletoe. Sure enough, the malevolent Santa Claus arrives in the mall just in time for the branch opening, though Miles – anticipating what will happen – keeps the misappropriated cash out of everyone's line of sight, innocuously hidden in the battered old lunchbox. At lunchtime, Fogelman returns with another large deposit from his business. Miles fills in an accurate deposit slip but then stashes the additional money in his lunchbox, leaving only a token amount in the bank's actual coffers. Sure enough, Santa appears in the branch exactly when Miles expected and uses a deposit note to demand all of the cash. The pressured clerk gathers all of the notes from his counter (conspicuously not including the contents of the hidden lunchbox), which Santa quickly stuffs into the pockets of his costume. However, this decidedly unjolly St Nick is still not satisfied: he had just seen Fogelman depositing a large amount of banknotes at that very counter, and is all too aware that the amount handed over by Miles comes nowhere near to matching it. At this point the bank's alarm goes off (triggered by Miles in an unseen manoeuvre), leading the security guard to pursue a fleeing Santa from the branch. Gunplay ensues as the fugitive races through the mall, commandeers a car near the entrance, and makes a fast getaway from the crime scene.

Miles and Julie are later interviewed by the local police about the robbery. Miles immediately spots the criminal responsible for the hold-up in a pile of police suspect photographs, but deliberately misidentifies the culprit to throw the police off the scent. The officer in charge of the investigation, Detective Willard (Ken Pogue), is suspicious that Miles hadn't alerted them sooner; once the bank alarm is triggered, the police are immediately informed and a closed-circuit camera is activated to help identify the robber. In each clerk's case, a hidden circuit is activated by removing a clip full of money from the cash drawer, but curiously Miles had already given several lower-denomination banknotes to the criminal before initiating the alarm. Julie points out that as operations manager at the branch, only she was aware of the robbery taking place just before the alarm sounded, and she explains that Miles's hesitancy was no doubt exacerbated by being held at gunpoint. The police are unconvinced, noting that the robber's pistol was still concealed at that stage of the hold-up, but Miles is able to dodge their reservations thanks to the threat of gunfire that had been scribbled by the criminal on one of the bank's deposit slips.

As Miles signs his witness statement, the detective again voices uncertainty over his account of proceedings. Why would the robber have hit his specific counter, where around $50,000 was being stored, when no other clerk in the bank would have had access to that level of cash? (Clearly Miles has reported the contents of his lunchbox – the previous and present day's transactions – as cash stolen in the robbery, along with the money that was actually taken by the felon.) Unruffled, Miles replies that every client who comes to the bank is aware that he is the vault teller; it is no secret that he would have more banknotes at his work station than any other employee. Grimly, Willard reflects that the flawless precision of the crime suggests that they are dealing with a professional crook and not an opportunistic amateur. Almost as an afterthought, the detective reminds Miles not to forget to collect his briefcase as he leaves the station – completely unaware of its contents. On the way home, Julie tells Miles that she has found the day's events to be an exhilarating departure from their usual humdrum workday. He smiles inscrutably, knowing only too well that he has outsmarted not only the felon but also his employers.

At a bar and nightclub in the city named the Silver Dollar Room, the Santa Claus robber – now revealed to be a violent professional thief named Harry Reikle – watches with aloof interest as a local TV news report recounts the details of the bank raid. However, his glacial calm soon turns to psychotic fury when he discovers that the actual amount reported stolen was $48,350, knowing that he had taken only a tiny fraction of that total. Belatedly realising what has happened, he becomes incensed and subjects a random woman (Nancy Simmonds) to a brutally vicious, misogynistic beating in a sauna, almost killing her in the process simply to sadistically vent his frustrations. This unprovoked savagery shocks the club's patrons. Unfortunately for Miles, as his face has been all over the news reports, it is very obvious who the eventual target of Reikle's violent exasperation is set to be.

Back at his apartment, Miles is meticulously separating the stolen cash into neat bundles and disguising the banknotes in makeshift cloth covers for concealment. Upon returning to work the next day, he discovers that he has become something of a minor celebrity, with clients queuing up to congratulate him on his TV and press appearances. Uncomfortable with all of the attention, Miles asks Packard if he can switch places with Julie for the day. As she takes up the customer-facing vault teller's position, Miles asks her for the keys to the safety deposit box receipts. In reality, however, he also surreptitiously swipes the master key for the strongboxes in the process. A customer (Nuala Fitzgerald) asks to be given access to her safety deposit box at the branch, but after Miles unlocks the relevant unit for her, he also (unseen by anyone) gains entry to an empty deposit box and stashes away all of the stolen money from the day before. By the time the customer is ready to leave the vault, there is no visual trace whatsoever of

Miles's furtive activity. Once home, he secretes the deposit box key in a half-eaten jar of jam in his fridge.

Miles pays a visit to his elderly father, who is being cared for in a nursing home. However, the older man is in the end stages of dementia and isn't even aware of his son's presence in the room, much less his identity. Miles then collects Julie, as arranged, to take her to Packard's Christmas party. Calling on her at her upmarket apartment, he spots a present from the bank manager with a label that makes clear the romantic attachment between the pair is still ongoing. They drive to Packard's classy suburban home, and Miles discovers that his colleagues Simonson and Louise are now an item too. He finds, to his discomfort, that he is a *cause celebre* at the party, with everyone keen to know how he managed to comport himself so calmly during the bank robbery. Jokingly, the guests ask what they would do if they had nearly $50,000 of other people's money to spend, but the diffident Miles simply replies that he would deposit it all in the bank for safety... though perhaps he might buy a blowfish for his aquarium first. During a dance with Packard's world-weary wife Vivien (Charlotte Blunt), Miles admits that he believes he has angered the branch manager by failing to foil the robbery sooner, but she simply shrugs off his concerns by telling him that her husband will learn to live with the reality of it.

Driving Julie back from the party, Miles has a frank conversation with his colleague and asks her if she is really in love with Packard. She replies that she doesn't really know one way or the other, and reflects that Vivien is almost certainly aware of her husband's various infidelities but has probably just come to expect it of him by now. Miles invites her to his apartment for a drink, and she reveals that the events of the past few days have made her see him in a different light; she has underestimated his versatility and courage under fire. She discloses the fact that she reciprocates his long-held affection for her, and they kiss. Just as the situation becomes more intimate, the phone rings. It is Reikle, who indirectly reveals that he is fully aware of Miles's deception. Miles hangs up and leaves the phone receiver off the hook, but finds that romance is suddenly the last thing on his mind. He breaks off the tryst, reasoning that they have both had a lot to drink and may come to regret it later. Julie is hurt by his change of heart, and can't understand his strange *volte-face*.

Miles drops Julie off at home (still seething at his inexplicable behaviour), but on returning to his apartment he is panicked to discover that the phone receiver is now back on the hook; clearly someone has gained entry to his home in his absence. The phone rings again, and Reikle reveals in-depth details of the interior of the bank clerk's home, proving that it was he who has broken in. While the criminal claims to admire Miles's ingenuity in outmanoeuvring him, he demands that the clerk return the money that he has kept for himself. Infuriated by the thief's audacity, Miles threatens to call the police, but Reikle asks him exactly what he intends to tell them; after all, he would be able to implicate the clerk in the crime if necessary. Revealing he is armed, he hints that he will be coming after Miles more directly soon, leading him to hurriedly barricade his apartment door. Unperturbed, Reikle continues the conversation through the letterbox, warning the teller that if he doesn't decide to co-operate then he will gain entry to his living space and extract the necessary information he needs via less civilised methods.

At work the next day, Miles finds himself the recipient of an unsubtly threatening postcard from Reikle, followed by a series of increasingly intimidating phone calls. Miles tries to shrug it off, but upon returning to his apartment he discovers that it has been ransacked and his angel fish killed with a knife. Reikle phones once again, and tells Miles that time has run out – they must now negotiate. Miles invites him up to his apartment, but secretly leaves his home via an alternative exit. While the criminal breaks into the clerk's home again, Miles uses a public callbox to ring his own landline and tells Reikle that he will not bargain with him. Displeased at having been outfoxed again, the felon races back out onto the street but can find no trace of Miles.

Little does Reikle know that the hunter has now become the hunted. As he heads to the subway, Miles is in close pursuit, jumping onto the same train and keeping a close eye on Reikle's carriage. He then tracks the thief all the way back to his own home in a run-down part of the city, and – taking note of the address – steals a nearby delivery van when its driver is offloading supplies at a convenience store. Miles then makes an anonymous phone call to the police, disguises his voice and reports the location of the stolen van at Reikle's location. Sure enough, the police arrive and take the livid criminal into custody.

Soon after, Julie and Miles receive calls from the police to say that they have a potential suspect for the robbery in custody; he has been arrested on an unrelated charge, but fits the profile of a professional robber. Sure enough, Reikle is present in the line-up, but Miles – knowing that he could be implicated in stealing the misplaced proceeds from the robbery – again lies that he doesn't recognise him as the thief from the bank. Detective Willard explains that the police were already looking for Reikle on account of his recent physical and sexual assault on the woman at the sauna, meaning that he is set to face serious charges for his indefensibly savage behaviour.

On leaving the police station, Miles again asks Julie out to dinner, but she is still hurt and confused over his suddenly standoffish behaviour after Packard's party. She coldly refuses his offer, and tells him curtly that she now considers him nothing more than one of her work colleagues. The security officer at the bank (Sean Sullivan), who has also been called to the station as a witness, wishes Miles a happy Christmas Eve as he leaves. The greeting seems to take the clerk aback slightly; having faced so much emotional turmoil over the past few days, the festivities have been the last thing on his mind.

A few months come and go, and Miles's father passes away. At the funeral, Miles meets a woman named Elaine (Celine Lomez) who introduces herself by saying that she had worked at the nursing home where his father was cared for. He offers to drive her home, and though their conversation is mainly composed of polite small-talk there is an obvious attraction between the pair. On returning home, Miles becomes alarmed when he discovers that the cleaner he hires, Mrs Evanchuk (Aino Pirskanen), has cleared out the contents of his fridge – including the jam jar with the safety deposit box key concealed within it. Unfortunately for him, the weekly waste collection uplift has just taken place, and he has no way of retrieving the misplaced key.

Back at the bank, Louise notes that the bank is about to open a brand new, heavily-reinforced subterranean vault in the city which will ensure greater safety of its holdings. The building is already under active construction. Miles innocuously mentions to Julie, who supervises the safety deposit boxes, that a customer has reported that they have lost their key and will need access to the contents of their strongbox. Glacially, she tells him that the only way to regain access to a deposit box when its key has been lost is to call in a locksmith.

Perturbed by the recent unexpected events, Miles takes himself to the park to think. There, he encounters Elaine again. She offers him a drink and explains that she expected to find him there because his father had mentioned that he used to bring Miles there as a child. This immediately provokes the clerk's suspicions, knowing that his father had been incommunicative for some time before he died. The pair enjoy each other's company, and eventually Miles invites Elaine to join him for dinner at a restaurant in the city. She begins to enquire about the Christmas robbery and how Miles had dealt with it, stating that his father had been very proud about the courage his son had shown. Elaine reveals that she had fallen for Miles when seeing his calm and collected demeanour on television. He offers to drop her off for her night-shift, but she reveals that she no longer works at the nursing home. Instead, Elaine is now a waitress in the employ of the Silver Dollar Room – Reikle's preferred hangout, though this is unknown to Miles.

As he enjoys a drink alongside the other clientele of the Silver Dollar Room, Miles decides on a whim to ask Elaine to be his guest at a marriage. The wedding he refers to is between his bank colleagues Louise and Simonson, which takes place a few days later. Following the ceremony, the happy couple enjoys a seaside reception at the beach. Simonson remarks that he is disappointed that their boss, Packard, didn't bother to attend in spite of being invited. Miles also points out that the branch will be very quiet while the newlyweds are away on honeymoon. Julie, who is also a guest, can't help but observe that Miles is accompanied by a beautiful young stranger, but he is reluctant to share any details about her, leading to some quiet speculation amongst his co-workers. By the time a polka band is accompanying the departure of the bride and groom, Miles and Elaine are already far away from the crowd, discussing plans for their own future.

Elaine heads back with Miles after the wedding, and the pair spend the night together. Later, however, he confronts her with some awkward truths. Distrustful of her story, he had called the nursing home, but no-one there had ever heard of her. If she hadn't known his father, why was she at his funeral... and how then had she deduced that Miles would later be at the park? Elaine reveals that she is really an associate of Reikle, who has entrusted her with keeping an eye on Miles while the thief is in prison. Reikle's hope was that the clerk would open up to Elaine and reveal the whereabouts of the stolen cash. However, Miles had quickly deduced the truth about Elaine, but was unwilling to reveal the connections he had drawn because he had genuinely become attracted to her. She laughs, realising not only that Miles had outsmarted Reikle but also that he has now outmanoeuvred her, too. Rather than simply playing a part in Reikle's game, her affection for the seemingly-innocuous bank clerk is genuine.

Elaine visits the cold-blooded Reikle in prison and lies that Miles has no clue about her real identity. The hardened criminal seems unconvinced by her assurances, and asks if she has managed to ascertain the location of the robbery cash yet. Elaine tells him that it is too early to extract that kind of information, but that she will continue to gain Miles's trust until he reveals everything. Infuriated, Reikle dismisses her, but grudgingly admits that Miles is a craftier adversary than he seems from his bland exterior.

When lunch hour arrives at the bank, Miles relieves Julie to allow her to have a break. He is surprised when she asks him to join her, suggesting a thaw in relations, but he politely declines. Elaine arrives, heavily disguised, and pretends to be the holder of the safety deposit box containing the stolen money. Knowing that he has only a narrow window of time until she returns, Miles responds that they will need to call in a locksmith given that she has 'lost' the key to the strongbox – the only way to open one of the units is to use the bank's key and the client's key at the same time. Packard, who is clearly attracted to Elaine, arrives to check that the procedure is being followed correctly (much to Miles's discomfort). The manager suggests waiting until Julie returns, but Elaine insists that action is taken immediately, claiming that her safety deposit box contains letters of a personal nature that she must access without delay. Convinced by her urgency, Packard authorises Miles to call in the locksmith.

Half an hour later, jovial locksmith Mr Perlman (Guy Sanvido) arrives as requested. Miles has become agitated, knowing that Julie is due back soon and keen that she not witness what is going on. The locksmith breaks the lock in no time and quickly works on replacing it with a new one. However, Miles panics on two fronts: Packard is paying much closer attention to the operation than he would like, and Elaine tries to stash the money into her handbag rather than returning it to the strongbox. She is annoyed when he insists on putting every note back where it came from, and – given her inability to stick to his plans – he is now apprehensive of trusting her with the key.

As Elaine is leaving, Packard holds up her departure by making a flirtatious effort to encourage her to make more use of the bank's services. This means that Julie's return to the branch overlaps with Elaine's exit, causing him to desperately improvise. Telling his confused colleague that they have denied each other's feelings for too long, he passionately kisses her – though this doesn't faze the departing Elaine, who knows that it is all part of the diversion. Taken aback by the sudden reignition of his romantic advances, Julie suggests that they meet that night after work, but Miles tells her that he isn't available... and what's more, she is going to be late in returning to her desk after lunch. Stupefied, Julie seems genuinely lost for words at his latest inexplicable turnaround in attitude.

Over a romantic meal at a restaurant that evening, Miles reveals to Elaine that he intends to split the money three ways with Reikle following his release from prison; one third will go to the thief, one third to Elaine, and he will retain the last third himself. Elaine laughs at his naïveté, pointing out that Reikle has killed before and will not hesitate to do so again. No matter what Miles proposes, the criminal will not rest until he has taken every penny of the stolen cash for himself. Miles is surprised by her attitude: if she knows that Reikle is so dangerous, why is she willing to risk her own safety (and perhaps her life) in order to romance a humble bank clerk instead? She replies that she needs change in her life, and believes that Miles might be the best way to achieve it. Having bested their adversary twice, he may just have the ability to do so one last time.

Elaine leaves the table to freshen up, but is shocked when she comes face-to-face with none other than Reikle. One of his other associates had managed to coerce the victim of his earlier violent crime into convincing the police that she had lied about the brutal cruelty that Reikle had perpetrated against her, giving the police no choice but to drop the charges. He immediately picks up on the fact that far from being pleased to see him, Elaine is alarmed and terrified by his presence.

While Miles remains at the restaurant table, puzzled by the amount of time his dinner partner has been absent, Reikle drives Elaine to the clerk's apartment and promptly trashes the place in a bout of rage. Elaine reveals that she has fallen in love with Miles and no longer fears Reikle's sadistic excesses. His suspicions confirmed, the vicious criminal repeatedly beats her and attempts to drown her in Miles's aquarium. When she breaks free, he goes into an enraged frenzy and smashes the fish-tank, then gores Elaine's neck on the shattered glass.

Shortly afterwards, Miles – who is still confused at Elaine's absence – returns home to hear the phone ringing in his apartment. He answers it to hear Reikle laughing hysterically... but then realises, to his horror, that Elaine's decapitated head is floating in what remains of his aquarium, her lifeless body crumpled beside it. As he suspected, Reikle is once again in the phone booth outside, amused at the teller's discomfort. Furious, Miles races to confront him, but the criminal is long gone. On returning to his apartment, he hears the phone ringing again – but this time it is Julie, concerned for his wellbeing after their erratic encounter earlier in the day. Miles manages to assuage her anxieties, but notices as he does so that Elaine had managed to hide the key to the safety deposit box on one of the pieces of his chess set before her murder, suggesting that Reikle still has no clue where the stolen money is being hidden.

Left with little choice, Miles embarks on the grisly task of removing Elaine's severed head from his shattered fish tank. He then conceals the body by wrapping it in his living room rug, covertly removes it from the apartment building (only narrowly avoiding the prying eyes of a newspaper delivery boy), and places it stealthily in the foundations of the new bank vault which he knows will soon be safely covered in concrete. As he removes himself from the scene, dishevelled and still numbed by shock, Miles realises that his disposal of the body has been witnessed from nearby by Reikle. The criminal again congratulates him on his intelligence, but notices that Miles has injured his leg in a fall from his apartment building while trying to avoid notice. By now, however, the once-meek clerk has had enough. When Reikle yet again threatens to murder him, Miles tells him that the money is being stored safely at the bank – and only he has access to it. The thief demands that it be withdrawn and given to him that night, but Miles has other ideas. He instead tells the thief that he must come to his counter at the bank, just as he did at Christmas when dressed as Santa Claus, and he will hand over all of the money knowing that he can't be as easily killed when surrounded by witnesses. Reikle knows when he's facing an impasse and reluctantly agrees to Miles's terms. As Reikle comments, they are both unwilling partners in this scheme, after all. In return, the clerk tells him in no uncertain terms that if he ever sees the criminal again once he has received the stolen money, it is *he* who will murder *him*.

Without time to change his clothes or freshen up his appearance, Miles heads to the bank before opening time and asks Julie to give him access to the safety deposit box. True to his word, he empties it of the cash and stores all of it in his briefcase. Julie is nonplussed, never having realised that Miles had valuables stored at the bank, and is suspicious of the sudden weight of his briefcase. The clerk is interrupted by Packard, who pompously dresses him down for his unkempt appearance and slovenly attitude. In response, Miles declares that he is leaving his job at the bank – and offers Julie the chance to join him.

Right on cue, Reikle arrives at the mall. He is smartly dressed as a middle-aged woman, keen to avoid being recognised by anyone as the felonious Santa who visited the branch at Christmas. He waits patiently in the queue once the bank opens, then angrily demands that Miles hold up his end of the bargain. The clerk does as he is asked and hands over the stolen money. Sneeringly, Reikle tells him that the game isn't over yet: eventually, he will find Miles and kill him for having dared to defy him for so long. In response, the clerk calmly passes him a deposit slip... upon which is scrawled a demand (in Reikle's own handwriting) to hand over the money or face the consequences. The robber discovers, to his dismay, that he has been set up for the third and final time. Miles triggers the alarm, and an incensed Reikle fires at point blank range with a gun concealed in his handbag. The security guard, however, is determined not to be outflanked again and shoots at Reikle, killing him as he attempts to flee the mall. As the felon dies on an escalator, he tries to tell the guard – with some incredulity – that Miles had given him the money from the bank, but not his own. The security man is baffled by his cryptic, dying words.

Injured by a flesh wound in his shoulder from Reikle's attack, Miles stumbles to the branch's doorway to be sure that his menacing adversary is finally dead at last. Julie calls for an ambulance to attend to her injured colleague, just as the police arrive and discover that Reikle's handbag contained a mere $2,821 in banknotes. Detective Willard, who recognises the (forged) handwriting on the deposit slip, realises that Reikle had been the same criminal behind the Santa Claus robbery the previous December and wonders why someone would return to the scene of the crime and sacrifice their life for such a relatively modest sum of money.

As Miles is stretchered into an ambulance, Julie hurriedly joins him – bringing his briefcase with her. She is aghast that he would put himself in harm's way against such an obviously dangerous opponent, but he seems content to simply know that he is now out of danger. Knowing that the blood loss is not the result of fatal injury, Miles asks Julie if she has looked inside his case. In response, she tells him that her dream of a more exciting existence may just be about to become a reality. The pair embrace, knowing that a new chapter is about to dawn in both their lives.

While *The Silent Partner* was miles away from a traditional Christmas movie, around half of the film does take place during the holiday season and very skilfully uses it as the background for its suspenseful storyline. While Christmas serves as the setting for the film's opening events, its portrayal in *The Silent Partner* is far from the typical festive cheer associated with the holiday season. Instead, the film uses the contrast between the Christmas festivities and the dark, tense atmosphere of the bank robbery plot in order to create uncertainty, anticipation and intrigue. Furthermore, the film explores themes of deception, greed and moral ambiguity, as Miles becomes increasingly entangled in the web of deceit surrounding Reikle's robbery. The festive season serves as a nerve-wracking backdrop for the characters' actions, highlighting the collocation between the joy and goodwill typically associated with Christmas and the more sinister motives at play within the story. Thus while not exactly a conventional slice of yuletide cinema, the holiday setting adds considerable depth and complexity to the storyline, enhancing the tension and atmosphere of the film while also touching on deeper themes of morality and deception alongside the sometimes incongruous festive environment. All of these qualities in combination made the film a highly distinctive addition to the subgenre of festively-situated thrillers.

Interestingly, for all its association with Christmas due to the nature of the robbery that is central to the plot, it is easy to overlook the fact that in actuality only part of the film is set during the festive season, with the concluding half being situated at Easter instead (as the promotional signs at the bank indicate). Just as Christmas is often depicted as a time of positive change in cinematic narratives, so too is Easter represented as a time of renewal, and this turns out to be the case in *The Silent Partner*. The film does, however, present some profound and problematic moral issues with which it invites viewers to engage. Clearly, the primary theme of the film is greed and the way that it has the capacity to lead an individual headlong into moral corruption. The conflict between Miles and Reikle is driven by a desire to retain what is not rightly theirs. While Reikle is clearly a dangerous criminal psychopath, however, Miles is a mild-mannered bank clerk who finds himself on a slippery ethical slope when he decides to subvert the robber's hold-up to keep the stolen money for himself. Clearly he reasons that if the money has been reported stolen as a result of Reikle's robbery, he has as much right to it as anyone, and thus he refuses to return it to the bank's vault where it rightly belongs. But while, on the face of it, this may seem to the teller as though it is a reasonable justification for his action as a kind of self-awarded recompense for having outwitted the thief, the law-breaking amorality on display ultimately raises the question of whether Miles's motivations are actually any more worthy than Riekle's had been. As Peter Hanson explains, the moral equivocality is just one of the reasons why the film's narrative is so compelling: 'The plot requires a considerable suspension of disbelief, and some viewers may be turned off by the lack of a tangible moral center – even though Harry is a monster, Miles is at the very least a reckless weasel who endangers everyone around him for petty reasons. Yet the movie remains interesting because of its unexpected rhythms and vivid performances'.[4]

It may well be that Miles believes that as the stolen money is large enough to be life-changing for an individual, yet an amount that is easily covered by the bank's insurance, he can attempt to justify his actions by rationalising that it simply won't be missed. (To put the matter into perspective, $50,000 in Canadian dollars in 1978 would be worth $217,168.03 in the present day when inflation is taken into account; at time of writing, that figure is equivalent to £120,997.34 in Pounds Sterling, or $159,755.32 in US dollars.) The reality, of course, is that his self-serving perception of the situation does not make his actions any less criminal in nature. Deception and misdirection thus become key themes throughout the film – not just in terms of characters misleading each other, but in Miles's case, even deceiving himself. It also has an impact on how the characters present themselves, with Reikle using unexpected costumes to mislead the bank staff, public and security cameras, while Miles cheats the robber himself by foreseeing events and stage-managing them to his own advantage by purloining the stolen cash. The narrative thus toys with the concept of duality in fascinating ways. Both Reikle and Miles are strange, distorted reflections of the other, with each man's assumed appearance seeming somewhat different from the reality behind their subterfuge. Miles's cool professionalism as a strait-laced bank teller reveals nothing of his side-line as an amateur thief, while Reikle is a murderous criminal who is given to constant violent and misogynistic excesses, yet hides his identity behind seemingly-benevolent disguises such as Santa Claus to escape detection.

The nature of the duality between the two characters is also reflected in the way that they each deceive others around them in order to achieve their respective aims and safeguard their secrets. This has led some critics, such as Glenn Erickson, to compare the film with classic literature: 'Curtis Hanson's taut script is a variation on [Joseph Conrad's 1909 short story] *The Secret Sharer*, in hard-boiled crime mode. [...] *The Silent Partner* is beautifully paced and plotted with sexy and shocking surprises'.5 The film embarks upon an exploration of the ways in which identity can be a malleable concept, especially when it collides with extreme circumstances. Miles may start the film as an introverted and reserved bank clerk, but – as the narrative progresses and the stakes continue to rise – he eventually metamorphoses into a resourceful and even merciless opponent. His struggle eventually ceases to be about protecting the stolen money and turns into a grudge match simply to stop Reikle from taking possession of it. However, to follow this course of action means putting Elaine at risk (as he again justifies his actions on shaky ethical grounds by reasoning that she was manipulating him before he manipulated her), and even his colleagues are conceivably placed in danger when he lures Reikle back to the bank like a spider ensnaring its prey in a web. Miles's increasingly cold-blooded machinations raise questions about whether anyone, in extreme enough situations, can be transformed into a morally fluid or even treacherous individual, again suggesting that he and Reikle may have more in common than is immediately obvious.

The psychological undercurrent which typifies the battle of wits between Miles and Reikle also raises the complicated subject of crime and punishment. Reikle's criminality is obvious: he is a sociopathic, murdering thief with no moral scruples and very little self-control. Miles, however, is represented very differently. By stealing from his employer, he is unquestionably also breaking the law, but he is not represented as a stereotypical villain. His change of personality makes him arrogant and self-serving, but while he becomes a less sympathetic character, the audience still finds him preferable to the violently sadistic Reikle who is much more obviously depraved and iniquitous. The film thus offers nothing concrete in the way of moral resolution, meaning that viewers must decide for themselves whether Miles is a triumphant everyman or a common criminal who simply has a more respectable façade compared to his cruel adversary. This sense of ethical abstruseness is also suggested by the film's subtle but damning treatment of the justice system, where the police are repeatedly fooled by Miles being one step ahead of their enquiries at all times. Because he anticipates their line of investigation, the fragile boundary between right and wrong is constantly obscured because while Miles is misleading them to keep his grip on the stolen cash, he is also trying to protect himself from Reikle's retribution. By the film's conclusion, it is left to the audience to ask themselves whether Miles deserves to start a new life with the embezzled money or if he should instead face punishment for assuming that criminal actions, if carried out in a way that is ingenious enough to deceive both his employers and the authorities, can be performed with impunity. As Ed Travis observes, 'Literally everything about *The Silent Partner* is good. The peak capitalism setting of a thriving shopping mall and bustling Canadian bank branch during a busy Christmas season is perfect for the total disregard for morality its characters display. [...] It forces us to reckon with matters of conscience, morality, and our nascent capability to go down dark paths at the blink of an eye. It explores not just the thrills and vices that can tempt us to do wrong, but also, as in Cullen's case, the seeming lack of any reason why we take a dark path in the first place'.[6]

As Travis suggests, the Christmas setting of the film becomes important for a number of reasons. The hugely increased number of cash transactions taking place at the height of the festive shopping season means a more lucrative raid for Reikle (something he is clearly gambling on by waiting for the proceeds of nearby businesses to be deposited before initiating the robbery), while the criminal's seemingly-innocuous Santa Claus disguise is the perfect deflection at a time of year where costumed charity collectors are commonplace. Yet *The Silent Partner* also explores personal isolation, loneliness and emotional seclusion – all factors which are inevitably heightened during the festive season, given its close association with family, friendship and community. (Another crime common at Christmas at the time, drink driving, is also addressed: Miles insults Julie by breaking off a romantic *tête-à-tête* with her, arguing that they are both too heavily inebriated to be responsible, and yet staggeringly thinks nothing of driving her home directly afterwards.)

We see in Miles a character who lives a solitary and essentially unsatisfied life, longing for a significant other but unable to initiate a fulfilling romantic relationship – a fact that is not helped by his strange inability to connect with others on an emotional level. This sense of intensified solitude may well help to explain his desire to purloin the bank's money when the opportunity arises: not only does it present him with the opportunity to widen his personal horizons by planning a new life away from his humdrum existence at the bank, but it also gives him the means to transcend the repetitiveness of his monotonous job, making him feel more alive simply by forcing himself to repeatedly improvise in order to evade detection and prosecution.

If Miles feels alienated from his ragtag collection of colleagues, he certainly has no desire to identify with the constantly-threatening Reikle. The psychological confrontation which breaks out between them leads to an endlessly shifting game of intimidation and dishonesty, compelling Miles to continually outsmart his adversary's lethal violence – something he achieves by using precise planning under extreme pressure. These dynamics raise the troubling issue of whether the real power is wielded through the ever-escalating threat of violence (as represented by Reikle), or cunning intellectual resourcefulness (as typified by Miles). Reikle's methodology of control has its origins in belligerence, hostility and aggressive coercion, whereas Miles' aptitude is drawn from brainpower and quick-thinking strategic planning. The film manages to brilliantly challenge traditional notions of power by demonstrating that brute force rarely tends to be the most effective way to achieve the most constructive ends. While Reikle employs fear and intimidation to dominate and terrorise others, Miles quickly discovers how to overcome his apprehension and distress in order to outwit his opponent. It is his capacity to keep a cool head even when facing great danger which eventually gives Miles the ultimate advantage over Reikle, who expects everyone to submit to his thuggish and violent behaviour simply through his malicious force of will.

The Silent Partner is a film densely packed with themes and subtexts, many of them probing into the murkier aspects of what it means to be human – not least the delicate line which lies between respectable people and violent criminals, and the way in which extreme situations can sometimes propel people into unexpected roles or to discover unanticipated depths. The film also toys with expectations in other ways, such as an example of Chekhov's gun in Miles's ornate chess set (which Elaine later uses to conceal the safety deposit box key from Reikle) and his elaborate living room rug (used by Elaine to taunt Reikle, but later employed by Miles to camouflage and dispose of her corpse). Even a seemingly-throwaway remark about the bank's new custom-built vault turns out to be relevant to the plot when Miles uses the building's foundations to hide Elaine's dead body from the authorities, while there is dark irony in the foreshadowing of Elaine reflecting that every time Miles looks at his aquarium, he will be sure to think of her – a prediction which tragically comes true when he is shaken and traumatised at the sight of her severed head floating in the water.

The film is chock full of memorable character moments which are incidental to the main action, including Michael Kirby's philandering bank manager Packard whose behaviour towards Miles becomes increasingly petty as he begins to resent his vault teller's growing popularity with the public. The warm romance between John Candy's Simonson and Gail Dahms's Louise, which plays out in the background, is also a touching counterpoint to the much more complicated relationships which occur between Miles and his two love interests, Susannah York's Julie and Celine Lomez's Elaine. Even those two romances contrast with each other: both women are highly intelligent and independent, yet very different in the dynamic they create with the famously unreadable Miles.

If *The Silent Partner* belongs to anyone, however, it is undoubtedly its two stars who made up the duelling, deadly double act of Miles and Reikle. Elliott Gould gave a bravura performance as the complex everyman Miles Cullen, lending a sense of undeniable believability to proceedings as the character gradually transforms from a commonplace administrator into a fast-thinking criminal tactician fighting for his life. At the time of the production, Gould had achieved major success thanks to performances in *Bob & Carol & Ted & Alice* (Paul Mazursky, 1969), *M*A*S*H* (Robert Altman, 1970) and *The Long Goodbye* (Robert Altman, 1973). Also active on television, during his long career he has been nominated for an Academy Award, two BAFTA Film Awards and a Golden Globe Award, alongside numerous other plaudits. Following the completion of *The Silent Partner*, Gould claimed to have arranged a private screening of the film for Alfred Hitchcock, who reputedly accepted the invitation and enjoyed the thriller's skilfully-crafted suspense.

Christopher Plummer excelled as the highly unpredictable Harry Reikle, alternating effortlessly between the character's charismatic charm and vicious, inhuman savagery. (Reikle also had the singular honour, as many commentators have noted, of being a Santa Claus with such a comprehensive grasp of profanity that he was in constant danger of ending up on his own naughty list.) Active on the stage since the late 1950s, Plummer first appeared on cinema screens in *Stage Struck* (Sidney Lumet, 1958), and then went on to enormous fame thanks to his appearance as Captain Georg von Trapp in *The Sound of Music* (Robert Wise, 1965). Among his many other noteworthy film performances of the time were *The Fall of the Roman Empire* (Anthony Mann, 1964), *Triple Cross* (Terence Young, 1966), *Battle of Britain* (Guy Hamilton, 1969), *Waterloo* (Sergei Bondarchuk, 1970) and *The Man who Would be King* (John Huston, 1975). He won the

Best Supporting Actor Academy Award in 2011 for his performance in *Beginners* (Mike Mills, 2010), and was nominated for the same honour on two other occasions. He also received wins and nominations at the BAFTA Film Awards, Emmy Awards, Golden Globe Awards, Grammy Awards, and several other industry awards ceremonies over the years of his remarkable career.

The Silent Partner also made excellent use of the city of Toronto as a filming location. The Eaton Centre – where much of the action takes place – had first opened its doors in 1977, and the film showcases the then-new location as the major downtown retail destination it was already proving to be. While the Eaton's department store chain went out of business in 1999, the centre retained its original name and continues to be a key commercial hub and tourist destination in the city. It is located on Yonge Street, between Dundas Street and Queen Street. Miles Cullen's apartment was located at Howard Street, while the waterfront restaurant where Miles and Elaine enjoy a romantic dinner together was Captain John's Harbour Boat Restaurant in Queens Quay West. The Silver Dollar Room, which Reikle uses both as a hangout and a kind of informal headquarters, was a famous live music venue which was located next to the main floor of the Hotel Waverly in Spadina Avenue. It had first opened in January 1959 and, while the building was demolished in 2018, there are plans to reopen the Silver Dollar Room with its well-known exterior neon sign and internal mural both reinstated as before once a new building is constructed on the original site.

The Silent Partner was to be a success with both critics and audiences, winning three Canadian Film Awards in the categories of Best Feature Film, Best Direction and Best Overall Sound while also being nominated for awards in Best

Performance by a Lead Actor, Best Performance by a Lead Actress and Best Art Direction. This critical admiration was reflected in many of the reviews of the time, including Roger Ebert of *The Chicago Sun-Times* who was especially fulsome in his praise:

> Along with half a dozen other lonely moviegoers, I was witness to a small miracle: To a thriller that was not only intelligently and well acted and very scary, but also had the most audaciously clockwork plot I've seen in a long time. *Silent Partner*'s plot, indeed, has such ironies and reversals and neatly inevitable triple-crosses that it's worthy of Hitchcock. [...] The movie was apparently one of those Canadian tax shelter deals in which the box office loot doesn't matter much anyway; everybody makes his money on the deal, and the movie is thrown to the wolves. And yet if we forget the logistics and the deal and the movie's obscurity, what we're left with is a small but wonderful gem of a thriller: A film in which complicated people and a very complicated plot come together in a mechanism that leaves us marveling at its ingenuity.[7]

Other commentators were more qualified in their praise, with *The Washington Post*'s Gary Arnold taking exception to the film's more extreme depictions of violence and the ethical ambiguity of the central premise: 'Before it takes an appalling turn for the vicious, *The Silent Partner* seems an uncommonly clever and gripping suspense thriller. Even after the story threatens to self-destruct, you fight the impulse to suffer a major letdown, for the sake of the swell nerve-racking time you've been having up to that point. [...] In addition to the three costars, Duke draws expert performances from several supporting players: Celine Lomez as a sultry girl-in-the-middle and Gail Dahms, Michael Kirby, John Candy and Michael Donaghue as Miles' co-workers. Billy Williams' lighting and Oscar Peterson's score are admirable enhancements, consistently encouraging a heightened sense of fearful anticipation. If only the filmmakers had anticipated the amoral traps in the story, *The Silent Partner* might have been a classic'.[8] Some critics, such as Janet Maslin of *The New York Times*, instead took aim at the performances, emphasising areas where the film had not matched its dizzying potential: 'Mr Plummer makes a terrific heavy, especially in an early scene in which his destructive potential seems to know no bounds. Unfortunately, the screenplay never makes full use of the maniacal power of his performance, nor does it allow the thief enough ingenuity to make his tricks really surprising. [...] Mr Gould is disappointing. Too often, he recites his lines as if he were explaining things to a small child with a hearing problem, exaggerating the teller's dullness to an almost insufferable degree. And too often, he makes a mockery of the character's old-maidishness, even though the audience needs to believe that this man's co-workers take him entirely at face value'.[9]

Re-evaluations of the film in more recent years have continued to commend its atmosphere and suspense, though often in different ways. Derek Smith, for instance, considered the film to be at its best when subverting audience expectation: '*The Silent Partner* playfully toys with the tropes of the thriller genre, counterbalancing its escalating tension and sense of impending violence with a dark humor and offbeat romanticism that accompanies Miles's growth into a more fearless, and eventually arrogant, man. It's a tricky tonal balance that, at times, recalls Jonathan Demme's *Something Wild*, especially in the surprising ways its dopey male protagonist copes with his impending collision with a relentlessly sadistic psychopath. Though Duke's film lacks the warmth and humanism of *Something Wild*, it's possessed of a similarly idiosyncratic edginess'.[10] Todd Garbarini, on the other hand, acclaimed the film for the way in which the inspired characterisation and dialogue elevated the feature from many of its contemporaries: '*The Silent Partner* [...] is an effective thriller that, to the eyes of today's viewer, may not seem all that intricate or even suspenseful. So many thrillers have been made in the intervening forty years, specifically heist-based movies, that *Partner* may seem derivative, insipid, or even dated given the presence of outmoded security equipment and the absence of omnipresent cell phones. This could not be further from the truth as there is a lot of subtext going on for even the most jaded cerebral viewer to enjoy here. [...] For the first time in any contemporary film that I can remember seeing, main characters ponder aloud as to the insignificance of their lives, wondering where they are going and what the meaning of life is all about'.[11] While relatively few reviewers have focused specifically on the film's festive setting, some – such as Johnny Shaw – have nonetheless ruminated on the importance of *The Silent Partner*'s depiction of loneliness over the holiday season which significantly permeates so much of its action:

> If movies are an indication of real life (they aren't), being alone for the winter holidays (or any holiday for that matter) is the worst thing that can ever happen to a person ever in their life ever. The depictions in film about the hardships of being alone

> on Christmas, New Year's, Valentine's Day, etc. are tried and true. Maybe there's something about all the supposed joyousness and festive spirit that bombards us during the time around Christmas. The idea that we're being left out of this manufactured fun. [...] *The Silent Partner* stands as one of the more underrated Christmas movies, but also one of those under-the-radar crime films from the 1970s that deserves more love.[12]

In its sharp divergence from traditional holiday fare, *The Silent Partner* was a truly standout Christmas thriller. The film's use of a festive setting to relate a complex story about crime, greed and deception provides a stark contrast to the typical warmth and sentimentality normally associated with Christmas movies. This thematic distinction naturally offered some insights into the relevance and evolution of Christmas movies during the 1970s. By setting a dark and suspenseful story against the backdrop of the holiday season, *The Silent Partner* reflected a more far-reaching trend throughout the decade towards questioning traditional genres and subverting long-held premises. The seventies was a decade marked by cynicism and a vigorous interrogation of established norms, influenced in no small part by the political and social upheavals of the time. *The Silent Partner* aligned with this wider trend by challenging the idea that Christmas stories must always focus on joy, community, family and redemption, instead presenting a much more multifarious, nuanced depiction of the moral and emotional intricacies of adult life.

The decade saw audiences expecting more complexity and realism from films, even in those genres that might traditionally be more closely associated with light-hearted entertainment. *The Silent Partner* suggested that the Christmas movies of this era could serve as a highly effective vehicle for exploring a darker, more subtle range of human emotions and situations, reflecting a profound shift in cultural sensibilities. The film illustrated how Christmas cinema in the 1970s began to expand beyond their conventional boundaries, incorporating elements of thrillers, horror and even social commentary. This expansion points to the broader experimentation and genre blending that characterised and refined the cinema of the decade. Thus the critical and commercial success of *The Silent Partner* suggested that by the end of the 1970s, Christmas movies were no longer confined to feel-good narratives and traditional themes, but could also be expected to explore more multifaceted and problematic themes, reflecting the changing tastes and social expectations of the audience during that tempestuous decade.

By this point, it was becoming clear that the 1960s and 1970s had contributed significantly to the Christmas movie genre in theatres. While the era hadn't produced as prolific an output of festive cinema in comparison with earlier or later decades, during this period Christmas movies evolved from sentimental, family-focused tales to include much broader genres, themes and storytelling techniques. Key contributions of this era had included the introduction of more diverse subgenres, where film-makers experimented with blending holiday season themes with different genres such musicals, comedies, thrillers and even horror tales and non-traditional stories. This period shifted from the classic sentimental and wholesome family-oriented Christmas films to much more eclectic presentations.

This era also witnessed the rise of Christmas movies which were aimed especially at families but with a level of production meant for the big screen, particularly in the 1960s. However, it was arguably the 1970s – a decade which has become known for its more experimental and auteur-driven cinema – which contributed more significantly to the genre by pushing the boundaries of what a Christmas movie could be. The idea that Christmas stories could be used as a background for more serious, mature themes emerged throughout this period, with several films from the era reworking classic Christmas stories while others were more acutely concerned with creating entirely original narratives – often strikingly contemporary in nature, and more in step with the prevailing cultural conventions of the time. Increasingly, audiences became accustomed to Christmas being employed more as a seasonal backdrop to a film's action rather than as its primary focus, but the festive ambience still nonetheless added to the film's atmosphere and emotional weight. Directors routinely used the holiday season to emphasise the loneliness, joy, or complexity of relationships during a time of year that has become closely associated with togetherness and community.

The 1960s and 1970s were transitional decades for the Christmas movie genre, characterised by the introduction of more diverse storytelling, a move away from strictly traditional, morally-upright festive tales and a resulting step towards experimentation with more complex or unambiguously adult themes. Musical interpretations of the genre flourished, fantasies and horror narratives began to emerge alongside festive dramas and comedies as emergent subgenres, while the holiday season setting was increasingly used to frame more varied stories of personal and societal conflict – sometimes in unconventional but highly distinctive ways. These stylistic changes and creative innovations laid the groundwork for the even more diverse range of Christmas films that would come in the following decade, when the genre was to enter a period of renewed cultural relevance and a new commercial golden age with audiences.

REFERENCES

1. Alan-Bertaneisson Jones, *I'm Dreaming of a Fright Christmas: A Guide to Seasonally-Themed Movies of the Macabre and Other Weird and Wacky Tinsel-Tinged Treasures and Turkeys* (Milton Keynes: AuthorHouse, 2010), p.92.

2. Sam Panico, 'Dismembercember: *The Silent Partner*', in *B&S About Movies*, 25 December 2022.
   <https://bandsaboutmovies.com/2022/12/25/dismembercember-the-silent-partner-1978/>

3. Derrick Bang, *Crime and Spy Jazz on Screen, 1950-1970: A History and Discography* (Jefferson: McFarland, 2020), p.112.

4. Peter Hanson, '*The Silent Partner*', in *Every '70s Movie*, 5 April 2013.
   <https://every70smovie.blogspot.com/2013/04/the-silent-partner-1978.html>

5. Glenn Erickson, '*The Silent Partner*', in *DVD Savant*, 31 March 2007.
   <https://www.dvdtalk.com/dvdsavant/s2265part.html>

6. Ed Travis, '*The Silent Partner*: An Unparalleled Thriller Classic', in Cinapse, 12 June 2019.
   <https://cinapse.co/2019/06/the-silent-partner-an-unparalleled-thriller-classic-blu-review/>

7. Roger Ebert, '*The Silent Partner*', in *The Chicago Sun-Times*, 30 March 1979.
   <https://www.rogerebert.com/reviews/the-silent-partner-1979>

8. Gary Arnold, '*The Silent Partner*: Nerve-Racking Game of Cat and Mouse', in *The Washington Post*, 12 October 1979.
<https://www.washingtonpost.com/archive/lifestyle/1979/10/12/the-silent-partner-nerve-racking-game-of-cat-and-mouse/>

9. Janet Maslin, 'Screen: Elliott Gould Stars in Daryl Duke's Thriller, *The Silent Partner*', in *The New York Times*, 11 May 1979.
<https://www.nytimes.com/1979/05/11/archives/screen-elliott-gould-stars-in-daryl-dukes-thriller-the-silent.html>

10. Derek Smith, 'Review: Daryl Duke's *The Silent Partner* on Kino Lorber Blu-ray', in Slant, 18 June 2019.
<https://www.slantmagazine.com/dvd/review-daryl-dukes-the-silent-partner-on-kino-lorber-blu-ray/>

11. Todd Garbarini, 'Review: *The Silent Partner*', in *Cinema Retro*, 17 September 2019.
<https://cinemaretro.com/index.php?/archives/10597-REVIEW-THE-SILENT-PARTNER-1979-STARRING-ELLIOTT-GOULD-AND-CHRISTOPHER-PLUMMER;-KINO-LORBER-BLU-RAY-SPECIAL-EDITION.html>

12. Johnny Shaw, 'Merry CrimesMas: Johnny Shaw on *The Silent Partner*', in *Hardboiled Wonderland*, 11 December 2019.
<https://spaceythompson.blogspot.com/2019/12/merry-crimesmas-johnny-shaw-on-silent.html>

13

Other Christmas Films of the 1960s and 70s

WHILE Christmas settings and situations were relatively few and far between in the cinema of the 1960s and 70s, there were nonetheless a few films throughout these decades which dealt either directly or indirectly with themes and scenarios related to the festive season. That being said, many of these movies were far from traditional yuletide fare. In the list below, I have compiled details of a number of other films which, though often not seasonal in and of themselves, nonetheless address or feature Christmas in one capacity or another – sometimes as merely a backdrop to the action, while in a few cases the festive season appears as an integral aspect of the plot or as part of a pivotal sequence:

1. *1900* (Bernardo Bertolucci, 1976)
2. *Aguirre, The Wrath of God* (Werner Herzog, 1972)
3. *All Fall Down* (John Frankenheimer, 1962)

4. *Annie Hall* (Woody Allen, 1977)
5. *Butterflies Are Free* (Milton Katselas, 1972)
6. *Captain Newman MD* (David Miller, 1963)
7. *The Christmas Martian* (Bernard Gosselin, 1971)
8. *The Christmas Tree* (Terence Young, 1969)
9. *Coup de Grâce* (Volker Schlöndorff, 1976)
10. *The Day Mars Invaded Earth* (Maury Dexter, 1963)
11. *The Day of the Locust* (John Schlesinger, 1975)
12. *Deep Red* (Dario Argento, 1975)
13. *Dondi* (Albert Zugsmith, 1961)
14. *Donovan's Reef* (John Ford, 1963)
15. *Eyes of Laura Mars* (Irvin Kershner, 1978)
16. *Female Trouble* (John Waters, 1974)
17. *Fitzwilly* (Delbert Mann, 1967)
18. *Fortune and Men's Eyes* (Harvey Hart, 1971)
19. *The French Connection* (William Friedkin, 1971)
20. *Get Yourself a College Girl* (Sidney Miller, 1964)
21. *Hardcore* (Paul Schrader, 1979)
22. *Hot Rods to Hell* (John Brahm, 1967)
23. *If I Ever See You Again* (Joseph Brooks, 1968)
24. *Johnny Got His Gun* (Dalton Trumbo, 1971)
25. *The Juggler of Notre Dame* (Milton H. Lehr, 1970)
26. *Kramer vs Kramer* (Robert Benton, 1979)
27. *The Last Picture Show* (Peter Bogdanovich, 1971)
28. *The Legend of Hell House* (John Hough, 1973)
29. *Looking for Mr Goodbar* (Richard Brooks, 1977)
30. *McCabe and Mrs Miller* (Robert Altman, 1971)
31. *My Night at Maud's* (Éric Rohmer, 1969)

32. *Nickelodeon* (Peter Bogdanovich, 1976)
33. *Ocean's Eleven* (Lewis Milestone, 1960)
34. *Performance* (Donald Cammell and Nicolas Roeg, 1970)
35. *Period of Adjustment* (George Roy Hill, 1962)
36. *The President's Analyst* (Theodore J. Flicker, 1967)
37. *Rabbit Test* (Joan Rivers, 1978)
38. *Rocky* (John G. Avildsen, 1976)
39. *Rosemary's Baby* (Roman Polanski, 1968)
40. *Shaft* (Gordon Parks, 1971)
41. *Starting Over* (Alan J. Pakula, 1979)
42. *Tales from the Crypt* (Freddie Francis, 1972)
43. *Taras Bulba* (J. Lee Thompson, 1962)
44. *Three Days of the Condor* (Sydney Pollack, 1975)
45. *Tommy* (Ken Russell, 1975)
46. *The Trouble with Angels* (Ida Lupino, 1966)
47. *The Umbrellas of Cherbourg* (Jacques Demy, 1964)
48. *Welcome to L.A.* (Alan Rudolph, 1976)
49. *What a Way to Go* (J. Lee Thompson, 1964)
50. *Will Penny* (Tom Gries, 1968)
51. *The World of Henry Orient* (George Roy Hill, 1964)
52. *Yours, Mine and Ours* (Melville Shavelson, 1968)

Filmography

THE APARTMENT (1960)

Production Company: The Mirisch Corporation.
Distributor: United Artists.
Director: Billy Wilder.
Producer: Billy Wilder.
Associate Producers: Doane Harrison and I.A.L. Diamond.
Screenplay: Billy Wilder and I.A.L. Diamond.
Original Music: Adolph Deutsch.
Cinematography: Joseph LaShelle.
Film Editing: Daniel Mandell.
Art Direction: Alexander Trauner.
Set Decoration: Edward G. Boyle.
Running Time: 125 minutes.
Main Cast: Jack Lemmon (C.C. 'Bud' Baxter), Shirley MacLaine (Fran Kubelik), Fred MacMurray (Jeff D. Sheldrake), Ray Walston (Joe Dobisch), Jack Kruschen (Dr Dreyfuss), David Lewis (Al Kirkeby), Hope Holiday (Mrs Margie MacDougall), Joan Shawlee (Sylvia), Naomi Stevens (Mrs Mildred Dreyfuss), Johnny Seven (Karl Matuschka), Joyce Jameson (The Blonde), Willard Waterman (Mr Vanderhoff), David White (Mr Eichelberger), Edie Adams (Miss Olsen).

POCKETFUL OF MIRACLES (1961)

Production Company: Franton Productions
Distributor: United Artists
Director: Frank Capra
Producer: Frank Capra
Associate Producers: Glenn Ford and Joseph Sistrom
Screenplay: Hal Kanter and Harry Tugend, based on a screenplay by Robert Riskin from a story by Damon Runyon
Original Score: Walter Scharf
Director of Photography: Robert Bronner

Film Editing: Frank P. Keller
Art Direction: Roland Anderson and Hal Pereira
Set Direction: Sam Comer and Ray Moyer
Costume Design: Edith Head and Walter Plunkett
Running Time: 137 minutes
Main Cast: Glenn Ford (Dave the Dude), Bette Davis (Apple Annie), Hope Lange (Elizabeth 'Queenie' Martin), Arthur O'Connell (Count Alfonso Romero), Peter Falk (Joy Boy), Thomas Mitchell (Judge Henry G. Blake), Edward Everett Horton (Hudgins), Mickey Shaughnessy (Junior), David Brian (Governor), Sheldon Leonard (Steve Darcey), Peter Mann (Carlos Romero), Ann-Margret (Louise), Barton Maclane (Police Commissioner), John Litel (Police Inspector McCrary), Jerome Cowan (Mayor), Jay Novello (Cortego), Frank Ferguson (Newspaper Editor), Willis Bouchey (Newspaper Editor), Fritz Feld (Pierre), Ellen Corby (Soho Sal), Gavin Gordon (Mr Cole), Benny Rubin (Flyaway), Jack Elam (Cheesecake), Mike Mazurki (Big Mike), Hayden Rorke (Police Captain Moore), Doodles Weaver (Pool Player).

SANTA CLAUS CONQUERS THE MARTIANS (1964)

Production Company: Jalor Productions.
Distributor: Embassy Pictures Corporation.
Director: Nicholas Webster.
Producer: Paul L. Jacobson.
Associate Producer: Arnold Leeds.
Executive Producer: Joseph E. Levine.
Screenplay: Glenville Mareth, based on a story by Paul L. Jacobson.
Original Music: Milton DeLugg.
Director of Photography: David L. Quaid.
Film Editing: Bill Henry.
Art Direction: Maurice Gordon.
Set Decoration: John K. Wright III.
Costume Design: Ramsey Mostoller.
Running Time: 81 minutes.
Main Cast: John Call (Santa Claus), Leonard Hicks (Kimar), Vincent Beck (Voldar), Bill McCutcheon (Dropo), Victor Stiles (Billy), Donna Conforti (Betty), Chris Month (Bomar), Pia Zadora (Girmar), Leila Martin (Momar), Charles Renn (Hargo), James Cahill (Rigna), Ned Wertimer (Andy Henderson), Doris Rich (Mrs Claus), Carl Don (Chochem/Von

Green), Ivor Bodin (Winky), Al Nesor (Stobo), Joe Elic (Shim), Jim Bishop (Lomas), Lin Thurmond (Children's TV Announcer), Don Blair (TV News Announcer), Tony Ross (Santa's Helper), Scott Aronesty (Santa's Helper), Ronnie Rotholz (Santa's Helper), Glenn Schaffer (Santa's Helper).

THE MAGIC CHRISTMAS TREE (1964)

Production Company: Orrin Enterprises
Distributor: Holiday Pictures
Director: Richard C. Parish
Producers: Jeffrey C. Hogue and Bruce Scott
Executive Producer: Fred C. Gerrior
Screenplay: Harold Vaughn Taylor
Original Score: Victor Kirk
Cinematographer: Richard Kendall
Running Time: 60 minutes
Main Cast: Chris Kroesen (Mark), Valerie Hobbs (Old Woman), Darlene Lohnes (Mark's Mother), Dick Parish (Mark's Father), Bill Willingham (Mark's Friend), Billy Schaffner (Mark's Friend), Robert Maffei (Greed), Dianne Johnson (Mark's Sister), Blanche Mickelson (Waitress), Howard Blevins (Santa Claus), Charles Nix (Fire Truck Driver).

THE CHRISTMAS THAT ALMOST WASN'T (1966)

Production Company: Bambi Productions/Childhood Productions
Distributor: Childhood Productions
Director: Rossano Brazzi
Producer: Barry B. Yellen
Associate Producer: A.J. Piccolo
Screenplay: Rossano Brazzi, from a story by Paul Tripp
Original Score: Bruno Nicolai
Cinematographer: Alvaro Mancori
Film Editing: Maurizio Lucidi
Production Design: A. Danilo Zanetti
Set Direction: G.F. Fantacci
Running Time: 89 minutes

Main Cast: Paul Tripp (Sam Whipple), Lidia Brazzi (Mrs Claus), Alberto Rabagliati (Santa Claus), Sonny Fox (Mr Prim), Mischa Auer (Jonathan, the Elf Foreman), John Karlsen (Blossom), Salvatore Furnari (Elf), Antonio De Martino (Elf), Gaetano Guacci (Elf), Adriano Cornelli (Elf), Francesco Doria (Elf), Fabrizio Arnaldo (Elf), Imperato Domenico (Elf), Rossano Brazzi (Phineas T. Prune).

THE LION IN WINTER (1968)

Production Company: Haworth Productions
Distributor: Embassy Pictures
Director: Anthony Harvey
Producer: Martin Poll
Associate Producer: Jane C. Nusbaum
Executive Producer: Joseph E. Levine
Screenplay: James Goldman, from a play by James Goldman
Original Score: John Barry
Director of Photography: Douglas Slocombe
Film Editing: John Bloom
Art Direction: Peter Murton
Set Direction: Lee Poll
Costume Design: Margaret Furse
Running Time: 134 minutes
Main Cast: Peter O'Toole (Henry II), Katharine Hepburn (Eleanor of Aquitaine), Anthony Hopkins (Richard), John Castle (Geoffrey), Nigel Terry (John), Timothy Dalton (Philip II), Jane Merrow (Alais), Nigel Stock (William Marshal), Kenneth Ives (Queen Eleanor's Guard), O.Z. Whitehead (Bishop of Durham), Fran Stafford (Lady in Waiting), Ella More (Lady in Waiting).

SCROOGE (1970)

Production Company: Waterbury Films/Cinema Center Films.
Distributor: Twentieth Century Fox Film Company/National General Pictures.
Director: Ronald Neame.
Producer: Robert H. Solo.
Associate Producer: David W. Orton.

Executive Producer: Leslie Bricusse.
Screenplay: Leslie Bricusse, based on a story by Charles Dickens.
Original Music: Leslie Bricusse.
Cinematography: Oswald Morris.
Film Editing: Peter Weatherley.
Art Direction: Bob Cartwright.
Production Design: Terry Marsh.
Costume Design: Margaret Furse.
Running Time: 113 minutes.
Main Cast: Albert Finney (Ebenezer Scrooge), Alec Guinness (Ghost of Jacob Marley), Edith Evans (Ghost of Christmas Past), Kenneth More (Ghost of Christmas Present), Paddy Stone (Ghost of Christmas Yet to Come), David Collings (Bob Cratchit), Frances Cuka (Ethel Cratchit), Richard Beaumont (Tiny Tim), Karen Scargill (Kathy Cratchit), Michael Medwin (Harry, Scrooge's Nephew), Mary Peach (Harry's Wife), Gordon Jackson (Tom, Harry's Friend), Laurence Naismith (Mr Fezziwig), Kay Walsh (Mrs Fezziwig), Suzanne Neve (Isabel Fezziwig), Anton Rodgers (Tom Jenkins), Geoffrey Bayldon (Pringle, the Toyshop Owner), Reg Lever (Punch and Judy Man), Keith March (Well Wisher), Marianne Stone (Party Guest), Derek Francis (Charity Collector #1), Roy Kinnear (Charity Collector #2), Molly Weir (Debtor #1), Helena Gloag (Debtor #2), Nicholas Locise (Goose Boy), Peter Lock (Urchin #1), Clive Moss (Urchin #2).

WHOEVER SLEW AUNTIE ROO? (1971)

Production Company: American International Pictures/Hemdale
Distributor: American International Picture
Director: Curtis Harrington
Producers: Samuel Z. Arkoff and James H. Nicholson
Associate Producer: John Pellatt
Executive Producer: Louis M. Heyward
Screenplay: Robert Blees and James Sangster, from an original screen story by David Osborn, with additional dialogue by Gavin Lambert
Original Score: Kenneth V. Jones
Director of Photography: Desmond Dickinson
Film Editing: Tristam Cones
Art Direction: George Provis
Running Time: 91 minutes

Main Cast: Shelley Winters (Mrs Forrest), Mark Lester (Christopher Coombs), Chloe Franks (Katy Coombs), Ralph Richardson (Mr Benton) Lionel Jeffries (Inspector Ralph Willoughby), Hugh Griffith (Mr Harrison, The Pigman), Rosalie Crutchley (Miss Henley), Pat Heywood (Dr Mason), Judy Cornwell (Clarine), Michael Gothard (Albie), Jacqueline Cowper (Angela Barnes), Richard Beaumont (Peter Brookshire), Charlotte Sayce (Katharine Forrest), Marianne Stone (Miss Wilcox).

SANTA AND THE ICE CREAM BUNNY (1972)

Production Company: R & S Film Enterprises
Distributor: R & S Film Enterprises
Director: R. Winer and Barry Mahon
Producer: Barry Mahon
Executive Producers: C.T. Robertson and Armand Cerami
Screenplay: Richard Winer, from stories by Hans Christian Andersen and Benjamin Tabart
Original Score: Ralph Falco and George Linsenmann
Cinematographer: Bill Tobin
Film Editing: Steve Cuiffo
Production Manager: Jon Williams
Running Time: 96 minutes
Main Cast: Version A: Jay Clark (Santa Claus), Shay Garner (Thumbelina), Pat Morrell (Mrs Mole), Bob O'Connell (Mr Digger), Ruth McMahon (Mother), Heather Grinter (Witch), Sue Cable (Flower Girl), Mike Yuenger (Flower Prince).
Main Cast: Version B: Jay Clark (Santa Claus), Mitchell Poulos (Jack), Dorothy Stokes (Jack's Mother), Christopher Brooks (Honest John), Renato Boracherro (Rosemary's Boyfriend), John Loomis (Giant), Sami Sims (Giant's Wife), George Wadsworth (Villager).

SILENT NIGHT, BLOODY NIGHT (1972)

Production Company: Armor Films Inc./Cannon Productions/Jeffrey Konvitz Productions/Zora Investments Associates
Distributor: Cannon Releasing Corporation
Director: Theodore Gershuny

Producers: Ami Artzi and Jeffrey Konvitz
Associate Producers: Lloyd Kaufman and Frank Vitale
Screenplay: Theodore Gershuny, Jeffrey Konvitz and Ira Teller, from a story by Jeffrey Konvitz and Ira Teller
Original Score: Gershon Kingsley
Cinematographer: Adam Giffard
Film Editing: Tom Kennedy
Art Direction: Henry Schrady
Running Time: 83 minutes
Main Cast: Patrick O'Neal (John Carter), James Patterson (Jeffrey Butler), Mary Woronov (Diane Adams), Astrid Heeren (Ingrid), John Carradine (Charlie Towman), Walter Abel (Mayor Adams), Fran Stevens (Tess Howard), Walter Klavun (Sheriff Bill Mason), Phillip Bruns (Wilfred Butler, 1929), Staats Cotsworth (Voice of Wilfred Butler), Ondine (Chief Inmate), Tally Brown (Inmate), Lewis Love (Inmate), Candy Darling (Guest), Harvey Cohen (Inmate), Hetty MacLise (Inmate), Jay Garner (Dr Robinson), Donelda Dunne (Marianne Butler, Age 15), Charlotte Fairchild (Guest), Michael Pendrey (Doctor), Alex Stevens (Burning Man), Barbara Sand (Guest), Lisa Richards (Maggie Daly), John Randolph Jones (Doctor), George Strus (Doctor), Grant Code (Wilfred Butler, Age 80), Debbie Parness (Marianne Butler, Age 8).

BLACK CHRISTMAS (1974)

Production Company: Film Funding/Vision IV.
Distributor: Warner Brothers Pictures/EMI Distribution.
Director: Bob Clark.
Producer: Bob Clark.
Co-Producer: Gerry Arbeid.
Associate Producer: Richard Schouten.
Executive Producer: Findlay Quinn.
Screenplay: Roy Moore.
Original Music: Carl Zittrer.
Director of Photography: Reg Morris.
Film Editing: Stan Cole.
Art Direction: Karen Bromley.
Running Time: 98 minutes.

Main Cast: Olivia Hussey (Jess), Keir Dullea (Peter), Margot Kidder (Barb), John Saxon (Lieutenant Fuller), Marian Waldman (Mrs Mac), Andrea Martin (Phyl), James Edmond (Mr Harrison), Douglas McGrath (Sergeant Nash), Art Hindle (Chris), Lynne Griffin (Clare), Michael Rapport (Patrick), Les Carlson (Bill Graham), Martha Gibson (Mrs Quaife), John Rutter (Laughing Detective), Robert Warner (Doctor), Syd Brown (Farmer), Jack Van Evera (Search Party), Les Rubie (Search Party), Marcia Diamond (Woman), Pam Barney (Jean), Robert Hawkins (Wes), Dave Clement (Cogan), Julian Reed (Jennings), Dave Mann (Cop), John Stoneham (Cop), Danny Gain (Cop), Tom Foreman (Cop).

THE SILENT PARTNER (1978)

Production Company: Carolco Pictures
Distributor: Pan-Canadian Film Distributors
Director: Daryl Duke
Producers: Joel B. Michaels and Stephen Young
Associate Producer: Curtis Hanson
Executive Producer: Garth H. Drabinsky
Screenplay: Curtis Hanson, from a novel by Anders Bodelsen
Original Score: Oscar Peterson
Director of Photography: Billy Williams
Film Editing: George Appleby
Production Design: Trevor Williams
Set Direction: Dave Deyell
Running Time: 106 minutes
Main Cast: Elliott Gould (Miles Cullen), Christopher Plummer (Reikle), Susannah York (Julie), Céline Lomez (Elaine), Michael Kirby (Charles Packard), Sean Sullivan (Bank Guard), Ken Pogue (Detective Willard), John Candy (Simonsen), Gail Dahms (Louise), Michael Donaghue (Berg), Jack Duffy (Fogelman), Nancy Simmonds (Girl in Sauna), Nuala Fitzgerald (Safety Deposit Box Woman), Guy Sanvido (Locksmith), Charlotte Blunt (Mrs Packard), Aino Pirskanen (Mrs Evanchuk), Michele Rosen (Young Woman in Bank), Ben Williams (Newsboy), Sandy Crawley (Detective #2), Jan Campbell (Little Boy's Mother), Jimmy Davidson (Little Boy), Eva Norman (Girl at Party), John Kerr (Detective #3), Sue Lumsden (TV Newswoman), Rev. Harry Amey

(Minister), Candace O'Connor (Bank Assistant), Stephen Levy (Freddie).

Bibliography

Adler, Renata, 'Screen: James Goldman's *Lion in Winter* Arrives: O'Toole and Katharine Hepburn Starred, Story of Mideast War Also Makes Bow', in *The New York Times*, 31 October 1968.
<https://www.nytimes.com/1968/10/31/archives/screen-james-goldmans-lion-in-winter-arrivesotoole-and-katharine.html>

Agajanian, Rowana, '"Peace on Earth, Goodwill to All Men": The Depiction of Christmas in Modern Hollywood Films', in *Christmas at the Movies: Images of Christmas in American, British and European Cinema*, ed. by Mark Connelly (London: I.B. Tauris, 2000), pp.143-164.

Aldgate, Anthony, and Jeffrey Richards, *Best of British: Cinema and Society from 1930 to the Present* (London: I.B. Tauris, 2002).

Allon, Yoram, Del Cullen and Hannah Patterson, eds, *Contemporary British and Irish Film Directors: A Wallflower Critical Guide* (London: Wallflower Press, 2001).

—, eds, *Contemporary North American Film Directors: A Wallflower Critical Guide* (London: Wallflower Press, 2000).

American Film Institute, The, 'Dialogue on Film: Billy Wilder and I.A.L. Diamond', in *Billy Wilder: Interviews*, ed. by Robert Horton (Jackson: University Press of Mississippi), pp.110-31.

Anderson, Jeffrey M., '*Black Christmas*: Slay Bells', in *Combustible Celluloid*, 2006.
<https://www.combustiblecelluloid.com/classic/blackxmas.shtml>

Anon., '*Black Christmas*', in *Variety*, 31 December 1974.
<https://variety.com/1973/film/reviews/black-christmas-1200423278/>

—, 'Film Reviews: *Pocketful of Miracles*', in *Variety*, 31 December 1960, p.6.

<https://variety.com/1960/film/reviews/pocketful-of-miracles-1200419917/>

—, '*The Apartment*', in *Variety*, 18 May 1960.
<https://variety.com/1960/film/reviews/the-apartment-1200419766/>

—, '*Santa Claus Conquers the Martians*', in *FilmFanatic.org*, 27 November 2006.
<https://filmfanatic.org/?p=1857>

—, 'The Wilder Touch: The Director Explains His Zany Method for Relaxing Actors', in *Life*, 30 May 1960, pp.40-41.

—, '*Whoever Slew Auntie Roo?*', in *Variety Reviews 1971-74* (New York: R.R. Bowker, 1983), pp.176-77.

Armstrong, Richard, *Billy Wilder, American Film Realist* (Jefferson: McFarland, 2000).

Arnold, Gary, '*The Silent Partner*: Nerve-Racking Game of Cat and Mouse', in *The Washington Post*, 12 October 1979.
<https://www.washingtonpost.com/archive/lifestyle/1979/10/12/the-silent-partner-nerve-racking-game-of-cat-and-mouse/>

Arnold, Jeremy, *Christmas in the Movies: 30 Classics to Celebrate the Season* (New York: Hachette Book Group, 2018).

Arrigo, Anthony, '*Black Christmas*: Collector's Edition', in *DVD Compare*, 9 January 2017.
<https://dvdcompare.net/review.php?rid=4557>

Ashby, Justine, and Andrew Higson, eds., *British Cinema, Past and Present* (London: Routledge, 2000).

Attebery, Brian, *Stories About Stories: Fantasy and the Remaking of Myth* (Oxford: Oxford University Press, 2014).

Austin, Joe, and Michael Nevin Willard, eds, *Generations of Youth: Youth Cultures and History in Twentieth-Century America* (New York: New York University Press, 1998).

Babington, Bruce, and Peter William Evans, *Biblical Epics: Sacred Narrative in the Hollywood Cinema* (Manchester: Manchester University Press, 1993).

Bang, Derrick, *Crime and Spy Jazz on Screen, 1950-1970: A History and Discography* (Jefferson: McFarland, 2020).

Blakley, Thomas, '*Scrooge* Musical Slant of Dickens' *Christmas Carol*', in *The Pittsburgh Press*, 4 December 1970, p.35.

Brayton, Tim, '*Santa and the Ice Cream Bunny*', in *Alternate Ending*, 6 April 2015.
<https://www.alternateending.com/2015/04/santa-on-the-beach.html>

Burns, Kevin, and William Tuttle, 'Greetings from Spider Island: Mill Creek's *Chilling Classics* 50-Movie Collection', in *The Video Basement*, 17 November 2014.
<https://videobasement.wordpress.com/2014/11/17/greetings-from-spider-island-mill-creeks-chilling-classics-50-movie-collection/>

Byfield, Ted, ed., *A Glorious Disaster: A.D. 1100 to 1300: The Crusades: Blood, Valor, Iniquity, Reason, Faith, The Christians: Their First Two Thousand Years*, Vol. 7 (Edmonton: The Christian History Project, 2008) p.73.

Canby, Vincent, '*Scrooge* Varies Ritual in Version at Music Hall', in *The New York Times*, 20 November 1970.
<https://www.nytimes.com/1970/11/20/archives/scrooge-varies-ritual-in-version-at-music-hall.html>

Carney, Raymond, *American Vision: The Films of Frank Capra* (Cambridge: Cambridge University Press, 1986).

Chapman, James, 'God Bless Us, Every One: Movie Adaptations of *A Christmas Carol*', in *Christmas at the Movies*, ed. by Mark Connelly (London: I.B. Tauris, 2000), pp.9-37.

Collins, Ace, *Stories Behind the Great Traditions of Christmas* (Grand Rapids: Zondervan, 2003).

Connelly, Mark, ed., *Christmas at the Movies* (London: I.B. Tauris, 2000).

—, 'Santa Claus: The Movie', in *Christmas at the Movies*, ed. by Mark Connelly (London: I.B. Tauris, 2000), pp.115-134.

Cook, David C., *The Inspirational Christmas Almanac: Heartwarming Traditions, Trivia, Stories, and Recipes for the Holidays* (Colorado Springs: Honor Books, 2006).

Cosindas, Marie, 'Gallery', in *Life*, 27 November 1970, pp.8-11.

Crouse, Richard, *The 100 Best Movies You've Never Seen* (Toronto: ECW Press, 2003).

Crowther, Bosley, 'Screen: Busy *Apartment*: Jack Lemmon Scores in Billy Wilder Film', in *The New York Times*, 16 June 1960.
<https://www.nytimes.com/1960/06/16/archives/screen-busy-apartmentjack-lemmon-scores-in-billy-wilder-film.html>

—, '*Screen: Dean Martin in* Texas Across the River: *Weak Western Spoof Has Local Premiere, 2 Other Movies Open at Theaters Here*', in *The New York Times*, 24 November 1966.
<https://www.nytimes.com/1966/11/24/archives/screen-dean-martin-in-texas-across-the-riverweak-western-spoof-has.html>

Crump, William D., *How the Movies Saved Christmas: 228 Rescues from Clausnappers, Sleigh Crashes, Lost Presents and Holiday Disasters* (Jefferson: McFarland, 2017).

—, *The Christmas Encyclopedia*, 3rd edn (Jefferson: McFarland, 2013).

D'Ecca, Artemisia, *Keeping Christmas Well* (Dublin: Phaeton Publishing, 2012).

Deacy, Christopher, *Faith in Film: Religious Themes in Contemporary Cinema* (Aldershot: Ashgate Publishing, 2005).

Derry, Charles, *Dark Dreams 2.0: A Psychological History of the Modern Horror Film from the 1950s to the 21st Century* (Jefferson: McFarland, 2009).

Detora, Lisa M., ed., *Heroes of Film, Comics and American Culture: Essays on Real and Fictional Defenders of Home* (Jefferson: McFarland, 2009).

DeVito, Carlo, *Inventing Scrooge: The Incredible True Story Behind Dickens' Legendary* A Christmas Carol (Kennebunkport: Cider Mill Press, 2017).

Dickens, Charles, *The Christmas Books* (Ware: Wordsworth Editions, 1995) [1852].

Docker, John, *Postmodernism and Popular Culture: A Cultural History* (Cambridge: Cambridge University Press, 1994).

Drew, Bernard, '*Who Slew Auntie Roo?* Continues Camp Horror', in *The Evening News*, 8 April 1972.

Druker, Don, '*The Lion in Winter*', in *The Chicago Reader*, 26 October 1985.
<https://chicagoreader.com/film/the-lion-in-winter-3/>

DuPée, Matthew C., *A Scary Little Christmas: A History of Yuletide Horror Films, 1972-2020* (Jefferson: McFarland, 2022).

Duralde, Alonso, *Have Yourself a Movie Little Christmas* (New York: Limelight Editions, 2010).

Ebert, Roger, 'Great Movies: *The Apartment*', in *The Chicago Sun-Times*, 22 July 2001.
<https://www.rogerebert.com/reviews/great-movie-the-apartment-1960>

—, '*The Lion in Winter*', in *The Chicago Sun-Times*, 4 November 1968.
<https://www.rogerebert.com/reviews/the-lion-in-winter-1968>

—, '*The Silent Partner*', in *The Chicago Sun-Times*, 30 March 1979.
<https://www.rogerebert.com/reviews/the-silent-partner-1979>

—, '*Scrooge*', in *The Chicago Sun-Times*, 20 November 1970.
<https://www.rogerebert.com/reviews/scrooge-1970>

Ellis, John, *Visible Fictions: Cinema, Television, Video* (London: Routledge, 1989) [1982].

Erickson, Glenn, '*Pocketful of Miracles*', in *DVD Savant*, 22 November 2014.
<https://www.dvdtalk.com/dvdsavant/s4663pock.html>

—, '*The Apartment: Collector's Edition*', in *DVD Savant*, 4 February 2008.
<https://www.dvdtalk.com/dvdsavant/s2503apar.html>

—, '*The Silent Partner*', in *DVD Savant*, 31 March 2007.
<https://www.dvdtalk.com/dvdsavant/s2265part.html>

—, '*Whoever Slew Auntie Roo?*', in *DVD Savant*, 5 September 2002.
<https://www.dvdtalk.com/dvdsavant/s586roo.html>

Fairclough, Norman, *Critical Discourse Analysis: The Critical Study of Language* (Harlow, Longman: 1995).

Felton, Bruce, *What Were They Thinking?: Really Bad Ideas Throughout History*, rev. edn (Guilford: Lyons Press, 2007).

Fishwick, Marshall W., *Popular Culture in a New Age* (Binghampton: Haworth Press, 2002).

Forbes, Bruce David, *Christmas: A Candid History* (Berkeley: University of California Press, 2007).

Frow, John, *Genre* (London: Routledge, 2006).

Garbarini, Todd, 'Review: *The Silent Partner*', in *Cinema Retro*, 17 September 2019.
<https://cinemaretro.com/index.php?/archives/10597-REVIEW-THE-SILENT-PARTNER-1979-STARRING-ELLIOTT-GOULD-AND-CHRISTOPHER-PLUMMER;-KINO-LORBER-BLU-RAY-SPECIAL-EDITION.html>

Garrett, Greg, *The Gospel According to Hollywood* (Louisville: Westminster John Knox Press, 2007).

Gaudion, Andrew, 'Capra's Last Laugh: *Pocketful of Miracles*', in *Filmhounds*, 21 September 2020.
<https://filmhounds.co.uk/2020/09/capras-last-laugh-pocketful-of-miracles-blu-ray-review/>

Gemünden, Gerd, *A Foreign Affair: Billy Wilder's American Films* (Oxford: Berghahn Books, 2008).

Giddings, Robert, and Erica Sheen, eds, *The Classic Novel: From Page to Screen* (Manchester: Manchester University Press, 2000).

Glavin, John, ed., *Dickens on Screen* (Cambridge: Cambridge University Press, 2003).

Gordon, Bill, '*Santa Claus Conquers the Martians* – with Pia Zadora', in *Worst Movies Ever Made*, 22 October 2012.
<https://worstmoviesevermade.com/santa-claus-conquers-the-martians-with-pia-zadora/>

Green, Stanley, *Hollywood Musicals Year by Year*, 2nd edn, rev. by Elaine Schmidt (Milwaukee: Hal Leonard, 1999).

Greenspun, Roger, '*Who Slew Auntie Roo?*' in *The New York Times*, 16 March 1972.
<https://www.nytimes.com/1972/03/16/archives/by-roger-greenspun.html>

Guida, Fred, A Christmas Carol *and Its Adaptations: A Critical Examination of Dickens' Story and Its Productions on Stage, Screen and Television* (Jefferson: McFarland, 2000).

Gunter, Matthew C., *The Capra Touch: A Study of the Director's Hollywood Classics and War Documentaries, 1934-1945* (Jefferson: McFarland, 2012).

Hales, Stephen D., 'Putting Claus Back into Christmas', in *Christmas: Philosophy for Everyone*, ed. by Scott C. Lowe (Chichester: Blackwell, 2010), pp.161-71.

Hallenbeck, Bruce G., *Comedy-Horror Films: A Chronological History, 1914-2008* (Jefferson: McFarland and Company, 2009).

Hamilton, Scott, and Chris Holland, '*The Magic Christmas Tree*', in *Stomp Tokyo*, 25 December 2005.
<http://www.stomptokyo.com/movies/m/magic-xmas-tree.html>

Hanson, Peter, '*Black Christmas*', in *Every '70s Movie*, 6 March 2011.
<https://every70smovie.blogspot.com/2011/03/black-christmas-1974.html>

—, '*Santa and the Ice Cream Bunny*', in Every '70s Movie, 25 December 2015.
<https://every70smovie.blogspot.com/2015/12/santa-and-ice-cream-bunny-1972.html>

—, '*Silent Night, Bloody Night*', in *Every '70s Movie*, 28 March 2015.
<https://every70smovie.blogspot.com/2015/03/silent-night-bloody-night-1972.html>

—, '*The Silent Partner*', in *Every '70s Movie*, 5 April 2013.
<https://every70smovie.blogspot.com/2013/04/the-silent-partner-1978.html>

—, '*Whoever Slew Auntie Roo?*', in *Every '70s Movie*, 16 January 2023.
<https://every70smovie.blogspot.com/2023/01/whoever-slew-auntie-roo-1972.html>

Hantke, Steffen, ed., *American Horror Film: The Genre at the Turn of the Millennium*, ed. by Steffen Hantke (Jackson: University Press of Mississippi, 2010).

Hardy, Phil, ed., *The Aurum Film Encyclopedia: Science Fiction* (London: Aurum Press, 1995).

Harty, Kevin J., *The Reel Middle Ages: American, Western and Eastern European, Middle Eastern and Asian Films about Medieval Europe* (Jefferson: McFarland, 2015).

Healey, Tim, *The World's Worst Movies* (London: Octopus Books, 1986).

Hill, John, and Pamela Church Gibson, eds, *The Oxford Guide to Film Studies* (Oxford: Oxford University Press, 1998).

Hischak, Thomas S., *American Literature on Stage and Screen: 525 Works and Their Adaptations* (Jefferson: McFarland, 2012).

Hjort, Mette, and Scott MacKenzie, *Cinema and Nation* (London: Routledge, 2000).

Hoffman, Robert C., *Postcards from Santa Claus: Sights and Sentiments from the Last Century* (New York: Square One Publishers, 2002).

Hollows, Joanne, and Mark Jancovich, eds, *Approaches to Popular Film* (Manchester: Manchester University Press, 1995).

Holsinger, M. Paul, ed., *War and American Popular Culture: A Historical Encyclopedia* (Westport: Greenwood, 1999).

Horton, Andrew, *Laughing Out Loud: Writing the Comedy-Centred Screenplay* (Berkeley: University of California Press).

Horton, Robert, ed., *Billy Wilder: Interviews*, (Jackson: University Press of Mississippi).

Hunter, Allan, ed., *The Wordsworth Book of Movie Classics* (Ware: Wordsworth, 1996) [1992].

Jacobson, Colin, '*The Apartment: Collector's Edition*', in *DVD Movie Guide*, 6 February 2008.
<http://www.dvdmg.com/apartmentce.shtml>

Jane, Sarah, 'TFS the Season: *The Magic Christmas Tree*', in *Talk Film Society*, 20 December 2017.
<https://talkfilmsociety.com/articles/tfs-the-season-the-magic-christmas-tree-1964>

Jawetz, Gil, '*The Lion in Winter*', in *DVD Talk*, 19 June 2001.
<https://www.dvdtalk.com/reviews/2383/lion-in-winter-the/>

Jeffers, H. Paul, *Legends of Santa Claus* (Minneapolis: Lerner Publishing Group, 2001).

Johnston, Hank, and John A. Noakes, eds, *Frames of Protest: Social Movements and the Framing Perspective* (Oxford: Rowman and Littlefield, 2005).

Jones, Alan-Bertaneisson, *I'm Dreaming of a Fright Christmas: A Guide to the Seasonally-Themed Movies of the Macabre and Other Weird and Wacky Tinsel-Tinged Treasures and Turkeys* (Milton Keynes: AuthorHouse, 2010).

Jones, Ken D., Arthur F. McClure and Alfred E. Twomey, *Character People* (New York: A.S. Barnes, 1977).

Jones, Kimberley, 'Holiday Viewing: *The Lion in Winter*', in *The Austin Chronicle*, 6 December 2017.
<https://www.austinchronicle.com/daily/screens/2017-12-06/holiday-viewing-the-lion-in-winter/>

Kael, Pauline, 'The Current Cinema' in *The New Yorker*, 9 November 1968, p.189.

Kalaga, Wojciech H., and Marzena Kubisz, eds, *Multicultural Dilemmas: Identity, Difference, Otherness* (Frankfurt am Main: Peter Lang, 2008).

Kane, Ian, 'Popcorn and Inspiration: *Pocketful of Miracles*: An Entertaining Comedy for the Holidays', in *The Epoch Times*, 21 December 2022.
<https://www.theepochtimes.com/bright/popcorn-and-inspiration-pocketful-of-miracles-an-entertaining-comedy-for-the-holidays-4916958>

Kehr, Dave, '*Pocketful of Miracles*', in *The Chicago Reader*, 26 October 1985.
<https://chicagoreader.com/film/pocketful-of-miracles/>

Knapp, Raymond, *The American Musical and the Performance of Personal Identity* (Princeton & Oxford: Princeton University Press, 2006).

Knauss, Will, '*Santa Claus Conquers the Martians*', in *Cool Cinema Trash*, 23 December 2014.

<https://jeffandwill.com/willknauss/2014/12/23/cool-cinema-trash-santa-claus-conquers-the-martians-1964/>

Krauss, David, '*Scrooge*', in *High-Def Digest*, 11 October 2011.
<https://bluray.highdefdigest.com/5705/scrooge_70.html>

—, '*The Lion in Winter*: 50th Anniversary Edition' in *High-Def Digest*, 13 March 2018.
<https://bluray.highdefdigest.com/45804/thelioninwinter.html>

Kuykendall, Jeff, '*Black Christmas*', in *Midnight Only*, 17 December 2016.
<https://www.midnightonly.com/2016/12/17/black-christmas-1974/>

Langford, Barry, *Post-Classical Hollywood: Film Industry, Style and Ideology Since 1945* (Edinburgh: Edinburgh University Press, 2010).

Leitch, Thomas M., *Film Adaptation and Its Discontents: From* Gone with the Wind *to* The Passion of the Christ (Baltimore: Johns Hopkins University Press, 2007).

Lester, Meera, *Why Does Santa Wear Red?... and 100 Other Christmas Curiosities Unwrapped* (Avon: Adams Media, 2007).

Linville, Susan E., *History Films, Women, and Freud's Uncanny* (Austin: University of Texas Press, 2004).

Long, Mike, '*Black Christmas*', in *DVD Sleuth*, 12 November 2008.
<https://www.dvdsleuth.com/BlackChristmasReivew/>

Loukides, Paul, and Linda K. Fuller, eds, *Beyond the Stars: Plot Conventions in American Popular Film* (Bowling Green: Bowling Green State University Popular Press, 1991).

—, eds, *Beyond the Stars: Studies in American Popular Film Volume 5: Themes and Ideologies in American Popular Film* (Madison: Popular Press, 1996).

Lovell, Mitch, '*Santa and the Ice Cream Bunny*', in *The Video Vacuum*, 19 November 2018.

<https://thevideovacuum.blogspot.com/2018/11/santa-and-ice-cream-bunny-1972.html>

Lowe, Scott C., ed., *Christmas: Philosophy for Everyone* (Chichester: Blackwell, 2010).

Magala, Slawomir, *Cross-Cultural Competence* (Abingdon: Routledge, 2005).

Mansour, David J., *From Abba to Zoom: A Pop Culture Encyclopedia of the Late 20th Century* (Kansas City: Andrews McMeel Publishing, 2005).

Maples, Gordon, '*Silent Night, Bloody Night*', in *Misan[trope]y*, 10 December 2015.
<https://misantropey.com/2015/12/10/silent-night-bloody-night/>

—, '*The Christmas that Almost Wasn't*', in *Misan[trope]y*, 25 December 2017.
<https://misantropey.com/2017/12/25/the-christmas-that-almost-wasnt/>

Marling, Karal Ann, *Merry Christmas!: Celebrating America's Greatest Holiday* (Cambridge: Harvard University Press, 2001) [2000].

Maslin, Janet, 'Screen: Elliott Gould Stars in Daryl Duke's Thriller, *The Silent Partner*', in *The New York Times*, 11 May 1979.
<https://www.nytimes.com/1979/05/11/archives/screen-elliott-gould-stars-in-daryl-dukes-thriller-the-silent.html>

Matthews, Kevin, '*The Christmas that Almost Wasn't*', in *For It is Man's Number*, 23 December 2023.
<https://foritismansnumber.blogspot.com/2013/12/the-christmas-that-almost-wasnt-1966.html>

McBride, Joseph, *Frank Capra: The Catastrophe of Success* (Jackson: University Press of Mississippi, 2011) [1992].

McGee, Patrick, *Cinema, Theory, and Political Responsibility in Contemporary Culture* (Cambridge: Cambridge University Press, 1997).

McGlynn, Sean, 'Fighting the Image of the Reluctant Warrior: Philip Augustus as Rex-not-quite-so-bellicosus', in *The Image and Perception of Monarchy in Medieval and Early Modern Europe*, ed. by Sean McGlynn and Elena Woodacre (Newcastle: Cambridge Scholars Publishing, 2014), pp.148-167.

—, and Elena Woodacre, eds, *The Image and Perception of Monarchy in Medieval and Early Modern Europe* (Newcastle: Cambridge Scholars Publishing, 2014).

Mechling, Jay, 'Rethinking (and Reteaching) the Civil Religion in Post-Nationalist American Studies', in *Post-Nationalist American Studies*, ed. by John Carlos Rowe (Berkeley: University of California Press, 2000), pp.63-80.

Miller, Toby, and Robert Stam, eds., *A Companion to Film Theory* (Oxford: Blackwell, 2004) [1999].

Mitchell, Jeremy, and Richard Maidment, eds., *The United States in the Twentieth Century: Culture* (London: Hodder and Stoughton, 1994).

Moore, Grace, *Insight Text Guides: Charles Dickens' A Christmas Carol* (St Kilda: Insight Publications, 2012) [2004].

Moore, Kenneth, *The Magic of 'Santa Claus': More Than Just a Red Suit!* (Martinez: Ken Moore Productions, 2006).

Moore, Tracy, 'Parents' Guide to *The Christmas That Almost Wasn't*', in *Common Sense Media*, 20 June 2023.
<https://www.commonsensemedia.org/movie-reviews/the-christmas-that-almost-wasnt>

Morrison, James, ed., *Hollywood Reborn: Movie Stars of the 1970s* (Piscataway: Rutgers University Press, 2010).

—, 'Shelley Winters: Camp, Abjection, and the Aging Star', in *Hollywood Reborn: Movie Stars of the 1970s*, ed. by James Morrison (Piscataway: Rutgers University Press, 2010), pp.120-37.

Muir, John Kenneth, *Horror Films of the 1970s* (Jefferson: McFarland, 2012).

Munby, Jonathan, 'A Hollywood Carol's Wonderful Life', in *Christmas at the Movies: Images of Christmas in American, British and European Cinema*, ed. by Mark Connelly (London: I.B. Tauris, 2000), pp.39-57.

Murphy, Robert, ed., *The British Cinema Book*, 2nd edn (London: British Film Institute, 2001).

Murray, Noel, '*Black Christmas*', in *The Onion A.V. Club*, 13 December 2006.
<https://www.avclub.com/black-christmas-1798202200>

Nash, Jay, *The Encyclopedia of Best Films: A Century of all the Finest Movies: Volume 4* (New York & London: Rowman and Littlefield, 2019).

Neale, Steve, *Genre and Hollywood* (London: Routledge, 2000).

Neff, Alan, *Movies, Movie Stars, and Me* (Bloomington: AuthorHouse, 2008).

Nelson, Andrew Patrick, 'Traumatic Childhood Now Included: Todorov's Fantastic and the Uncanny Slasher Remake', in *American Horror Film: The Genre at the Turn of the Millennium*, ed. by Steffen Hantke (Jackson: University Press of Mississippi, 2010), pp.103-118.

Nesseth, Nina, *Nightmare Fuel: The Science of Horror Films* (New York: Tor Publishing Group, 2022).

Newman, Kim, *Nightmare Movies: Horror on Screen Since the 1960s*, rev. edn (London: Bloomsbury, 2011).

Panico, Sam, 'Dismembercember: *The Silent Partner*', in *B&S About Movies*, 25 December 2022.
<https://bandsaboutmovies.com/2022/12/25/dismembercember-the-silent-partner-1978/>

—, 'Christmas Cinema: *Santa and the Ice Cream Bunny*', in *B&S About Movies*, 24 December 2017.

<https://bandsaboutmovies.com/2017/12/24/christmas-cinema-santa-and-the-ice-cream-bunny-1972/>

—, 'Christmas Cinema: *Silent Night, Bloody Night*', in *B&S About Movies*, 18 December 2017.
<https://bandsaboutmovies.com/2017/12/18/christmas-cinema-silent-night-bloody-night-1972/>

—, '*The Magic Christmas Tree*', in *B&S About Movies*, 25 December 2019.
<https://bandsaboutmovies.com/2019/12/25/the-magic-christmas-tree-1964/>

Panton, Gary, '*Black Christmas*', in *Movie Gazette*, 30 December 2003.
<https://movie-gazette.com/577>

Paszylk, Bartlomiej, *The Pleasure and Pain of Cult Horror Films: An Historical Survey* (Jefferson: McFarland, 2009).

Patel, Sonja, *The Christmas Companion* (London: Think Books, 2008).

Paulding, Barbara, Suzanne Schwalb and Mara Conlon, *A Century of Christmas Memories 1900-1999* (New York: Peter Pauper Press, 2009).

Phillips, Gene D., *Wilder: The Life and Controversial Films of Billy Wilder* (Lexington: The University Press of Kentucky).

Pickens, Jessica, 'Musical Monday: *Scrooge*', in *Comet Over Hollywood*, 5 December 2016.
<https://cometoverhollywood.com/2016/12/05/musical-monday-scrooge-1970/>

—, 'Musical Monday: *The Christmas That Almost Wasn't*', in *Comet Over Hollywood*, 20 December 2021.
<https://cometoverhollywood.com/2021/12/20/musical-monday-the-christmas-that-almost-wasnt-1966/>

Picou, Charleston, 'Film Review: *Magic Christmas Tree*', in *HorrorNews.Net*, 19 November 2018.
<https://horrornews.net/147398/film-review-magic-christmas-tree-1964/>

Powers, James, '*The Apartment: THR*'s 1960 Review', in *The Hollywood Reporter*, 15 June 2017.
<https://www.hollywoodreporter.com/movies/movie-news/apartment-review-1960-movie-1011488/>

Pulver, Andrew, 'My Favourite Christmas Film: *The Apartment*', in *The Guardian*, 23 December 2015.
<https://www.theguardian.com/film/filmblog/2015/dec/23/my-favourite-christmas-film-the-apartment>

Quart, Leonard, and Albert Auster, *American Film and Society Since 1945*, 3rd edn (Westport: Greenwood Publishing Group, 2002).

Reid, John Howard, *Hollywood Movie Musicals: Great, Good and Glamorous* (Morrisville: Lulu.com, 2006).

—, *Movies Magnificent: 150 Must-See Cinema Classics* (Morrisville: Lulu.com, 2005).

Rex, Jim, '*Santa Claus Conquers the Martians*', in *B&S About Movies*, 22 December 2019.
<https://bandsaboutmovies.com/2019/12/22/santa-claus-conquers-the-martians-1964/>

Rosewarne, Lauren, *Analysing Christmas in Film: Santa to the Supernatural* (Lanham: Lexington Books, 2018).

Rowan, Terry M., *Having a Wonderful Christmas Time Film Guide* (Morrisville: Lulu, 2014).

—, *Motion Pictures from the Fabulous 1960s* (Morrisville: Lulu, 2015).

—, *Motion Pictures from the Fabulous 1970s* (Morrisville: Lulu, 2015).

Rowe, John Carlos, ed., *Post-Nationalist American Studies* (Berkeley: University of California Press, 2000).

Ryan, James-Masaki, '*Pocketful of Miracles*', in *DVD Compare*, 20 September 2020.
<https://www.dvdcompare.net/review.php?rid=6344>

Ryan, Michael, and Douglas Kellner, *Camera Politica: The Politics and Ideology of Contemporary Hollywood* (Indianapolis: Indiana University Press, 1988).

Samuel, Raphael, *Theatres of Memory: Volume 1: Past and Present in Contemporary Culture* (London: Verso, 1994).

Santino, Jack, *All Around the Year: Holidays and Celebrations in American Life* (Champaign: University of Illinois Press, 1994) [1985].

—, *New Old-Fashioned Ways: Holidays and Popular Culture* (Knoxville: University of Tennessee Press, 1996).

Schickel, Richard, 'Critic's Roundup', in *Life*, 18 December 1970, p.6.

Schochet, Stephen, *Hollywood Stories: Short, Entertaining Anecdotes about the Stars and Legends*, 2nd edn (Los Angeles: Hollywood Stories Publishing, 2013).

Schwartz, Dennis, '*The Magic Christmas Tree*', in *Dennis Schwartz Movie Reviews*, 5 August 2019.
<https://dennisschwartzreviews.com/magicchristmastree/>

Sedensky, Ian, '*Silent Night, Bloody Night*', in *Culture Crypt*, 11 February 2014.
<https://culturecrypt.com/movie-reviews/silent-night-bloody-night-1972>

Shail, Robert, *British Film Directors: A Critical Guide* (Edinburgh: Edin

Shaw, Johnny, 'Merry CrimesMas: Johnny Shaw on *The Silent Partner*', in *Hardboiled Wonderland*, 11 December 2019.
<https://spaceythompson.blogspot.com/2019/12/merry-crimesmas-johnny-shaw-on-silent.html>

Shelley, Peter, *Grande Dame Guignol Cinema: A History of Hag Horror from* Baby Jane *to* Mother (Jefferson: McFarland, 2009).

Sherman, Dale, *The Worst We Can Find: MST3K, Rifftrax, and the History of Heckling at the Movies* (Lanham: Rowman and Littlefield, 2023).

Sikov, Ed, *On Sunset Boulevard: The Life and Times of Billy Wilder* (Jackson: University Press of Mississippi, 2017).

Simon, John, 'Divine Didactics', in *New York Magazine*, 23 November 1970, p.77.

Simpson, Paul, ed., *The Rough Guide to Cult Movies* (London: Haymarket Customer Publishing, 2001).

Sindelar, Dave, '*Santa and the Ice Cream Bunny*', in *Fantastic Movie Musings and Ramblings*, 6 June 2017.
<https://fantasticmoviemusings.com/2021/02/21/santa-and-the-ice-cream-bunny-1972/>

—, '*Santa Claus Conquers the Martians*', in *Fantastic Movie Musings and Ramblings*, 12 June 2005.
<https://fantasticmoviemusings.com/2016/09/25/santa-claus-conquers-the-martians-1964/>

—, '*Scrooge*', in *Fantastic Movie Musings and Ramblings*, 19 November 2008.
<https://fantasticmoviemusings.com/2018/06/19/scrooge-1970/>

—, '*Silent Night, Bloody Night*', in *Fantastic Movie Musings and Ramblings*, 30 June 2006.
<https://fantasticmoviemusings.com/2017/03/19/silent-night-bloody-night-1974/>

—, '*The Christmas that Almost Wasn't*', in *Fantastic Movie Musings and Ramblings*, 11 March 2018.
<https://fantasticmoviemusings.com/2018/03/11/the-christmas-that-almost-wasnt-1966/>

—, '*The Magic Christmas Tree*', in *Fantastic Movie Musings and Ramblings*, 18 January 2021.
<https://fantasticmoviemusings.com/2021/06/06/magic-christmas-tree-1964/>

—, '*Whoever Slew Auntie Roo?*', in *Fantastic Movie Musings and Ramblings*, 30 December 2015.

<https://fantasticmoviemusings.com/2015/12/30/whoever-slew-auntie-roo-1971/>

Smith, David H., '*Santa Claus Conquers the Martians*', in *It's Christmas Time at the Movies*, ed. by Gary J. Svehla and Susan Svehla (Baltimore: Midnight Marquee Press, 1998), pp.215-19.

Smith, Derek, 'Review: Daryl Duke's *The Silent Partner* on Kino Lorber Blu-ray', in *Slant*, 18 June 2019.
<https://www.slantmagazine.com/dvd/review-daryl-dukes-the-silent-partner-on-kino-lorber-blu-ray/>

Smith, Gary A., *Uneasy Dreams: The Golden Age of British Horror Films, 1956-1976* (Jefferson: McFarland, 2006).

Staiger, Janet, *Perverse Spectators: The Practices of Film Reception* (New York: New York University Press, 2000).

Stein, Ruthe, 'DVD Review: *The Apartment: Collector's Edition*', in *The San Francisco Chronicle*, 6 April 2008.
<https://www.sfgate.com/movies/article/DVD-review-The-Apartment-Collector-s-edition-3288284.php>

Strupp, Phyllis, *The Richest of Fare: Seeking Spiritual Security in the Sonoran Desert* (Scottsdale: Sonoran Cross Press, 2004).

Svehla, Gary J., and Susan Svehla, *It's Christmas Time at the Movies* (Baltimore: Midnight Marquee Press, 1998).

Swain, Chandler, 'Saving Santa: *The Christmas That Almost Wasn't*', in *Chandler Swain Reviews*, 19 December 2018.
<https://chandlerswainreviews.wordpress.com/2018/12/19/saving-santa-the-christmas-that-almost-wasnt-1966/>

Thomas, Kevin, 'Gothic Tale of a *Black Christmas*', in *The Los Angeles Times*, 6 August 1975, p.12.

Thomas, Tony, *A Smidgeon of Religion* (Bloomington: AuthorHouse, 2007).

Thompson, Frank, *American Movie Classics' Great Christmas Movies* (Dallas: Taylor Publishing Company, 1998).

Thompson, Howard, 'Children's Films Widening Market: Feature Movies at Weekend Matinees are Popular', in *The New York Times*, 13 February 1965, p.10.

—, 'Santa vs Martians', in *The New York Times*, 17 December 1964.
<https://www.nytimes.com/1964/12/17/archives/santa-vs-martians.html>

Tobias, Scott, '*The Apartment* at 60: Is This Billy Wilder's Finest Film?', in *The Guardian*, 15 June 2020.
<https://www.theguardian.com/film/2020/jun/15/the-apartment-billy-wilder-jack-lemmon>

Travis, Ed, '*The Silent Partner*: An Unparalleled Thriller Classic', in *Cinapse*, 12 June 2019.
<https://cinapse.co/2019/06/the-silent-partner-an-unparalleled-thriller-classic-blu-review/>

Turner, Graeme, *Film as Social Practice* (London: Routledge, 1999).

Van Heerden, Bill, *Film and Television In-Jokes: Nearly 2,000 Intentional References, Parodies, Allusions, Personal Touches, Cameos, Spoofs and Homages* (Jefferson: McFarland, 2008).

Verrati, Michael, '*Silent Night, Bloody Night* at 50: Reflecting on Five Decades of Festive Fright', in *Fangoria*, 16 December 2022.
<https://www.fangoria.com/silent-night-bloody-night-at-50-reflecting-on-five-decades-of-festive-fright/>

Watt, Kate Carnell, and Kathleen C. Lonsdale, 'Dickens Composed: Film and Television Adaptations, 1897-2001', in *Dickens on Screen*, ed. by John Glavin (Cambridge: Cambridge University Press, 2003), pp.199-207.

Weiler, A.H., 'Capra's *Pocketful of Miracles* Opens at Two Theaters Here', in *The New York Times*, 19 December 1961, p.39.
<https://www.nytimes.com/1961/12/19/archives/capras-pocketful-of-miracles-opens-at-two-theatres-here.html>

—, 'Screen: Murky Whodunit: *Black Christmas* is at Local Theaters', in *The New York Times*, 20 October 1975.
<https://www.nytimes.com/1975/10/20/archives/screen-murky-whodunitblack-christmas-is-at-local-theaters.html>

Werts, Diane, *Christmas on Television* (Westport: Greenwood Press, 2006).

Wilson, Chuck, 'Hepburn and O'Toole Roar Again in *The Lion in Winter*', in *The Village Voice*, 12 December 2016.
<https://www.villagevoice.com/hepburn-and-otoole-roar-again-in-the-lion-in-winter/>

Wilson, Richard, *Scrooge's Guide to Christmas: A Survival Manual for the Festively Challenged* (London: Hodder and Stoughton, 1997).

Winagura, Dale, 'Harrington: Curtis Harrington discusses *Games*, *What's the Matter with Helen?* and *Who Slew Auntie Roo?*', in *Cinefantastique*, Fall 1974.

Zad, Martie, '*The Lion in Winter*', in *The Washington Post*, 27 March 1994.
<https://www.washingtonpost.com/wp-srv/style/longterm/movies/videos/thelioninwinterpgzad_a09eof.htm>

Zipes, Jack, *The Enchanted Screen: The Unknown History of Fairy-Tale Films* (New York: Routledge, 2011).

Index

#

2001: A Space Odyssey (1968 film) 94, 333
2010: The Year We Made Contact (1984 film) 333
3:10 to Yuma (1957 film) 68

A

ABC (American Broadcasting Company) 135
Abel, Walter 283
Abley, Sean 98
Academy Awards ....
..35-36, 40, 68-69, 71, 166, 169-170, 173, 183, 200-201, 206, 208, 214, 238, 348, 375-376
Academy Film Archive .. 175, 215
Academy of Motion Picture Arts and Sciences (AMPAS) 46
Academy of Science Fiction, Fantasy and Horror Films Awards 337
Adams, Edie 13, 36
Adeste Fideles (song) 31
Adler, Renata 172
Adventures of Tom Sawyer, The (novel) 269

African Queen, The (1951 film) 169
After Hours Cinema (TV series) 299
Agony Booth, The (website) .....
.... 273
Aguirre, José Luis 78
Aldrich, Robert 68
Alfie (1966 film) 214
Alfred, Roy 98
Alice Adams (1935 film) 37
All About Eve (1950 film) 68
All the Right Noises (1971 film)
.... 332
Allen, Hannah 302
Allen, Irwin 183
Alphaville (1965 film) 93
Altman, Robert 375
Amateur, Der (1972 film) 346
Amazon Video (company) 141
American Christmas Carol, An (1979 TV movie) 3
American Cinema Editors Awards 72
American Film Institute, The .. 8
American International Pictures
.... 213
American Roulette (1966 short film) 280

American-International Pictures 239
Amityville Horror, The (1979 film) 303
Andersen, Hans Christian ... 245, 247, 251
Anderson, Jeffrey M. 339
Anderson, Michael 36
Andersson, Bibi 346
Ann-Margret 49, 56, 71, 125
Anthony, Joseph 36
Antonioni, Michelangelo 170
Anything Goes (stage musical) 93
Apartment, The (1960 film) 4, **7-44**, 72, 99
Appuntamento al Mare (novel) 333
Arbeid, Gerry 315
Argento, Dario 241, 323
Arkoff, Samuel Z. 213
Armstrong, Richard 29
Arnold, Gary 377
Around the World in Eighty Days (1956 film) 36
Arrigo, Anthony 336
Arsenic and Old Lace (1944 film) 46
Artzi, Ami 279
As You Like It (stage play) ... 147
Asner, Edward 3
Attenborough, Richard 170
Auer, Mischa 127, 135
Avanti! (1972 film) 35
Avildsen, John G. 35

B

Bacharach, Burt 41
Bacon, Lloyd 68
BAFTA Awards 40, 86, 169, 170, 173, 183, 200, 201, 206, 214, 333, 348, 375-376
Bambi Productions 123
Banacek (TV series) 347
Bang, Derrick 349
Baraka, Amiri 146
Barefoot Contessa, The (1954 film) 124
Barry, John 172-173
Bart, Lionel 182, 238
Bass, Jules 3
Battle of Britain (1969 film) 375
Battle of Love's Return, The (1971 film) 280
Battle of the Villa Fiorita, The (1965 film) 332
Bava, Mario 339
Baxter, Warner 47
Bay of Blood (1970 film) 339
Bayldon, Geoffrey 196, 201
Bazmee, Anees 72
BBC (British Broadcasting Corporation) 170, 238
Beaumont, Richard 185, 200, 217
Beautiful Day, The (song) 200
Beck, Vincent 81, 90
Becket (1964 film) 147, 166
Beginners (2010 film) 376

Begotten (1989 film) 301
Bell, Book and Candle (1958 film) 9, 34
Ben-Hur (1959 film) 238
Benjamin, Richard 169
Berlin, Irving 98
Bernier, Luc 301
Big Heat, The (1953 film) 68
Big Street, The (1942 film) 47
Bill, Tony 169
Birthday House (TV series) 124
Birthday Party, The (stage play) 297
Black Christmas (1974 film) 5, 295, **307-344**
Black Christmas (2006 film) 337
Black Christmas (2019 film) 338
Black Water Gold (1970 film) 333
Blackboard Jungle (1955 film) . 68
Blakley, Thomas 205
Blees, Robert 213, 236
Blevins, Howard 110
Blood Sisters (1973 film) 334
Bloodhounds of Broadway (1952 film) 47
Blowup (1966 film) 170
Blunt, Charlotte 356
Bob & Carol & Ted & Alice (1969 film) 375
Bodelsen, Anders 345-347, 349
Bogart, Paul 3
Bolt, Robert 172

Bonanza (TV series) 92
Bondarchuk, Sergei 375
Bonilla, George 99
Boorman, John 171
Boracherro, Renato 261
Boston Strangler, The (historical figure) 97
Boyle, Edward G. 33, 38
Bracknell, David 332
Brando, Marlon 47
Brayton, Tim 269, 271
Brazzi, Lidia 127, 136
Brazzi, Rossano 6, 123-125, 128, 135-136, 138, 142
Breffort, Alexandre 36
Brian, David 61
Bricusse, Leslie . 181, 183-184, 200, 203-204, 206-208
Bridge on the River Kwai, The (1957 film) 202
Bridges, James 35
Brief Encounter (1945 film) 8
Bringing Up Baby (1938 film) 169
Broadway Bill (1934 film) 47
Broccoli, Albert R. 171
Bronner, Robert J. 69
Brooks, Christopher 258
Brooks, James L. 36
Brooks, Richard 68
Brown, Tally 298
Browne, Wynyard 238
Buddy Buddy (1981 film) 35
Bug's Life, A (1998 film) 65
Burns, Kevin 300

Burnt Offerings (1976 film) ...303
Burt, Benny 18
Butterfly (1982 film) 93
Byfield, Ted 167

C

Cable, Sue 257
California Institute of Technology 46
Call, John 79, 90, 93
Camelot (1967 film) 182
Canadian Film Awards 337, 376
Canby, Vincent 205
Can-Can (1960 film) 36
Candy, John 349, 351, 374, 378
Canned Film Festival, The (TV series) 94
Cannes Film Festival 348
Cannon Films (company) 281
Capra, Frank...5, 45-49, 62-63, 65-67, 69-73, 99, 169
Card, The (1952 film) 202
Cardona, René 78
Carlson, Les 316
Carney, Raymond 65
Carolco Pictures 345, 347-348
Carpenter, Don 347
Carpenter, John 241, 323, 335
Carradine, John 283, 297, 300
Carroll, Kathleen 94
Cartwright, Bob 204
Cartwright, Robert 206
Cassidy, Katie 338

Castle, John 147, 149, 170
Catweazle (TV series) 201
CBS (Columbia Broadcasting System) 124
Chabert, Lacey 338
Chalk Garden, The (1964 film) 183
Chamberlain Brothers (company) 98
Chamberlain, Richard 208, 347
Chan, Jackie 72
Changeling, The (1980 film) 303
Changes (1964 short film) 170
Chaplin, Charlie 40
Charlie Brown Christmas, A (1965 TV feature) 2
Charlie Bubbles (1967 film) 199
Chenoweth, Kristin 41
Chicago International Film Festival 280
Chicago Sun-Times, The (newspaper) 172, 204, 377
Chicago, Chicago (1969 film) 334
Childhood Productions ... 123-125, 139
Children Shouldn't Play with Dead Things (1973 film) 308
China Syndrome, The (1979 film) 35
Chinatown (1974 film) 345

Christmas Carol, A (novella) 137, 139, 198, 202-203, 207-209
Christmas Evil (1980 film).....339
Christmas Story, A (1983 film) 308
Christmas that Almost Wasn't, The (1966 film).......6, **123-144**
Christmas that Almost Wasn't, The (poem) 123
Christmas to Remember, A (1978 TV movie)................... 3
Cimber, Matt............................ 93
Clark, Bob.....................................
5, 35, 307-309, 323-324, 326-327, 331, 335-338
Clark, Jay 249, 269
Clark, Jay Ripley..........................
.... See: Clark, Jay
Clarke, Arthur C..................... 333
Clavell, James 347
Close, Glenn 175
Code, Grant............................292
Collings, David................. 185, 201
Collins, Joan..............................238
Collinson, Peter.......................124
Columbia Pictures............... 47-48
Columbo (TV series) 69
Columbus, Christopher..........165
Comer, Sam 69
Conforti, Donna................. 81, 90
Connery, Sean 171
Conrad, Joseph....................... 370
Conversation, The (1974 film) 345
Cook, Fielder............................. 3

Coppola, Francis Ford............345
Corbett, Bill.............................. 114
Corman, Roger.......................297
Cornell, Pamela......................206
Cornwell, Judy 217, 238
Costa-Gavras (Konstantinos "Kostas" Gavras) 35
Costume Designers Guild Awards................................175
Cowan, Jerome......................... 59
Coward, Noel 8
Cowboy (1958 film)...................34
Craven, Wes............................339
Crichton, Charles 202
Criminal Symphony (1968 film) 125
Cromwell (1970 film)............. 202
Crosby, Bing........................ 46-47
Crowther, Bosley............... 38, 139
Crump, William D..........136, 247
Cuka, Frances...........................185
Cukor, George... 34, 169, 182, 214
Cunningham, Sean S. 339
Cup Fever (1965 film) 332
Curtis, Dan...............................303

D

Dahl, Roald 184
Dahms, Gail.............. 351, 374, 378
Dalton, Timothy ....
.... 147, 151, 171, 173
Danin, Will...............................347
Darling, Candy.......................298
Daves, Delmer............. 34, 68, 332

David and Lisa (1962 film)..... 333
David, Hal 41
Davidson, Jimmy 352
Davis, Bette 48-49, 68
Day, Doris.................................66
Days of Wine and Roses (1962 film)..35
De Palma, Brian 334
De Sade (1969 film)................. 333
Dead of Night (1974 film)..... 308
Dead to the World (1961 film).. 91
Death House...See: *Silent Night, Bloody Night* (1972 film)
Dell Comics (company)............98
DeLugg, Milton 98
DeMille, Cecil B......................298
Demme, Jonathan........... 170, 379
Desk Set (1957 film)................ 169
Deutsch, Adolph.......................33
Devil's Triangle, The (1971 film)... 247
Diamond, I.A.L.............. 7, 29, 38
Diary of Anne Frank, The (1959 film).......................................214
Dick Van Dyke Show, The (TV series)...................................124
Dickens, Charles...... 181-182, 198, 203, 205-206, 209
Directors Guild of America 46
Directors Guild of America Awards....................... 72, 146
Doctor Dolittle (1967 film)...182-183
Doctor Zhivago (1965 film) ..202

Dog Day Afternoon (1975 film) 345
Don, Carl............................80, 83
Don't Open Till Christmas (1984 film).........................339
Donaghue, Michael 378
Donen, Stanley....................... 199
Donnelly, Stephen 208
Donner, Richard 334
Double Life, A (1947 film) 214
Douglas, Kirk............................ 48
Dr Strangelove (1964 film) 94
Drew, Bernard 239
Druker, Don 174
Duffy, Jack...............................352
Duke, Daryl ...6, 345-348, 378-379
Dullea, Keir 312, 332-333
Dunk, Bert 326
Dunwich Horror, The (1970 film) 348
DuPée, Matthew C............... 295
Duralde, Alonso......... 79, 92, 273
Dutchman (1966 film)............146

E

Eaton's Department Store (company) 349, 376
Ebert, Roger ....
.... 32, 172-173, 204, 377
Edgar Allan Poe Awards 337
Edmond, James................. 312, 333
Edwards, Blake...................35, 183
Elic, Joe 85
Elmacı Kadın (1971 film)......... 72

Elvira, Mistress of the Dark ....
....299
Elwes, Cary 338
Emmy Awards...69, 91, 169-170, 175-176, 201, 214, 348, 376
Emperor's New Clothes, The (1966 film)......................... 308
Endfield, Cy............................. 333
Englund, George......................... 3
Entertainer, The (1960 film) ......
....199
Erickson, Glenn .. 28, 70, 239, 370
Erler, Rainer............................347
Evans, Edith 188, 201
Evans, Luke 208
Evening News, The (newspaper) 239
Excalibur (1981 film)...............171
Exorcist, The (1973 film).........241
Eyes of Laura Mars (1978 film)
....345

F

Fahrenheit 451 (1966 film) 93
Falk, Peter......................49, 69, 71
Fall of the Roman Empire, The (1964 film)...................202, 375
Fardin, Mohamad Ali............. 72
Farrell, Julia 301
Ferguson, Dustin......................301
Fiddler on the Roof (1970 film)
....184
Film Funding (company)........ 307
FilmFanatic (film website)...... 95

Finney, Albert.............................
184, 198-200, 202-203, 205-207
Fire Down Below (1957 film)..34
First Monday in October (1981 film) 183
Fitzgerald, Nuala 355
Fleischer, Richard.............182-183
Fleming, Ian.............................171
Fleming, Victor................69, 104
Flynn, Errol 248
For Your Eyes Only (1981 film)
....238
Ford, Glenn 48-49, 68, 71
Ford, John...................34, 69, 298
Foreman, Carl 199
Four Corners Records (company) 98
Fox, Sonny............................... 129
Fracastoro, Girolamo...............165
Francis, Derek 185, 201
Francis, Freddie.............. 213, 238
Franks, Chloe 216, 238
Franton Productions..................45
Fraser, Ian........................183, 206
French Connection, The (1971 film) 345
Friday the 13th (1980 film) ....
.... 296, 339
Friedkin, David 333
Friedkin, William............ 241, 345
Front Page, The (1974 film)....35
Frosty the Snowman (1969 TV feature)...................................3

Funny Thing Happened on the Way to the Forum, A (1966 film) 182
Furse, Margaret 204, 206

G

Games (1967 film) 215, 235
Garbarini, Todd 379
Garner, Shay 251-252
Gathering Storm, The (2002 TV movie) 200
Gathering, The (1977 TV movie) 3
Gaudion, Andrew 67
Gedayan Tehran (1967 film) 72
Gemünden, Gerd 31
Gershuny, Theodore.. 5, 279-281, 295, 300-302
Get Smart (TV series) 92
Gibson, Martha 314
Gilbert, Lewis 214, 333
Gilda (1946 film) 68
Gingerbread House, The .... See: *Whoever Slew Auntie Roo?* (1971 film)
Gleason, Jackie 48
Glen, John 171, 238
Glenville, Peter 147
Gloag, Helena 186
Godard, Jean-Luc 93
Golden Globe Awards 40, 68, 71, 93, 146, 169-170, 173, 175, 200, 201, 206, 214, 238, 332-333, 348, 375-376
Goldman, James 145-146, 148, 166-167, 172-174
Goldwyn, Tony 41
Gone Are the Days! (1963 film) 91
Gone with the Wind (1939 film) 69
Good Night, Dear Lord (song) 124
Goodbye, Mr Chips (1939 film) 184
Goodbye, Mr Chips (1969 film) 169, 184
Goodyear Television Playhouse, The (TV series) 124
Gordon, Bill 96
Gothard, Michael 216, 238
Gould, Elliott 349, 375, 378
Grammy Awards 376
Graves, Robert 170
Gravy Train, The (1974 film) 334
Great Escape, The (1963 film) 248
Great Expectations (1946 film) 202-203
Green, Guy 214
Greenspun, Roger 239
Griffin, Lynne 310
Griffith, Hugh 217, 238, 240
Grimm, Jacob 214
Grimm, Wilhelm 214
Grinter, Heather 251

Gua, Ah-Lei............................... 72
Guardian, The (newspaper) ... 39
Guess Who's Coming to Dinner?
  (1967 film).......................... 170
Guida, Fred.............................. 202
Guinness, Alec 187, 201-202
Gunter, Matthew C. 66
Guys and Dolls (1955 film)....... 47

H

Hairspray (1988 film) 93
Haller, Daniel 348
Halloween (1978 film).. 241, 296, 323-325, 335, 340
Hamer, Robert 202
Hamilton, Guy..........................375
Hamilton, Scott....................... 115
Hand that Rocks the Cradle, The (1992 film)...................348
Hangman's Knot (1952 film) ... 93
Hansel and Gretel (short story)
  .....214, 221, 223, 227, 232, 234, 236, 239, 240
Hanson, Curtis ....
  ....345, 347-349, 370
Hanson, Peter................................
  ....240, 272, 300, 324, 368
Happiness (song).....................200
Happy Anniversary (1959 film)
  93
Hard Feelings (1982 film).......347
Harmon, Darby 302
Harrington, Curtis...... 6, 213-215, 234-235, 239, 242

Harris, Richard 207
Harris, Rosemary.................... 145
Harry, Lou................................ 98
Harty, Kevin J........................ 166
Harvey, Anthony ....
  .... 4, 145-147, 163, 167, 172, 175
Hathaway, Henry.....................37
Hawks, Howard...................... 169
Haworth Productions 145
Hayes, Sean 41
HBO (Home Box Office)....... 141
Healey, Tim............................. 78
Hearst's International-Cosmopolitan (magazine).. 47
Heeley-Ray, Kenneth 337
Heeren, Astrid....................... 282
Heisler, Stuart........................... 68
Hemdale Productions............. 213
Henley, Drewe 170
Hepburn, Katharine 147, 149, 166, 168-169, 173-176
Here Comes the Groom (1951 film) 46
Herm, Klaus 347
Hess, David 339
Heywood, Pat 219
Hicks, Leonard 80, 90
High Noon (1952 film)............69
Hill, George Roy.....................182
Hiller, Arthur 170
Hilton, James........................... 332
Hindle, Art............................. 313
Hirt, Al.................................... 98
Hitchcock, Alfred 36, 324, 339, 375, 377

Hobbs, Valerie 105
Hogue, Jeffrey C. 103
Hole in the Head, A (1959 film) 46
Holiday, Hope 17
Holland, Chris......................... 115
Holly and the Ivy, The (1952 film).......................................238
Holly and the Ivy, The (stage play)......................................238
Homecoming: A Christmas Story, The (1971 TV movie) 3
Hoodlum Priest (1961 film).... 333
Hooper, Tobe 241
Hooray for Santa Claus (song) 98
Hope, Bob................................. 47
Hopkins, Anthony.......................
........................147, 149, 170, 173
Horse's Mouth, The (1958 film) 202
Horton, Edward Everett......... 57
Hough, John 213
House Without a Christmas Tree, The (1972 TV movie). 3
How the Grinch Stole Christmas (1966 TV feature) 3, 139
Howard, Andrew 175
Howard, Trevor.........................8
Hsu, Carl 302
Hsu, Claire.............................. 302
Hudson, Oliver........................338

Huggins, Roy........................... 93
Hughes, Ken........................... 202
Hume, Cyril.............................. 68
Humphreys, Alan 301
Hunt, Peter.............................. 171
Hurst, Brian Desmond ..182, 201, 203-204
Hussein, Waris........................ 334
Hussey, Olivia..........310, 329, 332
Huston, John 169, 375
Hyams, Peter........................... 333

I

I Claudius (TV series)...........170
I Hate People (song) 200
I Heard the Owl Call My Name (1973 TV movie)...............347
I'll Begin Again (song) 200
Internet Movie Database (website) 248, 349
Irma la Douce (1963 film) 36
Iron Butterfly (band)............. 247
Isasi-Isasmendi, Antonio 332
It Happened One Christmas (1977 TV movie) 3
It Happened One Night (1934 film) 46
It Should Happen to You (1954 film) 34
It's a Wonderful Life (1946 film) 45, 49, 62, 64, 69, 137, 327
Italian Job, The (1969 film)...124
Ivory, James.............................170

J

Jack and the Beanstalk (1970 film) 247, 249, 274
Jackson, Gordon 192, 201
Jackson, Lewis 339
Jacobson, Colin 39
Jacobson, Paul L. 77, 92
Jalor Productions................ 77, 92
James Bond film series 171
Jameson, Joyce 11
Jane, Sarah 117
Jarrott, Charles......................... 332
Jawetz, Gil................................. 174
Jeffries, Lionel 218, 238, 240
Jewison, Norman 184, 334
Johnson, Dianne 108
Jones, Alan-Bertaneisson 116, 281, 346
Jones, Chuck 3
Jones, Harmon 47, 93
Jones, Kenneth V. 237
Jones, Kimberley...................... 168
Jones, Shirley 48

K

Kael, Pauline............................. 172
Kaif, Katrina 72
Kane, Ian..................................... 71
Kanter, Hal 45, 49, 64
Karlsen, John 127, 136, 139
Kaufman, Lloyd....................... 280
Kaye, Danny 66, 124
Keach, Stacy 93
Keeping Up Appearances (TV show) 238
Kehr, Dave 63
Kemek (1970 film) 280
Kennedy, Burt 333
Kennedy, John F. 96
Kershner, Irvin 333, 346
Kid from Left Field, The (1953 film) 93
Kidder, Margot 310, 324, 332, 334, 337
Kind Hearts and Coronets (1949 film) 202
Kingsley, Gershon 294
Kinnear, Roy 186, 201
Kirby, Michael 350, 374, 378
Kjærulff-Schmidt, Palle 346
Klavun, Walter 283
Kleiser, Randal 3
Knauss, Will 92
Konchalovsky, Andrei............ 175
Konvitz, Jeffrey 279-280, 295
Kramer, Stanley 170
Krauss, David 148, 167, 207
Kroesen, Chris.......................... 105
Kruschen, Jack 11, 36, 40
Kubrick, Stanley................ 94, 333
Kumar, Akshay 72
Kuykendall, Jeff 331

L

L.A. Confidential (1997 film) 348

Lady for a Day (1933 film) 47, 49, 65-68
Ladykillers, The (1955 film) .. 202
Lambert, Gavin 213
Lande, Kay 124
Landsburg, Alan 333
Lanfield, Sidney 47
Lang, Fritz 68
Lang, Walter 36, 169
Lange, Hope 48, 50, 69
LaShelle, Joseph 38
Lau, Fred 39
Laughton, Charles 214
Laurel Awards 72
Lavender Hill Mob, The (1951) 202
Lawrence of Arabia (1962 film) 169, 202
Lax, Frances Weintraub 20
Lazenby, George 171
Le Ore Nude (1964 film) 333
Leachman, Cloris 3
Lean, David 8, 169, 202
Leech, John 205
Legend of Hell House, The (1973 film) 213
Leger, Suzie 302
Lemmon, Jack ... 9-10, 34-37, 39-41
Lemon Drop Kid, The (1951 film) 47
Leonard, Sheldon 52
LeRoy, Mervyn 34
Lester, Mark 182, 216, 238
Lester, Richard 182
Lever, Reg 186

Lewis, David 10, 37
Lewis, Jerry 66
Licence to Kill (1989 film) 171
Life (magazine) 38, 204
Light in the Piazza (1962 film) 125
Light, John 175
Lindsey, Gene 83
Lion in Winter, The (1968 film) 4, **145-180**
Lion in Winter, The (2003 film) 175
Lion in Winter, The (stage play) 145, 166-167, 172
Litel, John 59
Living Daylights, The (1987 film) 171
Logan, Joshua 37, 124, 182
Lohnes, Darlene 107
Lomez, Celine 359, 374, 378
Loncraine, Richard 200
London Weekend International (company) 201
Lonely Lady, The (1983) 93
Long Day's Journey into Night (1962 film) 169
Long Goodbye, The (1973 film) 375
Long, Mike 335
Lonsdale, Kathleen C. 202
Loomis, John 260
Los Angeles Times, The (newspaper) 335
Lost Horizon (1973 film) 332
Lovecraft, H.P. 348

Lovell, Mitch............................274
Lumet, Sidney.........169, 345, 375
Lux Video Theater (TV series)
....124
Lynch, Paul..............................339

M

M*A*S*H (1970 film)............375
Mackendrick, Alexander.......202
MacLaine, Shirley......................
...........................12, 35-36, 39-41
MacLane, Barton.....................59
MacMurray, Fred.........10, 37, 39
Macy's (company)..................138
Mad Men (TV series)...............9
Madame La Gimp (short story)
....47
Madame X (1966 film)...........333
Maffei, Robert........................110
Magic Christmas Tree, The
   (1964 film)................5, **103-122**
Magna Carta Libertatum
   (document)........................166
Mahon, Barry..............................
.....................245-249, 269, 273
Man for All Seasons, A (1966
   film).....................................173
Man for All Seasons, A (stage
   play)....................................172
Man of La Mancha (1972 film)
....170
Man who Would be King, The
   (1975 film)..........................375
Mandell, Daniel.......................39

Mankiewicz, Joseph L.......47, 68,
   124
Mann, Anthony..............202, 375
Mann, Peter.............................56
Maples, Gordon......................140
Mareth, Glenville........77, 90, 92
Marked Woman (1937 film)...68
Marsh, Terence (Terry).............
....204, 206
Marshall, George.....................36
Martin Marietta Company.....67
Martin, Andrea...............314, 337
Martin, Dean.......................... 48
Martin, Leila............................80
Marton, Andrew.................... 333
Maslin, Janet.........................378
Matchmaker, The (1958 film)....
....36
Mathis, Johnny......................124
Matthews, Kevin....................140
Mayer, Michael......................146
Mazursky, Paul......................375
McBride, Joseph.................49, 66
McCutcheon, Bill.........80, 90, 93
McGee, Nick............................98
McGlynn, Sean.......................171
McGrath, Douglas.................. 313
McMahon, Ruth....................251
Medak, Peter...................169, 303
Medwin, Michael...................184
Meet John Doe (1941 film)..... 46
Meet Whiplash Willie (1966
   film).......................................35
Melendez, Bill............................2
Merhige, E. Elias....................301

Merrow, Jane 147, 149
Meteor (1979 film) 183
Metro-Goldwyn-Mayer
 (company) 91
Meyers, Jonathan Rhys 175
Michael Myerberg Studios
 (company) 92
Michaels, Joel B 345
Michell, Keith 208
Miller, David 93
Million Pound Note, The (1954
 film) 183
Mills, Mike 376
Milton DeLugg and the Little
 Eskimos (band) 98
Minnelli, Vincente 36
Miracle on 34th Street (1947
 film) 139
*Miracles: The Canton
 Godfather* (1989 film) 72
Mirish Corporation, The 7
Miss Misery's Movie Massacre
 (TV series) 299
Missing (1982 film) 35
Mission Mars (1968 film) 91
Mister Roberts (1955 film) ....
 34-35
Mitchell, Thomas 49, 56, 69
Monroe, Marilyn 28
Monster Times, The (journal) ...
 94
Monsters (TV series) 280
Month, Chris 79
Montserrat (1971 film) 333
Moody, Ron 182

Moore, Clement Clarke 220
Moore, Grace 182
Moore, Roger 238
Moore, Roy 307, 309, 324, 331,
 337
Moore, Tracy 139
Moravia, Alberto 333
More, Kenneth 190, 201, 204
Moreno, José Elías 78
Moritzen, Henning 346
Morning Glory (1933 film) 170
Morrell, Pat 253
Morris, Oswald 184, 203
Morrison, James 235
Movie Macabre (TV series) ......
 299
Moyer, Ray 69
Mr Angel (1966 film) 247
Mr Deeds Goes to Town (1936
 film) 46
Mr Smith Goes to Washington
 (1939 film) 46
Mrs Doubtfire (1993 film) 65
Much Ado About Nothing
 (stage play) 147
Mui, Anita 72
Muir, John Kenneth 329
Murphy, Kevin 114
Murray, Noel 308
Music Man, The (stage musical)
 .... 13, 29
Musical Mutiny (1970 film) . 247
My Fair Lady (1964 film) 182
My Favorite Year (1982 film)
 169

Mystery Science Theater 3000 (TV series) 95, 114
Mystery Science Theater 3000: The Return (TV series) ... 141

N

Nagashima, Kizo 2
Naismith, Laurence 189, 201
Nash, Ogden 123
Neame, Ronald 4, 181, 183-184, 198-199, 201-205, 208-209, 214
Negulesco, Jean 124
Nelson, Andrew Patrick 325
Nelson, Mike 114
Nesor, Al 88, 90
Nesseth, Nina 326
Netflix (company) 141, 208
Neve, Suzanne 190, 200
New Wave Independent Pictures (company) 301
New York Daily News, The (newspaper) 94
New York Hall of Science 67
New York Herald-Tribune, The (newspaper) 94
New York Magazine (journal) 205
New York Times, The (newspaper) ... 38, 70, 94, 139, 146, 172, 205, 239, 334, 378
New Yorker, The (magazine) 172
Newell, Brian 98
Newley, Anthony 184, 208

Newman, Kim 323
Nicholson, James H. 213
Nicolai, Bruno 140
Night Gallery (TV series) 347
Night of the Dark Full Moon .... See: *Silent Night, Bloody Night* (1972 film)
Night of the Hunter, The 214
Night of the Juggler (1980 film) 298
Nightmare on Elm Street, A (1984 film) 339
Nix, Charles 109
Nixon, Richard M. 96
North Bank Entertainment (company) 301
Novello, Jay 56
Now, Voyager (1942 film) 68
Nunn, Trevor 145
Nutcracker, The (ballet) 70

O

O Come All Ye Faithful (song) 327
O'Connell, Arthur 56
O'Connell, Bob 253
O'Ferrall, George More 238
O'Grady, Brittany 338
O'Hara, Gerry 332
O'Hara, Jill 41
O'Neal, Patrick 282, 297
O'Toole, Peter ....
.... 146, 149, 166, 168, 173-176

Odessa File, The (1974 film).......
....183
Oliver! (1968 film).182, 184, 204, 206, 238
Oliver! (stage play).................238
Olivier, Laurence 147
Olivo, Robert .... See: Ondine (actor)
Olsson, Ann-Margret..................
.... See: Ann-Margret
On Golden Pond (1981 film).......
.... 170
On Her Majesty's Secret Service (1969 film)...........................171
On the Carousel (TV series) .....
....124
Ondine (actor) 298
One and Done Productions (company) 302
One Christmas (1994 TV movie)................................169
Orbach, Jerry...............................41
Ornadel, Cyril 184
Orrin Enterprises.....................103
Osborn, David.........................213
Other Half of the Sky, The: A China Memoir (1975 film).....
.... 36

P

Pakula, Alan J. 345
Panavision (company) 38, 48
Panico, Sam 115, 248, 270, 301, 347

Panton, Gary...........................336
Parallax View, The (1974 film)
....345
Paramount Pictures................ 48
Parish, Dick ....
...........See: Parish, Richard C.
Parish, Richard C. ....
.....................5, 103-104, 107, 115
Parrish, Robert 34
Paszylk, Bartlomiej................. 331
Patch of Blue, A (1965 film).......
....214
Patterson, James............ 283, 297
Patton, George S.................... 248
Paul and Michelle (1974 film)....
.... 333
Payday (1973 film).................347
Peach, Mary........................... 192
Peacock (company).................141
Peeping Tom (1959 film) 338
Pendrey, Michael....................289
Perry Mason (TV series)......124
Perry, Frank 333
Peterson, Oscar...............349, 378
Petrie, Daniel...........................238
Peyton Place (1957 film) 69
Phffft (1954 film) 34
Philadelphia Story, The (1940 film) 169
Phillips, Gene D. 34
Pickens, Jessica 125, 207
Pickwick (stage play).............184
Picou, Charleston...................116
Pinter, Harold.......................297

Pirates World (company) 246-247, 251, 257, 266-267, 271
Pirskanen, Aino 359
Pittsburgh Press, The (newspaper) 205
Place in the Sun, A (1951 film) 214
Plan 9 From Outer Space (1959 film) 94
Planet of the Apes (1968 film) 94
Plumb, James 301
Plummer, Christopher 349, 375, 378
Pocketful of Miracles (1961 film) 5, **45-76**, 99
Pogue, Ken 353
Polanski, Roman 345
Poling, Nick 98
Poll, Lee 172
Poll, Martin 145-146
Pollack, Sydney 346
Pollock, Sean 302
Poots, Imogen 338
Poseidon Adventure, The (1972 film) 183, 214
Poulos, Mitchell 257
Powell, Clinton 302
Powell, Michael 338
Powers, James 30
Preminger, Otto 280
President's Plane Is Missing, The (1973 TV movie) 347
Presley, Elvis 337
Preston, Robert 145

Price, Vincent 247
Prime of Miss Jean Brodie, The (1969 film) 183
Producers Guild of America Awards 175
Prom Night (1980 film) 339
Promises, Promises (stage musical) 40
Provis, George 237
Pryce, Jonathan 208
Psycho (1960 film) 331, 339
Pulver, Andrew 9
Purdom, Edmund 339

Q

Quackser Fortune Has a Cousin in the Bronx (1970 film) ... 334
Queen of Blood (1966 film) ... 215
Quezadas, Cesáreo 78
Quine, Richard 9, 34

R

R&S Film Enterprises 245
Rabagliati, Alberto 126, 135
Rankin, Arthur, Jnr. 3
Ransom! (1956 film) 68
Rapper, Irving 68
Reach for the Sky (1956 film) 201
Recreation Corporation of America (company) 247
Red Curtain Foundation for the Arts, The (company) 98

Reed, Carol............. 182, 184, 238
Reed, Julian 320
Reis, Irving 47
Reisz, Karel............................. 199
Remains of the Day, The (1993 film).................................... 170
Rendezvous in Space (1964 film) 67
Rex, Jim.....................................97
Reynolds, Debbie 215
Rich, David Lowell.................. 333
Rich, Doris................... 79, 90, 98
Richards, Lisa Blake...............286
Richardson, Ralph 216, 236, 238, 240
Richardson, Tony 199
Richie, Shane........................... 208
Ride the Pink Cloud.................... ......See: *Pocketful of Miracles* (1961 film)
Riding High (1950 film) 46-47
RiffTrax (company)......... 114, 274
Ripley, Jay............ See: Clark, Jay
Riskin, Robert 45, 47, 49
River Wild, The (1994 film) 348
Robards, Jason............................ 3
Robbins, Jerome 182
Robinson, Edward G. 46
Robson, Mark 34, 69
Rodgers, Anton 186, 200
Roemer, Larry 2
Rogers, Anton........................ 201
Romeo and Juliet (1968 film)...... 332

Ronild, Peter 346
Rosebud (1975 film)............... 280
Rosenbaum, Henry..................348
Rosenberg, Stuart 303
Rosewarne, Lauren................. 270
Ross, Herbert 36, 169, 184
Rowan, Terry 208
Royal Shakespeare Company 171, 199, 238
Rubie, Les...................................319
Rudolph the Red-Nosed Reindeer (1964 TV feature). 2
Ruggles, Wesley........................37
Ruling Class, The (1972 film) 169
Runyon, Damon........... 45, 47, 70
Ruth Foreman's Pied Piper Playhouse 249
Ryan, James-Masaki 64
Rydell, Mark............................170

S

Sabrina (1954 film)..................... 8
Saltzman, Harry 171
San Francisco Chronicle, The (newspaper)......................... 39
Sangster, James................ 213, 236
Santa and the Ice Cream Bunny (1972 film).................**245-278**
Santa Claus (1959 film)....78, 140
Santa Claus Conquers the Martians (1964 film)......6, **77-102**, 103, 140

Santa Claus Conquers the Martians (comic book).......98
Santa Claus Conquers the Martians (novelisation).....98
Santa Claus Conquers the Martians: The Musical (stage musical) 98
Santa Claus Versus the Zombies (2010 film) 99
Santa Claus: The Movie (1985 film)....................238
Santa's Christmas Elf (Named Calvin) (1971 film) 248
Sanvido, Guy 362
Sasdy, Peter 93
Saturday Night and Sunday Morning (1960 film) 199-200
Save the Tiger (1973 film).........35
Saxon, John.......................314, 333
Sayce, Charlotte......................216
Scargill, Karen 185
Schaffner, Billy 105
Schaffner, Franklin J. 93
Scharf, Walter...........................69
Schickel, Richard....................204
Schultze-Westrum, Edith 347
Schwartz, Dennis 104
Scorsese, Martin 345
Scott, Bruce 103
Screen Actors Guild Awards 170, 175
Scrooge (1951 film)...................182, 201, 204
Scrooge (1970 film).......4, **181-212**

Scrooge: A Christmas Carol (2022 film).........................208
Scrooge: The Musical (stage show)................................208
Searle, Ronald 203
Secret Sharer, The (short story) 370
Sedensky, Ian..........................299
Sellier, Charles E., Jr......279, 339
Seven Year Itch, The (1955 film) 8
Seven, Johnny........................... 22
Shadowlands (1993 film)........170
Shakespeare, William 172, 174, 332
Shannon, Aleyse 338
Shaughnessy, Mickey 54
Shaw, Johnny 379
Shawlee, Joan 10
Shelley, Peter...........................234
Sherman, Lowell 170
Sikov, Ed...................................37
Silence of the Lambs, The (1991 film) 170
Silent Night (song).....................294-295, 301, 309
Silent Night, Bloody Night (1972 film)..............5, **279-306**
Silent Night, Bloody Night (stage play)........................302
Silent Night, Bloody Night 2: Revival (2015 film) 301
Silent Night, Bloody Night: The Homecoming (2013 film)...301

Silent Night, Deadly Night
  (1984 film) 279, 339
Silent Partner, The (1978 film) ..
  .... 6, **345-386**
Silkosky, Ronald 348
Sim, Alastair 181, 199, 201, 208
Simmonds, Nancy 355
Simmons, Jean 47
Simon, John 199, 205
Simon, Neil 41
Sims, Sami 260
Sinatra, Frank 46-48
Sindelar, Dave ....
  ..... 96, 104, 139, 206, 240, 273, 294
Singh is Kinng (2008 film) 72
Sleeping Beauty (1963 film) ... 139
Slocombe, Douglas 172
Smith, David H. 94
Smith, Derek 378
Smith, Gary A 236
Smith, Hal 17
Smith, Jack 298
Smith, John 165
Solo, Robert H. 181
Some Came Running (1958 film)
  36
Some Like It Hot (1959 film) ......
  .... 8, 28, 35
Something Wild (1986 film) ....
  379
Sound of Music, The (1965 film)
  .... 182, 375
South Pacific (1958 film) ....
  .... 37, 124, 125

Spall, Rafe 175
Spencer, Herbert W. 206
Spy with a Cold Nose, The
  (1966 film) 238
Stage Struck (1958 film) 375
Stagecoach (1939 film) 69
Star, The (1952) 68
Starrett, Jack 334
State of the Union (1948 film)
  169
Steadicam (equipment) 326
Steele, Tommy 208
Stein, Ruthe 39
Stephen King's Golden Tales
  (TV series) 280
Stevens, Fran 283
Stevens, George 37, 214
Stevens, Mel 301
Stevens, Naomi 10, 36
Stewart, James 9, 45
Stewart, Patrick 175
Stiles, Victor 81
Stock, Nigel 149
Stokes, Dorothy 258
Stone, Marianne 217
Stone, Paddy 193
Stop Me ....
  .... See: *Black Christmas* (1974 film)
Stranger with a Gun (1958 film)
  36
Stravinsky, Igor 172
Stuart, Mel 184
Sullivan, Sean 359
Summertime (1955 film) 125

Summertime Killer (1972 film) 332
Superman: The Movie (1978 film) 334
Suspiria (1977 film) 241
Swain, Chandler 137
Sweet Kill (1973 film) 348
Szwarc, Jeannot 238

T

Tabart, Benjamin 245, 249
Tænk på et tal ....
.... See: *Think of a Number* (novel)
Tænk på et tal (1970 film) 346
Tai-Pan (1986 film) 347
Takal, Sophia 338
Take My Life (1947 film) 183
Tales from the Crypt (1972 film) 213, 238
Tales from the Darkside (TV series) 280
Tales of Tomorrow (TV series) 135
Talk Film Society (website) ....
.... 117
Taxi Driver (1976 film) 345
Taylor, Harold Vaughn ....
.... 103, 113
Tchaikovsky, Pyotr 70
Teller, Ira 279-280, 295
Terms of Endearment (1983 film) 36
Terry, Nigel 147, 149, 171

Texas Chain Saw Massacre, The (1974 film) 241
Thank You Very Much (song) 200, 206-207
Thin Red Line, The (1964 film) 333
Think of a Number (novel) ....
.... 346-347, 349
Thomas, Kevin 335
Thompson, Howard 94
Thorn Birds, The (TV miniseries) 347
Thoroughly Modern Millie (1967 film) 182
Three Coins in the Fountain (1954 film) 124
Three Days of the Condor (1975 film) 346
Thumbelina (1970 film) ....
.... 247, 249, 273-274
Till, Eric 3
To All a Good Night (1980 film) 339
Tobias, Scott 39
Tolentino, Roberto 302
Tom Jones (1963 film) 199-200
Tony Awards 69, 93, 145, 170, 297
Torn, Rip 347
Trachtenberg, Michelle 338
Trail of the Lonesome Pine, The (1936 film) 37
Trauner, Alexander 33-34, 38
Travis, Ed 371-372
Tribute (1980 film) 35

443

Triple Cross (1966 film).........375
Tripp, Paul ....
..........123-124, 126, 135, 138-139
Tripp, Ruth Enders................124
Trouble with Harry, The (1955)
.... 36
True Confession (1937 film) ... 37
Truffaut, Francois.................... 93
Tubby the Tuba (song)..........124
Tugend, Harry 45, 49, 64
Tuna, Feyzi...............................72
Tunes of Glory (1960 film)...202
Turning Point, The (1977 film)
.... 36
Tuttle, William 300
Twain, Mark..........................269
Twilight Zone, The (TV series)
....124
Two for the Road (1967 film)
....199

U

Ullman, Nate..........................246
United Artists (company) ....
.... 37, 48
United States Copyright Office
....298
US Army 91
US Army Signal Corps...........46
US Department of Agriculture
.... 91
US Library of Congress
    National Film Registry 40
US Supreme Court.................325

V

Van Evera, Jack 319
Van Heerden, Bill..................298
Variety (magazine)......37, 38, 70,
    239, 334
Verrati, Michael....................298
Victor/Victoria (1982 film) ....
....184
Victors, The (1963 film) 199
Vidor, Charles.......................... 68
*Violent World of Sam Huff,
    The* (TV series) 91
Vision IV (company).............307
Visit from St Nicholas, A
    (poem) 220
Von Braun, Werner 96
Voyage to the Prehistoric Planet
    (1965 film) 215

W

Waldman, Marian 311, 333
Waldorf (novel)......................146
Walk in My Shoes (TV series)
.... 91
Walsh, Kay 189, 201
Walston, Ray 11, 37
Walt Disney Company................
.... 246-247
Waltons, The (TV series).. 3, 92
Wannberg, Ken...................... 349
Ward, Rachel..........................347
Warhol, Andy........................298
Washam, Ben 3

Washington Post, The (newspaper) 377
Waterloo (1970 film) 375
Waterman, Willard 12
Waters, John 93
Watt, Kate Carnell 202
Webster, Nicholas 6, 77, 91-92
Weiler, A.H. 70, 334
Weinstein, Drew 302
Weir, Molly 186, 201
Welles, Orson 3, 93
Wertimer, Ned 79
West of Montana (1964 film) 333
West Side Story (1961 film) 182
Whammo (company) 88
What Ever Happened to Baby Jane? (1962 film) 68, 239
What's the Matter with Helen? (1971 film) 214-215, 235
White Christmas (song) 98
White, David 12
Whitehead, O.Z. 156
Who Slew Auntie Roo? ....See: *Whoever Slew Auntie Roo?* (1971 film)
Whoever Slew Auntie Roo? (1971 film) 6, **213-244**
Wilder, Billy 4, 7-9, 34-41, 99
Wilder, Gene 184
Williams, Billy 378
Willingham, Bill 105
Willy Wonka and the Chocolate Factory (1971 film) 184

Wilson, Chuck 174
Winer, Richard ....
.... 245-248, 273-274
Winkler, Henry 3
Winter, Edward 41
Winters, Shelley 214, 216, 235-236, 239-240
Winters, Shirley 239
Wise, Robert 182, 375
Wizard of Oz, The (1939 film) 104, 115
WNBC (television station) ... 124
Wojeck (TV series) 347
Wonderful Land of Oz, The (1969 film) 248
Wong, Glen 337-338
Wood, Ed 94
Wood, Sam 184
World's Worst Movies, The (book) 78
Woronov, Mary 281, 297
Wrye, Donald 3
Wyler, William 238

Y

Yarbrough, Glenn 140
Yellen, Barry B. 123
York, Susannah 349, 374
You Can't Take It with You (1938 film) 46
You... You... (song) 200
Young, Stephen 345
Young, Terence 375
Yuenger, Mike 257

445

Z

Zad, Martie 147
Zadora, Pia 79, 93, 95
Zeffirelli, Franco 332
Zinnemann, Fred 69
Zipes, Jack 236
Zittrer, Carl 337
Zora Investments Associates (company) 298

Acknowledgements

I am most grateful to my family, Julie Christie and Mary Melville, and to my friends Amy Leitch, Stuart Hall, Professor Roderick Watson, Eddy and Dorothy Bryan, Katie Donnelly, Alex Tucker and Kelley Nave, Ian and Anne McNeish, Dr Colin M. Barron and Vivien Barron, Vincent and Elizabeth Connell, Robert Murray and Eleanor Jewson, Scott and Caroline Boulton, and Joy Furmage for their fellowship and encouragement throughout the course of this project.

With the greatest of thanks, as ever, to my wonderful friends Joe and Mary Moore of the North Pole Press, who always keep the Christmas spirit alive all the year round!

About the Author

Dr Thomas Christie has many years of experience as a literary and publishing professional, working in collaboration with several companies including Cambridge Scholars Publishing, Crescent Moon Publishing and Applause Books. A passionate advocate of the written word and literary arts, over the years he has worked to develop original writing for respected organisations such as the Stirling Smith Art Gallery and Museum and a leading independent higher education research unit based at the University of Stirling. Additionally, he is regularly involved in public speaking events and has delivered guest lectures and presentations about his work at many locations around the United Kingdom.

Tom is a Fellow of the Royal Society of Arts and a member of the Royal Society of Literature, the Society of Authors, the Federation of Writers Scotland and the Authors' Licensing and Collecting Society. He holds a first-class Honours degree in English Literature and a Master's degree in Humanities with British Cinema History from the Open University in Milton Keynes, and a Doctorate in Scottish Literature awarded by the University of Stirling. He is currently an Associate Lecturer with Forth Valley College's Stirling Campus.

Tom is the author of a number of books on the subject of modern film which include *Liv Tyler: Star in Ascendance* (2007), *The Cinema of Richard Linklater* (2008), *John Hughes and Eighties Cinema: Teenage Hopes and American Dreams* (2009), *Ferris Bueller's Day Off: Pocket Movie Guide* (2010), *The Christmas Movie Book* (2011), *The James Bond Movies of the 1980s* (2013), *Mel Brooks: Genius and Loving It!: Freedom and Liberation in the Cinema of Mel Brooks* (2015), *A Righteously Awesome Eighties Christmas: Festive Cinema of the 1980s* (2016), *The Golden Age of Christmas Movies: Festive Cinema of the 1940s and 50s* (2019), *John Hughes FAQ* (2019) and *A Totally Bodacious Nineties Christmas: Festive Cinema of the 1990s* (2022).

His other works include *Notional Identities: Ideology, Genre and National Identity in Popular Scottish Fiction Since the Seventies* (2013), *The Spectrum of Adventure: A Brief History of Interactive Fiction on the Sinclair ZX Spectrum* (2016), *Contested Mindscapes: Exploring Approaches to Dementia in Modern Popular Culture* (2018) and *A Very Spectrum Christmas: Celebrating Seasonal Software on the Sinclair ZX Spectrum* (2021). He has also written a crowdfunded murder-mystery novel, *The Shadow in the Gallery* (2013), which is set during the nineteenth century in Stirling's historic Smith Art Gallery and Museum, and – in collaboration with archaeologist Dr Murray Cook – *Scotland's Christmas: Festive Celebrations, Traditions and Customs in Scotland from Samhain to Still Game* (2023).

Additionally, Tom has written two Scottish travel guides in partnership with his sister, Julie Christie, which are entitled *The Heart 200 Book: A Companion Guide to Scotland's Most Exciting Road Trip* (2020) and *Secrets and Mysteries of the Heart 200 Route* (2021).

For more details about Tom and his work, please visit his website at:
www.tomchristiebooks.co.uk

Also Available from Extremis Publishing

A Very Spectrum Christmas
Celebrating Seasonal Software on the Sinclair ZX Spectrum

By Thomas A. Christie

Throughout the 1980s, thousands of British children were lucky enough to discover a Sinclair ZX Spectrum under their Christmas trees and soon found their eyes opened to a virtual world of wonder. But Santa Claus did more than deliver computers – sometimes he appeared on them, too.

From the author of *The Spectrum of Adventure* and *A Righteously Awesome Eighties Christmas*, this book delves into the Spectrum's extraordinary pantheon of seasonal games: the good, the bad, the surprising, the unabashedly surreal and the occasionally rather tenuous.

From the machine's formative days in the early eighties right through to the latest independent releases, *A Very Spectrum Christmas* takes a look at what makes a truly memorable festive title for the vintage home micro-computer... as well as unearthing a few games that may have become lost in the mists of Christmas past for good reason.

Fully illustrated with colour screenshots of all the games under discussion, *A Very Spectrum Christmas* is a treasure trove of yuletide software experiences – where eighties nostalgia collides with modern day homebrew innovation with frequently unexpected results!

Also Available from Extremis Publishing

A Righteously Awesome Eighties Christmas
Festive Cinema of the 1980s
By Thomas A. Christie

The cinema of the festive season has blazed a trail through the world of film-making for more than a century, ranging from silent movies to the latest CGI features. From the author of *The Christmas Movie Book*, this new text explores the different narrative themes which emerged in the genre over the course of the 1980s, considering the developments which have helped to make the Christmas films of that decade amongst the most fascinating and engaging motion pictures in the history of festive movie production.

Released against the backdrop of a turbulent and rapidly-changing world, the Christmas films of the 1980s celebrated traditions and challenged assumptions in equal measure. With warm nostalgia colliding with aggressive modernity as never before, the eighties saw the movies of the holiday season being deconstructed and reconfigured to remain relevant in an age of cynicism and innovation.

Whether exploring comedy, drama, horror or fantasy, Christmas cinema has an unparalleled capacity to attract and inspire audiences. With a discussion ranging from the best-known titles to some of the most obscure, *A Righteously Awesome Eighties Christmas* examines the ways in which the Christmas motion pictures of the 1980s fit into the wider context of this captivating and ever-evolving genre.

Also Available from Extremis Publishing

The Golden Age of Christmas Movies
Festive Cinema of the 1940s and 50s

By Thomas A. Christie

Today the Christmas movie is considered one of the best-loved genres in modern cinema, entertaining audiences across the globe with depictions of festive celebrations, personal reinvention and the enduring value of friendship and family. But how did the themes and conventions of this category of film come to take form, and why have they proven to be so durable that they continue to persist and be reinvented even in the present day?

This book takes a nostalgic look back at the Christmas cinema of the 1940s and 50s, including a discussion of classic films which came to define the genre. Considering the unforgettable storylines and distinctive characters that brought these early festive movies to life, it discusses the conventions which were established and the qualities which would define Christmas titles for decades to come.

Examining landmark features of the period, *The Golden Age of Christmas Movies* delves into some of the most successful festive films ever produced, and also reflects upon other movies of the time that—for one reason or another—have all but disappeared into the mists of cinema history. Considering films which range from the life-affirming to the warmly sentimental, *The Golden Age of Christmas Movies* investigates the many reasons why these memorable motion pictures have continued to entertain generations of moviegoers.

Also Available from Extremis Publishing

A Totally Bodacious Nineties Christmas
Festive Cinema of the 1990s

By Thomas A. Christie

If the 1980s had been the decade that had brought festive cinema out of its wilderness period and back into the public consciousness as never before, the 1990s would continue to reinvigorate the genre while also returning with fresh purpose to the central themes of its post-war Golden Age. The result would be a mixture of originality and traditionalism which was to prove successful at the box-office as well as reinforcing the relevance of the Christmas movie amongst critics and commentators.

From the author of *The Golden Age of Christmas Movies* and *A Righteously Awesome Eighties Christmas*, this book explores some of the most prominent festive films of the nineties—as well as discussing some of the decade's more unusual yuletide features. Moving from madcap comedies to family dramas, by way of many other subgenres in-between, the topics which arose throughout the Christmas cinema of the decade are considered along with some unexpected movie facts.

The 1990s marked a period of lightning-fast technological development and substantial cultural change, which had wide-ranging effects on the world of cinema. *A Totally Bodacious Nineties Christmas* will take you on a journey through the festive movies of this tempestuous era, blending nostalgia for the nineties with an examination of how that decade's films had a major impact on the genre which persists even to the present day.

For details of new and forthcoming books from Extremis Publishing, including our monthly podcast, please visit our official website at:

www.extremispublishing.com

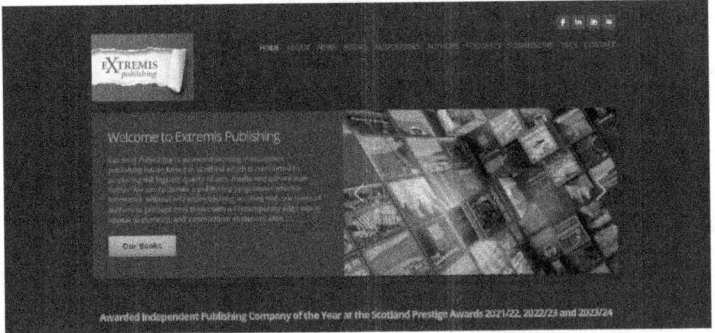

or follow us on social media at:

www.facebook.com/extremispublishing

www.linkedin.com/company/extremis-publishing-ltd-/

www.ingramcontent.com/pod-product-compliance
Lightning Source LLC
Chambersburg PA
CBHW072143070526
44585CB00015B/992